The Media and Aid
in Sub-Saharan Africa

News coverage on Africa is closely connected not only with how Western audiences see the continent, but also with how a wide Western audience builds its opinion on issues that carry consequences for the public's and governments' support and policy towards development aid. The Western media reinforce a picture of a continent that drowns in chaos, is dominated by conflicts, diseases, corruption and failed democratisation. Whose interests lie behind that? How does foreign news on sub-Saharan Africa emerge, which actors are relevant in its making, and on the basis of what interests do these actors shape the coverage that is then presented as 'neutral information' to a broad international audience?

Closely examining the relationship between foreign correspondents of international news media and humanitarian organisations, Lena von Naso shows how the aid and media sectors cooperate in a unique way in Africa. Based on more than 70 interviews with foreign correspondents and aid workers operating across Africa, the book argues that the changing nature of foreign news and of aid is forcing them to form a deep co-dependency that is having a serious and largely unnoticed effect on Western news coverage.

This comprehensive examination of a new paradigm will interest students and scholars of media and journalism, African studies, development and humanitarian studies and the aid and media communities operating across Africa.

Lena von Naso received her PhD in Political Science, Peace and Conflict Studies at Augsburg University, Germany in 2016.

Author bio

Dr. Lena von Naso studied international literature and political science at Ludwigs-Maximilians-Universität München, Germany, and at Universidad de Buenos Aires, Argentina, and received her PhD in political science from the Department of Political Science, Peace and Conflict Studies at Augsburg University, Germany. She has worked as University Lecturer and Research Associate in political science, as a journalist and writer, and as researcher in aid and development contexts, including work for the UN. She is currently based in East Africa working as an independent researcher.

Routledge Contemporary Africa

The Development of African Capital Markets
A Legal and Institutional Approach
Boniface Chimpango

China, Africa and Responsible International Engagement
Yanzhuo Xu

Joke-Performance in Africa
Mode, Media and Meaning
Edited by Ignatius Chukwumah

The Media and Aid in Sub-Saharan Africa
Whose News?
Lena von Naso

The Media and Aid in Sub-Saharan Africa

Whose News?

Lena von Naso

LONDON AND NEW YORK

First published 2018
by Routledge
2 Park Square, Milton Park, Abingdon, Oxon OX14 4RN

and by Routledge
711 Third Avenue, New York, NY 10017

Routledge is an imprint of the Taylor & Francis Group, an informa business

© 2018 Lena von Naso

The right of Lena von Naso to be identified as author of this work has been asserted by her in accordance with sections 77 and 78 of the Copyright, Designs and Patents Act 1988.

All rights reserved. No part of this book may be reprinted or reproduced or utilised in any form or by any electronic, mechanical, or other means, now known or hereafter invented, including photocopying and recording, or in any information storage or retrieval system, without permission in writing from the publishers.

Trademark notice: Product or corporate names may be trademarks or registered trademarks, and are used only for identification and explanation without intent to infringe.

British Library Cataloguing-in-Publication Data
A catalogue record for this book is available from the British Library

Library of Congress Cataloging-in-Publication Data
Names: Naso, Lena von, author.
Title: The media and aid in Sub-Saharan Africa : whose news?/Lena von Naso.
Other titles: Routledge contemporary Africa series.
Description: New York : Routledge, 2018. | Series: Routledge contemporary
Africa series | Includes bibliographical references and index. | Abstract in German.
Identifiers: LCCN 2017048617 | ISBN 9781138575462 (hardback) | ISBN 9781351271806 (e-book)
Subjects: LCSH: Foreign correspondents – Africa, Sub-Saharan. | Mass media and public opinion – Africa, Sub-Saharan. | Humanitarian assistance – Africa, Sub-Saharan – Societies, etc. – Influence. | Human rights – Africa, Sub-Saharan – Societies, etc. – Influence. | Africa, Sub-Saharan – Press coverage. | Africa, Sub-Saharan – Public opinion. | Africa, Sub-Saharan – In mass media.
Classification: LCC P96.A37 N37 2018 | DDC 070.449967 – dc23
LC record available at https://lccn.loc.gov/2017048617

ISBN: 978-1-138-57546-2 (hbk)
ISBN: 978-1-351-27180-6 (ebk)

Typeset in Times New Roman
by Apex CoVantage, LLC

Contents

Figures and tables ix
Preface xi
Preface in German xiii
Selected acronyms xv
Acknowledgement xvii

1 Introduction: coverage of Africa, foreign correspondents and humanitarian organisations — 1
  1.1 Research interest and hypotheses 7
  1.2 Overview of research design and data 10

2 State of research — 20

3 Theoretical concepts — 29
  3.1 One single theory of journalism? 29
  3.2 What reality does journalism display? 31
  3.3 Theories of news selection 34
  3.4 Methodological individualism and its combination with network analysis 37

4 Media and aid – sectors and actors: basic assumptions — 48
  4.1 Foreign correspondents as political actors 48
  4.2 Based in sub-Saharan Africa 59
  4.3 The relationship between journalism and public relations 64
  4.4 Humanitarian organisations – roles and tasks 68
  4.5 Embedded journalism – embedded with the military and embedded with the humanitarian sector? 79

5 Research design and methodology — 98

6 Research findings — 118

6.1 Framework and conditions defining the interactions – journalists 118
6.2 Framework and conditions defining the interactions – humanitarian organisations 143
6.3 Overview of the interactions 163
6.4 Challenges in the interactions 182
6.5 Importance of the interactions 189
6.6 Contextualising aid embedding in the light of the research results 200
6.7 Influence on coverage 213
6.8 Blurring of lines 241

7 Summary and conclusion — 251

8 Outlook — 261

Index 264
Annex 267

Figures and tables

Figures

0.1	Gado (2010)	xviii
3.1	Macro-micro-macro scheme, modified	40
4.1	Donations by image type	76
5.1	Numerical breakdown of interviewees	101
5.2	Data analysis	112
6.1	Map of common geographic division of Western media coverage of Africa	120
6.2	The true size of Africa	121
6.3	Working experience of correspondents working in Africa – freelancers and retainers only	122
6.4	Working experience of correspondents working in Africa – staff only	122
6.5	The editors' understanding of Africa	130
6.6	Correspondents' self-identification with roles – different media nationalities	135
6.7	Correspondents' self-identification with roles – freelancers and retainers only	136
6.8	Correspondents' self-identification with roles – staff only	137
6.9	Frequency of contact with OHHs – identification with the role 'advocate of socially disadvantaged people' and those correspondents who want to 'change something' with their reporting	141
6.10	Frequency of contact with OHHs – identification with all other roles but 'advocate' and those who want to 'change something'	142
6.11	Dependency on OHHs perceived by correspondents – identification with the roles 'advocate' and 'change something'	144
6.12	Dependency on OHHs perceived by correspondents – identification with all other roles but 'advocate of socially disadvantaged people' and 'change something'	145
6.13	Importance of contact with the media from the OHHs' perspective	146

Figures and tables

6.14	Dependency on the media and correspondents perceived by OHHs	151
6.15	The network of foreign correspondents	164
6.16	Importance of OHHs in comparison to other partners from the correspondents' perspective	167
6.17	Type of contact with correspondents from OHHs' perspective	168
6.18	Type of contact with OHHs from correspondents' perspective	169
6.19	Importance of personal contacts with correspondents from the OHHs' perspective	175
6.20	Correspondents avoiding OHHs	189
6.21	Reasons for avoiding certain OHHs	191
6.22	Importance of OHH and dependency on them – from correspondents' perspective	193
6.23	Dependency on OHHs – correspondents with less than four years of experience	194
6.24	Dependency on OHHs – correspondents with four to six years of experience	195
6.25	Dependency on OHHs – correspondents with seven or more years of working experience in Africa	196
6.26	Frequency of interactions between OHHs and correspondents	198
6.27	Dependency on OHHs perceived by correspondents – freelancers and retainers only	199
6.28	Dependency on OHHs perceived by correspondents – staff only	199
6.29	Correspondents' dependency on OHHs – British outlets only	210
6.30	Correspondents' dependency on OHHs – American outlets only	211
6.31	Correspondents' dependency on OHHs – German-speaking outlets only	212

Tables

| 5.1 | Media outlets included in the study | 102 |
| 5.2 | Humanitarian organisations included in the study | 102 |

Preface

This book takes a look behind the scenes of foreign news production on the African continent. It closely examines the relationships between two major players involved in its emergence: foreign correspondents and humanitarian organisations. Based on scientific evidence, I argue that the cooperation between the aid and the media sectors in sub-Saharan Africa has created a 'new normal' that has a worrying influence on Western news coverage. With evidence from the field, based on more than 70 in-depth interviews, this book analyses why and how journalists and humanitarian organisations interact, and what consequences that bears for reporting. Besides providing scientific research, the book gives practical examples and lets the actors in the field speak.

The changing nature of foreign news and of aid is forcing humanitarians and journalists to form an 'unholy alliance' of deep co-dependency that is having a serious and largely unnoticed effect on Western news coverage. This *aid embedding* is in many cases comparable to journalists embedded with the military. The mutual dependency is widely discussed among people working in the aid and development sector, as well as amongst journalists and their editors. Yet, so far there has not been any in-depth research on the issue, and no evidence to prove the trend for which single journalists account. I found a worrying blurring of lines between the two sectors taking place. However, Western news audiences are largely unaware of the fact that much of what is presented to them as 'neutral information' or 'coverage' from Africa, actually regularly comes close to following agendas of humanitarian organisations, which are often perceived as only 'doing good' in the public's view. Foreign correspondents have faced heavy budget cuts in recent years, yet they need to travel to be able to report. As a result, they often rely on humanitarian organisations to give them access to remote areas, including conflict zones, and to provide transportation, security, statistics, contacts and expertise. My research finds that the independence of journalists' reporting is often compromised because travel is recurrently facilitated by humanitarian organisations, and often partly or even fully financed by them. Not only are the places and people viewed through a humanitarian lens, many journalists also cannot reach their destination without the assistance of aid organisations. Meanwhile, the numbers and budgets of humanitarian organisations are growing and the competition over funding is getting harsher. In this situation, humanitarian organisations rely on media coverage to dynamise their donations and to build a 'brand'. They invest in public relations, and produce material that is then offered to the media. This material is regularly published word-for-word in newspapers, often without a hint of its provenance.

A broad international audience is unaware of the working reality of journalists reporting on Africa; and even less do they know of the consequences this reality has for news coverage. With media reports, often then echoed through social media, driving the formation of most Westerners' impressions of contemporary Africa, the book highlights for the first time the latest conditions under which those reports emerge. The thoughts about these changes of the actors involved in both industries – media and aid – are presented in their own words. The cooperation between humanitarians and journalists is uncovered, and it is shown how it not only influences the reporting and shapes the way Westerners see the African continent, but also affects decisions made in aid and development policy. It is the first data-driven examination of a new paradigm that will interest – if not worry – anyone interested in international affairs, aid and humanitarian interventions, global fundraising, public relations and news media.

Preface in German

Krisenfokussierte Berichterstattung dominiert die Nachrichten über Subsahara-Afrika. Das Bild eines homogen im Chaos versunkenen Kontinents voller Warlords, Piraten, Massenvergewaltigungen, Korruption, ethnischer Konflikte, fehlgeschlagener Demokratisierungsversuche und Erkrankungen wie Ebola überwiegt: Die Vorstellung von einem Kontinent, der sich selbst nicht aus der Misere befreien kann, sondern auf Hilfe der westlichen Welt angewiesen ist. Diese Art der Berichterstattung ist mitverantwortlich daran, dass das Bild von Afrika als verlorener Kontinent fortgeschrieben wird. Deshalb ist es wichtig, nach den Ursachen für diese Form der Berichterstattung zu forschen, denn Berichterstattung trägt zur politischen Meinungsbildung bei. Fast immer werden Personen des westlichen Kulturkreises herangezogen, um in westlichen Medien Konfliktlagen in Subsahara-Afrika zu beurteilen. Jüngste Analysen zeigen, dass fast zwei Drittel aller Quellen, die für Berichte verwendet werden, nicht afrikanisch sind, wobei Vertreter von Hilfsorganisationen eine prominente Rolle spielen, und fast immer ausschließlich positiv dargestellt werden. Dies ist kein Zufall. Während die Hilfsbranche seit dem ersten Jahrzehnt des 21. Jahrhunderts einen rasanten Aufschwung erlebt, ist die Anzahl der AuslandskorrespondentInnen erheblich zurückgegangen. Ich argumentiere in diesem Buch, dass sich die Interessen von Medien- und Hilfsbranche in den Krisenthemen treffen, und dass sich in Subsahara-Afrika zwischen den beiden Branchen und ihren Akteuren ein stabiles Netzwerk entwickelt hat, von dem beide profitieren, das sich aber stark auf die Unabhängigkeit des Berichterstattens auswirkt. Durch die Medien können Hilfsorganisationen Glaubwürdigkeit erlangen und ihre Spendenakquise dynamisieren; im Gegenzug sind Hilfsorganisationen mit ihren guten Informations- und Kontaktnetzwerken von großer Bedeutung für JournalistInnen, wenn diese Statistiken, Einschätzungen, oder logistische Hilfe benötigen. Häufig bieten Hilfsorganisationen KorrespondentInnen mit geringen Reisebudgets an, ihre Recherchetrips in schwer zugängliche Gebiete logistisch zu unterstützen und die Reise teil- oder komplett zu finanzieren, wodurch wiederum die Heimatredaktionen eher gewillt sind, den Trips zuzustimmen. Die Akteure haben aufgrund der Rahmen- und Strukturbedingungen ihrer jeweiligen Branche wenig andere Wahl, als die enge Kooperation mit Hilfsorganisationen weiter auszubauen. In vielen Fällen ist die Abhängigkeit so stark, dass man von *Aid embeds* sprechen kann. Unterdes verschwimmen die

Grenzen zwischen Medienberichterstattung und Öffentlichkeitsarbeit von Hilfsorganisationen auf eine Art und Weise, die für RezipientInnen kaum zu durchschauen ist. Diese Studie gibt Einblick in die Akteursbeziehungen zwischen AuslandskorrespondentInnen und einer ihrer wichtigsten Quellen und Partner, Not- und Entwicklungshilfeorganisationen.

Die politische Dimension von Auslandsberichterstattung als vierte Gewalt und ihr Einfluss auf westliche Not- und Entwicklungshilfe, sowie ihre wichtige Rolle, andernfalls nicht demokratisch legitimierte NGOs und UN-Organisationen zur Rechenschaft zu ziehen, setzt voraus, dass die Berichterstattung unabhängig und kritisch ist und sein kann. Die Veränderungsprozesse, denen Auslandsberichterstattung und Hilfsorganisationen gleichermaßen unterliegen, drängen AuslandskorrespondentInnen und PR-Mitarbeiter von Hilfsorganisationen dazu, enge Kooperationen einzugehen, die sie abhängig voneinander machen und die mediale Berichterstattung stark beeinflussen. In manchen Fällen der Kooperation ist die Abhängigkeit so stark, dass man nicht mehr von unabhängigem Berichterstatten sprechen kann. Umso erstaunlicher, dass die meisten Medien-Rezipienten nichts von diesen Kooperationen und ihren Auswirkungen wissen. Dieses Buch blickt hinter die Kulissen: Wie sind diese Kooperationen vor Ort gestaltet und wie werden sie durch in ihr jeweiliges System bedingt? Welchen Einfluss haben sie auf das Berichterstatten über das subsaharische Afrika, mit welchen Konsequenzen?

Selected acronyms

Adeso	African Development Solutions
AFP	Agence France-Presse
Amisom	African Union Mission in Somalia
AP	The Associated Press
ARD	Arbeitsgemeinschaft der öffentlich-rechtlichen Rundfunkanstalten der Bundesrepublik Deutschland
BBC	British Broadcasting Corporation
Cafod	Catholic Agency for Overseas Development
Care	Cooperative for Assistance and Relief Everywhere
CNN	Cable News Network
Comms	Communications department
CSM	Christian Science Monitor
DFID	(UK) Department for International Development
DPA	Deutsche Presseagentur
Echo	European Commission's Humanitarian Aid and Civil Protection Department
EU	European Union
FAZ	Frankfurter Allgemeine Zeitung
Gavi	The Vaccine Alliance
GBP	Great British Pounds
HRW	Human Rights Watch
Humanitarians	Employees working for humanitarian organisations
ICRC	International Committee of the Red Cross
IDP	Internally Displaced Person
IFRC	International Federation of Red Cross and Red Crescent Societies
IOM	International Organization for Migration
IRC	International Rescue Committee
Irin	Integrated Regional Information Networks
MSF	Médecins Sans Frontières/Doctors Without Borders
(I)NGO	(International) Nongovernmental Organisation
NZZ	Neue Zürcher Zeitung
Ocha	(UN) Office for the Coordination of Humanitarian Affairs

ODA	Official Development Assistance
OECD	Organisation for Economic Cooperation and Development
OHH	Organisation for Humanitarian Help, humanitarian organisation
Oxfam	Oxford Committee for Famine Relief
PR	Public Relations
SRF	Schweizer Fernsehen und Radio
SZ	Süddeutsche Zeitung
TAZ	Tageszeitung
UN	United Nations
UNDP	United Nations Development Programme
UNHAS	United Nations Humanitarian Air Service
UNHCR	United Nations High Commissioner for Refugees
Unicef	United Nations Children's Fund
USD	United States Dollars
VOA	Voice of America
WFP	World Food Programme
WHO	World Health Organization
ZDF	Zweites Deutsches Fernsehn

Note 1: I use British English spelling in this book, unless I am citing from a text that uses American spelling, or when referring to an organisation whose name uses American English.

Note 2: The title of this thesis was created before I read Carroll Bogert's "Whose News? The Changing Media Landscape and NGOs," Human Rights Watch World Report, 2011. I acknowledge similarities between aspects of the title of my book and her report.

Acknowledgement

I want to express my gratitude to all journalists and aid workers who participated in the research that this book is based upon, giving me their precious time for long interviews and sharing their experiences and perspectives. I would also like to thank everyone who supported me during the years that this book needed to take shape, and who encouraged me to keep following the initial spark of fascination about the topic, from the idea to its implementation and completion.

xviii *Acknowledgement*

Truth is violence, reality is war, news is conflict.

Hartley (2000: 40)

Figure 0.1 Gado (2010) Tanzania elections 2010

Reference

Hartley, John (2000) "Communicative Democracy in a Redactional Society: The Future of Journalism Studies", in: *Journalism* 1.

1 Introduction

Coverage of Africa, foreign correspondents and humanitarian organisations

News coverage of sub-Saharan Africa in Western media is dominated by reporting that focuses on crises. Africa mostly appears as a continent homogeneously drowning in chaos, full of warlords, mass rapes, corruption, ethnic conflicts, famines, failed democratisation, pirates, HIV, and epidemics such as Ebola. For years, public fatigue relating to news from Africa has been criticised (Krems 2002; Clark 2004; Mükke 2009a). The lack of interest regarding sub-Saharan Africa is a phenomenon in many Western industrialised nations. Unreasonably high negativism (De Beer 2010), so-called crisis-focused coverage,[1] is considered a likely cause of this (Van der Gaag 2007: 185; Plewes & Stuart 2009: 24f; see also Luger & Pointner 1996; Dilg 1999). Rarely does the news cover progress, successful local economic structures, cultural events, or African personalities as role models; and if correspondents suggest covering any of these stories, Western editors are often not interested in running them (Mükke 2003).[2] The dominant perception is that the continent cannot release itself from misery and is dependent on Western support. This one-sided reporting is in large part responsible for reinforcing the image of Africa as a hopeless continent in the minds of large audiences (many studies argue in favour of this coherence, see e.g. Plewes & Stuart 2009: 24ff; see also DFID 2000; VSO 2001; Van der Gaag 2007). This is especially so if the audiences have no experience of places in Africa to help contextualise the information that the media and campaigns of humanitarian organisations provide, which is the case for most Western audiences (George Alagiah in Clark 2004: 695; see also Glennie, Straw & Wild 2012: 8ff).

We live in a media society where fictional and 'real' actuality conglomerate in a "contemporary reality", generated by mass media (Merten 2004: 17).[3] The very few reports on sub-Saharan Africa contribute substantially to reinforcing the picture of Africa as a hopeless continent. Many studies have shown how dominant and enduring this crisis focus remains in audiences' perception.[4] The issue of reporting is thus closely interconnected with the formation of political opinion on foreign issues and can influence the political agenda, if the media are understood as having *agency*. The media frequently report on incidents because they are on the political agenda; equally, some issues are on the political agenda because they have already been spread to the populace by the media. Studies on the so-called *CNN effect* show how media coverage indirectly impacts policy making via its influence on political elites, usually by reflecting public opinion and creating pressure to act, by adding issues to the public discourse, or by creating a public climate that encourages or discourages politicians to act in a certain way. Despite controversial discussions about whether the media has a direct causal effect on policy making, its indirect influence is widely accepted.[5] What kind of social responsibility thus comes with news coverage? The German Federation of Journalists published the following statement regarding the special mission journalists have in our society:

> To uphold and extend these freedoms, all journalists are called upon to exercise utmost diligence during their work, to respect human dignity, and to adhere to basic principles as defined in the Press Codex of the German Press Council [Deutscher Presserat]. Journalists can only fulfil their tasks of providing information and commentary and of fostering public checks and balances when they are free of legal restrictions and constraints that hinder these principles.
>
> (Deutscher Journalisten Verband 2012: 2)

Starting from the premise that media coverage can have an influence on events themselves, I thus am of the opinion that coverage bears political and social responsibility (see also Chouliaraki 2006; Chouliaraki 2012; for the argument that media shape and reconfigure disasters and their social relations, see Cottle 2014). Underlying my investigation on foreign news covering of sub-Saharan Africa and its connection with the aid sector is an understanding of normative media theory, in a representative liberal tradition. Media do not necessarily have to only present facts and objective views, but the reporting should be balanced and – if it is interpretative – give a context and understanding. Journalists are not only

> external observers but also part of 'the reality' that they report on. [...] Under certain circumstances, they change the 'reality' that they report on, even if they do not intend to do so. There are reciprocal effects between 'the reality' and the journalistic depiction of it that cannot be adequately accounted for by the question as to whether the media portray reality 'correctly' or 'incorrectly'.
>
> (Kepplinger 2004, 2. edition: 100)

Journalism, as I understand it, is supposed to be impartial and solution-oriented. It is problematic that in the field, journalists can be caught in the dilemma between impartiality and humanity that might conflict with professional obligations (Gjelten 2001). In such cases, reporting because of its crucial role of holding governments, institutions, businesses, and individuals to account, should always give impartiality preference over lobbying for a cause, however seemingly good it may be. Journalists also have to consider the potential impacts that their reports may have, attend to the causes of a conflict, focus on solutions, reflect on their own position and role, and provide implicit transparency (Bilke 2008).

The *CNN effect* shows the importance of media coverage and the critical role of media serving as a regulating control in Western democracies. Because the coverage has political consequences, the questions of why reporting on sub-Saharan Africa assumes this strongly crisis-focused manifestation, under which circumstances the coverage originates, and what actors are involved in its emergence, are very important. Especially since studies show that if a broader public is to be engaged with developing countries' issues, intrinsic values must be addressed, instead of "enhancing the status of Northern 'givers' relative to Southern 'receivers', and delivering messages focused on giving money or taking easy actions" (Darnton 2011: 2). However, people from the Western cultural sphere are almost invariably consulted when it comes to assessing conflict situations for Western media (Schmoll 1998: 3; Krems 2002; Smith, Edge & Morris 2006; Alam 2007: 59). Two thirds of sources used in news reports are not African (Mükke 2009b: 116) with representatives of humanitarian organisations playing a prominent role as the second most common main actors (Mükke 2009b: 258). It is striking how often they feature in news reports, and are framed exclusively as positive actors (Alam 2007: 59; Mükke 2009b: 114). Additionally, catastrophes in sub-Saharan Africa have to be very serious for the international media market to take notice of them (Mükke 2003: 84; see also VSO 2001; Smith, Edge & Morris 2006; Stollenwerk 2011). The news threshold, the hurdle that events must overcome to be newsworthy, is high. A high news threshold is followed by an increasing crisis focus, resulting in an even higher threshold, and so on. A positive feedback loop occurs. The Kenyan professor Wambui Mwangi criticises: "To get comparable attention [comparable to an event in Western industrial nations], a lot of African deaths are necessary. This disparity is profoundly racist" (Grill 2007: 126). While it is the media that make disasters visible to a broader audience, both the media and humanitarian organisations are key to "the mediation of distant suffering and the global production and dissemination of images and stories of disasters and atrocities" (Orgad & Seu 2014: 8), and both together shape moral responses to this distant suffering. Spohrs showed that de-escalation oriented framing of news is later reflected in the mental patterns of its readers (Spohrs 2006: 1). By proving this, he delivered evidence that news coverage can have a direct impact on recipients and that conflict sensitivity can be transmitted through texts. Other large-scale audience research also precisely identifies the origin of the audience's perceptions in the media, and in the way the media present humanitarian issues; that is also the case, yet to a lesser extent, for studies on humanitarian organisations' campaigns (VSO 2001; Opinion Leader Research 2002; Höijer 2004; Glennie, Straw & Wild 2012). Studies show that larger organisations with significant budgets to widely spread their messages tend to use more "pornography of poverty" material that then sticks in the public's minds (Plewes & Stuart 2009: 29). We see that media coverage can have significant effects on the audiences, but few studies research in depth its origination processes, conditions of production, and its structures, and it is important to close that gap. We need to focus on the actors relevant in the originating process of news. However, until now the scientific debate on news coverage of sub-Saharan Africa has primarily focused on content analysis. So far, we lack studies investigating why this kind of material is produced, and studies that include the actors that are involved in its production process.

An ongoing development drives the global news market. The global cutback of foreign correspondent posts in Western media is alarming, and is associated with diminishing interest in comprehensive and knowledgeable presentation of foreign news. Prominently placed foreign stories in British newspapers decreased by 80 percent from 1979 to 2009 according to a study by M. Moore (2010: 17), and there is little evidence that this trend might change. For news from sub-Saharan Africa, with its considerably higher news threshold, this development comes with severe consequences: there are very few reports about the African continent south of the Sahara in the Western media. Note that more than 30 percent of foreign correspondents for American media covering sub-Saharan Africa think the continent should receive more attention (Wu & Hamilton 2004: 527; also Ricchiardi 2005). They especially believe that positive news should be covered more, since not everything is negative[6] in Africa, despite its association with backwardness not least since the publication of Joseph Conrad's *Heart of Darkness*.[7] The increasing number of blog entries, travel novels, memoirs, and other publications produced by foreign correspondents besides news stories is beginning to advance a more positive picture of Africa south of the Sahara.[8] The Africa correspondent of the German newspaper Frankfurter Allgemeine Zeitung remarks:

> The situation in Africa has generally improved significantly. The wars in Mozambique, Angola, Ivory Coast, Sierra Leone, and Liberia have ended. The economic growth on the continent is on an average six percent a year. Roads are being built everywhere.
>
> (Scheen 2008)

The media, however, have for centuries concentrated on 'hard news', covering up-to-date and consequential news that are relevant to the audiences (Weichert & Kramp 2011: 14). Certainly one of the media's tasks is to point out problematic issues. But because the crisis focus is so immanent in Western news on sub-Saharan Africa, my research interest sprang from the assumption that aspects other than those generally responsible for global news production, such as *news values*, and unreconstructed stereotypes about Africa, play a significant role in the concentration on crises in sub-Saharan African news (see Chapter 2, 3, and Chapter 4, section 4.2). Those existing theories cannot explain satisfactorily why the media coverage of sub-Saharan Africa is so persistently negative, or why the coverage consistently ranks lower than news from less developed countries in Asia and South America (Lange 2003: 88f).

Because of the marked decrease of Western foreign correspondents in Africa, even media of record sometimes use so-called *parachute journalists*;[9] the working reality of journalists changes constantly (Hamilton & Jenner 2004; Sambrook 2010), and the news-making process has become ever faster, while requiring more workforce to be able to supply the media's digital presence with new material constantly. This is due to the development of the information technology and infrastructure mainly since 2000 that allows reporters to file anything from anywhere at any time, exacerbating their influence (Shrivastava & Hyde-Clarke 2004), and due to the online presence of news media. The digitalisation of news puts more pressure on correspondents to react immediately to events, and to prioritise crises. In addition to media outlets competing against each other and increasing the speed of news, also audiences have higher demands since they can compare reports from different outlets directly, and may for example demand that 'their' newspaper or broadcaster reports on issues that other outlets report on already. This is a challenge for correspondents, not only but especially in sub-Saharan Africa. A correspondent covering sub-Saharan Africa for German media, for example, is responsible for an average of 33 countries (Mükke 2009a: 43), while travel budgets shrink. This trend is the same for other Western media nationalities. Additionally, sub-Saharan Africa is seen as a springboard for careers; in the beginning most correspondents may have journalistic experience but little or no knowledge about Africa (Mükke 2003: 83; Wu & Hamilton 2004: 522; Wanene 2005; Junghanns & Hanitzsch 2006), and their editors often know less, and are not interested in giving space to well-researched pieces beyond stereotypical African stories. These factors combine to produce a situation that provides humanitarian organisations with powerful possibilities to influence journalistic work, because, in contrast to the decrease in foreign correspondents, humanitarian organisations have experienced a rapid boom since the first decade of the twenty-first century – influenced with a lasting effect by the unprecedented political and fundraising response to the BBC coverage about the 1984 famine in Ethiopia (Franks 2013: 71–87). The boom in the humanitarian sector is reflected in the budgets, in the sharp increase in the number of international NGOs, local NGOs, and governmental organisations and in their increasing professionalisation (de Jonge Oudraat & Haufler 2008: 11). Between 2006 and 2010 INGOs' humanitarian funding income rose from USD 2.8 billion to 8.7, with ten out of 20 key recipient countries being sub-Saharan African, which received more than 62 percent of the 20 key recipients' total budget (Stoianova 2012: 5,11). And this does not even include UN organisations. In accordance with the growing number and professionalism of INGOs, the funding from governments to INGOs and the outsourcing of government services to INGOs has increased, and as a result, so has their political influence (Werker & Ahmed 2008: 77ff). The largest amongst the humanitarian organisations have a very significant amount of money at their disposal. Unicef, for example, spends 55 percent of its average overall annual budget of USD 3.3 billion on sub-Saharan Africa (UNICEF 2010, 2011, 2012) and is one of the main multilateral Official Development Assistance receivers.[10] Care International, as Mükke researched, globally has a budget of around USD 500 million a year (Mükke 2011: 25). Oxfam raised more than USD 1 billion in one year (Oxfam 2014: 68), and is planning to grow; it wants to raise USD 560 million more, and recruit three million new donors in the 5 years until 2020 (I_74).[11] The ICRC issued an initial appeal for USD 1.5 billion for operations worldwide in 2016 – excluding costs for the headquarters and costs that occurred during the year – of which USD 609 million were needed for operations in Africa (ICRC 2015).[12]

Mükke (2009b: 263f) plausibly assumes a correlation between the increase in crisis-focused news coverage and the increasing amount of aid money. The interests of the media and the aid sector seem to intersect in the field of 'crisis themes': the media perform a key role for the aid sector when it comes to the "normative representation of aid, acquiring donations, and the employment of aid as an instrument for realising political and economic objectives" (Mükke 2009b: 262) because they can lend credibility to the organisations; and because "[j]ournalism serves as a bridge linking aid agencies and the work that they do in the field, with publics and potential donors" (Cottle & Nolan 2007: 863) to the respective organisation. The professionalisation of humanitarian organisations has been accompanied by an increase in economic competition between them. At the same time the changing role for foreign correspondents is apparent. Yet, how are these two developments related when at first sight they seem to be independent of one another? "Much of the reporting on Africa that *does* occur originates from within the framework of aid and is facilitated by aid organizations", Franks concludes from her research (Franks 2010: 82; see also Cottle & Nolan 2007: 863; Wright 2016). But how does that actually take place? The Kenyan writer and journalist Binyavanga Wainaina remarks sarcastically in an article published in The Guardian with the title *How Not to Write about Africa*:

> Nairobi is a good place to be a foreign correspondent. There are regular flights to the nearest genocide, and there are green lawns, tennis courts, good fawning service. [. . .] To make your work easier, you need, in your phone, the numbers of the country directors of every European aid agency: Oxfam, Save the Children. To find these numbers is not difficult: chances are these guys are your neighbours, your tennis partners. [. . .] In this age, all local knowledge is carried by aid organisations. These organisations speak human rights, and because they do so, we know that they are good, objective and truthful. So, if a foreign correspondent needs to know what exactly is going on in Sudan, their weekly lunch with the Oxfam guy will identify the most urgent issues.
> (Wainaina 2012: 1f)

A BBC news report by Michael Buerk on the 1984 famine in Ethiopia had a global resonance because of two factors that are also relevant to this study. First, the directive by Buerk's editors "to find some starving Africans [. . .] to run in parallel with a piece on BBC News" (Franks 2013: 19). And second, the fact that Buerk called the Oxfam press office because his report was supposed to air before a story by a competing television broadcaster that was still in production, so time was running out. As he called Oxfam's press office, they suggested he report from a region close to where they were already operating (Gill 1986: 93), even though it was not in the "epicentre" (Franks 2013: 19) of the hunger catastrophe. But the story was a means to make the interests of the media and humanitarian sector meet. Just as the humanitarian organisations factor in the work of journalists, journalists prepare cost-benefit-analyses when they decide which issue to report about, how much time to spend on it, and what means and resources to use. Humanitarian organisations are attractive for journalists on three levels, which cannot clearly be separated:[13] on the organisational-logistical level, on the level of information content, and on an economical level. These three levels overlap; if journalists, for example, use the means of transportation or translators that humanitarian organisations provide, it can bring advantages on all three levels.

Against this background, I argue in this book that it is because of the interactions in the dense network between foreign correspondents and humanitarian organisations that the news coverage on sub-Saharan Africa is largely crisis-focused. First, I explore why it is beneficial from both the media's and aid sector's perspectives to form this 'unholy alliance', based on the framework in which they each work. I present the standpoints of the actors involved, map the interactions and analyse what they look like in detail. Based on these findings, I explain why this alliance in many cases influences the news coverage to an extent that it cannot be called independent journalism.

1.1 Research interest and hypotheses

The interactions between the media and humanitarian sector are a plausible explanation for the provenance of conflict-focused coverage that has not been thoroughly scientifically studied (Franks 2008; Mükke 2011). Against this background, this research gives detailed insight into the emergence and conditions of current international news production in sub-Saharan Africa. It focuses on *actor relationships* between foreign correspondents as producers of news coverage, and one of their most important sources and partners, humanitarian organisations. To explain the interactions between these two, I explore the reasons for cooperation from both perspectives, from an organisational as well as an individual standpoint. In an explorative micro-analysis with an inductive design I then analyse the interactions in detail, and conclude with their influence on news coverage.

There is no commonly used accepted definition of *humanitarian organisation* (see ideal-typical NGOs: Kuhn 2000: 24; Frantz & Martens 2006). Often, a conceptual distinction between humanitarian and development aid is made. Humanitarian work is often understood as emergency relief, a crisis intervention aiming at providing financial and material, existential support to people in need, addressing basic needs to save lives during a limited period of time. For emergency aid, organisations mostly work around governments or fill in their role when they cannot or do not provide this existential support themselves (Macrae 2012); development aid, in contrast, is referred to as long-term efforts to influence and change the conditions of people's lives for the better by building and supporting structures and systems. Development aid is mostly delivered through NGOs and the governments in the countries that receive the development aid. While conceptually there is a clear distinction between humanitarian/emergency and development aid, in practice, myriad different organisations working in the aid sector define very differently what humanitarian assistance is, and also "their classification of what constitutes humanitarian activities" varies widely from "more long-term approaches" to emergency response (Stoianova 2012). In the context of this study, the term *humanitarian organisation* explicitly includes both these concepts, as most organisations have projects for emergency relief as well as development aid. Although the conceptual framework of both is different, one aiming at immediate help, the other aiming at setting up structures that can be self-contained, and although they are funded separately, on the ground these processes often overlap, when humanitarian operations are about to be completed and development operations start. At the same time, many crises in conflict-affected and fragile states go far beyond emergency relief (Simon Levine in Anyangwe 2015). Also, since it is easier to fundraise for emergencies, more and more organisations make appeals during emergencies but instead of thematic funding make clear in their appeals that the donations will be used for different projects at different times, in order to be more flexible and be able to use the money where it is needed most.[14] I define humanitarian organisations (*OHHs*, short for *Organisations for Humanitarian Help*) as international, implementing aid organisations – nongovernmental (INGOs), as well as organisations of the United Nations – that fall in the broad categories of both emergency and development aid, as well as humanitarian affairs. OHH thus encompasses UN organisations such as Unicef, as well as INGOs such as Save the Children or Doctors Without Borders, as well as human rights organisations such as Human Rights Watch. I will explain in Chapter 5 why such a wide understanding of the term is beneficial for the research design I chose. OHHs understood in this sense are formally organised, internationally operating entities, which are funded through either public or private means or a mixture of both; their stated aim is to carry out disaster emergency relief on the one hand, and development aid on the other hand, for people who cannot overcome such difficulties through their own means. OHHs also have in common that they are to a great extent financed by donations in addition to governmental support; they thus rely on positive news reports regarding their work, and therefore also on good contacts to journalists on an actor level.

The following central questions have priority: **what do the actor relationships between foreign correspondents and the staff of humanitarian organisations in sub-Saharan Africa look like? What importance do these interactions have for the news reporting, and more specifically: what influence do they have on the crisis-focused reporting on sub-Saharan Africa?**

Regarding the second question and generally, I proceed from the assumption that independence in the investigation and production process of news has a positive influence on the quality of news coverage. Unbiased, impartial reporting always has to be the aim. In the course of answering these primary research questions, a number of subordinate questions are to be answered. Who interacts with whom? Who does not interact? For what reasons? What form do the interactions assume on an organisational-logistical and economic level, as well as on the level of information content? What do working routines look like? What kinds of motives and cost-benefit analyses underlie the interactions? Where do the interests of both groups intersect, and where do they differ? What does that imply? What role do personal and private contacts play? What impact do they have on news production? What self-understandings and role conceptions inform the conduct of the individual actors and what impact does this have on interactions with the other group? What are the challenges, and what are the advantages of the interaction from both perspectives? What role do humanitarian organisations play in general in the production process of media content? What are other relevant players, and how relevant are they from a news production perspective in comparison to humanitarian organisations?

The research looks at the interactions on an actor level as well as at conditions inherent in the system of both journalism and public relations in the aid sector that influence the actions of the individuals on a micro-level. Finally, in order to be able to determine the degree of dependence between foreign correspondents and the personnel of humanitarian organisations, I situate the actor relationships within a wider context of relations of dependence, comparing them in structural terms with *embedded journalism*.[15] Are foreign correspondents and the personnel of humanitarian organisations dependent on one another in ways comparable to embeds and military troops? What does this mean on the macro-level for the picture of Africa generated in the media? Recent publications speak of an incestuous relationship between the aid and media sectors (Franks 2008; Mükke 2011; see also Gibbon 1996; Leigh 2015; Green 2016; Wright 2016). Is this claim entirely supportable? To what extent can conceptual characteristics of *embedding* be transferred to the structural cooperation between the humanitarian and media sectors?

My central heuristic hypotheses underlying the above questions are:

(1) There is a structural coupling of motives and interests of foreign correspondents and humanitarian organisations that is potentially dangerous for the coverage. A structural cooperation has developed between foreign correspondents and humanitarian organisations, which is reasonable for the concerned actors, but normatively disastrous for the picture of Africa portrayed in the media. Their reciprocal relationship of dependency can be compared structurally to that between embeds and the military.

(2) The foreign correspondent acts increasingly as a *homo socio-oeconomicus*. The cooperation with humanitarian organisations is, out of lack of alternatives, a logical consequence of the increasing *economisation* of journalism. It is not the correspondent's self-perceived role as a journalist that leads to cooperation with the aid sector, but rather the conditions and structures defining the correspondent's work, even if the reporting is at risk of taking on a significantly selective viewpoint through the cooperation.

(3) The image of Africa as a continent of catastrophes, which the media often convey, serves the interest of humanitarian organisations in acquiring donations. Functional relationships with journalists provide humanitarian organisations with the possibility of distinguishing and 'ennobling' certain strategic contents as "impartial information" (de Waal 1997: 84), which thereby escalates the acquisition of donations. The programmes of humanitarian organisations thus receive a quasi "informal stamp" of credibility and reliability (Bogert 2011: 3).

I start from the premise that the interaction between the humanitarian and the media sectors is one of a mutual dependency, with both enabling each other's work, with neither side overweighing and determining the other for their own benefit. Only with this premise can I analyse the interactions in an unbiased way.

1.2 Overview of research design and data

I researched the interactions between humanitarian organisations and correspondents in an explorative micro-analysis with an inductive design. The relationships between single actors were studied on a micro-level with regard to the system – journalism and humanitarian/development aid, within which individual actors perform – by means of empirical communicator research (Bentele, Brosius & Jarren 2003). Taking *methodological individualism* as a basis of understanding the relation between individuals and their social context (Esser 1993), I assume that the macro-phenomenon, one-sided, crisis-focused news reporting, is explainable through micro-analysis of motivations, expectations, and actions of individuals interacting with each other. I follow the understanding that social phenomena 'reproduce' through reciprocal expectations and expectations of what the other is expecting, and individuals take actions within a social context orienting themselves towards others' selections of actions and their expectations (Esser 1999, 2000a, 2000b, 2000c, 2003, 2004; Greshoff 2008). Within this framework of methodological individualism, I start from the premise that individuals are socio-economic actors.[16]

In order to understand the actions of the individuals, their motives, expectations, preferences, views, role perception, expectation of the others' behaviour, not only individuals but also their social and institutional framework need to be researched. Then we can understand how individual interactions within that framework can aggregate to a macro-phenomenon. Network research and guideline interviews with open questions are the method of choice for this study.[17] It is important to stress that in this view the actions actors perform are confined and influenced by their institutional framework; at the same time the actions chosen also influence the framework. I combine this approach with network analysis (see Kropp 2010), understanding the network as a supra-individual pattern of interactions, and use the network as help to explain the aggregation of individual interactions to the macro-phenomenon. For this, participants were questioned about their relationships, closeness and frequency of contacts, and expansion of their network. The relationships in the network analysis in combination with the model of methodological individualism – other than in more 'traditional' network-analyses – do not in principal take priority over individual motives and characteristics of individuals. I understand the network as a consolidation of wider, stabilised interactions between individuals.

I use an interdisciplinary approach to study the production processes of news, and the practices, aims, perspectives, and constraints of both the humanitarian and media sector, individually and in interaction with each other. Orgad and Seu also argue in favour of an interdisciplinary study for a similar undertaking to study perspectives on the ground that have not been studied (Orgad & Seu 2014: 28). At this point, I only provide a basic overview of the research design as a preliminary orientation; details are explained in Chapter 5 about the design and methodology of this study. The data was gathered in a multilevel approach with a comparative design. The interactions of correspondents of American, British, and German-speaking media outlets and staff of humanitarian organisations were analysed at the micro-level by means of *analysis of ego-centred networks* and a combination of qualitative *semi-structured guideline-* and *problem-centred interviews*, as well as through questionnaires. Thanks to the comparative design, an independent variable – the nationality of the media for which the correspondents work – could be controlled methodically. Pre-research in Nairobi suggested that there were essential differences between the media policies of British, American, and German-speaking media houses, which have an effect on the relationships with humanitarian organisations.[18] For this study, interviews were first conducted with permanent employees, stringers, freelancers, and agency journalists of international leading media organisations with a presence in sub-Saharan Africa. Many of the interviews took place in Nairobi, chosen for its prime location for correspondents and hub for aid projects in East and Central Africa. Following this, applying the same method, humanitarian organisations' personnel were interviewed, mostly communication officers, spokespeople, and programme managers, whose organisations the journalists interviewed in the first step identified as important partners or sources.[19] An initial selection of interviewees was made in pre-research test interviews. The main semi-structured interviews were supplemented by ego-centred network analysis (Wolf 2004) to reveal the journalists' network, motives for cooperation and procedures, and to reconstruct typical patterns of behaviour. Additionally, a few experts working on African issues and correspondents with extensive working experience, but who have worked on continents other than Africa were interviewed to gain a more abstract view on the processes, and a broader outside perspective on long-term trends. Furthermore, selected individuals working in strategic positions in the fundraising departments at the headquarters of humanitarian organisations were interviewed to provide additional information on the organisations' financial perspectives, and their connection to the public relations departments, and to communications officers, who are the ones mainly in contact with correspondents on the ground.

Chapter 1 gives an introduction to the issue, the research questions, and a short overview of the study's design. Chapter 2 presents the state of research in brief. Chapter 3 then elucidates the theoretical understanding of journalism, how journalism portrays reality, and what aspects can influence coverage. Generally, I assume that the macro-phenomenon of coverage focussing on negative issues can be explained via the analysis of micro-actions of individuals that form a network consisting of journalists and people working for humanitarian organisations. This is why Chapter 4 outlines characteristics of the media and the aid sector, and explains the context in which their individual actors work: foreign correspondents and staff or consultants of humanitarian organisations, their working conditions, their working routines, their role concepts, motives, their expectations and understanding towards the other sector and its individuals. Through the comparison with the phenomenon of embedded journalism in Chapter 4, section 4.5, the actor relationships are put into an extended context of a relationship of dependency. On the macro-level, the research examines the phenomenon of crises-focused coverage and the image of Africa in the media, created through the decisions and actions of individual actors on a micro-level. Chapter 5 presents at full length the research design, methods, and the criteria for sample selection strategy. Chapter 6 then gives a detailed insight into the empirical research: sections 6.1 and 6.2 explain the framework that defines the interactions, 6.3 to 6.4 give an overview of the studied interactions, the partners involved, how the interactions take place, and what challenges occur in the field. Sections 6.5 and 6.6 delve into dependencies that these interactions create and compares the relationships to embedded journalism, arguing that journalists from a certain level of dependency on humanitarian organisations can be called aid embeds. Section 6.7 then discusses the impact that the interactions have on news reporting. Section 6.8 argues that the lines between aid and media sector become increasingly blurred. Chapter 7 summarises the findings. Chapter 8 presents a short outlook on future trends in the news and aid sector, and stresses how crucial it is for both news media and audiences to realise the importance of well-funded, unbiased reporting that does not have to rely on the goodwill of humanitarian organisations carrying their own agenda.

Notes

1 Crisis-focused coverage refers to the dominance of topics of crises, conflicts, catastrophes, wars, and illnesses in the media. The voyeuristic display of people as poor and helpless is also referred to as the "pornography of poverty" (Plewes & Stuart 2009: 23). The more crisis-focused stories are, the harder it becomes to publish other coverage, and the bigger the catastrophes must be for the media market to take notice of them.
2 Positively framed reports in print media are likely to feature successful aid projects, while longer documentaries on Africa on television most often show flora and fauna as well as "established clichés about the 'mythical Africa' or 'the land of adventures'" (Krems 2002: 130f).
3 The author of this book did all translations from German into English and from French into English with a focus on the content.
4 Adamson (1993); Alam (2007). On the German mass-media context, see Luger and Pointner (1996), Schmoll (1998), Dilg (1999), Mükke (2004); on British media, see e.g. VSO (2001), Smith, Edge, and Morris (2006), Seu (2011), Birrell (2012a); On American media, see Sartor (2011). For a comparative content analysis of German, British and American media, see De Beer (2010).
5 Some scholars criticise that the policy-media interaction model explaining the *CNN effect* – the media influencing political action – is too simplistic (Jakobsen 2000). Robinson, however, argues convincingly that the question of the media's influence on policy making remains relevant despite all scholarly precaution toward research including dependent and independent variables, and despite all scepticism with regard to whether it can be scientifically proven how policy makers would have acted differently if the coverage would have been different (Robinson 2002:2f).
6 For a differentiated analysis of favourable developments in sub-Saharan Africa see, for example, Birrell (2012a), Kappel et al. (2013).
7 *Heart of Darkness* by Joseph Conrad (2007 [1899]).

8 Among many others: *The Shadow of the Sun: My African Life* by Ryszard Kapuściński (2001); *Die schwarze Sonne Afrikas* [Africa's black sun] by Michael Birnbaum (2001); *Das Prinzip Trotzdem* [The principle of nevertheless] by Michael Bitala (2007); *Ein Fahrrad für die Flussgötter. Reportagen aus Afrika* [A bike for the river Gods. Reporting from Africa] by Birgit Virnich (2010); *Mein afrikanisches Tagebuch. Reise durch einen Kontinent im Aufbruch* [My African diary. Travelling through an awakening continent] by Marietta Slomka (2011); *Der unterschätzte Kontinent: Reise zur Mittelschicht Afrikas* [The underestimated continent: visiting Africa's middle class] by Bettina Gaus (2011). See also Dausend (2000), Moore (2010). The quality of publications varies. Similar in form but considerably different in quality are the publications by Bettina Gaus and Marietta Slomka: although both journalists take a personal, almost diary-like viewpoint in their books on sub-Saharan Africa mentioned above, Gaus displays well-researched background knowledge, whereas Slomka partly uses anecdotal commonplaces that cannot be proven.

9 *Parachute journalists* are journalists who do not live in the foreign country or region permanently but are sent there to cover breaking news, mostly in crisis situations. Thus, many of them do not have background knowledge and cannot rely on the network that journalists based in the region might have. Parachute reporting has concomitant limits; see Ricchiardi (2006).

10 Official Development Assistance (ODA) is monetary flow to multilateral organisations designated to certain countries or areas, which are listed on the OECD Development Assistance Committee, (short: DAC) as ODA-recipients. This budget number is an average of the Unicef annual budgets from 2009 to 2011.

11 The interviews conducted for this book are all anonymised through numbers. In most cases I still refer to the position that the interviewee has, or the organisation he or she works for, and – when it is a journalist – whether he or she is a freelancer. This information, however, is only added in cases where these facts do not reveal the interviewee's anonymity.

In favour of readability I removed the pauses, which are indicated in the transcripts, from the quotations in this text. I also smoothed sentences if an interviewee got muddled. In the transcripts, however, all sentences are indicated exactly as uttered, so that before citing an interviewee, I could always assure that the meaning of the quotation was not changed.

12 All currency exchange rates calculated via xe.com at time of writing.

13 The following distinctions were developed according to my research data but can also be found in Mükke (2009b: 276ff).

14 This was also the idea behind the Central Emergency Response Fund (CERF), which was incepted in 2006 to pool financing of private and government donors to be able to react timely to crises worldwide.

15 For further information see Chapter 4, section 4.5, and Chapter 6, section 6.6. This is just a short overview: The term *embedded journalism* (or *embed* if talking about the journalists him/herself, see Oxford Dictionary Online) is used to describe the attachment of journalists to the frontline combatants of a military unit during conflict. The practice itself is referred to as *embedding*, the journalists are called *embeds*. On a grand scale this idea of embedded frontline journalism was institutionalised in coalition forces in the Iraq War in 2003. The troops provided access to the war theatre, and the reporter moved with the respective unit in which he or she was embedded, and received military protection, board, and lodging. In such a situation journalists can gather facts and impressions directly on-site with a reduced risk to their safety, while the military gains influence on the coverage to a certain extent (Löffelholz 2016; Dietrich 2007).

16 More about the premise on actor's choices in Chapter 3.

17 For more details on the methodology, see Chapter 5.

18 Test interviews with key actors in Nairobi in December 2010 and January 2011.

19 Interviews across sub-Saharan Africa between March and September 2014. Additional interviews regarding fundraising and specifics about embedded journalism were conducted in 2015.

References

Adamson, Peter (1993) "Charity Begins With the Truth: Too Much Bad News About the Developing World Gives a Distorted Picture", *The Independent*, URL: www.independent.co.uk/voices/charity-begins-with-the-truth-too-much-bad-news-about-the-developing-world-gives-a-distorted-picture-says-peter-adamson-2323657.html [2.2.2015].

Alam, Shahidul (2007) "The Visual Representation of Developing Countries by Developmental Agencies and the Western Media", in: *Policy & Practice – A Development Education Review*, 59–65.

Anyangwe, Eliza (2015) "Is it Time to Rethink the Divide between Humanitarian and Development Funding?", *The Guardian*, URL: www.theguardian.com/global-development-professionals-network/2015/dec/04/funding-humanitarian-assistance-development-aid [10.1.2017].

Bentele, Günter, Brosius, Hans-Bernd and Jarren, Otfried (2003) *Öffentliche Kommunikation. Handbuch Kommunikations- und Medienwissenschaft*, Wiesbaden.

Bilke, Nadine (2008) *Qualität in der Krisen- und Kriegsberichterstattung. Ein Modell für konfliktsensitiven Journalismus*, Wiesbaden.

Birnbaum, Michael (2001) *Die schwarze Sonne Afrikas*, München.

Birrell, Ian (2012a) "Our Image of African is Hopelessly Obsolete", *The Observer*, 26.8.2012, URL: www.ianbirrell.com/our-image-of-africa-is-hopelessly-obsolete/–more-1456, [18.2.2012].

Birrell, Ian (2012b) "The Aid Business has Grown Fat. It's Time there was Proper Scrutiny", *The Spectator*, [18.2.2012].

Bitala, Michael (2007) *Das Prinzip Trotzdem: Afrikansiche Augenblicke*, Wien.

Bogert, Carroll (2011) "Whose News? The Changing Media Landscape and NGOs", Human Rights Watch Wolrd Report.

Chouliaraki, Lilie (2006) *The Spectatorship of Suffering*, London, New Delhi.

Chouliaraki, Lilie (2012) *The Ironic Spectator: Solidariy in the Age of Post-Humanitarianism*, Cambridge.

Clark, D. J. (2004) "The Production of a Contemporary Famine Image: the Image Economy, Indigenous Photographers and the Case of Mekanic Philipos", in: *Journal of International Development* 16, 693–704.

Conrad, Joseph (2007 [1899]) *Heart of Darkness*, London.

Cottle, Simon (2014) "Rethinking Media and Disasters in a Global Age: What's Changed and Why it Matters", in: *Media, War & Conflict* 7(1), 3–22.

Cottle, Simon and Nolan, David (2007) "Global Humanitarianism and the Changing Aid-Media Field. 'Everyone was Dying for Footage'", in: *Journalism Studies* 8(6), 862–878.

Darnton, Andrew (2011) *Finding Frames: New Ways to Engage the UK Public in Global Poverty*.

Dausend, Peter (2000) "Der schönste Kontinent der Welt", *Die Welt*, 05.08.2000, URL: www.welt.de/526636 [22.5.2013].

de Beer, Arnold (2010) "News from and in the 'Dark Continent'", in: *Journalism Studies* 11(4), 596–609.

de Jonge Oudraat, Chantal and Haufler, Virginia (2008) "33 AICGS Policy Report", *Global Governance and the Role of NGOs in International Peace and Security*, Baltimore: American Institute for Contemporary German Studies, Johns Hopkins University.

de Waal, Alex (1997) *Famine Crimes. Politics and the Disaster Relief Industry in Africa*, Bloomington, IN.
Deutscher Journalisten Verband (2012) "Vocational Profile – Journalist", DJV Wissen 4.
DFID, Department for International Development (2000) "Viewing the World. A Study of British Television Coverage of Developing Countries", London: DFID, URL: http://webarchive.nationalarchives.gov.uk/+/http:/www.dfid.gov.uk/pubs/files/viewworldfull.pdf [15.12.2013].
Dietrich, Sandra (2007) *Embedded journalism. Ursprünge, Ziele, Merkmale, Probleme und Nutzen von 'Embedding' am Beispiel des Irak-Krieges 2003*, Saarbrücken.
Dilg, Ute (1999) "Schwarzafrika: Weißer Fleck auf dem Nachrichtenglobus. Die Berichterstattung über Afrika südlich der Sahara in der überregionalen deutschen Presse. Eine Inhaltsanalyse", in: *Communicatio Socialis. Internationale Zeitschrift für Kommunikation in Religion, Kirche und Gesellschaft* 32(3), 241–260.
Esser, Hartmut (1993) *Soziologie. Allgemeine Grundlagen*, Frankfurt/M.
Esser, Hartmut (1999) Situationslogik und Handeln. *Soziologie. Spezielle Grundlagen*, ed. Vol 1, Frankfurt.
Esser, Hartmut (2000a) *Institutionen*, Frankfurt.
Esser, Hartmut (2000b) "Opportunitäten und Restriktionen", *Soziologie. Spezielle Grundlagen*, ed. Vol. 4, Frankfurt.
Esser, Hartmut. (2000c) "Soziales Handeln", *Soziologie. Spezielle Grundlagen*, ed. Vol. 3, Frankfurt.
Esser, Hartmut (2003) "Die Rationalität der Werte. Die Typen des Handelns und das Modell der soziologischen Erklärung", in: Gert Albert (Ed.), *Das Weber-Paradigma*, Tübingen, 153–187.
Esser, Hartmut (2004) "Akteure und soziale Systeme", in: Thomas Schwinn (Ed.), *Differenzierung und soziale Ungleicheit*, 271–283.
Franks, Suzanne (2008) "Getting into Bed with Charity", in: *Brisith Journalism Review* 19(3), 27–32.
Franks, Suzanne (2010) "The Neglect of Africa and the Power of Aid", in: *International Communication Gazette* 71(1), 71–84.
Franks, Suzanne (2013) *Reporting Disasters. Famine, Aid, Politics and the Media*, London.
Frantz, Christiane and Martens, Kerstin (2006) *Nichtregierungsorganisationen (NGOs)*, Wiesbaden.
Galtung, Johan (1997) "Der Frieden ist das erste Opfer des Krieges – deshalb Friedensjournalismus. Thesen von Johan Galtung", M Menschen Machen Medien 11.
Galtung, Johan (1998) "Friedensjournalismus: Was, warum, wer, wie wann, wo?" *Krieg, Nationalismus, Rassismus und die Medien*, Münster, 3–20.
Galtung, Johan (2002) "Peace Journalism – a Challenge", in: Wilhelm Kempf and Heikki Luostarinen (Eds.), *Journalism and the New World Order. Studying War and the Media*, Vol. 2, Göteborg, 259–272.
Galtung, Johan and Fischer, Dietrich (2003) "Kriegsberichterstattung kann Konflikte verlängern", in: *Medienjournal* 27(2).
Galtung, Johan and Ruge, Mari H. (1970) "The Structure of Foreign News. The Presentation of the Congo, Cuba and Cyprus Crisis in four Norwegian Newspapers", in: Jeremy Tunstall (Ed.), *Media Sociology*, Urbana, IL.
Gaus, Bettina (2011) *Der unterschätzte Kontinent: Reise zur Mittelschicht Afrikas*, Frankfurt/M.
Gibbon, Joanna (1996) "Aid Meets the Press", in: *The Magazine of the International Red Cross and Red Crescent Movement* 1.
Gill, Peter (1986) *A Year in the Death of Africa: Politics, Bureaucracy and the Famine*, London.

Gjelten, Tom (2001) "Finding the Right 'Moral Attitude'. Journalists Can Best Serve Victims of Crisis by Balancing Humanity and Professionalism", in: *Media Studies Journal* 15(1), 72–76.

Glennie, Alex, Straw, Will and Wild, Leni (2012) "Understanding Public Attitudes to Aid and Development", *ODI and Institute for Public Policy Research & Overseas Development Institute*, URL: www.odi.org/sites/odi.org.uk/files/odi-assets/publications-opinion-files/7708.pdf [23.8.2015].

Green, Andrew (2016) "The Thorny Ethics of Embedding with Do-Gooders", *Columbia Journalism Review*, URL: www.cjr.org/first_person/the_ethics_of_embedding_with_do-gooders.php [8.2.2016].

Greshoff, Rainer (2008) "Strukturtheoretischer Individualismus", in: Georg Kneer and Markus Schroer (Eds.), *Handbuch Soziologische Theorien*, Wiesbaden, 445–467.

Grill, Bartholomäus (2007) "Auf verlorenem Posten? Als Korrespondent in Afrika", in: Gerhard Göhler, Cornelia Schmalz-Jacobson and Christian Walther (Eds.), *Macht und Medien. Über das Verhältnis von Politik und Kommunikation*, Frankfurt/M., 119–136.

Hamilton, John Maxwell and Jenner, Eric (2004) "Foreign Correspondence: Evolution, Not Extinction", in: *Nieman Reports: The Nieman Foundation for Journalism at Harvard* (Fall).

Höijer, Brigitta (2004) "The Discourse of Global Compassion: The Audience and Media Reporting of Human Suffering", in: *Media, Culture & Society* 26(4), 513–531.

ICRC (2015) "Key Data Appeals 2016 Breakdown and 2015–2016 Comparative Data", *ICRC Appeal Online*, URL: http://reliefweb.int/sites/reliefweb.int/files/resources/2016_appeals_keydata_rex2015_609_final.pdf.

Jakobsen, Peter Viggo (2000) "Focus on the CNN Effect Misses the Point: The Real Media Impact on Conflict Management is Invisible and Indirect", in: *Journal of Peace Research* 37(2), 131–143.

Junghanns, Kathrin and Hanitzsch, Thomas (2006) "Deutsche Auslandskorrespondenten im Profil", in: Institut Hans Bredow (Ed.), *Medien & Kommunikationswissenschaft*, Vol. 54(3), Baden-Baden, 412–429.

Kappel, Robert and Pfeiffer, Birte (2013) "Performanzanalyse Subsahara-Afrika", *GIGA*, URL: www.bundesbank.de/Redaktion/DE/Downloads/Bundesbank/Hauptverwaltungen_Filialen/studie_performanzanalyse_subsahara_afrika.pdf?__blob=publicationFile [27.11.2013].

Kapuscinski, Ryszard (2001) *The Shadow of the Sun: My African Life*, Camberwell.

Kepplinger, Hans (2004, 2nd. edition) "Problemdimensionen des Journalismus. Wechselwirkung zwischen Theorie und Empirie", in: Martin Löffelholz (Ed.), *Theorien des Journalismus. Ein diskursives Handbuch*, Wiesbaden, 87–106.

Krems, Olaf (2002) *Der Blackout-Kontinent. Projektion und Reproduktion eurozentristischer Afrika- und Afrikanerbilder unter besonderer Berücksichtigung der Berichterstattung in deutschsprachigen Massenmedien*. Dissertation at the Westfälischen Wilhelms Universität zu Münster, Münster.

Kropp, Per (2010) "Methodologischer Individualismus und Netzwerkforschung. Ein Diskussionsbeitrag", in: Christian Stegbauer (Ed.), *Netzwerkanalyse und Netzwerktheorie*, 145–154.

Kuhn, Marco (2000) *Humanitäre Hilfe in der Europäischen Gemeinschaft. Entwicklung, System und primärrechtlicher Rahmen*, Berlin.

Lange, Silvia (2003) "Vor Afrika – aber hinter Asien", in: *Message. Internationale Zeitschrift für Journalismus* 2, 88–89.

Leigh, Tamara (2015) "Aid Workers or Journalists: Who Should Report the News?", *IRIN*, URL: http://newirin.irinnews.org/extras/2015/2/11/aid-workers-or-journalists-who-should-report-the-news [2.1.2016].

Löffelholz, Martin (2016) "Embedded Journalism", in: *Encyclopaedia Britannica*, URL: https://www.britannica.com/topic/embedded-journalism [10.2.2015].

Luger, Kurt and Pointner, Andreas (1996) "Die 'Gesichter Afrikas'. Ein Kontinent in der Konstruktion österreichischer Printmedien", in: Österreichischen Gesellschaft für Kommunikationsfragen (Ed.), *Medien Journal*, Vol. 4, Salzburg, 4–29.

Macrae, Joanna (2012) "Relationship between Humanitarian and Development Aid. The Continuum is Dead, Long Live Resilience", *NGO Voice (Voluntary Organisation in Cooperation in Emergencies)*.

Merten, Klaus (2004) "Mikro, Mikro-Makro oder Makro? Zum Verhältnis von Journalismus und PR aus systemischer Perspektive", in: Klaus-Dieter Altmeppen, Ulrike Röttger and Günter Bentele (Eds.), *Schwierige Verhältnisse. Interdependenzen zwischen Journalismus und PR*, Wiesbaden, 17–36.

Moore, Jina (2010) "The White Correspondent's Burden. We Need to Tell the Africa Story Differently", *Bosten Review Online*, 2.8.2012, [22.5.2013].

Moore, Martin (2010) "Shrinking World: The Decline of International Reporting in the British Press", in: *Media Standards Trust*, URL: http://mediastandardstrust.org/publications/shrinking-world-the-decline-of-international-reporting-in-the-british-press/ [16.05.2013].

Mükke, Lutz (2003) "Einzelkämpfende Allrounder. Eine Studie über Korrespondenten in Nairobi", in: *Message. Internationale Zeitschrift für Journalismus* (2), 82–87.

Mükke, Lutz (2004) "Schwarzweißes Afrika: Über das Entstehen Afrika-bezogener Nachrichten im Zerrspiegel deutscher Massenmedien", in: *Africa Spectrum* 39(2), 277–289.

Mükke, Lutz (2009a) "Allein auf weiter Flur: Korrespondenten in Afrika", in: *APuZ* 34–35, 39–45.

Mükke, Lutz (2009b) *'Journalisten der Finsternis': Akteure, Strukturen und Potenziale deutscher Afrika-Berichterstattung*, Köln.

Mükke, Lutz (2011) "Humanitär embedded: Wie symbiotische Beziehungen zwischen Hilfsorganisationen und Medien Qualitätsjournalismus aushöhlen", in: *PR und Journalismus – Zwischen Kooperation und Konfrontation. Dokumentation einer Fachkonferenz der Rudolf-Augstein-Stiftungsprofessur für Praxis des Qualitätsjournalismus, Unversität Hamburg und des Netzwerks Recherche*, 23–30.

Opinion Leader Research (2002, October) "Making Sense of the World: A Joint BBC News – DFID Study of Public Perceptions of Television News Coverage of Developing Countries".

Orgad, Shani and Seu, I. Bruna (2014) "The Mediation of Humanitarianism: Toward a Research Framework", in: *Communication, Culture & Critique* 7, 6–36.

Oxfam (2014) "Annual Report 2013–2014", *Oxfam*, URL: www.oxfam.org/en/file/oxfam-annual-report-2013-2014pdf [24.8.2015].

Plewes, Betty and Stuart, Rieky (2009) "The Pornography of Poverty: A Cautionary Fundraising Tale", in: *Ethics in Action: The Ethical Challanges or International Human Rights Nongovernmental Organizations*, 23–37.

Ricchiardi, Sherry (2005) "Déjà Vu", in: *American Journalism Review (AJR)* (February/March).

Ricchiardi, Sherry (2006) "The Limits of the Parachute", in: *American Journalism Review (AJR)* (October/November), 40–47.

Robinson, Piers (2002) *The CNN Effect: The Myths of News, Foreign Policy and Intervention*, New York, NY.

Sambrook, Richard (2010) *Are Forein Correspondents Redundant? The Chancing Face of International News*, Oxford.

Sartor, Tricia (2011) "Little Coverage of Sub-Saharan Africa", in: *Pew Research Center*, URL: www.journalism.org/numbers/little-coverage-subsaharan-africa/ [10.12.2013].

Scheen, Thomas (2008) "Ich hatte Angst um mein Leben", *Frankfurter Allgemeine Zeitung* [17.11.2008].

Schmoll, Anka (1998) "Die Wa(h)re Nachricht über Afrika. Stereotype und Standardisierung in der Fernsehberichterstattung", in: Wilhelm Kempf and Irena Schmidt-Regener (Eds.), *Krieg, Nationalismus, Rassismus und die Medien*, Münster, 89–96.

Seu, I. Bruna and Orgad, Shani (2014) *Mediated Humanitarian Knowledge: Audiences' Reactions and Moral Actions*, Final Report, University of London, URL: http://www.bbk.ac.uk/psychosocial/FinalReportBruna.pdf [22.10.2015].

Shrivastava, Meenal and Hyde-Clarke, Nathalie (2004) "International Media Regime and News Management: Implications for African States", in: *Politikon* 31(2), 201–218.

Slomka, Marietta (2011) *Mein afrikanisches Tagebuch. Reise durch einen Kontinent im Aufbruch*, München.

Smith, Joe, Edge, Lucy and Morris, Vanessa (2006) "Reflecting the Real World? How British TV Portrayed Developing Countries in 2005", 2.11.2013, URL: www.vso.org.uk/news/pressreleases/reflecting the real world.asp [12.3.2014].

Spohrs, Monika (2006) "Über den Nachrichtenwert von Friedensjournalismus – Ergebnisse einer experimentellen Studie", in: *Conflict & Communication Online* 5(1).

Stoianova, Velina (2012) "Private Funding. An Emerging Trend in Humanitarian Donorship", *Global Humanitarian Assistance Report*, Briefing Paper, URL: https://de.scribd.com/document/287839036/Private-Funding-an-Emerging-Trend [10.3.2015].

Stollenwerk, Julia (2011) "Schwarzseherei für den 'schwarzen' Kontinent?", *Medien Monitor. Online-Magazin für den aktuellen Medienjournalismus*, 20.4.2011, URL: www.medien-monitor.com/Schwarzseherei-fuer-den-schwa.1754.0.html [8.10.2013].

UNICEF (2010) "Unicef Annual Report 2009", URL: www.unicef.org.hk/upload/News Media/download/international/Annual_Report_2009.pdf [12.12.2011].

UNICEF (2011) "Unicef Annual Report 2010", URL: www.unicef.at/fileadmin/media/Ueber_UNICEF/UNICEF_International/UNICEF_Annual_Report_2010_EN_052711.pdf [12.12.2011].

UNICEF (2012) "Unicef Annual Report 2011", URL: www.unicef.org/nutrition/files/UNICEF_Annual_Report_2011_EN_060112.pdf [12.12.2011].

Van der Gaag, Nikki (2007) "Images in Fundraising", in: Jill Mordaunt and Rob Paton (Eds.), *Thoughtful Fundraising: Concepts, Issues and Perspectives*, 184–198.

Virnich, Birgit (2010) *Ein Fahrrad für die Flussgötter: Reportagen aus Afrika*, München.

VSO (2001) *The Live Aid Legacy. The Developing World Through Brisith Eyes – a Research Report*, VSO.

Wainaina, Binyavanga (2012) "How not to Write about Africa in 2012 – a Beginner's Guide", *The Guardian Online*, 3.6.2012, URL: www.guardian.co.uk/commentisfree/2012/jun/03/how-not-to-write-about-africa [12.3.2014].

Wanene, Wilson (2005) "An American Correspondent Brings Africa Out of the Shadows", in: *Nieman Reports: The Nieman Foundation for Journalism at Harvard* (Summer).

Weichert, Stephan and Kramp, Leif (2011) *Die Vorkämpfer. Wie Journalisten über den Ausnahmezustand berichten*, Köln.

Werker, Eric and Ahmed, Faisal (2008) "What Do Nongovernmental Organisations Do?", in: *The Journal of Economic Perspectives* 22(2), 73–92.

Wolf, Christof (2004) "Egozentrierte Netzwerke. Erhebungsverfahren und Datenqualität", in: Andreas Diekmann (Ed.), *Methoden der Sozialforschung. Sonderheft der Kölner Zeitschrift für Soziologie und Sozialpsychologie*, Vol. 44, 244–273.

Wright, Kate (2016) "These Grey Areas", in: *Journalism Studies* 17(8), 989–1009.

Wu, H. Denis and Hamilton, John Maxwell (2004) "US Foreign Correspondents: Changes and Continuity at the Turn of the Century", in: *Gazette: The International Journal for Communication Studies* 66(6), 517–532.

2 State of research

Although the cooperation between humanitarian and media sector is widely discussed among people working for both sectors, academic research has surprisingly large gaps regarding this subject. If the subject area is more broadly defined, then relevant studies can be found from various disciplines that use considerably different approaches. This chapter aims to give a rough overview of the literature on the periphery of this research topic, and how it benefited my study. Conclusions and more detailed documentation of the cited sources and their approaches will follow in the respective themed sub-chapters. In the first subsection of this chapter, I give an overview of research on Africa coverage that has mostly been dealt with in the form of quantitative content analyses. The second subsection shines a light on the actor-focused research of journalists, and the lack of studies incorporating these actors in a wider network. In this spirit, the third subsection looks into the lack of studies between (IN)GOs as PR entities and their connection to news reporting. The fourth subsection gives an overview of studies on embedded journalism. And the final and fifth subsection looks at research on power relationships between PR and journalism.

Coverage of sub-Saharan Africa has so far primarily been the subject of quantitative content analyses, and there have been a small number of qualitative content analyses in communication studies (e.g. Masha 1970; Ngegwa 1982; Luger & Pointner 1996; Schmoll 1998; Wimmer 2003). Both only take into consideration the completed 'product', and do not provide information about its emergence, which is the focus of this book. A recent literature review puts it this way: "The academic literature on the process of producing messages about distant suffering and the assumptions, structures, influences, intentions, and expectations that their producers bring to the task, is slight" (Orgad & Seu 2014: 22). This book focuses on all of the latter. In terms of content analyses, Terrell provides a historical overview of the content of American coverage of Africa, and notes its focus on negative issues and its general discontinuity (Terrell 1989: 133). Brookes analyses how stereotypes of Africa developed historically (Brookes 1995). A study by the Department for International Development offers an overview of British television coverage of developing countries (DFID 2000). Convincing is a long-term trend that Wimmer evidences: after the Africa-euphoria of the 1990s, the coverage of African institutions declines, whereas that of international institutions and

NGOs increases (Wimmer 2003: 344ff). The phenomenon of crisis-focused news is the subject of research by Franzke (2000), who concentrates on the role of news agencies, the volume edited by Cipitelli (2003), the study by Moeller (2006), who focuses on the effect this has on the audiences, the book *New News out of Africa* by the journalist Charlayne Hunter-Gault (2007),[1] and de Beer (2010), who compares British, American and German media coverage. Other studies show that sources used in news analyses are mostly non-African, and that international humanitarian organisations play a prominent and mostly positive role in them (Mükke 2009b: 114, 116, 285; Alam 2007; Krems 2002; Smith, Edge & Morris 2006). For this study, I built on the results of these content analyses, and thus take as a given that negative, crisis-focused news of sub-Saharan Africa are dominating, and that humanitarians often feature as exclusively positive players in the coverage.

Actor-focused studies on foreign correspondents are rare,[2] and hardly any explicitly address the relationship between foreign correspondents and humanitarian organisations. Very few mention their cooperation at least as a secondary issue. Only Mükke (2009b) so far has presented a systematic and comprehensive media-studies analysis of the actors and structures involved in foreign news coverage of sub-Saharan Africa. Mükke's findings are essential to my analysis. Via content analyses of German print media, Mükke determined how important INGOs and organisations of the UN are as sources for media coverage. Additionally, he points out that content analyses can "only give a vague idea of the working reality and network of relationships between correspondents [. . .] and relief organisations" (Mükke 2009b: 258). Thus Mükke interviewed correspondents and their editors about role models and about their daily working reality, supporting the content analysis. He investigated the economic situation of correspondents and convincingly shows how it can lead to unwanted dependencies. Mükke describes the work of foreign correspondents as a triangle between their own aims, editors, and agencies. To some extent, he outlines *public relations* strategies of relief organisations (Mükke 2009b: esp. 113–124, 159–165, 256–290, 488–495) and sheds light on "relief organisations as complex of sources" (Mükke 2009b: 256ff). However, he does not analyse the phenomenon thoroughly and only focuses on German journalists. Mükke's research provides reference points for my inquiry, but his broad-based study addresses the relationship between foreign correspondents and humanitarian organisations only at its peripheries, and does not include the perspective of aid organisations.

Measured against the increase in humanitarian organisations, it is surprising how little NGOs and UN organisations have been studied in terms of their communication outputs related to the *agency* and power to push for change that comes with it (Waisbord 2011). Given that media still are one of the main output channels for humanitarian organisations' messages, more research should be done on humanitarian organisations' influence on media. And given the power that this channel position gives media actors, their influence on the behaviour and strategies of humanitarian organisations should come into focus equally. Franks (2008, 2013) tracks the conditions that led to dependencies between the media and humanitarian organisations in a case study of the Ethiopian food crisis in 1984. She analyses factors that made the media take notice of the event, and investigates the impact that this – in this case one-time – coverage had on political action, and donations to humanitarian organisations (Franks 2013: esp. 133–160). Taking her considerations of direct impact of media coverage on political action, and drawing on her results of the case study, I investigate the dependencies between humanitarian organisations and foreign correspondents more widely, uncovering general patterns going beyond one case. Franks (2008, 2013), Cottle (2014; 2007, 2009), Powers (2016c, 2016a, 2015), and Wright (2016b) have published articles about the nexus between international media and aid. Franks (2008) describes the phenomenon of symbiosis between aid organisations and media as 'embedding' but does not conceptualise beyond description, which would enable drawing useful comparisons to military embedding. In more recent research, she highlights aid organisations' need to fundraise and its connection with media coverage, and achieves a milestone in studying in-depth the case of the reporting on the 1984 famine in Ethiopia, proving its role in the political response to the famine (Franks 2010). Cottle and Nolan (2007, 2009) study how media's needs shape the way aid organisations organise their public relations, and how these organisations produce material; yet their results are based on a very small sample that is regionally restricted to aid employees working in one developed country. Cottle, Pantti and Wahl-Jorgensen (2012) and Cottle (2014) investigate how development in media technologies together with the changing ideas of how a 'disaster' is defined, shape disasters, and play an important role in communicating them. They also discuss how emotions such as compassion and anger impact journalists, and how journalists' writing of disasters provides possibilities for social and political change and transformation. Finally, they investigate the role of social media in disasters' visibility. The book raises the important question whether objectivity is possible at all, a question that will be raised in this book again. Overall, Cottle, Pantti and Wahl-Jorgensen's book studies the media's involvement in disasters on a much more abstract level. We lack a mapping analysis of the actors and their relationships in the field. Powers (2016a) argues that judging whether the expectations that one may have towards both journalism and public relations of NGOs, and their interactions, highly depends on the theoretical normative approach. I will get back to this in Chapter 4, in a subsection of 4.4. Powers also makes a claim for NGOs increasingly "rival[ing] the resources" for journalism (Powers 2016b: 401; 2015). Wright (2016b, 2016a) focuses on freelance journalists and their connection with aid organisations; she works with a very small sample, which enables her to highlight individual cases and point out their role in the "erosion" of boundaries between the sectors; the small sample, however, does not allow for a wider view on structural changes and tendencies, or for empirical proof of this blurring of lines beyond individual accounts. Useful for my investigation is Benthall's (2010) investigation of the functional chain of influence in crises, the resulting media coverage, and the consequences for humanitarian help ("disasters-media-humanitarian aid").[3] I will explain more about this chain, and the meaning of crises, the following media coverage and its importance for humanitarian organisations, in Chapter 4, in the subsections on public relations and its professionalisation, and on the meaning of media for the humanitarian sector. Scientific studies aside, there are several reports on the issue from the perspective of journalists and humanitarian organisations. In her book *The Crisis Caravan: What's Wrong With Humanitarian Aid*, the Dutch journalist Linda Polman (2011) polemically, but in substance rightly, criticises poorly conceived aid missions, and the role that media presence plays when it comes to the selection of missions. The French journalist Claire Guillot (2012) reports in *Le Monde* on the cooperation between photojournalists and INGOs, and how they can very easily lead to involuntary dependencies. Guillot argues that journalism becomes difficult to differentiate from advertising or public relations. Carroll Bogert, then deputy executive of Human Rights Watch and a former journalist, speaks of a "symbiosis" between journalists and INGOs (Bogert 2011: 2) due to the INGOs' need to advertise their brands, and tough working conditions for correspondents. Richard Munz, who worked as a doctor with the ICRC in crisis areas for many years, describes the media reports that first emerge from a crisis area as a double-edged sword. On one hand they are responsible for increasing donations; on the other hand they provide unsubstantiated data that lack an overview of the situation on the ground. And once the numbers of people affected by an event are public, it is difficult to correct them (Munz 2007: 30).

Research on the phenomenon of embedded journalism can be divided into two groups. One descriptively depicts the relationship between journalists and the military (Paul & Kim 2004; Schwarte 2007). Some of these studies employ questionable normativity in their approaches (Tuosto 2008). The other group analyses articles by embeds regarding their attitude towards the military, criticising their loss of objectivity (Pfau 2004; Mans, Meindersma & Burema 2008). I can build on research of Brandenburg (2005) and Dietrich (2007), as well as on empirical studies by the Pew Research Center (PRC Pew Research Center 2003) and Cardiff University (Lewis et al. 2004) insofar as they reveal characteristics, advantages, and challenges of embedded reporting. I will use the characteristics they determined to develop a concept of embedded journalism as a situational dependence-relationship between journalists and a third party, detached from its original military context.

Research regarding power relations between the humanitarian sector and journalism have mainly been carried out as *input-output-analyses*, which consider press releases sent to the media by people working in public relations as input, and journalistic texts using those releases and other public relations material as output, putting input and output into proportion. Press conferences, discussions with journalists, and, above all, private and social relationships, are usually not considered in these analyses (Altmeppen, Bentele & Röttger 2004: 92), even though they are required for successful public relations (Altmeppen, Bentele & Röttger 2004: 11). These content analyses frequently assume that the media is instrumentalised and determined by aid organisations' public relations departments (this is called "determination", see esp. Baerns 1991). This suggests that the 'bad' public relations departments of humanitarian organisations try to influence the 'good' media in their favour. Other than these approaches that follow Baern's determination hypothesis, I start from the proposition that aid organisations' public relations and journalism have a reciprocal influence on each other, and share a mutual dependency. Other scholars have called this "interdependency", "symbiosis", or "structural coupling" (see listed in the order of the named concepts: Ruß-Mohl 1994; Bentele, Liebert & Seeling 1997; Merten 2004; Altmeppen 2004). Unlike the studies with the focus on the textual inputs and outputs, I focus on the actors. In contrast to normative research approaches in the sense of a determination from the PR personnel towards the journalists (Laudan 1984; Gysin 2000), I favour an unbiased approach that analyses the relationships against the background of socio-economic behaviour of the individual actors. I start from the premise that the two enable one another, and make each other's work possible. I assume that it is necessary to research the interactions in the field as balanced as possible to receive information from all perspectives, including all possible power relationships. Only with this approach can we determine whether one side dominates over the other. Questions about what journalism requires, what role it should have in society, and what differentiates it from public relations, are fundamental to understand the structure of actor relationships and the actions of journalists and aid workers. Löffelholz (2004) and Hanitzsch, Altmeppen and Schlüter (2007) provide essential theoretical background about these issues. Following their outlook, I will explain in Chapter 3 upon which theoretical background my investigation is built.

Notes

1 See also references in the introductory chapter.
2 Junghanns and Hanitzsch (2006) display a general analysis of the occupational field with a focus on foreign correspondents, their career progression, qualifications, role models, and self-perceptions. For similar investigations of Japanese correspondents, see Nafroth (2002). In this context, the ethnographical study of Hannerz (2004) is also interesting: it seeks to define the 'species' of foreign correspondent, also including the respective home editors in its analysis. In terms of American correspondents, the analyses by Kruglak (1955), Maxwell (1956), Hess (1996), and Hamilton & Wu (2004) should be mentioned. Hamilton and Wu investigate correspondents' qualification profiles, their language skills, and the time correspondents spent travelling, but the study is very general. Hamilton and Jenner (2004) provide a theoretical basis for research on foreign correspondents. Actor-focused communicator studies on foreign correspondents covering certain areas are nevertheless rare. Hannerz (2004) gives an overview of journalism culture in Indonesia. Hanitzsch and Junghanns (2006) undertake a descriptive, explorative occupational field analysis of German foreign correspondents, through an online survey that mainly aimed at investigating the self-conception of foreign correspondents in comparison to journalists working at the editorial headquarters. Lange (2002) investigates the working realities and the role-perceptions of correspondents in Latin America, and Bengelstorff (2002) in Africa. Bengelstorff's qualitative interview research focuses on journalists' ambiguous relationships with news agencies but does not reach in-depth correspondents' networks of relationships. So far, there is no study that compares actors working for news outlets in different countries and their relationships with humanitarian organisations revealing differing trends in media policies.

3 Similarly, Gill (1986: 93f) demonstrates that the news coverage of Ethiopia displays connections to journalists' collaborations with Oxfam and Save the Children. De Waal's research (1997: 82ff) shows on which levels the two sectors are dependent on one another.

References

Alam, Shahidul (2007) "The Visual Representation of Developing Countries by Developmental Agencies and the Western Media", in: *Policy & Practice – A Development Education Review*, 59–65.

Altmeppen, Klaus-Dieter, Bentele, Günter and Röttger, Ulrike (2004) "PR und Journalismus. Eine lang andauernde und interessante ‚Beziehungskiste'", in: Klaus-Dieter Altmeppen, Günter Bentele and Ulrike Röttger (Eds.), *Schwierige Verhältnisse. Interdependenzen zwischen Journalismus und PR*, Wiesbaden, 7–16.

Altmeppen, Klaus-Dieter (2004) *Schwierige Verhältnisse Interdependenzen zwischen Journalismus und PR*, Wiesbaden.

Baerns, Barbara (1991, 2nd. edition) *Öffentlichkeitsarbeit oder Journalismus? Zum Einfluss im Mediensystem*.

Bengelstorff, Anja (2002) *Auslandskorrespondenten in Afrika südlich der Sahara. Eine qualitative Kommunikatorstudie zu Rollenverständnis und Arbeitsrealität*. Magisterarbeit. FU Berlin, Berlin.

Bentele, Günter, Liebert, Thomas and Seeling, Stefan (1997) "Von der Determination zur Intereffikation. Ein integriertes Modell zum Verhältnis von Public Relations und Journalismus", in: Günter Bentele and Michael Haller (Eds.), *Aktuelle Entstehung von Öffentlichkeit. Akteure – Strukturen – Veränderungen*, Konstanz, 225–250.

Benthall, Jonathan (2010) *Disasters, Relief and the Media*, Herefordshire.

Bogert, Carroll (2011) "Whose News? The Changing Media Landscape and NGOs", Human Rights Watch Wolrd Report.

Brandenburg, Heinz (2005) "Journalists Embedded in Culture: War Stories as Political Strategy", in: Lee Artz and Yahya Kamalipour (Eds.), *Bring 'em on: Media and Politics in the Iraq War*, Lanham, 225–238.

Brookes, Heather Jean (1995) "'Suit, Tie and a Touch of Juju' – The Ideological Construction of Africa: A Critical Discourse Analysis of News on Africa in the British Press", in: *Discourse & Society* 6(4), 461–494.

Cipitelli, Claudia (2003) *Nur Krisen, Kriege, Katastrophen? Auslandsberichterstattung im deutschen Fernsehen: Dokumentation der 21. Tutzinger Medientage*, München.

Cottle, Simon and Nolan, David (2007) "Global Humanitarianism and the Changing Aid-Media Field. 'Everyone was Dying for Footage'", in: *Journalism Studies* 8(6), 862–878.

Cottle, Simon and Nolan, David (2009 November 16) "How the Media's Codes and Rules Influence the Ways NGOs Work", in: *Nieman Journalism Lab*. URL: http://www.niemanlab.org/2009/11/simon-cottle-and-david-nolan-how-the-medias-codes-and-rules-influence-the-ways-ngos-work [10.3.2014].

Cottle, Simon, Pantti, Mervi and Wahl-Jorgensen, Karin (2012) *Diasters and the Media*, New York, NY.

Cottle, Simon (2014) "Rethinking Media and Disasters in a Global Age: What's Changed and Why It Matters", in: *Media, War & Conflict* 7(1), 3–22.

De Beer, Arnold (2010) "News from and in the 'Dark Continent'", in: *Journalism Studies* 11(4), 596–609.

de Waal, Alex (1997) *Famine Crimes: Politics and the Disaster Relief Industry in Africa*, Bloomington, IN.

DFID, Department for International Development (2000) "Viewing the World. A Study of British Television Coverage of Developing Countries", London: DFID, URL: http://webarchive.nationalarchives.gov.uk/+/http:/www.dfid.gov.uk/pubs/files/viewworldfull.pdf [15.12.2013].

Dietrich, Sandra (2007) *Embedded Journalism. Ursprünge, Ziele, Merkmale, Probleme und Nutzen von, Embedding' am Beispiel des Irak-Krieges 2003*, Saarbrücken.

Franks, Suzanne (2008) "Getting into Bed with Charity", in: *Brisith Journalism Review* 19(3), 27–32.

Franks, Suzanne (2010) "The Neglect of Africa and the Power of Aid", in: *International Communication Gazette* 71(1), 71–84.

Franks, Suzanne (2013) *Reporting Disasters. Famine, Aid, Politics and the Media*, London.

Franzke, Michael (2000) "'Aber die Agenturen haben nichts gemeldet . . .' Das Problem, über Probleme der ‚Dritten Welt' zu berichten", in: Stefan Brüne (Ed.), *Neue Medien und Öffentlichkeiten. Politik und Tele-Kommunikation in Afrika, Asien und Lateinamerika*, Hamburg.

Gerhards, Jürgen and Neidhardt, Friedhelm (1993) "Strukturen und Funktionen moderner Öffentlichkeit. Fragestellungen und Ansätze", in: Wolfgang R. Langenbucher (Ed.), *Politische Kommunikation: Grundlagen, Strukturen, Prozesse*, Wien, 52–88.

Gill, Peter (1986) *A Year in the Death of Africa: Politics, Bureaucracy and the Famine*, London.

Guillot, Claire (2012) "Photographes en terrain miné", *Le Monde*, 6.10.2012.

Gysin, Nicole (2000) *Der direkte Draht zur Welt? Eine Untersuchung über Auslandskorrespondentinnen und -korrespondenten Deutschschweizer Prinzmedien*. Dissertation am Institut für Medienwissenschaften, Bern.

Hamilton, John Maxwell and Jenner, Eric (2004) "Foreign Correspondence: Evolution, Not Extinction", in: *Nieman Reports: The Nieman Foundation for Journalism at Harvard* (Fall).

Hanitzsch, Thomas, Altmeppen, Klaus-Dieter and Schlüter, Carsten (2007) "Zur Einführung: Die Journalismustheorie und das Treffen der Generationen", in: Thomas Hanitzsch, Klaus-Dieter Altmeppen and Carsten Schlüter (Eds.), *Journalismustheorie: Next Generation. Soziologische Grundlegung und theoretische Innovation*, Wiesbaden, 7–23.

Hannerz, Ulf (2004) *Foreign News: Exploring the World of Foreign Correspondents*, Chicago.

Hess, Stephen (1996) *International News and Foreign Correspondents*, Washington.

Hunter-Gault, Charlayne (2007) *New News out of Africa*, London.

Junghanns, Kathrin and Hanitzsch, Thomas (2006) "Deutsche Auslandskorrespondenten im Profil", in: Institut Hans Bredow (Ed.), *Medien & Kommunikationswissenschaft*, Vol. 54 (3), Baden-Baden, 412–429.

Kepplinger, Hans (2004, 2nd. edition) "Problemdimensionen des Journalismus. Wechselwirkung zwischen Theorie und Empirie", in: Martin Löffelholz (Ed.), *Theorien des Journalismus. Ein diskursives Handbuch*, Wiesbaden, 87–106.

Kirschstein, Frank (1996) "Liveberichterstattung im, 'Feuerwehrstil'. Auswirkungen neuer Technologien auf die Auslandsberichterstattung", in: Miriam Meckel and Markus Kriener (Eds.), *Internationale Kommunikation. Eine Einführung*, Opladen, 229–240.

Krems, Olaf (2002) *Der Blackout-Kontinent. Projektion und Reproduktion eurozentristischer Afrika- und Afrikanerbilder unter besonderer Berücksichtigung der*

Berichterstattung in deutschsprachigen Massenmedien. Dissertation at the Westfälischen Wilhelms Universität zu Münster, Münster.

Kruglak, T. E. (1955) *The Foreign Correspondents: A Study of the Men and Women Reporting for the American Information Media in Western Europe*, Washington DC.

Lange, Silvia (2002) "Auf verlorenem Posten?", *Deutschsprachige Auslandskorrespondenten in Lateinamerika. Eine qualitative Kommunikatorstudie zur Arbeitsrealität und Rollenverständnis*. Magisterarbeit, FU Berlin.

Laudan, Peter (1984) "Die Rolle des Auslandskorrespondenten im Informationsfluß aus der Dritten Welt", in: Helmut Asche (Ed.), *Dritte Welt für Journalisten: Zwischenbilanz eines Weiterbildungsangebotes. Im Auftrag des Modellversuchs Journalisten-Weiterbildung an der Freien Universität Berlin*, Saarbrücken, 223–229.

Lewis, Justin, Threadgold, Terry, Brookes, Rod and et al (2004) *Too Close for Comfort? The Role of Embedded Reporting During the 2003 Iraq War: Summary Report*, Cardiff.

Löffelholz, Martin (Ed.) (2004) *Theorien des Journalismus. Ein diskursives Handbuch*, Wiesbaden.

Luger, Kurt and Pointner, Andreas (1996) "Die 'Gesichter Afrikas'. Ein Kontinent in der Konstruktion österreichischer Printmedien", in: Österreichischen Gesellschaft für Kommunikationsfragen (Ed.), *Medien Journal*, Vol. 4, Salzburg, 4–29.

Mans, Ulrich, Meindersma, Christa and Burema, Lars (2008) "Eyes Wide Shut? The Impact of Embedded Journalism on Dutch Newspaper Coverage of Afghanistan", HCCSS-report 08–002.

Masha, F. I. (1970) "Tanzania in the United States", in: *Grassroots Editor* 11(2), 22–23.

Maxwell, J. William (1956) "US Correspondents Abroad: A Study of Backgrounds", in: *Journalism Quarterly* 33, 346–348.

Merten, Klaus (2004) "Mikro, Mikro-Makro oder Makro? Zum Verhältnis von Journalismus und PR aus Systemischer Perspektive", in: Klaus-Dieter Altmeppen, Ulrike Röttger and Günter Bentele (Eds.), *Schwierige Verhältnisse. Interdependenzen zwischen Journalismus und PR*, Wiesbaden, 17–36.

Moeller, Susan (2006) "Regarding the Pain of Others: Media, Bias and the Coverage of International Disasters", in: *Journal of International Affairs* 59(2), 173–196.

Mükke, Lutz (2009b) *'Journalisten der Finsternis': Akteure, Strukturen und Potenziale deutscher Afrika-Berichterstattung*, Köln.

Munz, Richard (2007) *Im Zentrum der Katastrophe. Was es wirklich bedeutet, vor Ort zu helfen*, Frankfurt/M.

Nafroth, Katja (2002) *Zur Konstruktion von Nationenbildern in der Auslandsberichterstattung: Das Japanbild der deutschen Medien im Wandel*, Münster.

Ngegwa, Catherine Wagithi (1982) "Coverage of Zimbabwe in Newsweek and The New York Times 1965–66 and 1979–80", University of Missouri School of Journalism.

Orgad, Shani and Seu, I. Bruna (2014) "The Mediation of Humanitarianism: Toward a Research Framework", in: *Communication, Culture & Critique* 7, 6–36.

Paul, Christopher and Kim, James (2004) "Reporters on the Battlefield. The Embedded Press System in Historical Context", URL: www.rand.org/pubs/monographs/2004/RAND_MG200.pdf [22.11.2012].

Pfau, Michael et al. (2004) "Embedding Journalists in Military Combat Units: Impact on Newspaper Story Frames and Tone", in: *J&MC Quarterly* 81(1), 87–88.

Polman, Linda (2011) *The Crisis Caravan. What's Wrong With Humanitarian Aid*, New York, NY.

Powers, Matthew (2015) "Contemporary NGO-Journalism Relations: Reviewing and Evaluating an Emergent Area of Research", in: *Sociology Compass* 9(6), 427–437.

Powers, Matthew (2016a) "Beyond Boon or Bane. Using Normative Theories to Evaluate the Newsmaking Efforts of NGOs", in: *Journalism Studies Online*.

Powers, Matthew (2016b) "The New Boots on the Ground: NGOs in the Changing Landscape of International News", in: *Journalism* 17(4), 401–416.

Powers, Matthew (2016c) "NGO Publicity and Reinforcing Path Dependencies: Explaining the Persistence of Media-Centred Publicity Strategies", in: *The International Journal of Press/Politics* 21(4), 490–507.

PRC Pew Research Center (2003) "War Coverage Praised, but Public Hungry for Other News", URL: www.people-press.org/2003/04/09/war-coverage-praised-but-public-hungry-for-other-news/ [23.11.2012].

Ruß-Mohl, Stephan (1994) "Symbiose oder Konflikt: Öffentlichkeitsarbeit und Journalismus", in: Otfried Jarren (Ed.), *Medien und Journalismus*, Vol. 1, 313–326.

Schmoll, Anka (1998) "Die Wa(h)re Nachricht über Afrika. Stereotype und Standardisierung in der Fernsehberichterstattung", in: Wilhelm Kempf and Irena Schmidt-Regener (Eds.), *Krieg, Nationalismus, Rassismus und die Medien*, Münster, 89–96.

Schwarte, Kristina Isabel (2007) *Embedded Journalists – Kriegsberichterstattung im Wandel*, Münster.

Siemes, Annette (2000) *Auslandskorrespondenten in Polen. Nachbarschaftsvermittler zwischen Rollenverständnis und Arbeitsrealität*, Bochum.

Smith, Joe, Edge, Lucy and Morris, Vanessa (2006) "Reflecting the Real World? How British TV Portrayed Developing Countries in 2005", 2.11.2013, URL: www.vso.org.uk/news/pressreleases/reflecting the real world.asp.

Terrell, Robert L. (1989) "Problematic Aspects of U.S. Press Coverage of Africa", in: *International Communication Gazette* 43, 131–153.

Tuosto, Kylie (2008) "The 'Grunt Truth' of Embedded Journalism: The New Media/Military Relationship", in: *Stanford Journal of International Relations* 10(1), 20–31.

Waisbord, Silvio (2011) "Can NGOs Change the News?", in: *International Journal of Communication* 5, 142–165.

Wimmer, Jeffrey (2003) "Das Ende der 'Dritten Welt'? Ein Vergleich der Berichterstattung über Afrika in der deutschen Presse 1991 und 2001", in: *Communicatio Socialis. Internationale Zeitschrift für Kommunikation in Religion, Kirche und Gesellschaft* 4, 337–352.

Wright, Kate (2016a) "Moral Economies. Interrogating the Interactions of Nongovernmental Organizations, Journalists, and Freelancers", in: *International Journal of Communication* 10, 1510–1529.

Wright, Kate (2016b) "These Grey Areas", in: *Journalism Studies* 17(8), 989–1009.

Wu, H. Denis and Hamilton, John Maxwell (2004) "US Foreign Correspondents: Changes and Continuity at the Turn of the Century", in: *Gazette: The International Journal for Communication Studies* 66(6), 517–532.

3 Theoretical concepts

This chapter deals with the theories and approaches underlying my study. In the beginning I ask whether one single theory of journalism exists, how journalism portrays reality, and which reality that may be. Following this question, in the second section I explain the gatekeeper, news value, and framing theory of news selection, and why they inform my research but do not give satisfactory explanations for the interactions between media and the aid sector in sub-Saharan Africa. In the third section I describe the structural-individualistic approach of this study, and how the actors, which portray the reality discussed in the introduction, fit into a wider context of actors' interactions and macro-phenomena such as crisis-focused reporting. The fourth section explicates how this actor-focused approach and network analysis are combined. These sections on the underlying theoretical concepts aim to make clear how this approach focussing on individual actors and their (inter-) actions can answer my research questions. They aim to make my general scientific understanding transparent.

3.1 One single theory of journalism?

At the very beginning of Löffelholz's volume "Theorien des Journalismus" (2004c) that gathers the most influential theories, he states that there is no generally accepted theory of journalism (Löffelholz 2004a). German and French scholars in particular appear nevertheless to be searching for a *"grande théorie* of journalism" (Löffelholz 2004a: 20), and they approach the topic from a perspective that is considerably oriented towards theory (Löffelholz 2004b: 19), whereas Anglo-American researchers rather tend to apply *grounded theory* (Hanitzsch, Altmeppen & Schlüter 2007: 10). Existing theories on journalism do not cohere. The search for a consistent "(constructivist systems-based) theory" that unites all levels nevertheless continues (Löffelholz 2004b: 53). In many cases, so-called theories are not theories in a narrow sense but systems of concepts and nomenclatures that rather help to "sort their subjects, than to explain them, and have a heuristic rather than prognostic function" (Löffelholz 2004b: 60). One theory of journalism – a superstructure theory that captures, systemises, and explains the reality of journalism in all its facets – does not exist. There are however different perspectives and methods to approach the phenomenon of journalism.

Two areas of journalism research evolved that for a long time were considered to contradict one another: actor and systems theory. According to Neuberger, an approach using actor-based theory inhibits the outlook on larger contexts, while approaches using systems theory do not keep the journalistic actor in mind, and instead let him or her dissolve in structural perceptions (Neuberger 2004). Recent integrative concepts try to combine both perspectives, understanding journalism as "communicative acting" (Bucher 2004), as a "system-related actor constellation" (Neuberger 2004; see also Schimank 2007), or as a network of interacting actors (Quandt 2007; Schlüter 2007). Attempts to combine journalistic actors, their actions, and the concept of journalism as a system with an integrative concept only prove to be successful when the focus is shifted away from structural functionalism (Altmeppen 2000; Quandt 2007). Referring to action-theoretical methodologies (Bucher 2004), I thus use an approach that operates with the term *system* but accredits great importance to the actor, and turns its back on the tradition of Luhmann. Instead I understand journalism as a *milieu* ("tribe of journalists", Hannerz 2004: 3); recent studies have similarly integrative approaches (Rühl 1969; Hanitzsch 2004, 2007; Schäfer 2004; Raabe 2005; Willems 2007). I do not perceive the actor as a biological individual but as an actor within a social and institutional network that determines and enables his or her actions, while, at the same time, those actions also shape the framework. My interest lies in describing the actions of individual actors, and their structural context, and patterns of behaviour beyond individuals. Through this approach, I link the perspectives of the system and the individual subject, understanding them as complementing one another,[1] rather than as being dichotomous (see also argument by Sharrock & Button 1991: 162ff).

Building upon the idea that journalism postulates different concepts of reality, my understanding of journalism has a media-normative foundation. That means that I proceed from a concept of journalism not as it *is* but as it *ought to be*. Judging from audience studies, this is what most audiences not only expect from journalism, but also how they think journalism *is*, which is why it is crucial to point out practices that undermine this understanding – too close ties between media and aid that are discussed in this book being one of them. Journalism, in my view, should enable the reader, viewer, or listener to build his or her own opinion on the basis of comprehensive, unbiased reporting that provides a balanced context. It should portray reality in all its facets as adequately as possible. In my view, journalism is a form of communication with the audience. It informs the audience about issues, events, and characters that matter politically, socially, culturally, or economically, by laying out facts in all their complexity, making them publicly available, explaining their context, and putting them into perspective. The latter is crucial for people who usually do not expose themselves to these issues or to these places in such great detail as journalists do. The media's role is to objectively inform, critique, control, reveal, educate, and to help form opinions and decisions by empowering the audience through increasing their level of awareness, knowledge, and understanding. According to Bucher (2004: 263), journalism is "communicative acting". He distinguishes real acting ("*actions*") from possible actions ("*patterns of actions*"). The actions of individual journalists are indices to underlying patterns of actions. The actions cannot be understood without considering the patterns of actions that are defined by the respective social subsystem (Bucher 2004: 268), and by the institutional framework in which they take place. The structures, i.e. the framework that defines reporting and its product, the news, do not exist by themselves but are only constituted within a certain operational social framework, and can only be affirmed "in social behaviour patterns" (Raabe 2004: 115). Structures and actions determine, restrict, and enable each other at the same time, and for the purpose of this book I look at their interlink with structures and actions of actors of humanitarian organisations. To understand the interactions between actors of the media and aid sector, not only journalistic role expectations and self-perception – normative structures as Raabe calls them – but also humanitarians' perception of the journalists' role view are relevant. This type of expectation of second degree is called 'expectation-expectation', and can reveal that the self-perception and the foreign perception do not necessarily match, and can also give clues to why actors interact in a certain way. For the empirical study this meant that the roles and tasks of foreign affairs reporting, and of the work of humanitarian organisations should be researched from both perspectives to find out whether their views about each other match, what structures and patterns could be determined in the interactions, and what the greater social and institutional context looked like. The aim was to reveal patterns of journalists' and humanitarians' actions, their interactions, as well as generative structures of their actions (Raabe 2004: 115ff).

3.2 What reality does journalism display?

The perception of 'reality' is one thing. The portrayal of that 'reality' is another. The question how media display reality is relevant not only in comparison to what it ought to display, if we apply a media-normative foundation considering journalism as an important means to inform audiences, to hold governments, and – relevant for this study – humanitarian organisations to account. Etymologically, the word *journal* derives from the French *le jour*, thus it is news concerning daily events. From there, the job description *journalist* evolved referring to someone who works for the press (Klosa, Scholze-Stubenrecht & Wermke 1997: 315, keyword 'Journal'). The German Federation of Journalists (DJV) emphasises the importance of journalism for politics and for a healthy society by stressing the importance of journalistic participation for any democracy:

> The job of a professional journalist is to publish facts, trends, and issues that are of general, political, economic, or cultural importance to society. By providing comprehensive information in all forms of media, journalists create a basis on which every member of a society can recognise the forces influencing his or her life and can participate in forming public opinion. These are preconditions for the functioning of a democratic state [. . .]. To uphold and extend these freedoms, all journalists are called upon to exercise

utmost diligence during their work, to respect human dignity, and to adhere to basic principles as defined in the Press Codex of the German Press Council (Deutscher Presserat). Journalists can only fulfil their task to provide information and commentaries, and to foster public checks and balances, when they are free of legal restrictions and constraints that hinder these principles.
(Deutscher Journalisten Verband 2012: 2)

Journalism is supposed to be free and independent, unbiased, reliable, and multifaceted (Lünenborg 2012: 5). Its basic principles are transparency and the separation of news content from advertisements and public relations (German Press Council 2008: § 7). Unlike the latter, journalism should mirror events beyond personal interests as realistically as possible, and inform adequately about background context. But how is it possible to judge the adequacy of the portrayal of a certain event, if at all? How can you 'measure' reality in order to compare it to the coverage? Having posed this question, it is necessary to explain my understanding of science. If we were to conceive news coverage as the product of a complex media system where several gatekeepers select events and portray them according to individuals' and the system's preferences, then coverage would necessarily be in conflict with its proclaimed aim to mirror reality (Reese 2001: 179). Schulz argues that depicting one-to-one the frequency and intensity of events is not the media's only task anyway (Schulz 1989). Nevertheless, we expect news coverage to be an adequate and, at least in part, verifiable representation of reality (Kepplinger 1993). But how can we evaluate its adequacy? First, journalists would likely apply different factors in answer to this question than people affected by the events or audiences (see argument by Kepplinger 2004, 2nd edition: 100f). Second, from a meta-theoretical perspective, the question is whether one thinks that 'reality' is measurable at all, which is crucial to the ability to then compare the identified reality with the coverage about it. While realists assume the existence of a social reality regardless of news coverage, which can in parts be measured through indicators (Kepplinger 1989), radical constructivists hold the opposite belief that impartial reality does not exist by itself but is always a subjective construction. The constructivist perspective thus denies the potential for impartial cognition (i.e. the cognitive inaccessibility of reality, Merten 1990). In analogy to the way we conceive science, we can also conceive the journalistic reconstruction of reality. While supporters of naïve realism believe that you can at least get close to the reality through news coverage, constructivists deny in the first place that coverage like this exists, since all statements in coverage are made on a basis of individual socio-culturally predefined observations: "Everything that is said [in journalistic work] is, one way or the other, constructed or reconstructed" (Rühl 1992: 121). Ruling out constructivists' perspectives completely seems naïve, even if we assume that the media attempt to depict reality as impartially as possible. Even if you reject the ideas of radical constructivism, it is apparent that news coverage is subject to processes of selection. On an actor level, both the events that the journalist selects and how he or she perceives and decides to contextualise them (on journalists as gatekeepers see the subsection on gatekeeping), depend on personal and economic interests that themselves are determined by networks, the institutional framework that the journalist is working in, and social imprinting. On an institutional level, media routines, news values (see the subsection on news value theory) and again personal interests and social imprinting of editors, decide the newsworthiness of an event and how it is *framed* in the end product; on the side of the news consumers, the recipient, his or her social imprinting, and his or her prior knowledge, determine how reality depicted in the media assembles into an individual overall picture perceived as 'reality'. Nevertheless, a radical constructivist perspective is not helpful. If one assumes that the media construct reality, and inner-media reality and extra-media reality are inseparable, the issue of adequacy of news coverage becomes obsolete. Radically denying an extra-constructed reality that could be approached scientifically means rejecting the debate on quality journalism as well. Kepplinger states:

> Those who deny the possibility of comparing journalistic representations of reality with the respective reality, also deny the possibility that scientists can draw a comparison between journalistic representations of reality and their object of representation. Thus, they position themselves outside of empirical research.
>
> (Kepplinger 2004, 2. edition: 96)

Yet, scientific research working beyond empirical observations faces the difficulty of not being able to compare its hypotheses with an objectively quantifiable, complex reality. Even if 'truth' does not exist, methods of evaluating representations of reality exist; the place of 'truth' is then substituted by criteria like 'credibility' and 'diversity' as standards (Weischenberg 1993: 132) enabling the ability to draw conclusions within a specific cultural area of reference. "Verification [thus becomes] a comparison of statements, instead of a comparison of facts. It objectifies the statements without gaining full objectivity" (Haller 1993: 144). Objectivity is then – as I understand it from a less radical constructivist perspective – not an ultimate but an abstract aim. In order to avoid misunderstandings, it is useful to distinguish between the description (news depicts reality) and the normative requirement (news is supposed to depict reality as truthfully as possible) in discussions about the veracity of media content (Bentele 1993b: 156). Following Bentele's argument, reality is not constructed itself but the coverage of events is. Only via the media does reality become reality in the audiences' view (Bentele 1993a: 179). Avoiding the two contradictory extreme positions that fall short, Bentele (1992) convincingly suggests a *re-constructivist approach*, which – although it might not allow objective verification of reality – makes it subjectively comprehensible: coverage is credible if the concept of reality is confirmed by other participants of the discourse. Reality undergoes selection and construction processes, and then becomes news reality (Bentele 1993b: 167); news is thus a "re-construction of reality" (Merten 2004: 17). For this study, I wanted to find out which reality Western media display of sub-Saharan Africa, and how the interactions between media and aid sector shape this media reality. To understand this reality and the interactions between media and aid that shape it better, I present in the next section theories of news production, of actor-focused journalism, and my approach to understand actors, as well as the theoretical background of the relationship between public relations and journalism.

3.3 Theories of news selection

In the following subsections I will elucidate different theories of news selection that lead to standard explanations as to why news generally tends to be crisis-focused in order to further answer the question of what reality journalism displays. I use these theories to understand the processes in my empirical research better. However, they do not have the potential to give a plausible explanation of the predominating negative Africa coverage. Do correspondents select what they cover and how? Are they reporting their unbiased, second-order observations on site? Are they bystanders, or are they involved in the events on the ground?

Gatekeeper theory

One theory of news selection I refer to in my empirical study is the *gatekeeper theory* (White 1959), which frames the role of journalists in a triangle between events, news production and the product 'news', and its role in the political system. The gatekeeper theory assumes that news does not depict reality but rather conveys specific stereotypical segments of reality that are the result of selections based on conventions (see e.g. Hambückers 2008: 57). It explains the process of news selection with a focus on communicators who decide which events do or do not pass their 'gates' to then become news. This so-called *gatekeeping* is the selection and further processing of events through media organisations (McQuail 2005: 308f) and their actors, and takes place on both an individual and on a system level. On an individual level journalists work as *gatekeepers* deciding which information will reach the public and how. For this decision, individual preferences and media-specific factors such as organisational, economical, and institutional restraints influencing the selection are important. Only those events that pass the gatekeepers are displayed as 'the reality' in news. On an organisational level, editors are gatekeepers. The process of news selection takes place on the basis of personal attitudes and values, economic premises and media-specific factors, that is organisational, economic, and institutional restraints. Traditional gatekeeper research assumes journalists are the sole decision makers. However, gatekeepers do not make their decisions in a vacuum but within a socially structured context (Scholl & Weischenberg 1998: 40). In the process of news production many actors are involved on different levels. The sociologist Warren Breed points out that journalists often internalise their editor's attitude, which makes it difficult to differentiate who is the actual gatekeeper in the end (1973). I assume that whether the individual journalist can be considered active or passive in his or her gatekeeping role depends on the journalist's self-perception in combination with the influence of lobbyists, editors, and structural restraints influencing the coverage. I explicate that further in this book. Scientific studies on the role of foreign correspondents as gatekeepers have produced contradictory results: Sange and Marten argue that editors already make a selection by choosing a certain correspondent, which can be understood as "pre-selection for a certain orientation of the coverage" (Marten 1987: 23f; see also Sange 1989: 70). Siemes (2000: 42) and Lange (2002: 184) consider the gatekeeping competence of foreign correspondents limited; they see news agencies and editorial headquarters as actual gatekeepers. Bengelstorff and Franzke's studies conclude with similar results, finding editors to be the main gatekeepers that have little interest and knowledge regarding Africa (Franzke 2000: 116, 119f; Bengelstorff 2002: 86). Neudeck (1977: 17) and Mükke (2009b: 110ff) think that the editorial headquarters' interest in crisis-focused topics is one of the main factors weakening the gatekeeping competence of Africa correspondents, and that mainly coverage written in the headquarters is crisis-focused. Interestingly, Wimmer's study contradicts these results, saying that it is mainly correspondents' reporting that is negative in its judgement of African issues (Wimmer 2003: 348). To what extent are foreign correspondents in Africa gatekeepers? And what role do humanitarian organisations play in the gatekeeping debate? Could they also be seen as gatekeepers distributing information to and withholding information from journalists, and therefore shaping the news? My contribution to the gatekeeper theory is to see to what extent correspondents act as gatekeepers in sub-Saharan Africa, and whether humanitarian organisations have gatekeeping powers too.

News value theory, or what makes the headlines?

Another prominent theory of news selection is the *news value theory* (Galtung & Ruge 1970; Staab 1990; Harcup & O'Neill 2016), which begins one step earlier with the perception of events. It aims to explain what factors influence news selection and thus coverage. I use this theory to investigate how much freedom correspondents and humanitarian organisations have to influence which events get covered, and ask them which events have the highest news value in their perception. According to news value theory, news is the result of selection decisions. Since a significant number of events and selections have to be made, selection criteria facilitate journalistic work. The more criteria – so-called *news factors* – apply to an event, the greater the probability that the media take notice of it, and that the event becomes news (*additivity hypothesis*). Some events have a greater *news value* than others (Galtung & Ruge 1970; Harcup & O'Neill 2010). During the selection process one criterion can be compensated by others (*complementary hypothesis*). Factors that hardly matter in national news, such as 'affinity', 'proximity', and 'status', play an important role in foreign news. Coverage of a foreign country is proportional to the importance of that country to the international relations of the news outlet's home country, and to the similarity of the foreign country to the news outlet's home country in terms of economic, cultural, and political development. The more similar to the home country, the more likely it is that news from the foreign country will be covered (Hagen 1998: 148; Schmidt &

Wilke 1998: 176f). The greater the perceived difference between the culture that is to be reported about, and the culture for which the reporting takes place, the bigger the catastrophe has to be, or the more people have to die, for the event to make the news (Lange 2002: 184). Exceptions, such as coverage due to special interests of editors or correspondents, or special *human interest* coverage (Klosa, Scholze-Stubenrecht & Wermke 1997: 315, key word 'Journal'), prove that rule. Content analyses of Africa coverage show that above all, the factors 'relevance', 'conflict', and 'ethnocentrism', as well as 'scale of damage', 'prominence', and 'surprise' have a significant influence (Mükke 2009b: 127). *Timing* also plays a role with regard to the extent that an event is noticed by the media, and to the level of response to the coverage (Franks 2013: 32). Hardly any 'positive' events in sub-Saharan Africa get covered since "the news factor success has an insignificant influence in comparison to the factors damage and conflict" (Mükke 2009b: 127). Mükke points out that negative news reporting is a general trend, but is especially relevant in foreign news (Mükke 2009b: 77). "The news factors 'personalisation', 'negativism' and 'surprise' lead [. . .] to overstressing the conflict element in foreign news reporting" (Mükke 2009b: 77), and single events receive more attention than continuous ones (Mükke 2009b: 142). The absolute nature of news value theory was often criticised (see for example Kepplinger 1998), but the theory is still widely used. It is widely accepted now that also social and economic aspects and the journalists' general political "views also have a significant influence on the coverage" (Kepplinger 2004, 2. edition: 98). Whether something gets covered also depends on its quality, the competition between different media outlets, and whether the origin of a catastrophe is easy to explain (Franks 2013: 32).

The news value theory serves as background information for my study. The theory on its own does not satisfactorily explain why the reporting of sub-Saharan Africa is so persistently negative, and more so than in other regions that meet similar criteria. In Africa events have a high news value if they involve conflicts, cause a considerable amount of damage, and involve powerful nations, organisations, or prominent actors (Mükke 2009b: 165ff). In my research, I therefore asked what events correspondents perceived as important, irrelevant of whether they actually had influence on the selection of events, and of whether the event lead to coverage. To find out more about the interaction between correspondents and humanitarians, I compared these 'perceived' news values that they applied to certain events to how humanitarian organisations' 'perceived' news values.[2] I was interested to find out whether these perceived news values matched, and whether they influenced the interactions between correspondents and humanitarian organisations.

Framing theory and news-bias research

Framing theory (e.g. Scheufele 2003) applies at a point after the selection of event has already taken place, thus at a point later than the news value theory. Framing theory combines concepts of news selection and media impact: journalists *frame* events or topics in a certain way. A *frame* is a pattern of interpretation:

the journalist presents and contextualises an event in a certain way in his or her report by creating a social and cognitive frame of reference, selecting, stressing, or omitting certain aspects of the individually perceived reality. The *framing* of a topic suggests a certain interpretation of the event (see e.g. Sommer & Ruhrmann 2010), by "structuring a topic in a specific way and thus directing the information-handling and opinion-making" (Hambückers 2008: 67). It ensures that old patterns of interpretation remain or that new patterns of interpretation prevail (Scheufele 2003: 104); with a change in values, frames can change in the long run (Ruhrmann 2005: 318). Thus, how sub-Saharan Africa is perceived by news audiences depends not only on the selection of events that are then covered, but also very much on the framing of events as they appear in the news.

News-bias research operates on a similar level as the framing theory. It has shown a correlation between the beliefs of communicators, their ways of selecting the news, and potentially inadequate representations of events (Schönbach 1977). Framing theory and news-bias research are relevant for my study insofar as I assume that the ubiquitous positive framing of the aid industry in articles, which content analyses of media reports have clearly proven, can also be revealed on an actor level, which is yet to be proven. For triangulation, the second actor group will be asked about their opinion of the first actor group, and the other way round, and what they think is the respective other group's opinion about themselves. Including the third-order view will help to get a broader picture of the actors' views and their interactions.

3.4 Methodological individualism and its combination with network analysis

Instead of understanding journalism as a system in Luhmann's sense, which is not beneficial for this inquiry, I use a structural-individualistic approach: the focus lies on actors integrated in a specific social and institutional framework that determines their actions, and that is shaped by the actors' actions at the same time. In this actor-performance focused approach, journalism, as well as public relations of humanitarian organisations consists of *actions*; it is a *system* of *interacting actors*. Actors I define as people who are specialised in a certain domain, act against this background, and make (strategic) decisions following particular interests and objectives, and with command over operational resources and normative orientations (Jarren & Donges 2006: 119). In this book, such actors are foreign correspondents (staff and freelancers), as well as employees and consultants of humanitarian organisations who serve as contact persons for these journalists, mainly programme managers and people working in public relations in the communication departments of humanitarian organisations. The actor model is that of a *homo socio-oeconomicus* (Lindenberg 1985: 100ff; Esser 1993).[3] That means the actors are social beings operating within a context of social relationships, their own expectations of the actions' outcome, and expectations of the others' expectations. Within a framework of certain material, social, and institutional restrictions that they face, they have different options as to how to act at their proposal, and choose the option that – according to their expectations after being evaluated with regards to their aim(s), consciously, or sometimes sub-consciously – subjectively perceived promises the most benefit and the least effort. While making decisions, the socio-oeconomic man is resourceful and can find new ways to solve his/her problems (resourceful-restrictive-evaluating-emotional-maximising man RREEMM, Esser 1993: 238). Within this understanding of the journalists as social, rational actors I also want to build on the reflections of Fengler and Ruß-Mohl (2005), who convincingly use a theoretical-economic approach for communicator research, specifically for analysing journalistic acting. They reveal on a theoretical level that what leads to journalists' decisions regarding reporting is mostly economic considerations, and only to a much lesser extent personal belief or the job's ethics. However, Fengler and Ruß-Mohl do not verify their theoretical approach empirically. In what way do foreign correspondents and humanitarians act as *homines socio-oeconomici* in their interactions?[4] Actions can also be explained by meanings that the actors agree upon in the process of interaction (Raabe 2004: 118). *Actor relationships* I understand as personal and professional contacts on a micro-level that consist of individual actions between the actors, and in attitudes and understandings that these actors have regarding each other. The actor relationships are part of general relationships between the different sectors for which these actors work.

Outcomes that actors expect of their actions, and interactions, as well as what they expect their interaction counterpart to do, are fundamental in this approach of methodological individualism, and are a starting point for rational choices that actors make. Since social acting is defined by subjective interpretations of a specific situation, the reconstruction of subjective rationality in the actions of the actors and the actor's network is essential. In order to reconstruct this subjective rationality, I also investigate the actor's self-perception and role (I explain this connection in Chapter 4, section 4.1 in the subsection on journalists' self-perception and under Chapter 4, section 4.4 in the subsection on humanitarian organisations' self-perception), and how they perceive their counterpart's role. This sociological approach permits the connection with empirical research on journalism (Reinemann 2007), and thus the connection with approaches like the news value theory and framing theory that I presented in the last subsections.

In this approach, the focus lies on individuals and actions of individuals working in the humanitarian and media sector, as well as their interactions, but the rationale behind this approach is to look at social phenomena that happen on the macro-level, resulting from individual actions on the micro-level that aggregate to a new or changed phenomenon on the macro-level. This model is referred to as macro-micro-macro-scheme that Esser (Esser 2004: 15ff) developed in further advancement of Coleman's "bathtub model" (Coleman 1986: 1322), and was modified in the version used here by Kropp (2010). A macro-phenomenon 'I' influences the changing actions and interactions of individuals – correspondents and humanitarians – on the micro-level whose actions are mutually oriented towards one another and bound to expectations and expectation-expectations. The actions of these individuals that are oriented towards one another aggregate to a new macro-phenomenon 'II'. The macro context is thus explained implicitly via the (1) logic of the situation, that is restrictions which individuals face in their material, institutional, and cultural framework; the (2) logic of selection that leads to a decision on how to act based on the individual's understanding of the situation, the evaluation of expected and likely outcomes – with the aim to maximise them – and the consequences of the outcomes; and the (3) logic of aggregation, in which individuals' actions that are oriented towards others aggregate to the new macro-phenomenon (Esser 1999: 259; 2000a: 8–14; 2000c: 6; Kropp 2010: 147), see Figure 3.1.

The distinction between the levels of micro and macro in this model is an analytical distinction that enables systematic explanations (for the argument in this whole past paragraph, see Kropp 2010). The model helps to explain collective social phenomena via the actions and interactions of individuals (Greshoff 2009: 109, 119). If I use the term *individuals* I do not mean individual human beings, but individuals as *social actors* that act within a framework that enables or disables certain actions, and a network of interactions with other social actors. The motivations for the individual's actions cannot be analysed detached from the framework, or detached from other players in the network. I consider it important to contextualise the actors in a network of actor relationships and a socially structured functional context, instead of treating them as if they acted in a vacuum. My approach focuses on the individual and structural factors without seeing this as a contradiction.[5] How do correspondents and staff of humanitarian organisations perceive their own actions, and to what extent do they think they are determined by the demands of their own and the others' sector? What material and institutional framework do the actors feel restricted by, and to what extent can they be resourceful within these restrictions? In order to clarify the concept of individual actors that I use, and to understand the background of their action patterns, I will explain roles and tasks of correspondents in Chapter 4, section 4.1 and of humanitarian organisations in Chapter 4, section 4.4.

As described above, I examine the actors' behaviour in their social and professional work context to reveal how foreign correspondents and humanitarians interact. An actor-focused methodological individualism approach alone is however not sufficient because I also consider the interactions beyond the micro-scale to be important, as they form a wider network consisting of stable relationships beyond a singular interaction. Choosing a micro-level perspective with a focus on individual actors, even when applying the macro-micro-macro model complicates the monitoring of trends in foreign reporting on a larger scale. I therefore look at the whole as more than just the sum of its parts; not only the individual but also "its relationships to others and its contextualisation within a structure" (Jansen 1999: 16) is of interest. The interests, resources, and most important actions of actors, depend on their context. Taking structural restrictions into account helps to understand the actions of individuals, which is why in Chapter 6 I include reflections on the framework that defines journalists' and humanitarians' work, generally, and specifically in sub-Saharan Africa. The framework defining their interactions is discussed in separate sections, in 6.1 and 6.2.

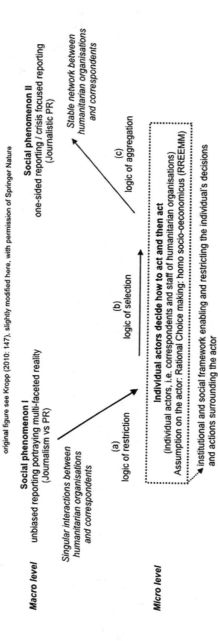

Figure 3.1 Macro-micro-macro scheme, modified

Original graphic by Kropp, Per (2010) "Methodologischer Individualismus und Netzwerkforschung. Ein Diskussionsbeitrag", in: *Netzwerkanalyse und Netzwerktheorie*, 145–153, 147; with permission of Springer Nature.

In journalism research – in contrast to social sciences – the concept of network has been discussed surprisingly little (Quandt 2005: 75; 2007: 376; see also Altmeppen 1999; Altmeppen 2000; Neuberger 2004). Studying the interactions, I use a network theoretical approach. A network is a "structure consisting of a number of elements [...] and their interconnections. The social sciences primarily depict social networks, in which the linked elements are people (actors). In these networks, the links between these elements depict social relationships" (Quandt 2007: 377). I understand a network in this context as consisting of stabilised interactions between actors of the humanitarian and the media sector. Interactions are any type of contact taking place between the two, as long as they are mutual. In more traditional network analysis, the focus purely lies on the relationships and the position of the actors within the network, and is not compatible with a focus on the actors themselves, questioning their actions and motives. So at first sight, qualitative research and network analysis seem to contradict one another, since the latter often implies standardised research with a large set of data and elaborated model calculations (Hollstein 2006: 12). In contrast, I do not research the purely formal network structures, such as for example an individual's position within the network (Holzer 2013), but instead study actors' actions and interactions, and, at the same time I allow for network perspectives, so as to establish a further explanation of the aggregated interactions that link the micro- and macro-level.[6] Following Kropp's (2010: 150) reflections on a fruitful combination of methodological individualism and network perspective, I see the micro-macro-model as "heuristic to categorise the role of social networks" in the correlation between micro and macro level. Exploring the importance of the actor relationships for the news coverage, and their influence in the crisis-focused reporting on sub-Saharan Africa is my second research question. For this investigation, the network – consisting of interactions that consolidate, and to be explored in order to answer the first research question – is part of the explanation:[7] The nature of the network, in which the actors are embedded, makes certain actions on the micro-level possible or not, and these actions lead to the macro-phenomenon of one-sided, crisis-focused reporting, of which in turn both actor groups in the network profit.

In this chapter I explained my underlying understanding of news and news production, my general understanding of interactions, and how changing actors' choices of behaviour can change macro phenomena. I also discussed theoretically how this understanding is compatible with network analysis, and fruitful for this explorative investigation. In the following chapter, I will subsequently explore in more detail the framework within which the actors operate, with a regional focus on sub-Saharan Africa, which shapes the actors' decisions to perform certain actions in a unique way. The actors in this study are correspondents of large international Western news media as well as employees of humanitarian organisations, so in the next chapter I explore the framework that restricts and enables both separately, and also look at the specific conditions in sub-Saharan Africa that shape their interactions. Investigating the network of correspondents, and which humanitarian organisations they consider necessary, I also explore how the nature of this network directs a certain way and angle of reporting in the journalists' view.

Notes

1 See also Kepplinger's attempt to make empirical research and theoretical approaches compatible by regarding journalism as inhomogeneous system of actors, a system of rules that consists in people, organisations, and institutions. He defines journalism as a subsystem of mass communication whose conditions, types, and effects are the results of journalistic work (Kepplinger 2004). See also Gerhards and Neidhardt (1993) who combine actor and systems theory in their analysis of public policy communication discourses.
2 Foreign correspondents and the staff of humanitarian organisations working in communications departments were asked how newsworthy they considered certain events.
3 The perspective of economical determinism originally derives from business ethics and assumes "that individuals largely display similar patterns of behaviour in economic, political and social contexts" (Fengler & Ruß-Mohl 2005: 27). In all contexts the actors have various options to act at their disposal. They agree to barter relationships, while giving priority to their own interests and choosing the option that satisfies expected benefits (e.g. Kunz 1996). Not only economic benefits play a role but also social benefits, such as for example prestige. For further discussions about this controversial approach and the *rational choice theory* that evolved from it, see e.g. Zimmerling (1994).
4 I use the term 'humanitarians' to designate the personnel of humanitarian organisations or consultants working for them. I also use it to differentiate between the organisational level (humanitarian organisation) and the actor level (humanitarians, people working for a humanitarian organisation, no matter what position they may have).
5 Compare also with the argumentation of Bucher, who understands journalism as "communicative acting" (Bucher 2004: 267) and shows that journalistic actions also imply system characteristics, and that they emerge from the context of a social system. According to Bucher, the action-theoretical approach should not cut actors down to individuals, and investigate their acting or performance patterns, but instead the actor's performance patterns within their system (Bucher 2004: 267). In stating this, Bucher explicitly criticises Rühl (1980) and the research that follows Rühl's approach. Also, third-degree phenomena are especially of interest in journalism. These phenomena are, says Bucher, the result of individual actions in the social system but not the result of individuals' intentions (Bucher 2004: 263f). Actions can only be evaluated through observation and by contextualising them (Bucher 2004: 271f).
6 Scholars often seek a conjunction of micro- and macro-perspectives but they also often view such conjunctions critically. The attempt to combine both perspectives is accused of diluting both (Quandt 2005: 74). Quandt rightly points out that the "identification of action theory with the micro level and systems theory with the macro level" (ibid.) is unreasonable because the relationships between structure and action are then ignored.
7 See Kropp 2010: 148.

References

Altmeppen, Klaus-Dieter (1999) *Redaktionen als Koordinationszentren. Beobachtungen journalistischen Handelns*, Opladen.
Altmeppen, Klaus-Dieter (2000) "Entscheidungen und Koordinationen. Dimensionen journalistischen Handelns", in: Martin Löffelholz (Ed.), *Theorien des Journalismus. Ein diskursives Handbuch*, Wiesbaden, 293–310.
Bengelstorff, Anja (2002) *Auslandskorrespondenten in Afrika südlich der Sahara: Eine qualitative Kommunikatorstudie zu Rollenverständnis und Arbeitsrealität. Magisterarbeit*, FU Berlin, Berlin.

Bentele, Günter (1992) "Fernsehen und Realität – Ansätze zu einer rekonstruktiven Medientheorie", in: Knut Hickethier and Irmela Schneider (Eds.), *Fernsehtheorien: Dokumentation der GFF-Tagung 1990*, Berlin, 45–65.

Bentele, Günter (1993a) *Theorien Öffentlicher Kommunikation. Problemfelder, Positionen, Perspektiven*, München.

Bentele, Günter (1993b) "Wie wirklich ist die Medienwirklichkeit? Einige Anmerkungen zum Konstruktivismus und Realismus in der Kommunikationswissenschaft", in: Günter Bentele and Manfred Rühl (Eds.), *Theorien öffentlicher Kommunikation. Problemfelder, Positionen, Perspektiven*, München, 152–171.

Breed, Warren (1973) "Soziale Kontrolle in der Redaktion: eine funktionale Analyse", in: Jörg Aufermann, Hans Bohrmann and Rolf Sülzer (Eds.), *Gesellschaftliche Kommunikation und Information. Forschungsrichtungen und Problemstellungen. Eine Arbeitsbuch zur Massenkommunikation*, Frankfurt, 356–387.

Bucher, Hans-Jürgen (2004) "Journalismus als kommunikatives Handeln. Grundlagen einer handlungstheoretischen Journalismustheorie", in: Martin Löffelholz (Ed.), *Theorien des Journalismus. Ein diskursives Handbuch*, Frankfurt/M., 263–285.

Coleman, James (1986) "Social Theory, Social Research, and a Theory of Action", in: *The American Journal of Sociology* 91(6), 1309–1335.

Deutscher Journalisten Verband (2012) "Vocational profile – Journalist", in: *DJV Wissen* 4.

Esser, Hartmut (1993) *Soziologie. Allgemeine Grundlagen*, Frankfurt/M.

Esser, Hartmut (1999) "Situationslogik und Handeln." in: *Soziologie. Spezielle Grundlagen* ed. Vol 1, Frankfurt.

Esser, Hartmut (2000a) *Institutionen*, Frankfurt.

Esser, Hartmut. (2000b). "Soziales Handeln." in: *Soziologie. Spezielle Grundlagen*, ed. Vol. 3, Frankfurt.

Esser, Hartmut (2004) "Akteure und soziale Systeme", in: Thomas Schwinn (Ed.), *Differenzierung und soziale Ungleicheit*, 271–283.

Fengler, Susanne and Ruß-Mohl, Stephan (2005) *Der Journalist als 'Homo oeconomicus'*, Konstanz.

Franks, Suzanne (2013) *Reporting Disasters. Famine, Aid, Politics and the Media*, London.

Franzke, Michael (2000) "'Aber die Agenturen haben nichts gemeldet . . .' Das Problem, über Probleme der ‚Dritten Welt' zu berichten", in: Stefan Brüne (Ed.), *Neue Medien und Öffentlichkeiten. Politik und Tele-Kommunikation in Afrika, Asien und Lateinamerika*, Hamburg.

Galtung, Johan and Ruge, Mari H. (1970) "The Structure of Foreign News. The Presentation of the Congo, Cuba and Cyprus Crisis in four Norwegian Newspapers", in: Jeremy Tunstall (Ed.), *Media Sociology*, Urbana, IL.

Gerhards, Jürgen and Neidhardt, Friedhelm (1993) "Strukturen und Funktionen moderner Öffentlichkeit. Fragestellungen und Ansätze", in: Wolfgang R. Langenbucher (Ed.), *Politische Kommunikation. Grundlagen, Strukturen, Prozesse*, Wien, 52–88.

German Press Council (2008) *German Press Code*, Vol Version of 13.03.2013.

Greshoff, Rainer (2009) "Das 'Modell der soziologischen Erklärung' in ontologischer Perspektive - das Konzept von Harmut Esser", in: Jens Greve, Annette Schnabel and Rainer Schützeichel (Eds.), *Das Mikro-Makro-Modell der soziologischen Erklärung*, Wiesbaden, 108–144.

Hagen, Lutz (1998) "Die Beobachtung Deutschlands in ausländischen Medien als Funktion des Nachrichtenfaktors Nähe. Eine Analyse von Zeitungs- und Fernsehnachrichten", in: *Publizistik* 43, 143–157.

44 Theoretical concepts

Haller, Michael (1993) "Journalistisches Handeln: Vermittlung oder Konstruktion von Wirklichkeit?", in: Günter Bentele and Manfred Rühl (Eds.), *Theorien öffentlichker Kommunikation. Problemfelder, Positionen, Perspektiven*, München, 137–151.

Hambückers, Martin (2008) *Medien, Politik, Demokratie eine interkulturelle Perspektive*, Nordhausen.

Hanitzsch, Thomas (2004) *Journalismus in Indonesien: Akteure, Strukturen, Orientierungshorizonte, Journalismuskulturen*, Wiesbaden.

Hanitzsch, Thomas (2007) "Die Struktur des journalistischen Feldes", in: Thomas Hanitzsch, Carsten Schlüter and Klaus-Dieter Altmeppen (Eds.), *Journalismustheorie: Next Generation. Soziologische Grundlegung und theoretische Innovation*, Wiesbaden, 239–262.

Hanitzsch, Thomas, Altmeppen, Klaus-Dieter and Schlüter, Carsten (2007) "Zur Einführung: Die Journalismustheorie und das Treffen der Generationen", in: Thomas Hanitzsch, Klaus-Dieter Altmeppen and Carsten Schlüter (Eds.), *Journalismustheorie: Next Generation. Soziologische Grundlegung und theoretische Innovation*, Wiesbaden, 7–23.

Hannerz, Ulf (2004) *Foreign News: Exploring the World of Foreign Correspondents*, Chicago.

Harcup, Tony and O'Neill, Deirdre (2010) "What Is the News? Galtung and Ruge Revisited", in: *Journalism Studies* 2(2), 261–280.

Harcup, Tony and O'Neill, Deirdre (2016) "What Is News? News Values Revisited (Again)", in: *Journalism Studies Online*.

Hollstein, Betina (2006) "Qualitative Methoden und Netzwerkanalyse – ein Widerspruch?", in: Betina Hollstein and Florian Straus (Eds.) Qualitative Netzwerkanalyse, 11–35.

Holzer, Boris (2013) "Netzwerktheorie", in: Georg Kneer and Markus Schroer (Eds.), *Handbuch Soziologische Theorien*, Wiesbaden, 253–276.

Jansen, Dorothea (1999) *Einführung in die Netzwerkanalyse: Grundlagen, Methoden, Anwendungen*, Opladen.

Jarren, Otfried and Donges, Patrick (2006, 2. edition) *Politische Kommunikation in der Mediengesellschaft. Eine Einführung*, Wiesbaden.

Kepplinger, Hans (1989) "Theorien der Nachrichtenauswahl als Theorien der Realität", in: *APuZ Beilage B* 15(89), 3–16.

Kepplinger, Hans (1993) "Erkenntnistheorie und Forschungspraxis des Konstruktivismus", in: Günter Bentele and Manfred Rühl (Eds.), *Theorien öffentlicher Kommunikation*, München, 118–125.

Kepplinger, Hans (1998) "Der Nachrichtenwert der Nachrichtenfaktoren", in: Christina Holtz-Bacha and Helga Weisbecker (Eds.), *Wie die Medien die Welt erschaffen und wie die Menschen darin leben*, Opladen, 19–106.

Kepplinger, Hans (2004, 2nd. edition) "Problemdimensionen des Journalismus. Wechselwirkung zwischen Theorie und Empirie", in: Martin Löffelholz (Ed.), *Theorien des Journalismus: Ein diskursives Handbuch*, Wiesbaden, 87–106.

Klosa, Annette, Scholze-Stubenrecht, Werner and Wermke, Matthias (Eds.). (1997) *Duden, Etymologie*, Mannheim.

Kropp, Per (2010) "Methodologischer Individualismus und Netzwerkforschung. Ein Diskussionsbeitrag", in: Christian Stegbauer (Ed.), *Netzwerkanalyse und Netzwerktheorie*, 145–154.

Kunz, Volker (1996, 2nd. edition) *Empirische Ökonomik. Handlungstheoretische Grundlagen der Erklärung politischer und sozialer Prozesse*, Marburg.

Lange, Silvia (2002) "Auf verlorenem Posten?", *Deutschsprachige Auslandskorrespondenten in Lateinamerika. Eine qualitative Kommunikatorstudie zur Arbeitsrealität und Rollenverständnis. Magisterarbeit*, FU Berlin.

Lindenberg, Siegwart (1985) "An Assessment of the New Political Economy: Its Potential for the Social Sciences and for Sociology in Particular", in: *Sociological Theory* 3(1), 99–114.
Löffelholz, Martin (2004a) "Krisen- und Kriegskommunikation als Forschungsfeld. Trends, Themen und Theorien eines hoch relevanten, aber gering systematisierten Teilgebiets in der Kommunikationswissenschaft", in: Martin Löffelholz (Ed.), *Krieg als Medienereignis II. Krisenkommunikation im 21: Jahrhundert*, Wiesbaden, 13–55.
Löffelholz, Martin (2004b) "Theorien des Journalismus. Eine historische, metatheoretische und synoptische Einführung", in: Martin Löffelholz (Ed.), *Theorien des Journalismus. Ein diskursives Handbuch*, Wiesbaden, 17–64.
Löffelholz, Martin (Ed.) (2004c) *Theorien des Journalismus: Ein diskursives Handbuch*, Wiesbaden.
Lünenborg, Margreth (2012) "Qualität in der Krise?", in: *APuZ* 29–31(Qualitätsjournalismus), 3–8.
Marten, Eckhard (1987) "Zwischen Skepsis und Bewunderung. Zum Tätigkeitsprofil, Selbstverständnis und Deutschlandbild amerikanischer Auslandskorrespondenten in der Bundesrepublik Deutschland", in: *Publizistik* 32(1), 23–33.
McQuail, Denis (2005 [1983]) *Mass Communication Theory. An Introduction*, 5. ed., Los Angeles.
Merten, Klaus (1990) "Inszenierung von Alltag, Kommunikation, Massenkommunikation, Medien", in: Deutsches Institut für Fernsehstudien an der Universität Tübingen (Ed.), *Funkkolleg, Studienbrief*, Weinheim-Basel, 79–108.
Merten, Klaus (2004) "Mikro, Mikro-Makro oder Makro? Zum Verhältnis von Journalismus und PR aus systemischer Perspektive", in: Klaus-Dieter Altmeppen, Ulrike Röttger and Günter Bentele (Eds.), *Schwierige Verhältnisse. Interdependenzen zwischen Journalismus und PR*, Wiesbaden, 17–36.
Mükke, Lutz (2009b) *'Journalisten der Finsternis'. Akteure, Strukturen und Potenziale deutscher Afrika-Berichterstattung*, Köln.
Neuberger, Christoph (2004, 2nd. edition.) "Journalismus als systembezogene Akteurkonstellation. Grundlagen einer integrativen Journalismustheorie", in: Martin Löffelholz (Ed.), *Theorien des Journalismus: Ein diskursives Handbuch*, Frankfurt/M, 287–303.
Neudeck, Rupert (1977) *Den Dschungel ins Wohnzimmer: Auslandsberichterstattung im bundesdeutschen Fernsehen*, Frankfurt/M.
Quandt, Thorsten (2005) *Journalisten im Netz: Eine Untersuchung Journalistischen Handelns in Online-Redaktionen*, Wiesbaden.
Quandt, Thorsten (2007) "Netzwerkansätze: Potenziale für die Journalismusforschung", in: Klaus-Dieter Altmeppen, Thomas Hanitzsch and Carsten Schlüter (Eds.), *Journalismustheorie: Next Genernation*, Wiesbaden, 371–392.
Raabe, Johannes (2004, 2nd. edition) "Theoriebildung und empirische Analyse. Überlegungen zu einer hinreichend theorieoffenen, empirischen Journalismusforschung", in: Martin Löffelholz (Ed.), *Theorien des Journalismus. Ein diskursives Handbuch*, Wiesbaden, 107–128.
Raabe, Johannes (2005) *Die Beobachtung journalistischer Akteure. Optionen einer empirisch-kritischen Journalismusforschung*, Wiesbaden.
Reese, Stephen (2001) "Understanding the Global Journalist: A Hierarchy-of-Influences Approach", in: *Journalism Studies* 2(2), 173–187.
Reinemann, Carsten (2007) "Subjektiv rationale Akteure: Das Potential handlungstheoretischer Erklärungen für die Journalismusforschung", in: Thomas Hanitzsch and et al (Eds.), *Journalismustheorie: Next Generation*, Wiesbaden, 47–67.

Rühl, Manfred (1969) *Die Zeitungsredaktion als organisiertes soziales System*, Bielefeld.
Rühl, Manfred (1980) *Journalismus und Gesellschaft Bestandsaufnahme und Theorieentwurf*, Mainz.
Rühl, Manfred (1992) "Theorien des Journalismus", in: Roland Burkhard and Walter Jörnberg (Eds.), *Kommunikationstheorien: Ein Textbuch zur Einführung*, Wien, 117–320.
Ruhrmann, Georg (2005) "Nachrichtenselektion", in: Siegfried Weischenberg, Hans Kleinsteueber and Bernhard Pörksen (Eds.), *Handbuch Journalismus und Medien*, 317–320.
Sange, Ralf (1989) "Japanische Auslandskorrespondenten in der Bundesrepublik Deutschland. Qualifikationsmerkmale, Arbeitsbedingungen und Berufseinstellungen", in: *Publizistik* 34(12), 62–77.
Schäfer, Sabine (2004) "Journalismus als soziales Feld. Das relationale Denken Pierre Bourdieus als Grundlage für eine Journalismusforschung", in: Martin Löffelholz (Ed.), *Theorien des Journalismus. Ein diskursives Handbuch*, Wiesbaden, 321–334.
Scheufele, Bertram (2003) *Frames – Framing – Framing-Effekte. Theoretische und methodische Grundlegung des Framing-Ansatzes sowie empirische Befunde zur Nachrichtenproduktion*, Wiesbaden.
Schimank, Uwe (2007) "Handeln in Konstellationen: Die reflexive Konstitution von handelndem Zusammenwirken und sozialen Strukturen", in: Klaus-Dieter Altmeppen, Thomas Hanitzsch and Carsten Schlüter (Eds.), *Journalismustheorie: Next Generation*, Wiesbaden, 121–138.
Schlüter, Carsten (2007) "Rollen und Rahmen der Interaktionsordnung: Journalismus aus der Perspektive seiner Interaktionen", in: Klaus-Dieter Altmeppen, Thomas Hanitzsch and Carsten Schlüter (Eds.), *Journalismustheorie: Next Generation*, Wiesbaden, 327–346.
Schmidt, Dagmar and Wilke, Jürgen (1998) "Die Darstellung des Auslands in den deutschen Medien. Ergebnisse einer Inhaltsanalyse 1995", in: Siegfried Quandt and Wolfgang Gast (Eds.), *Deutschland im Dialog der Kulturen: Medien, Images, Verständigung*, Konstanz, 167–181.
Scholl, Armin and Weischenberg, Siegfried (1998) *Journalismus in der Gesellschaft: Theorie, Methodologie und Empirie*, Opladen.
Schönbach, Klaus (1977) *Trennung von Nachricht und Meinung: Empirische Untersuchung eines journalistischen Qualitätskriteriums*, Freiburg i. B.
Schulz, Winfried (1989) "Massenmedien und Realität", in: Max Kaase and Winfried Schulz (Eds.), *Massenkommunikation: Theorien, Methoden, Befunde*, Opladen, 135–149.
Sharrock, Wes and Button, Graham (1991) "The Social Actor: Social Action in Real Time", in: Graham Button (Ed.), *Ethnomethodology and the Human Science*, Cambridge, 137–176.
Siemes, Annette (2000) *Auslandskorrespondenten in Polen. Nachbarschaftsvermittler zwischen Rollenverständnis und Arbeitsrealität*, Bochum.
Sommer, Denise and Ruhrmann, Georg (2010) "Oughts and Ideals – Framing People with Migration Background in TV news", in: *Conflict & Communication Online* 9(2).
Staab, Joachim Friedrich (1990) *Nachrichtenwert-Theorie formale Struktur und empirischer Gehalt*, Freiburg (Breisgau), München.
Weischenberg, Siegfried (1993) "Die Medien und die Köpfe. Perspektiven und Probleme konstruktivistischer Journalismusforschung", in: Günter Bentele and Manfred Rühl (Eds.), *Theorien öffentlicher Kommunikation. Problemfelder, Positionen, Perspektiven*, München, 126–136.
White, David (1959) "The 'Gatekeeper': A Case Study in the Selection of News", in: *Journalism Quarterly* 27, 383–390.

Willems, Herbert (2007) "Elemente einer Journalismustheorie nach Bourdieu", in: Klaus-Dieter Altmeppen, Thomas Hanitzsch and Carsten Schlüter (Eds.), *Journalismustheorie: Next Generation*, Wiesbaden, 215–238.

Wimmer, Jeffrey (2003) "Das Ende der 'Dritten Welt'? Ein Vergleich der Berichterstattung über Afrika in der deutschen Presse 1991 und 2001", in: *Communicatio Socialis. Internationale Zeitschrift für Kommunikation in Religion, Kirche und Gesellschaft* 4, 337–352.

Zimmerling, Ruth (1994) "Rational Choice-Theorien: Fluch oder Segen für die Politikwissenschaft?", in: Ulrich Druwe and Volker Kunz (Eds.), *Rational Choice in der Politikwissenschaft. Grundlagen und Anwendungen*, Opladen, 15–34.

4 Media and aid – sectors and actors

Basic assumptions

Correspondents and humanitarians are acting within a framework-lock that is restricting and enabling their actions at the same time. This framework, see sections 4.1 and 4.4, is related to the micro-level but goes beyond it. It determines the actors' behaviour but the actors' behaviour can also shape the framework. Framework in this context means material, institutional, and social restrictions that actors operate within, and general social and institutional expectations that the actors face. This chapter highlights diverse components of this framework for the international media and for the aid sector and its actors working in sub-Saharan Africa. The first section deals with correspondents as political actors, their roles and tasks, their self-perception, and their place within the journalistic system. The second section looks at the framework specific to the conditions correspondents working in sub-Saharan Africa face. The first two sections thus deal with what Greshoff calls "the institutional structures" in Esser's structural-theoretical social theory (Greshoff 2013: 450). The third section then addresses the Africa-specific relationships between correspondents and humanitarian organisations, and the material advantages this relationship brings. This, in Esser's model, is what Greshoff calls "material structures", consisting of material interests and opportunities (Greshoff 2013: 450). The fourth section discusses – in analogy to the first – the roles and tasks of humanitarian organisations, their actors' self-perception, and their material pressures that created a development towards professionalisation of the public relations sector. Finally, the fifth section compares the relationship between humanitarian organisations and correspondents to the relationship between correspondents and military troops. This last section on the framework defining actions of actors from both humanitarian and media sector in sub-Saharan Africa, theoretically contextualises the relationship of dependency between the actor groups, and discusses embedding with humanitarian organisation in analogy to embedding the military.

4.1 Foreign correspondents as political actors

Correspondents are social actors, who have *social capital* at their disposal (Bourdieu 1986): relationships, reputation, patterns of action conditioned by socialisation, moral concepts, and other constitutive criteria, which result in a specific perception and understanding of reality, according to prior formative influences. The limited and biased news coverage of sub-Saharan Africa preserves audiences' negative perceptions of Africa. "Our society is more and more engaged with itself, the unknown other is disturbing [. . .] [but keeping it unknown is] the psychological root of xenophobia and racism. [. . .] Good foreign reporting is part of political hygiene", says correspondent Sonia Mikich (Mikich 2003: 125) who considers it important to confront the audience with the 'other'. Why Western reporting about Africa is often negative is of social relevance. It is closely interconnected with the formation of public opinion on foreign issues. Surveys show that the general public is poorly informed about developing countries and processes of development aid (Glennie, Straw & Wild 2012: 8), leaving an even greater knowledge gap for the media to fill. At the same time, most people form their ideas about developing countries from the media (Glennie, Straw & Wild 2012: 21). Foreign correspondents are 'political actors' if we conceive news as an institutionalised form of political mass communication. In their role at the interface between politics and public, the media have the potential to put pressure on political processes (Hafez 2001). News coverage is an important element of democratic structures (Göhler 1995). The power media has is "not a state of invariable possession" (Altmeppen 2007: 424), but bound to specific context. Thus only specific outlets or journalists, concludes Altmeppen, can become opinion-makers with regard to a specific audience at a specific point in time (Altmeppen 2007: 424). Foreign correspondents, however, contribute significantly to whether, and to what extent, local or regional situations are thrust into the full glare of international attention. Irrespective of the international community's decision whether to intervene in a conflict or emergency, foreigners of different professions are already on site. Among others, these are staff members of UN organisations, governmental relief organisations, nongovernmental organisations performing development assistance and emergency relief, and journalists. What chances and challenges does this co-presence of foreign practitioners bring? Prima facie one might think that all of them, as foreigners, are non-participants and not – or at least not primarily – involved in emergency or conflict situations. Their programmatic and professional ethos demands that they are multi-partial, which is true for most humanitarian organisations, and especially true for journalists. Are they? Can they be? According to the humanitarian organisations' self-perception, their role in many cases is to be supportive and neutral. Despite this fact, however, most staff of humanitarian organisations are at the same time part of peace- and state-building missions or emergency operations, and they are in the field with the explicit mandate to influence the proceedings. They have a major impact on the events on site. The line between non-involvement and engagement is very fine. The mere symbolic presence of professional foreigners leaves lasting marks on the local conflicts, for example if their support is systematically misused for private issues of one party, or if a conflict party behaves in a specific way only to win international media's attention thinking this will then trigger more aid funding (Polman 2010: 175). More importantly, research has produced significant evidence that the fundraising strategies and pictures many humanitarian organisations use to raise funds have a share in perpetuating clichés about Africa (Adamson 1993) and Africans as "helpless victims" (Crisp 2011: 1).[1] Moreover, these foreign professionals on the ground often have major influence as to what extent the local or regional (conflict) situation is taken into account by the international community, and if it is brought to the global public's notice at all. Studies in different cultural contexts show that the way media frames actors can influence which ones "qualify for 'our' support" (Horsti 2013: 2). Regarding the audiences' perceptions on sub-Saharan Africa, foreign correspondents play an especially important role in this process, besides humanitarian organisations, which are often the first to be on site to supply emergency assistance. Together with humanitarian organisations, journalists coin the ways in which the public talks about the situation. To a significant level they control the vocabulary used in international debates and in public discourse, for example if the terms 'war', 'peace', or 'conflict' are applied. Foreign correspondents and humanitarian organisations define which actors are perceived as 'actors' on the international stage in the first place,[2] and they have the *prerogative of interpretation* for the actor categories. Not only do they define the categories but they also assign which actor falls into which category. This is highly important: depending on the actor's status, local actors are perceived or ignored as actors on the stage of international affairs. For local actors this is relevant insofar as these external categories determine the possibility to participate on the international stage, to be supported, and to benefit from international networks and funding. The international media, with their supposed non-involved correspondents on site, observing the events unbiased according to journalistic principles, nevertheless generate a 'white Western' sovereignty of interpretation in collaboration with humanitarian organisations. This not only applies to the actor categories, but generally to thinking patterns behind the concept of development aid. Development is a "normative term, which builds upon theoretical assumptions of the cause of underdevelopment and models of socioeconomic transformation that indicate the standard progress; it bundles together concepts of societal, economic, and political change that should be aimed for" (Kevenhörster & Boom 2009: 19).[3] Which countries are provided with aid is largely a political question; political and strategic considerations of the donor country play an equally important role as economic needs of the recipient (Alesina & Dollar 2000: 33). Apart from the recipient country's needs, also the colonial past of both the recipient and donor nation, the level of democratisation of the recipient nation, and political ties, amongst other things, play a role (Alesina & Dollar 2000: 54ff). How these recipient countries and their needs are portrayed in the media thus has a political dimension, given that media coverage can influence policy making, as explained in the next subsection using the example of the British Cabinet Office and the coverage of the Ethiopian famine. The Western sovereignty of interpretation is important for the international framing of conflicts, which humanitarian organisations create in collaboration with the media in many cases.[4] Humanitarians are popular interview partners for international media since they often have a similar cultural background as the journalists and audiences, and conversations can take place without an interpreter (Franks 2013: 32; see also Munz 2007). "[I]NGOs accept that they themselves have helped to create over-simplified and stereotyped images [...]", since they cannot live without them (Franks 2013: 34f, 37). The media can also be advantageous for actors in conflict regions who profit from conflicts. Conflicts are running through a "process of mediatisation" (Eilders & Hagen 2005: 217). By depicting conflict processes in a certain way, stressing specific aspects, not mentioning them, or evaluating them differently, the media can influence for example whether interventions are seen as legitimate or illegitimate in public discourse, how conflicts are perceived, and how disasters are rated.

With all these influences, the bar raised for journalistic work is high; journalism takes on an important task in our society and has committed itself to a code of ethics. Reese says that how journalism is perceived depends on its contribution to a democratic society (Reese 2001: 175). Hardly any other profession is evaluated according to such strict normative and ethical perspectives. "[W]e evaluate media performance against the major social values of freedom, equality, and order" (Reese 2001: 175). Is it (at all) possible, asks Reese, to develop principles of journalistic practice that have universal validity and seem sustainable across different nations? (Reese 2001: 175). National media systems have developed under different conditions and according to their historical situations. It is important to keep this in mind when analysing journalists' behaviour (Reese 2001: 177). In my comparative research design, the nationality of the outlet for which the journalists work, is not of interest itself but gives 'context' for other phenomena that I investigate (Kohn 1989: 22ff), such as the individual's attitude, different editorial policies, or crisis-focused reporting in varying manifestations.

Tasks of media and correspondents, and the role of social media

I define foreign correspondents as journalists who work longer term in a different country from the one where their outlet is based. They work for media of record in print, online, television, or news agencies, and are responsible for covering sub-Saharan Africa, regardless of whether they are staff, working on a retainer, or freelancers. In contrast to most journalists working at the editorial headquarters, foreign correspondents must be all-rounders, capable of covering, explaining, and commenting on all "political, economical, culturally and socially heterogeneous" events (Junghanns & Hanitzsch 2006: 17), and providing background information to acquaint their audiences with the foreign country. Studies show that the training profile for foreign correspondents is not very specific. The choice of deploying someone to work as a correspondent is not linked to his or her specific knowledge about the respective region. Posts abroad are rather offered at specific moments in a journalist's career (Neudeck 1990: 18). Foreign correspondents usually have above-average domestic work experience (Junghanns & Hanitzsch 2006: 13; see also Wu & Hamilton 2004). However, Africa is considered an entry-level post for correspondents, and correspondents often start without significant knowledge about the continent (Mükke 2004: 279). As mentioned earlier, the humanitarian sector has experienced a rapid boom since the first decade of the twenty-first century, while there has been a marked decrease in the number of foreign correspondents. The conditions for the two actor groups are moving in opposite directions, also in terms of funds available to them. Correspondents are responsible for covering large, inhomogeneous patches, containing diverse countries and cultures. Junghanns and Hanitzsch (2006: 16)[5] found in their study that foreign correspondents worldwide cover more than seven countries. Africa represents the extreme: one correspondent covers an average of 33 countries (Mükke 2009a: 43),[6] while travel budgets are diminishing. Nevertheless, I do not assume that foreign correspondents will become extinct, because it is still a prestigious job,[7] and journalists are seen as eyewitnesses (see also Sambrook 2010). They help to contextualise and evaluate events within the increasing information overload that characterises our globalised world. Never before were world affairs so interwoven and dependent on information. Hamilton and Jenner consequently make a case for vanishing boundaries between local and foreign topics, and therefore the necessity of a broader understanding of foreign reporting (Hamilton & Jenner 2003). Even though it is true that domestic reporters due to globalisation often add international aspects to their stories, I do not support the conclusion that one could draw from Hamilton and Jenner's argument, that due to globalisation of markets, information flows, and international aspects to many domestic topics, domestic and foreign reporters essentially do the same job. A domestic reporter covering domestic topics with additional information on their international connections, still focuses on domestic angles. Another argument for a broader understanding of foreign reporting is the rise of what Hamilton and Jenner call the "do-it-yourself journalism" that modern technology and the ability to upload information accessible to anyone enabled (Hamilton & Jenner 2003: 17, 19, 21). This type of amateur reporting doubtlessly changed the media landscape. These reports can be used as sources in mainstream media, and more importantly, hold traditional media to account by counterbalancing them through voices from the ground. However, this "do-it-yourself journalism" does not carry the same authority as traditional reporting does. Traditional journalists and the media they work for are still seen as the authority in a never-ending stream of information available to audiences. My data shows that social media, blogs, and other means to disseminate information do not have anywhere near the same importance for humanitarian organisations as traditional media do, especially with regards to cooperation with humanitarian organisations. Social media are used to mediate directly to audiences, but according to my research only traditional media are seen to increase the brand and fundraising significantly because of the perceived neutrality that traditional media carry. Material that humanitarian organisations produce and disseminate over their own channels and social media is not seen to create the same visibility as traditional news. "Polymedia events", which Madianou defines as events that start in the media, and then unfold over other platforms and have a large impact ('go viral') are very rare (Madianou 2013: 263). This is why this book focuses on traditional media mainly, and only here and there delves into use of social media. Foreign reporting is still seen as the authoritative guide in a flood of information available. Mikich considers reporting on foreign affairs an early-warning system for conflicts and catastrophes. Citizens need high-quality information that is put into context in order to react based on a background of knowledge, instead of reacting according to emotions and stereotypes (Mikich 2003: 120).

Since correspondents do not act in a vacuum, the following subsection will also shed light on the role of the media system. The influential power that the media have on politics has been much discussed. In regards to development and relief aid, the so-called *CNN effect* is relevant: Boutros Boutros-Ghali, then UN Secretary-General, said in 1995 regarding CNN's role: "We have 16 members in the Security Council: the 15 country members plus CNN" (Franks 2013: 5). Tony Blair attributed an important role to CNN, applicable to similar media of record, in 1999: "We are continually fending off the danger of letting wherever CNN roves, be the cattle prod to take a global conflict seriously" (Blair 1999). Franks traced the powerful influence of BBC's Ethiopian famine coverage in 1984, but argues that the CNN effect only takes place under certain circumstances.[8] Before Buerk's BBC report aired, the global public did not take notice of coverage of the famine for over a year (Franks 2013: 12–18). Sometimes only massively recited media coverage can enable policy makers to respond to events, even if they knew about them earlier ("enabling effect", Robinson 2002: 40).

Whether the media have any direct or even indirect influence on political decisions,[9] even putting aside whether the relation of cause and effect can be proven, and whether the CNN effect can itself be proven in studies looking for cause-effect relations, it is certain that the media play an important role in politics and society. Philip Seib, in his book *The Global Journalist*, instead of continuing with the discussion of whether the effect is directly and causally determinable or not, instead convincingly distinguishes between a direct and an indirect impact on policy; he argues that impact is no less existent when it is hard to prove: "News coverage does not, in itself, determine policy, despite what proponents of the 'CNN effect' might contend. But it does wield influence in the democratic interaction between public and government" (Seib 2002: 121). According to Frank's research, the indirect impact on the political agenda and government ministries is clearly provable, namely in the case of the Ethiopian famine when media coverage effected public pressure on the British Cabinet Office (Franks 2013: 54ff). Apart from this, Franks cites an unpublished report that includes a Member of Parliament's statement on the Ethiopian famine:

> We knew of the famine problem obviously before it broke, I think it would be fair to say we had not quite realised the impact it would have on public opinion once the pictures came through. That of course influenced government policy. It would be silly to pretend that it didn't. With the news coverage the famine became a domestic political issue to which we felt we had to respond.
> (Franks 2013: 54)

Frank's case study shows another point relevant to investigating the interests of humanitarian organisations: even though the BBC's coverage of the Ethiopian famine resulted in a provable CNN effect – that is creating public awareness and then specific government actions (Franks 2013: 50), – the situation on the ground changed little: "So in this case it appears that although there was a CNN effect which might have prompted humanitarian action by government, it was primarily for short-term domestic political effect, in response to public opinion within Western countries" (Franks 2013: 70).

Journalistic self-perception

I assume that the journalists' self-perception significantly shapes their work and especially their relationships with humanitarian organisations (see also Bengelstorff 2002; Mükke 2009b). A correspondent who understands him- or herself as 'neutral reporter' acts differently from one who understands him- or herself as 'advocate of socially disadvantaged people' (Mükke 2009b: 181). Mükke points out that the self-image of foreign correspondents has changed over time, and has recently been under a lot of "pressure to adapt to changed conditions of societal, economic, and institutional frames" (Mükke 2009b: 178). According to his research, ten role-perceptions determine the actions of German Africa correspondents (Mükke 2009b: 181f, 196). Eighty percent of the correspondents who Mükke interviewed see themselves as 'mediating-analytical' correspondents who report reflectively and provide background information.[10] Seventy percent see themselves as 'interpreters between cultures', highlighting positive aspects, denying stereotypes, and trying to counterbalance crisis-focused coverage. The same percentage understand themselves as 'brokers of issues', having to pitch and promote their stories, which means that economic perspectives and self-promotion play significant roles. About 60 percent perceive themselves as 'reporters', stressing unbiased reporting on site. The same amount perceives their role as pure 'informers', and 50 percent as 'editorial managers'. Only one correspondent understood his role as 'investigative' (Mükke 2009b: 181f). The latter sees the reason for stereotypical coverage of German media to follow from a lack of investigative reporting: "I believe the picture of Africa is very superficial in the German media because there is no space for investigative journalism" (Mükke 2009b: 196). However, the problem with Mükke's role concept is that he does not explain thoroughly why he uses these role concepts in the first place. Researching which roles correspondents identify with in their work, however, is important. These roles give an insight into how correspondents view their own responsibilities and tasks, how they interact with their surroundings, and how they position themselves towards editors and their audiences. As I understand Mükke's use of roles, they do not necessarily contradict one another; instead the main task journalists think to fulfil shifts into focus, while other tasks fade into the background. The informational role implies that the journalists see their main task in gathering and presenting information; they remove themselves from the equation. The mediating-analytical journalists see their main task in providing their audiences an analytical understanding of the people, places, and issues about which they write. The role of the interpreter between cultures has a similar background insofar as it also stems from the idea of having to bridge a gap between the culture of Western audiences, and sub-Saharan people and issues reported about. The role of the editorial manager describes journalists who mainly see their task in managing content, possibly but not exclusively from their desks; similarly the broker of issues deals with content, but from a freelancer perspective who has to pitch and 'sell' stories to outlets for them to be published; the role of the provocateur highlights that some journalists see their task mainly in confronting and provoking their audiences with topics that challenge their views. The role of the reporter stresses the perspective that journalists are primarily giving account of events, in either written or spoken form. The role of an investigative reporter speaks for itself: the journalists see themselves primarily as watchdogs that uncover inconsistencies, corruption, and other hidden issues of general interest. The missionary-advocacy role I renamed as advocate of socially disadvantaged people, implying that journalists want to change something for the better with their reporting by advocating in the name of socially disadvantaged people. Lastly, pre-interviews for this study showed that journalists did not identify with the role as diplomat and politician, which is why it was dropped. Journalists were instead given the opportunity to add any other role that they think described their work better. One aim of this study was to find out whether correspondents of American and British media outlets identified with the same self- and role-perceptions as the German correspondents, whether these self-perceptions could be linked to the correspondents' relationships with humanitarian organisations, and whether the correspondents' self-perception and the humanitarians' concept of the journalists' self-perception matched.

The journalist as one brick in the building

News values, gatekeeping, and the journalists' self-perception, which together result in a certain news bias, are not the only defining features that shape news coverage. The correspondents do not work in a vacuum but are integrated into the media system and its institutional dimensions. In the following subsections I therefore shed light on roles of editorial work and news agencies so as to contextualise the journalists' work.

The editorial headquarters

Editorial headquarters also have a gatekeeping function: they directly influence the correspondent by "ordering reports on specific topics, and accepting or refusing topics suggested by the correspondents" (Bengelstorff 2002: 103). As early as 1917 Karl Bücher wrote:

> News and essays, which are the content of the manifold modern newspaper, obtain their final form through the editors. [. . .] The perception that a 'chief editor' or an 'editorial conference' decides upon each piece, only applies in cases of doubt; otherwise, in the case of large papers, this is merely a fiction, and the abstract term 'editorial' dissolves in reality into a number of people who are only invisible for the reader behind the mist of this abstraction.
> (Bücher 1926: 31–44)

The gap between "the influence of the media, respectively journalism on the one side, and the relative powerlessness of individual journalists on the other side" is increasing (Kepplinger 2004, 2. edition: 103). Correspondents consider themselves to be lone fighters and perceive their relationship to their editors largely as a difficulty since they receive little support, are poorly supervised, and feel abandoned (Mükke 2009b: 152f; Weichert & Kramp 2011: 217). According to foreign correspondents, many editors do not know enough about Africa (Mükke 2009b: 352), and nevertheless – or therefore – prefer certain stereotypical topics. Weichert and Kramp (2011: 218) found in their study on correspondents in crisis areas around the world that the editors sometimes confuse "the editorial support at the headquarters [. . .] with substantial patronisation". Reese's *hierarchy-of-influences* model (Reese 2001) shows that editors usually aim at different goals than individual journalists.[11] Editors for example focus more on editorial policy in order to guarantee economic efficiency (see Meldrum 2010), whereas correspondents often want to mirror events on the ground that they consider important, regardless of their economic value to the news outlet. The correspondent is dependent on his or her editors who must agree to commission reports, while at the same time the correspondent's position on the ground and insider-knowledge grant him or her a monopoly position over the editors' knowledge, which is only challenged by news agencies.[12] It is likely that the editors ask a correspondent to write about topics that involve wars, conflicts, and catastrophes (Bengelstorff 2002: 105), and to report on issues that competing media or agency reports have already covered. However, the direct influence of the editorial headquarters on the correspondent is low; more significant is the indirect influence. The editors' preferred angle for coverage is mainly executed indirectly: correspondents often act in the spirit of anticipatory obedience, meeting the editorial line knowing the priorities of their editors, and assuming to know which topics will get published (Reese calls this "self-policing", Reese 2001: 182). The correspondent's gatekeeping competence also depends on his or her experience, the editors' Africa competence – which comes down to individual people (Mükke 2009b: 355) – and the type of event to be covered. If the event is not urgent, correspondents are primary gatekeepers, according to Mükke's research. In contrast, the coverage of late-breaking events is

> often stimulated by the public relations of humanitarian organisations and TV or agency reports on crises, conflicts, and catastrophes, in which cases the news circulation between the major media of record and the editorial headquarters cuts off the gatekeeping-position of journalists in Nairobi from the beginning and might even require a specific bias in the coverage.
>
> (Mükke 2004: 282)

In addition to this, de Waal speaks of an "aid angle", a perspective that includes humanitarian organisations, which many editors require (see Meldrum 2010). I assume that the less experience a correspondent has working in Africa, and the less Africa competent the editors are, the more other reports, public relations, and agency news dominate their news agenda (see also de Waal 1997: 82). A correspondent of a British outlet and former chair of the Foreign Correspondents Association of East Africa (FCAEA) reported: "[The editors] seem to just follow whatever the news agenda of the wires or the BBC or other newspapers is. It's very rare now to be breaking a foreign news story" (I_14). Specifically asked whether the editors were communicating that explicitly and whether they were requiring reports on particular issues, which had been brought up by other media or news agencies, he answered:

> Yeah, exactly. Which is a great shame. It makes my job very dull. And the excitement of doing the job is because you are going somewhere and speaking to people that wouldn't be reached by international media and telling their story. That's the point of being here. You are literally corresponding from a foreign place. And that's not happening at the moment. To be honest, I could do this job from London; there is no reason for me to be in Nairobi. [. . .] So the question has to be asked why I am here at all. If all I'm doing is sitting in my office on the phone and on the wires [. . .]. There must be some level of prestige left, so that the big papers [. . .] around the world have correspondents based in what they would class to be the important places.
>
> (I_14)[13]

It can be a challenge for correspondents when the editors do not have significant knowledge of sub-Saharan Africa, and largely rely on news agencies. A correspondent based in South Africa for a German media outlet explains: "I have been asked things like to 'just quickly pop down to Windhoek'. And I said, 'do you know where Windhoek is? That is like [. . .] driving from Frankfurt to Moscow. You can't just do it that quickly'" (Mükke 2009b: 354). The connection to the editors, and the personal or content-related feedback for journalists is very important nevertheless (Weichert & Kramp 2011: 28). This is not only because foreign reporting is physically and mentally demanding, but also because it is impossible for correspondents to keep an eye on all events and developments in their huge and inhomogeneous patch. Thirty percent of the German correspondents interviewed by Mükke (2009b: 357) felt their editors engaged with them only about their stories' content, if at all, and offered little extra support. Correspondents of larger British and American media, for example The New York Times, CNN, and the BBC, seem better off in terms of editorial support. German editors often orient themselves towards these media and toward news agencies when commissioning stories to their correspondents (Weichert & Kramp 2011: 135). The authors of a broad study on the portrayal of developing countries on British television suggest strongly that correspondents should regularly review their assumption that their editors are not interested in reports that challenge stereotypes (Smith, Edge & Morris 2006; see also de Waal 1997: 83; Franks 2013: 70); otherwise the correspondents may pre-emptively abide by a falsely-assumed editorial policy, meaning that more diverse reports may never be pitched in the first place. I will explore what role the editors play in the process of news selection, and how they perceive humanitarian organisations in the correspondents' view later on in this book. I also want to investigate whether there is a difference between correspondents of German-speaking, American, and British media interacting with humanitarian organisations, presumably due to different reporting traditions.[14]

The journalist and news agencies

International news agencies, as touched upon in the previous subsection, are also important factors deciding what issues to place on the agenda. As more posts for correspondents are closed down, the role of news agencies becomes more important (Ricchiardi 2008). In this subsection, I explain what influences news agencies, so-called 'wires' or 'wire services', have on other correspondents' agendas.

News agencies act as an "intermediary between the news and the media" (Weischenberg 2005: 311, keyword 'Nachrichtenagenturen'). They do not address the public directly, but work as service providers delivering information and content for other media. Correspondents use them as one source among others. Many editors monitor the wires constantly, and consider the topics the agencies have run so important that they ask their own correspondents to cover those stories, and turn down other stories, simply because they have not yet been covered by agencies, and thus seem to be less safe a bet (Franzke 2000). This results in outlandish alliances between Africa correspondents and agency journalists on the ground. A correspondent of a British outlet – and he is not an exception – stated in an interview that he frequently asks his journalist friends at news agencies to cover issues that he would like to report on, for his editors to then 'allow' him to write about them (I_14). Mükke's study shows similar occurrences (Mükke 2009b: 238). The media's reproduction of reports created by news agencies, which then influence other media, creates a so-called autopoietic system. It sometimes does not follow the event but the news agencies' news selection (Weichert, Kramp & Matschke 2012: 25). Media headlines then try to outbid each other (Munz 2007: 30).[15] Due to time pressure, especially in crisis situations agency reports are used, which is problematic; these "official data regarding victims, goods supplies, or statistics on refugees are often stated unverified" (Weichert & Kramp 2011: 31; also Bickel 2008: 120). It is hard for journalists using these agency reports, under pressure from their home editors, to re-examine such data. As amplifiers, agency journalists have a wide reach. Their relationship with humanitarian organisations is therefore very important for this study. Due to their wide reach, they have a special position. Due to pressure to deliver up-to-date news all the time, agency journalists nonetheless rarely travel to research stories (Mükke 2003: 84). German agency reports on Africa often refer to one source only.[16]

> Most of the working time of an agency journalist is not allotted to [...] investigations on the ground, or ad-hoc-reports on unexpected events, but to the sighting and handling of press releases. [...] [The senders] aim to use the wide reach and credibility of news agencies to create a broad public awareness in their interest.
> (Weischenberg 2005: 14, keyword 'Agenturjournalismus')

Agency correspondents revise and reword press releases from third parties usually carefully; nevertheless we can assume that humanitarian organisations' influence through this gate is significant.

In this past section I argued that reporting has an effect on political reaction to events, and that the way journalists see themselves and understand their role, plays into their reporting and their relationships with humanitarian organisations. Taking both together, it shows that the analysis of journalists' understanding of their role and the way they act it out in practice in the field, and their view on humanitarians as well as how their relationship with them takes shape in practice has political relevance. Correspondents and humanitarian organisations together shape the way audiences see events, and in what vocabulary these events are talked about as they have the *prerogative of interpretation* of these events. I also argued that you cannot look at correspondents alone but also have to consider the editorial network in which they are integrated. This network is supposed to give support to the correspondent and counterbalance one-sided reporting. Instead, it is common that editors of Western news know little about Africa and correspondents feel left alone. Due to reduced pay of staff correspondents, news agencies become more and more important. This puts significant pressure on these agencies to report up-to-date news, and opens gateways for humanitarian organisations to influence reporting.

4.2 Based in sub-Saharan Africa

Journalists very regularly produce content under deadline pressure. They mourn the lack of sufficient resources to verify data and investigate closely. The logic of the 'journalism' system becomes more evident when the system and its actors reach their capacity limit (Weichert & Kramp 2011: 25ff). Correspondents working in sub-Saharan Africa reach this limit regularly. This section therefore sheds light on the conditions under which correspondents in sub-Saharan Africa work.

Researching the interactions between journalists and humanitarian organisations largely in Nairobi and then claiming the findings apply across sub-Saharan Africa seems presumptuous. However, on closer inspection, it is not. The majority of international Africa correspondents are based in only four cities: Cairo, Nairobi, Cape Town, and Johannesburg. Nearly all Africa's 54 countries are covered from these cities. The small number of correspondents based in West Africa, who are largely working for Francophone media, are negligible, especially considering that West Africa is in nearly all cases of English- and German-speaking media outlets also covered from Nairobi, Cape Town, or Johannesburg. This study does not address the Maghreb-countries in North Africa that are primarily influenced by Arab culture. Leaving aside the Maghreb region, and thus also Cairo as a base for reporters covering North Africa and the Middle East, this study includes reporting on 49 independent nations, commonly referred to as sub-Saharan Africa, all of which are mostly covered out of three cities. Among development organisations, sub-Saharan Africa is often considered as one distinct cultural area: a group of countries with broadly similar cultural characteristics, historical experiences, problems, and structural characteristics, despite their lack of socio-economic homogeneity, which is completely neglected by the term. Most journalists based in South Africa work from Johannesburg. Some of those working in Johannesburg were interviewed for this study. Most of the investigation was, however, carried out in Nairobi, which functions as a microcosm for this study, mirroring the interactions between correspondents and humanitarian organisations in all of sub-Saharan Africa. A significant number of correspondents use it as a base to travel to other countries. Most regional head offices of humanitarian organisations are based there as well. I will explain this and the choice of Nairobi further in Chapter 5.

Sub-Saharan Africa as projection screen

Reports on Africa have a long history. I will briefly summarise different phases of Western Africa perception to make the current coverage easier to understand against the background of deep-rooted stereotypes.[17] Krems distinguishes ten phases, in which global development shaped Europeans' picture of Africa(ns), resulting in contradictory projections (for the following listing see Krems 2002: 51–133):

> (1) The image of the "black devil [. . .] in the context of faith-based conflicts" in the High to Late Middle Age. (2) The image of the exotic 'blackamoor' as prestige object in high society of the Renaissance. (3) The 'primitive African' as slave in the Early Modern Age. (4) The African as an assumed transitional link between animals and humans in the Early Enlightenment. (5) The image of a prototypical African with the aid of whom, and to whose benefit, it was possible to explain the educational ideal of Enlightenment. (6) The Romantic image of a 'noble savage', living in utopian accordance with nature, which functioned as projection surface for nostalgia. (7) The image of the 'dark continent', influenced by Joseph Conrad's novella,[18] in the context of colonisation of unknown parts of the continent, which consolidated in the Western collective memory. (8) The image of the African 'who should become civilised', which was shaped through colonial ideology and evangelisation, and which was also a projection surface for sexuality (the 'potent African', the 'voluptuous African woman'). The process of decolonisation was tainted with violations of human rights (Klose 2013) – mainly the Mau Mau uprising, the Congo Crisis, famines in the Sahel region and Ethiopia, as well as intrastate conflicts in former Biafra, Namibia, Mozambique, and Angola among others – and shaped (9) the image of a continent in crisis and in need of Western donors. Since then the media have produced (10) a more heterogeneous image of Africa, while the "generally negative image of the continent of crises and catastrophes [. . .] that destroys itself works well" (Krems 2002: 136) for (development) aid policy.

Despite the obvious change of the Africa image over the centuries, negativity permeates across the images. Krems explicitly highlights the travel reports, "encyclopaedias, and universal history books, that have shaped that perception with concepts such as 'barbarism versus civilisation', 'wilderness versus culture', 'cannibalism', and 'polygamy'" since the eighteenth century (Krems 2002: 67). These encyclopaedias created and consolidated a reality. Many of the stereotypes mentioned still influence the way we see the continent today, and many people cannot overwrite their perceptions with their own experiences in African countries, lacking the experience. The former correspondent of the German public television broadcaster ARD, Richard Klug, said about his editors: "Sometimes there are people who believe that I am not sitting in my office in a city with a certain number of inhabitants but with my laptop under a tree, and next to me a woman is threshing millet" (Mükke 2009b: 355). If already editors view it that way – how could audiences have a different perception? The former Africa correspondent of the German newspaper Süddeutsche Zeitung, Arne Perras, sees it as a correspondent's duty to modify and refuse fuelling these clichés. While Perras does not believe that ignoring existent conflicts is the solution, he argues that development needs to be just as much in the spotlight (Perras 2010).[19]

At the same time, humanitarian organisations shape the perception Western audiences have of Africa. Peter Adamson, former journalist and then senior adviser to Unicef based in Oxford, said:

> Whenever I give a talk in a school or college, I distribute a questionnaire. What percentage of the world's children, it asks, do you think are starving – defined as 'visibly malnourished'? The answer is usually 50 to 75 percent. The real answer is 1 to 2 percent.
>
> (Adamson 1993, para. 1)

He believes fundraising images to be one cause of this phenomenon (Adamson 1993; for these numbers see also Alam 2007: 59).

Differences in the Africa coverage between media of the United States, the UK, and Germany can partly be explained by their colonial histories, which I will not discuss here. Martin Plaut, the former Africa editor for BBC World Service News, said that, in contrast to the American media, he and his colleagues could rely on the knowledge of their readers and viewers since the BBC reports constantly on, for example, Sudan (Weischenberg 2005: 311, key word 'Nachrichtenagenturen'), which made it easier to use fewer stereotypes. However, colonial history does not give a satisfying explanation to the research puzzle of why foreign reporting on Africa is often that negative and stereotypical.

In the introduction and the subsection on the quality debate regarding media coverage I already discussed the role that the media and humanitarian organisations play in terms of shaping the image of the African continent held by news audiences, and by audiences informed through websites, data, handouts, or films produced by humanitarian organisations. Also, I explained earlier how the prerogative of interpretation of the situation on the ground lies with both, media and humanitarian organisations. Sam Hopkins, a visual artist based in Nairobi and London, who studied the display of INGO logos that are omnipresent in Africa, says they are "a distillation of an ideology. They [INGOs] perpetuate images and notions of suffering in charity, which most people that spent time in any African country know represent only a small part of reality" (Darby 2015). Interestingly, Hopkins describes that narratives humanitarian organisations use find a way beyond Western audiences to shape even how Africans see their own world, which, after interviewing humanitarian workers with African backgrounds for this study, I believe to be true. Hopkins experienced that young Kenyans he invited for a film workshop, when asked about what issues they wanted to make films, all answered using aid terminology, and all mentioned INGO topics. It shows, Hopkins says, how humanitarian organisations influence people's thinking of what is desirable to do and how to speak about it (Darby 2015). The media then spread these topics to a broader audience. Thus, counter narratives are needed both to tell and to inspire less one-sided stories. This study therefore investigates whether the actors of media and aid sector think that their interactions play a part in the continuation of these clichés, and how they perceive their own roles perpetuating crisis-focused news coverage of Africa.

Working conditions of correspondents and their relationships with humanitarian organisations

Close to half of the correspondents reporting from Africa cover 49 countries (Mükke 2009b),[20] while the other half cover fewer. Freelance correspondents cover more than their employed colleagues. The bases Nairobi, Cape Town, and Johannesburg clearly structure the reporting: most often, German correspondents work in East Africa and Southern Africa (Mükke 2009b: 198). The same is true for other international correspondents including American and British ones (Wanene 2005; Kumar 2011). The French media are more likely to cover French-speaking West Africa, and, in contrast to other international media, they tend to have a base there (mostly in Dakar, Senegal, or Abidjan, Ivory Coast). Juxtaposed against the size of the area correspondents cover, is their often small travel budget. Many correspondents never set foot in a third of the countries they cover (Mükke 2003: 83; 2009b: 219), which raises issues of credibility, since they are still classified as eyewitnesses (Sambrook 2010), and travelling and investigating on the ground provide journalistic independence. Content analyses show that the reporting is imbalanced: more than half of all African countries are hardly ever covered (Mükke 2003: 43). The correspondents do not lack intentions but financial and logistical hurdles discourage them. In addition to the size of the area to be covered, many sub-Saharan African countries have poor infrastructure, which means the editors would have to pay significant expenses to enable travelling (Mükke 2009b: 222; see also Scheen 2007: 27). A correspondent of a British outlet recounts that he used to travel an average of 40 weeks per year, whereas in 2011 he was on the road for investigations for only three weeks. Within these, his paper paid only one journey, while INGOs, the UN, and companies covered the expenses for the other trips (I_14). This development has a strong impact on the interactions with humanitarian organisations, and the dependency on them.[21] Other difficulties in reporting from African countries can include strict censorship (Péus 1977: 87f) and even life-threatening dangers. The attempted kidnapping of SZ correspondent Arne Perras in Somalia, the hostage-taking of the FAZ correspondent Thomas Scheen in Eastern Congo, the accusation of the photographer Phil Moore of being a spy while held in custody in Burundi, and the imprisonment of Al Jazeera correspondent Peter Greste in Egypt are only four examples out of many from correspondents working from Nairobi and South Africa covering sub-Saharan Africa (Scheen 2008; Perras 2009; Moore 2016; Al Jazeera 2015, 2016). How often a correspondent travels also depends on his or her role perception, on whether he or she is staff or freelancer (Mükke 2009b: 217), and on experience. A significant number of correspondents complain about the marginal support they get from their editors (Franzke 2000: 116, 119; Mükke 2009b: 352f). The perception of distance from the editors is not only negative, however: it also provides a window of opportunity for more "independence [. . .] of editorial restraints" (Bengelstorff 2002: 20). The geographical distance from the home country and home editors can, on the other hand, lead to the so-called *Hong Kong syndrome* (Scharf & Stockmann 1998: 77), in which correspondents consider poor research justifiable since it is hard to check facts. In surveys of correspondents, "media, aid organisations/UN, ordinary people, and [. . .] government representatives" (Mükke 2009b: 243) are mentioned as important sources of information for their reports. Content analyses show that correspondents use non-African sources remarkably often (Mükke 2009b: 122), especially the UN and nongovernmental aid organisations (Mükke 2009b: 124). Fritsch criticises the tendency of journalists to orientate their coverage toward "the viewpoint of elites" (Fritsch 2008: 15), which would explain why information from the UN, which is seen as an authority, is often used without being verified, which also my data's study shows. Löffelholz points out that "unilateral reference to official statements" (Löffelholz 2004: 33) is potentially dangerous. Yet, many reports on crises feature humanitarian organisations only (Mükke 2009b: 259).

Most difficult for correspondents is the ongoing reduction of posts, which leaves the few remaining posts covering ever larger areas. Even the NZZ, known for its foreign news, recently cut posts (Zitzelsberger 2009). Parachute journalists, who are sent from the home country temporarily to cover an event abroad, are more likely to search for evidence that affirms their pre-existing stereotypes, I assume, than foreign correspondents permanently stationed in the location. At the same time the parachutists may be able to offer fresh insights into the situation not perceived by correspondents who have been living on the continent for a long time, says Thilke, former correspondent of Der Spiegel (Mükke 2009b: 359, 361). In contrast, Grill, former Africa correspondent for Die ZEIT, now for Der Spiegel, remarks:

> You notice how often you are hoodwinked by your own projections. My colleagues from the 'quick response force' [parachute journalists] seem to have

fewer qualms about this, and that is entirely apart from the fact that they do not have time for thorough preparation and in-depth investigation.

(Grill 2007: 123)

Parachute journalists are not necessarily pushing more prejudices; they sometimes have more experience of different countries than correspondents stationed in Africa who do not have sufficient travel budget. Often, however, they lack the context of stories and local contacts that long-term correspondents stationed in a foreign country have.

Germany, Switzerland, the UK, and the United States, where the media outlets that this study investigates are based, have different traditions regarding the intensity of research and the transparency of sources. While investigative journalism has a long tradition in the United States and is considered indispensable for democracy, with journalism awards and foundations protecting quality standards (Weischenberg 2005, keyword 'quality'), in Germany it was almost not present at all before 2016's Panama Papers (Esser 1997; Redelfs 2003, 2007). It is likely, however, that fewer personal and financial resources, and seemingly less interest of the audiences in longer background reports, affect the dependency on sources and information networks provided by humanitarian organisations (Christoph Reuter of the magazine Stern, in Weichert & Kramp 2011: 131). War and crisis reporting also has a more important status in the United States and the UK than in Germany (Weichert & Kramp 2011: 78), which might also affect the editors' willingness to support costly research on critical issues, or reporting in dangerous areas that could more easily be carried out with the logistical help of humanitarian organisations.

This section shed light on how Western perceptions of the African continent throughout influenced reporting, and how even today location-specific aspects play an important role in reporting on sub-Saharan Africa. In the study results part of this book, I will explain in more detail how these location-specific aspects add to difficulties in reporting and lead to tight networks with humanitarian organisations adding their own interests and biases to stories.

4.3 The relationship between journalism and public relations

The conditions of foreign reporting have a direct impact on the humanitarian sector as the media are "an important channel for communicating messages" (Bogert 2011: 1) for humanitarian organisations.[22] Journalistic working conditions make it rational to collaborate with humanitarian organisations on the ground. The relationships between humanitarian organisations and the media are complex and ambivalent in nature (Bogert 2011: 2); each needs the other, but both function very differently. Scientific studies often fail to acknowledge that their characteristics, roles, and production processes are based on very different conditions and use them interchangeably (Orgad & Seu 2014: 22f also stress this failure of analyses of humanitarian narratives). Both sectors might inform about deplorable states of affairs. Quality journalism would report a deplorable situation without bias, whereas a humanitarian organisation might present the same situation so as to challenge public opinion to change the situation, to solicit donations, or to encourage political action (Bogert 2011: 7).

How do the interactions between journalists and staff working in humanitarian organisations' public relations departments take place, and upon what mechanisms are they based? General theories on power relationships between public relations (*PR*) and journalism can be divided into two categories. The first includes all approaches that assume public relations instrumentalise journalism (*determination*, see Baerns (1991)), or the other way round (*mediatisation*). The second includes approaches that assume a mutual influence and dependency (*interdependency, symbiosis, intereffication, structural coupling*).[23] Baern's *determination hypothesis* (1979, 1985)[24] – later criticised as too one-sided, for example by Szyszka (1997, 2004) – resulted in determination studies that focused on journalism, manipulated by public relations. Journalism was considered important, altruistic, and to be supported from an ethical viewpoint. However, these studies ignore economic perspectives of journalism and inadequately reduce the complex interrelation (Bentele, Liebert & Seeling 1997).

To look at the interactions as unbiased as possible, I assume that foreign correspondents and humanitarian organisations need each other, enable each other, and adapt to each other's needs. In this approach I integrate the actor understanding with an actor-focused and action-theoretical approach, focussing on relationships on different communication levels between individual and institutional actors. I investigate journalists and PR-communicators; audiences and other communicators play only a tangential role. Concentrating on actors' performance also simplifies the *operationalisation* of the theoretical claims. *Inductions* and *adaptions* are relevant for the interactions between journalism and public relations. *Inductions* are "intended communication stimuli which are directional [. . .], initiated from one side and – if picked up – have measurable impact on the complementary side" (Bentele & Nothhaft 2004: 73). *Adaptions* are expressions for "communicative or organising actions in order to adapt" (Bentele, Liebert & Seeling 1997: 241). There are different types of induction (Bentele & Nothhaft 2004: 75f): *text induction* means the thematic initiative of public relations can be detected in the journalistic output, such as in the citing of data or statements; *initiative induction* means that the public relations only provide thematic stimulation without journalism adopting its components directly; and *evaluating induction* is used if there is a general tendency toward judgements on issues. Proving the presence of inductions is challenging. Evaluating induction does not need a PR output in the first place, for example. It also has to be determined whether the alleged text induction is a comprehensive journalistic report or not (Bentele & Nothhaft 2004: 77). A so-called *adaption effort* takes place when a humanitarian organisation selects topics according to the likelihood of earning media coverage (see also considerations by Mükke 2003: 87). How humanitarian organisations choose topics according to their representability in the media is "linked to the success of an organisation [. . .], but it also determines its credibility" (Ricchiardi 2005: 6).

Until now, there have primarily been content analyses of *induction processes* in the form of input-output analyses drawing a picture of the relationship between the two sectors. These analyses put into proportion the input – press releases sent by public relations departments to journalists – and the output, journalistic texts using this material (Scholl 2004: 42f; see also Luger & Pointner 1996; Schmoll 1998; Dilg 1999; Waisbord 2011). So far, research has not thoroughly investigated press conferences, background briefings, and most importantly personal and social relationships (Altmeppen, Bentele & Röttger 2004: 92), even though they constitute successful public relations (Altmeppen 2004: 11). Few comprehensive studies map the complex relationship between public relations and journalism with a methodological approach, such as studies considering the relationship on an individual and institutional level at the same time (Altmeppen, Bentele & Röttger 2004: 10f). This is where this book comes in. The approach of seeing PR and journalism as enabling each other is criticised for disguising antagonistic elements in the relationship of both sectors ("systems") in favour of a "partner ideology that discards boundaries" (Ruß-Mohl 1994: 169). I disagree this is necessarily the case. Seeing journalism and public relations as an "exchange relation" (Merten 2004: 24), enabling and depending on each other, does not mean that there are no power relations between them. Bentele, Liebert, and Seeling, who generated the idea that the two enable each other, say that seeing the relationship between public relations and journalism as only a power relationship, in which public relations determines media coverage, is too simple (Bentele, Liebert & Seeling 1997: 237, 240). Induction and adaption processes flowing from the media's to public relations' side should also be considered (Bentele & Nothhaft 2004: 73). Regarding my empirical study I conclude that *communication stimuli* should be investigated on both sides. So the question is: to what extent do employees of humanitarian organisations adapt to media-specific procedures, or the preferences of individual journalists? Do they for example purposefully serve news factors? Or do they anticipate selection criteria of journalists (adaption, thus playing by journalistic rules)? Do people working in public relations departments of humanitarian organisations know most correspondents personally? And how do they evaluate this contact?

The role of humanitarian organisations in news coverage – what do journalists get out of it?

Due to difficult working conditions, in sub-Saharan Africa correspondents are especially reliant upon contact networks, a variety of sources, and logistical support. This makes them more susceptible to the information humanitarian organisations provide. Foreign correspondents are forced to think economically. They carry out cost-benefit calculations when deciding what topic to investigate, what resources to use, and how thoroughly to do investigations. In those calculations, humanitarian organisations appeal on three different levels that cannot always accurately be separated (Mükke 2009b: 267): (1) on a logistical level, because they have access to dense local and global contact networks, to human and logistical resources, and in many cases good contacts to government officials. They can provide drivers, transport, and interpreters, facilitate journalists' travel to remote areas, and provide security to move around the respective area; (2) humanitarian organisations are also appealing on an informational and content level, because they have extensive contacts, information, and sources, and collect data themselves, which is valuable if journalists need figures or estimations; and (3) lastly, humanitarian organisations are appealing on an economic level because they are valuable partners for journalists working on their own as they, out of their own interest, provide information promptly. They offer correspondents working on tight budgets the opportunity to travel to aid projects, partially covering the travel costs, or funding them through quid pro quos, so that the correspondents' editors are more likely to agree to coverage.[25]

Humanitarian organisations' contact network opens doors to government officials and local authorities, and helps to find interviewees in local communities. Since the correspondents have to cover a huge patch, many humanitarians have better up-to-date knowledge of local situations than journalists (Guillot 2012). According to Mükke, 80 percent of the German correspondents make use of direct contacts to humanitarian organisations (Mükke 2009b: 270). Larger organisations provide logistical help on a grand scale and images, saving media outlets the cost of sending a photographer. "Nowadays everyone wants to work with us. We are professionals in terms of picture production, we have more money, and more experience", says John Novis, director of photography with Greenpeace (Guillot 2012). This extended statement from a correspondent of a British outlet I interviewed illuminates the issue:

> I think [. . .] [humanitarian organisations] are now becoming the lifeline for journalists who want to reach areas where news is happening. So if you were going to Somalia or even South Sudan, Eastern Congo, a lot of people – especially if you've not been there before – a lot of journalists would chose to go with an aid organisation. And that doesn't mean they are paying for your flights or whatever, you'd still pay for your flight, probably pay for the accommodation [. . .] But they will then pick you up from the airport. They will have a Land Cruiser to drive you around, there will be a translator, a driver, and they will set up people, projects for you to see, that kind of thing. Because, of course, they need the publicity to get the money and the rest of it, so it makes sense. And we need to be able to reach those places, so I think it would be much, as I said before about travelling this year, it was much easier for me to get the paper to agree to send me somewhere if they didn't have to pay anything. So if an aid agency is paying a flight for me to Northern Uganda or at least is paying for your fuel, your car, your driver to take you around and see what they're doing, the paper is much more interested in that. But it does mean you don't get to do your own reporting and to speak to people outside of the control of that aid agency. And even as simple as translators, if I'm on a job with Unicef or with Caritas, whatever, in Eastern Congo, they are giving me a car and a driver. First I'd be driven up to an IDP camp in a white Land Cruiser with a Caritas sticker on the side, I'm clearly a foreigner. So the first impression is: This guy is an aid worker, which has to colour the way

that people are approaching us. Because even though it's difficult to explain the concept of what journalism is to people who don't read newspapers, you could still get across the idea that I'm trying to tell the outside world what's happening to you and your people around here. But if they think you're an aid worker, they will answer the questions in a certain way because they want more money. And they want more help. And they want whatever else.

(I_14)

Leaving aside support for logistics, content, and costs, the loss of separation between a journalist's role to report impartially, and their human concern in face of human suffering is precarious. From this follows the lack of separation between the journalistic role and human concern, when facing human suffering. Some journalists consider it "necessary and just [to appeal for donations], [...] since journalists often are faster to appear on-site than humanitarian organisations" (Katrin Sandmann, formally working for N24, cited by Weichert & Kramp 2011: 89). The photographer Matthias Bruggmann states: "Ideologically we are very close to humanitarian organisations" (Guillot 2012). The former BBC correspondent George Alagiah describes the reciprocal dependency and the informal agreement on pictures and stories with public appeal:

> Relief agencies depend upon us for publicity and we need them to tell us where the stories are. There's an unspoken understanding between us, a sort of code. We try not to ask the question too bluntly: 'Where will we find the most starving babies?' And they never answer explicitly. We get the pictures just the same.
>
> (Franks 2013: 12–18)

Others have a more critical view: "You should not allow yourself to be exploited, not even for a good cause" (Christoph Maria Fröhder, ARD, cited by Weichert & Kramp 2011: 89).

Since freelancers have less budget and are more dependent on outlets commissioning them, I assume they are more likely to use networks in the field, and are generally more susceptible to outside influence. This raises the following questions: what are the correspondents' motives for interacting with humanitarian organisations, and what challenges do they see? Do correspondents think their reporting is compromised by their interactions with humanitarian organisations? Does the type of employment have an impact on the journalists' interaction with humanitarian organisations?

4.4 Humanitarian organisations – roles and tasks

Having discussed journalistic roles, I now move to discussing roles and tasks of humanitarian organisations. It is difficult to define the term *humanitarian organisation* (see also definition of NGOs by Kuhn 2000; Martens 2002). Under the term humanitarian organisations, I define both INGOs and (inter-) governmental organisations, such as organs of the UN that provide emergency assistance, development aid, and who generally deal with humanitarian affairs. Humanitarian organisations are formally organised entities that operate and advocate nationally and internationally. They are state or privately financed, and their proclaimed aim is emergency and disaster relief, or development aid on an international scale, in cases where the afflicted cannot overcome the problems by themselves. Humanitarian organisations have in common that they are mostly donation funded. Their wide-reaching public profile depends on in-house advocacy, news reports, and functioning relationships to journalists. In Anglophone literature these organisations are sometimes summarised under the term *humanitarian agencies*, or *aid agencies*. A large number of the organisations are often also called *relief organisations*, although most also do development and not exclusively emergency relief (Benthall 2010: 23). Organisations mainly doing development aid tend to "avoid the discourse of humanitarianism in favour of the discourses of relief and development" (Orgad & Seu 2014: 8), whereas humanitarianism is mainly associated with emergency relief (Barnett 2011: 10). Historically, some scientists argue that NGOs resulted from government failure to provide particular services (Fisher 1997; Werker & Ahmed 2008), and that a trend for donor governments to outsource their services to INGOs evolved (Werker & Ahmed 2008: 77; Macrae 1996). Since I focus on interactions between the media and humanitarian organisations as partners, I purposely do not differentiate between emergency relief and development aid – the latter focusing on the problems' causes with a broader objective, while the first tends to focus on symptoms. Neither do I differentiate between the different forms of development aid, which is why I use the term *humanitarian* to make my broader approach clear. This is mainly due to the design of this study, which takes into consideration all organisations working in the aid sector interacting with correspondents, no matter what their self-proclaimed aim is, or what their organisational structure looks like.[26] I also intentionally do not differentiate between different donor models, i.e. public, private, or hybrid forms. It is part of the study to examine whether correspondents are conscious of these differentiations, and whether that affects their behaviour toward different humanitarian organisations.

The humanitarian sector has become an important business. Johns Hopkins University estimated in 2003 that there were already between 37,000 and 55,000 international NGOs working worldwide in the field of development, human rights, and peacekeeping (de Jonge Oudraat & Haufler 2008: 11). In 2011, EU countries alone spent USD 57.6 billion on worldwide development aid (Europäische Kommission 2012), and OECD members spent USD 202.2 billion on Official Development Assistance (ODA) (OECD n.d.). The situation in sub-Saharan Africa is particularly remarkable; one dollar in every four that OECD members spent on development aid in 2011 went to sub-Saharan Africa; Germany's contribution alone was USD 2.3 billion (OECD n.d.).[27] The public outrage in Germany over the 2008 "Unicef scandal"[28] showed that the public was not yet aware of the professionalisation of aid organisations that function increasingly like large commercial enterprises. As such, they do not collect coins in collection boxes anymore and pay commissions.[29] But the aid industry finds it difficult to speak openly about its professionalisation (Munz 2007: 178).

But even though the public knows little about the histories of these organisations, their modes of operation, proclaimed aims, mandates, and what the money is actually spent on, their support is still unabated. In 2012, despite the economic crisis, 85 percent of EU citizens were of the opinion that development assistance was important, and 60 percent thought that aid should be either kept stable or increased (European Commission 2012: 5,7). 'Development assistance'[30] is justified by industrialised nations' declared aim of supporting developing countries, as proclaimed compensation for "undesirable developments caused by the era of colonialism" (Andersen 2011: 105), as part of peacekeeping including the control of refugee and IDP movements, by the "general principle of solidarity", and as part of "the safeguarding of jobs through reinforced exports into developing countries" (Andersen 2011: 105f).[31] Development aid and emergency relief also create many jobs. The flow of the large amounts of money, with many projects and jobs connected to those funds, is, however, strongly dependent on the limited degree that the public – that is individual, institutional, and governmental donors – is aware of problems in developing countries, and the money that humanitarian organisations say is needed to 'fix' them.

Humanitarian organisations' self-perception

Literature on humanitarian organisations' self-perception is scarce (Shawcross 1984; Riddell & Robinson 1992) and the interest in examining the structure of humanitarian organisations and their operationalisation is comparatively new (Benthall 2010: 123). The focus of most studies lies more on organisations as institutions, and less on their staff. The focus is shifting more and more onto individuals influencing their respective organisations (Blackmore 2009: 13), but humanitarians' motives are diverse (Lieser 2013: 295ff).[32] In the work of humanitarian organisations, employees' "private" and "professional" attitudes often mix (Fechter 2012: 1388), and also interactions between humanitarians and correspondents take place in grey areas between private and professional relationships.[33] These relationships are often based on shared values and the shared experience as expatriates in a developing country. A study carried out at King's College London sheds light on the background motives for humanitarian and commercial engagement in crisis areas beyond philanthropy (Kent & Burke 2011). How a humanitarian organisation perceives itself – that is how it sees its role, position, and brand – can be understood via its history, its background, its mandate, and its source of funding.[34] I will examine in this study to what extent correspondents consider the factors that can have an impact on an organisation's self-perception when choosing their interaction partners. Since the range of factors that can have an impact – beyond those mentioned in each organisation's statutes – is very broad, I will only give a few examples here. One aspect of institutional self-conception is safeguarding one's own agenda and maintaining independence from governments' interests. Oxfam, for example, receives funds from both DFID and the European Commission, among others. Nevertheless, Oxfam's policy is that governmental means must not exceed 10 percent of its total revenue (Benthall 2010: 89). The organisation thinks that only through this policy can it keep a certain degree of independence. An example of the role that an organisation's background can play in its self-perception, and then also in its foreign perception is World Vision: it is often criticised for its explicit commitment to evangelical Christianity, whereas Cafod and other large humanitarian organisations with a religious background draw a clear line between missionary and humanitarian work (Benthall 2010: 157).

The way an organisation interacts with the public is another facet of the self-concept and the established practice: Bentele distinguishes between Oxfam, Save the Children, and World Vision on the one hand, and Care International on the other. The first are outspoken, whereas the latter shows the tendency to approach governments directly, and does not have an official public voice ("mediatized" versus "pre-media NGO", Benthall 2010: 157). The media thus may play a less prominent role for Care (Benthall 2010: 167f). In this study I examined whether correspondents differentiate between humanitarian organisations funded only through donations, those with a governmental mandate, and those with a religious background, see Chapter 6, section 6.3.

Aiming at self-preservation

Humanitarian organisations rely to a great degree on media attention and the resulting donations. With regard to large disasters, media coverage has a significant influence on donations and where they flow (Cooper 2011: 8; see also Walter 2006). Even critics do not question the fact that crisis-focused stereotypical reporting garners more donations (Plewes & Stuart 2009: 30, 36). This can lead to humanitarian organisations "exaggerating their estimated figures of refugees and victims of famine to give the people tired of donations a wake-up call" (Grill 2007: 126). Marcel Vos, director of marketing and communications at MSF Holland, admits that the figures are occasionally exaggerated because small numbers are less impressive (Polman 2010: 59f). It is not only aid projects that depend on the flow of donations. Humanitarian organisations also have to sustain themselves and their employees. Many jobs depend on this sector – more than 240,000 in Germany alone (Europäische Kommission 2012). According to calculations from Johns Hopkins University in a study of 35 countries, the total funds of the non-profit sector would, if the sector were a country, make it the seventh largest economy in the world (Salamon, Sokolowski & List 2003). Self-preservation sometimes becomes the main focus of an organisation. Hence an employee of the American organisation Refugee Help reports on his work in Goma: "It's perhaps embarrassing to admit [. . .] but much of the discussion between head-quarters and the field is focused on contracts: securing them, maintaining them, and increasing them. The pressure was on: 'Get more contracts!'" (Cooley & Ron 2002: 26). Another employee from Refugee Help's headquarters states that the question asked most while he was in the field was how the competition for donors was progressing (Cooley & Ron 2002: 26). A rising number of humanitarian organisations increases the competition for donations (Benthall 2010). It gets more difficult to sustain one's position in the market (Frantz & Martens 2006: 64; Munz 2007), to attract funding, to win the media's attention, and to survive as an organisation. A successful and professional public relations department consequently becomes central. This is also the case because humanitarian organisations have changed from purely operational, i.e. delivering aid, to proactive advocacy groups that also apply pressure on politics. However, this shift towards advocacy has not yet been recognised by broader audiences.

Public relations

At the same time that the advocacy role of humanitarian organisations has become more important, their communication departments have grown, to keep up with the increased size of the organisations, and to work towards more public awareness and greater funds. In order to secure the organisations' future, crisis-focused coverage is needed: "When you're fundraising you have to prove there is a need. [. . .] If you're not negative enough, you won't get funding", states the head of a US-based INGO in Kenya, according to Rothmyer's study (Rothmyer 2010: 11). The communications, fundraising, and advocacy departments can be grouped under the term public relations. They all serve the wider purpose of communicating and interacting with the public and policy makers, always adhering to the organisations' aims, increasing their brand awareness, and making the organisations' goals public. Public relations, in contrast to short-term advertising, create "the foundation for organisations to successfully act in the long run through establishing long-term steady communication contacts" (Röttger 2005: 373). The goals of public relations are, alongside image building, increased control of public attention, and the encouragement of partners' and clients' loyalty. For this, well-maintained contacts with "multipliers (e.g. journalists), a precise idea of one's self-concept, [. . .] and a high degree of creativity are important, [as well as] transparency and confidence-building" (*Gabler Wirtschaftslexikon Online* n.d.). There are five types of public relations (Grunig & Hunt 1984; Avenarius 2008): public relations as persuading, public relations as informing, public relations as publicity, public relations as dialogue, and public relations as a win-win-situation. Research on public relations so far is limited to commercial organisations, and there is insufficient research on INGOs' public relations up to this point (Benthall 2010: 89).

In theory, it is easy to distinguish between journalism and public relations. In practice, however, the lines are blurred increasingly – for example where freelance journalists also work temporarily or on contract in public relations, or in the professionalised, strategic public relations of organisations that publish their releases directly, without making the source and background clear so that they are almost indistinguishable from journalistic texts to the recipient's eye (Lünenborg 2012: 8; for the argument of blurring lines between PR and journalism, also see Cottle & Nolan 2007). Note also the phenomenon of freelancing foreign correspondents accepting short-term contracts as public relations consultants for humanitarian organisations, since they are well paid (Lilienthal & Schnedler 2012: 16; see also Voss 2007; Green 2016), which I will get back to towards the end of this book. Studies show that Western audiences learn much of their 'knowledge' about Africa not only from the media but also from fundraising campaigns (Alam 2007: 60), which suggests that humanitarian organisations mainly fulfil the 'informing' and 'publicity' types of public relations. Humanitarian organisations "show a strong correlation between public relations work and lobbying" (Voss 2007: 287). Altogether the meaning of public relations is significant. Merten even states: "If a certain topic is not chosen by PR-people, it will not appear in the news" (Merten 2004: 33). I doubt this statement in its stridency. Nevertheless, I am convinced that journalism no longer has a monopoly on the procurement and the production of information. Public relations play a more and more important role and are becoming indispensable to the process of reporting, as my study results show.

Africa attracts more aid than anywhere else yet the news threshold for coverage is very high. This is why the public relations departments of humanitarian organisations must make significant efforts to draw the attention of potential donors and the general public to their organisations' work, and to the needs of a project country, with journalists as propagators of the message. The goal is not only to raise awareness, but also to acquire donations. The harmful effects of the focus on crises and the stereotypically negative images that fundraising campaigns used, which it is assumed led to audiences' exhaustion with development topics, were extensively discussed in the 1990s. Following these discussions, many organisations and governmental institutions developed codes of conduct for reporting about people in the developing world, and how problems should be presented in a non-stereotypical, non-prejudiced, non-pathetic, and non-objectifying way.[35] However, studies show that there is little difference between the images in the 1990s and those appearing in 2000 (Clark 2004).

Despite humanitarian organisations' professionalised public relations – including via channels like Twitter or their websites – there is greater competition for donations, and the mainstream media still confers valuable credibility (Cottle & Nolan 2009). Compared to in-house public relations that are often identified as such, media reports are seemingly unbiased. Positive reports about aid projects and the situation on the ground thus become invaluable in funding appeals. How humanitarian organisations organise their internal processes increasingly conforms to functional media processes. Media attention can become more important than the sustainability of a project (I_56), which can have a significant impact on economic and social development, and on peace-building processes. Humanitarian organisations often take on core responsibilities that should be carried out by governmental authorities, and thus unwillingly undermine the state. They can also be part of donor countries' political strategy, steered according to their respective geopolitical and military strategic interests (Davies 2006).[36] Content analyses of press releases show weak actors in need of support of strong humanitarian organisations as predominating (Salazar-Volkmann 1997: 260). Successful donations, according to a study on charity advertising billboards, require emotions, stereotypes, and the simplification of context (Albrecht & Albrecht 2004: 14f). The images "do not inform the public [. . .] but instead advocate for immediate action that is depoliticised and replaces the challenge of taking political action by simply making donations" (Guillot 2012). Without images, however, no donations (Gibbon 1996). In this, the interests of the media and humanitarian organisations intersect, since the media also use images that humanitarian organisations provide for free.

Within the last decade, there has also been a shift in budgeting in terms of humanitarian organisations increasingly becoming advocacy groups. More money is spent on communications and public relations. Many organisations have their own media teams, and the number of employees sometimes exceeds those at foreign desks. Save the Children UK has more than a dozen in-house media staff at its headquarters, as well as field-based communications staff (Leigh 2015). The interviews for my study revealed that some humanitarian organisations employ emergency communication officers who are specifically trained to communicate in emergency situations according to their organisations' media policy.[37] The increasing financial pressure and competition among humanitarian organisations, and the "scepticism in the West and the developing world about foreign aid and humanitarian intervention, have produced radical changes to [I]NGOs' communication practices" (Orgad & Seu 2014: 23). Yet, a better understanding of the newly-evolved production of humanitarian content is needed (Orgad & Seu 2014: 23). Waisbord, who researched South American NGOs' ability to set news agendas, argues that the organisations' practice to adapt to media's needs and package information according to the media's logic is a sign of weakness of their public relations (Waisbord 2011: 144). I could not disagree more. Rather I see their ability in adapting their strategies and approaches, and their creativity in packaging their core messages in different shapes seemingly tailored to the media's needs, as their greatest strength. And my study of the actor's relations also reveals that they do so very successfully.[38]

Powers usefully points out that in order to judge whether public relations of NGOs meet the expectations we pose on them, we first have to determine the normative frame in which we observe their communication aims. I see the public relations as advocacy tool to raise awareness and to generate donations, in what Powers calls "participatory tradition" (Powers 2016: 6). However, humanitarian organisations present themselves increasingly as impartial experts, producing their own content, commissioning more and more research that feeds into news production. This self-presentation as unbiased experts does in my view, however, often not reflect the reality on the ground. Rather than presenting events from various angles, these organisations due to the nature of their work tend to focus on crises, and what needs to be done. Chouliaraki also argues that the focus rather than on informing the public lies on creating "compassion" with the victims (Chouliaraki 2012: 273). Although one of the self-proclaimed aims of humanitarian organisations' is to neutrally inform the public, the increasing professionalisation of their public relations – which I will talk about in the following subsection and in the subsection *How do interactions take place* – pushes the advocacy role forward, and increasingly leads to activism-focused strategies. Because humanitarian organisations in this advocating role function are source and partners for journalists in the field, whereas journalists in a liberal understanding ought to be impartial, the interactions between them become problematic when they are not made transparent. The interactions then threaten the idea of journalistic independence.

The meaning of media for humanitarian organisations – professionalised PR and fundraising

With the exponentially increasing number of humanitarian organisations, especially in sub-Saharan Africa, and the resulting increase in competition for funding, the media become an essential means to communicate the organisations' messages, and dynamise the fundraising processes. Franks cites the humanitarian crisis in the Congo in 2006 as an example of humanitarian organisations' dependency on the media. Only a few donations were generated because of the lack of media coverage: USD 10 per capita. In contrast, USD 1,000 per capita was raised for the victims of the Asian tsunami of 2004 because of massive media coverage (Franks 2008: 29). After an emergency has struck, when logistics are still coordinated, the more media is involved, the better for the humanitarian organisations (Munz 2007: 51). Especially at the beginning of a crisis, it is difficult to estimate the scale of the disaster. Citing exact numbers at this stage is nearly impossible (Munz 2007: 53). However, media reports require contextual numbers. Humanitarian organisations' staff that are interviewed on-site by journalists, find themselves forced to give out numbers, for example of casualties. These numbers, once in the public domain, are extremely difficult to adjust downwards (Munz 2007: 30, 52ff, 127), and often the parties involved have little interest in doing so, because the exaggeration of crises attracts further media attention (Cooper 2011: 8), and thus also donations (Plewes & Stuart 2009: 30; Rothmyer 2010: 12). The more casualties, the easier to pass the news threshold, and the greater therefore is the public's likelihood to donate. Fundraising specialist Jeff Brooks states that negative images still 'sell' better (Brooks 2011). This is shown in Figure 4.1, with children's different expressions influencing success in fundraising. Media are not only seen as a means to an end but as partners with similar objectives. Sylvana Foa, former director of Public Affairs for WFP says: "Journalists are our natural allies, they are the original advocates of the underdog and were championing the victims way before humanitarian aid became an issue. We can't function without them" (Gibbon 1996). Following this view, the ICRC asks whether humanitarian organisations should be responsible to make sure that journalists can report safely from crisis areas (ICRC 2012).

Humanitarian organisations can put pressure on governments' agendas through media reports if they see the need for action. Peter Fuchs, then director general of the ICRC, explains that the ICRC tried to publicise stories about the 1991 situation in Somalia, to put pressure on governments and the UN to take action. Only when they finally managed to get pictures into The New York Times was the public discourse changed (Gibbon 1996). This shows how closely the success of humanitarian organisations' public relations is related to media coverage.

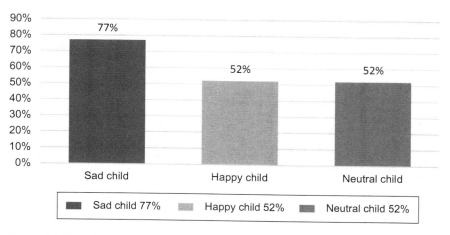

Figure 4.1 Donations by image type

Source: Brooks, Jeff (2011) from URL: www.futurefundraisingnow.com/future-fundraising/2011/07/index.html [12.1.2016]; with the author's permission.

The media also play an important role between humanitarian organisations competing for donors (Polman 2010: 34; Franks 2008: 30). Making their own logo visually prominent is crucial for humanitarian organisations' brand visibility (Cottle & Nolan 2007). To receive media attention, humanitarian organisations try to accommodate the correspondents' needs and tailor their procedures to match the media's demands (Cottle & Nolan 2009). At the same time, humanitarian organisations' in-house public relations are becoming ever more professional. Franks calls this the "growing media sophistication of [I]NGOs" (Franks 2010: 97). In addition to press releases and information material, humanitarian organisations supply free pictures and footage.[39] The increasing media power that humanitarian organisations gain by producing their own information material can be at the expense of conflict prevention because their material tends to be one-sided and restricted to the victim's perspective (Kennedy 2009; Shaikh 2011). Only where there are victims, are donations needed. Larger organisations spend a significant budget on external public relations consultants (Voss 2007: 1111) – often journalists, or former journalists who are recruited. Journalistically qualified experts thus write many of the reports that humanitarian organisations provide as information material. Communication staff that have worked as journalists before know from their own experience how the media market works. The *branding* of the organisation in the media, providing and packaging footage and information material, and using celebrities to appeal to the media (Franks 2013: 81f), are all signs that humanitarian organisations increasingly adapt to the media's production logic. According to Mükke, 90 percent of the correspondents working for German media outlets in sub-Saharan Africa use information provided by humanitarian organisations (Mükke 2009b: 279); mostly because no other information is available for the respective topics. Other sources confirm this: "[I]NGOs have become very important actors in terms of photojournalism, at least for major international reporting in situations of war, famine, and catastrophes" (Guillot 2012). Larger organisations hand out so-called guidelines and instructions for journalists, explaining how ethically justified reporting or interviewing should take place (UNICEF n.d.; McIntyre 2002). MSF, UNHCR, ICRC, or Oxfam also offer training workshops and conferences for journalists, bringing media and aid staff together to share their perspective of how joint missions between journalists and humanitarians can help overcome problems in developing countries. Humanitarian organisations also curate customised *media packages* for those media that they have a long-time partnership with for so-called World Days that are supposed to direct public attention to specific issues (Cottle & Nolan 2009: 868). By "occupying specific issues, and running effective publicity campaigns" (Salazar-Volkmann 1997: 260f), the organisations build up an image that distinguishes them from their competitors. Media reports on aid projects generate greater attention from potential donors than in-house press releases, which is why journalists are offered travel to crisis areas. Those are places they could otherwise only reach with significant difficulties, at great expense, and possibly risking their lives, as many interviews in my study revealed.

The British journalist Ian Birrell writes on this topic:

> Last year when I asked Christian Aid about spending £16,722 taking journalists to India and Nicaragua, the charity responded that the resulting coverage was equivalent to advertising worth £161,000. It was a gratifyingly honest response. But nothing illustrates better how such groups are manipulating the media.
>
> (Birrell 2013)

From a fundraising perspective, not only news stories that mention the organisations facilitating media visits to their work are useful; even reports from the field without a mention of the organisation can serve indirectly to raise donations: "If there is full page with photos of refugees, people will immediately make donations [. . .]. That is very useful for us, more than a page of advertisement", says Bruno De Cock, the International Photo Editor and co-editor of the Ethical Guidelines at MSF France (Guillot 2012).

However, external pressures on humanitarian organisations and on the media are high, and neither sees the interactions between them entirely positively. Ian Piper, former spokesman for the ICRC, who has in the past also worked for the BBC World Service, says: "It's as if both sides suddenly got the impression that they were being abused by the other, that their integrity was being threatened by the other's attitude. Perhaps both are less idealistic now" (Gibbon 1996). Many journalists, Piper concludes, had only realised a short time ago that humanitarian organisations do not only do good, but also have their own agenda (Gibbon 1996).

Carroll Bogert, deputy executive director of external relations of Human Rights Watch, talks about animosities on the other side:

> They [INGOs] frequently feel that in the rush of the news cycle, key facts may get forgotten or taken out of context, and the headline-grabbing aspects of the story may not be the most [. . .] important angles for their own advocacy.
>
> (Bogert 2011: 2)

To improve cooperation with journalists, a British study recommends to humanitarian workers: "Become storytellers, when engaging the media, not issue-sellers" (Smith, Edge & Morris 2006: 3). In her book that looks behind the scenes of the aid industry, Polman writes that the mutual dependency between media and humanitarian organisations can have a significant impact on the course of conflicts. She offers the example of rebels in Sierra Leone who understood the principle of humanitarian help, and abused it for their own interests. "If you only use enough violence, aid will come. If you use more violence, more aid will come" (Polman 2010: 188). It is not only because of this that the media bear a particular responsibility. Franks verifies the direct effect of – partly misleading – media reports on public opinion, the aid sector, and the action of the British government with reference to the BBC's reporting on the 1984 famine in Ethiopia:

> It acted as an international siren [. . .], and eventually spurred on the biggest humanitarian relief effort the world had ever seen and a spectacular new strand of raising funds and awareness. [. . .] It was an example of a huge and worldwide news event, but one, which ultimately involved major misunderstandings and misconceptions. [. . .] The media perception of the famine in Ethiopia was far from accurate.
>
> (Franks 2013: 2)

Beyond the BBC case study, Franks points to the effect of various other misinterpretations of media reports with serious consequences, such as too little funding or over-funding (Franks 2013: 2). De Waal invented the term "humanitarian Gresham's Law" to identify the phenomenon of humanitarian organisations reducing complex, moral contexts to a simple charitable imperative, to make them more easily representable in the media (de Waal 1997: 138, 196). Studies show that media reports are crucial to humanitarian organisations' fundraising and publicity efforts, as donors "continue to value media coverage as a platform to learn about advocacy demands" (Powers 2015: 490).

In this past section, I argued that humanitarian organisations have become large entities, that – although their self-perception varies and so does their outspokenness – have to keep their self-preservation in mind at all times. Negative news sells better to the public and brings more funding, and is thus for what most humanitarian organisations aim. Over the past decade, humanitarian organisations developed highly professionalised PR machinery that feeds into news reporting on Africa. In this study, I therefore look in detail into how this relationship between the PR and communications team of humanitarian organisations and correspondents works, and investigate what the correspondents' perspective about this is.

4.5 Embedded journalism – embedded with the military and embedded with the humanitarian sector?

In order to categorise the interactions, and their level of dependency, in this section I will schematise journalistic embedding with the military, and then transfer it to journalists' embedding with humanitarian organisations. I use the concept of embedding to position the interactions between humanitarian organisations and foreign correspondents on a scale of dependency, with *aid embedding* being the strongest form of dependency. I start from the assumption that a close form of cooperation and dependency between humanitarian organisations and foreign correspondents has evolved, which can be compared to embedded journalism in certain circumstances that I will highlight in this section.[40] I explore this assumption further using the research results in Chapter 6, section 6.6.

Although it existed before that, the idea of embedded frontline journalism was institutionalised on a grand scale for the first time for the coalition forces in the Iraq War in 2003 (Multi-National Force – Iraq).[41] The idea is that a journalist is embedded with a unit to gain access to the war theatre; he or she moves with the unit and receives military protection, board, and lodging. From the military's perspective, the strategy behind the concept is to "create proximity, create trust, create advantages – and journalists will thank you with a [. . .] more loyal coverage" (Löffelholz 2003: 11), which can also be applied to humanitarian organisations. The military hopes to exert significant influence over the coverage of war, which gives the concept of embedding political importance. Journalists in return can gather facts and impressions directly on the ground, and from the frontlines, while mitigating the risks to their lives. Embedded reporting is cost-effective and cuts down reporting expenditure, but limits the ability to report neutrally and to dissociate from the events on the ground. An advantage of embedded reporting from the media's perspective is that correspondents gain access to regions that otherwise would be difficult if not impossible, and very expensive to reach. Journalists can be present on the ground, rather than having to rely only on press conferences and official governments' statements. However, embeds' reporting can be biased since they cannot include other sources beyond the soldiers' and the journalist's own perspective (Brandenburg 2005: 232). Investigating independently is difficult because the freedom of movement is limited.[42] Instead, a perception of the reality is gathered "at the eye-level of a tank driver" (Bütler 2004: 51). Marjorie Miller of the Los Angeles Times states on her work as an embed: "We didn't want to be in bed with the military but we certainly wanted to be there" (Tuosto 2008: 21). Preserving journalistic objectivity is difficult despite all good intentions, since the concept of embedding implies that journalists are physically and psychologically tied to the troops. Journalists have to integrate into the military "to receive support in terms of resources and information" (Brandenburg 2005:

231).⁴³ Which journalists are selected as embeds depends on the circulation range and rating of the news outlet (Paul & Kim 2004: 53).⁴⁴

Embedded journalism provably leads to troop-focused reporting with a positive perspective on the military (Brandenburg 2005: 233f). More particularly, Brandenburg determines that the journalists' opinion on the military in general does not change during the embedding; the attitude towards the troops, however, does – provably towards more support for the troops (Brandenburg 2005: 233), since the journalists come to identify with them. Often, embeds visit so called *media boot camps* to prepare for the field. Identification with the soldiers, and the rapprochement of perception with their views, can start from this early stage of engagement. In crisis areas, embedded journalists and their troop eat, sleep, and experience dangerous situations together, which can reinforce the journalists fraternisation and identification with the soldiers (Pfau 2004; Ricchiardi 2003). Military embeds are not allowed to leave the unit and investigate independently (Dietrich 2007: 70); they have to follow the *Ground Rules* (United States Department of Defense 2003). The logistical and security-related dependency on the soldiers makes critical coverage difficult, and the perspective on the battlefield is limited. "It was very strange [. . .] because no matter how much you guard against it, you start to identify with the people that you're embedded with, particularly when you're being shot at" (Mohan 2003: 262), a journalist testifies. In some cases official censorship is performed, especially but not only when reports could jeopardise the security of the troops (Dietrich 2007: 71). We can assume that the adaptation to the others also leads to self-censorship from the journalists' side. However, it has not yet been researched with a broader sample whether any violation of the rules by an embedded journalist jeopardises the military's future decisions on granting him or her an embedded status again (Dietrich 2007: 73), but individual accounts show that this is the case (La Fleur 2003: 4; Zeide 2005: 1318; Kamber & Arango 2008). Official documents state that "any violation of the ground rules could result in termination of that media's embed opportunity", without specifying whether that may have an effect on future embedding for the journalist and his or her media outlet too (United States Department of Defense 2006: §3M).

Transferring the idea of embedding onto the aid sector, power relationships similar to the ones between troops and embeds occur that can lead to censorship and self-censorship. For example, when humanitarian organisations in conflict areas claim security reasons for withholding information, or when they threaten not to invite journalists again to travel with them if they publish a certain story of which an organisation does not approve. Humanitarian organisations, unlike the military, however, do not have a direct lever to influence correspondents or their reports about the organisations and their projects. They nevertheless expect a "quid pro quo" (Franks 2013: 142), and have ways to claim it. An important component to achieve this is the 'social control', which I understand as a form of indirect or self-censorship in analogy with the form of indirect and self-censorship reporters embedded with the military exhibit: the journalist is not likely to jeopardise the relationship because he or she wants to be invited on press trips or trips facilitated by humanitarian organisations in the future, and needs to make use of the information and network of contacts that that respective humanitarian organisation provides. Franks reports in her study that World Vision sent a letter expressing disappointment that Michael Buerk's reportage on Ethiopia did not mention that World Vision facilitated his visit and made the reportage possible. This letter caused controversy at BBC headquarters (Franks 2013: 143f), and there are many similar cases. However, the dependency between humanitarian organisations and correspondents embedded with them is mutual: humanitarian organisations need media coverage, and journalists need access to remote or dangerous places. The pay-off for humanitarian organisations to embed correspondents is influence on coverage, and thus on potential donors and policy makers. In analogy to Bütler's image of the reality being gathered "at the eye level of a tank driver" in the case of a military embed (Bütler 2004: 51), one could say that correspondents embedded with humanitarian organisations construct reality at the eye level of the driver of a Toyota Land Cruiser, the cliché vehicle of choice for humanitarians in the field, and for correspondents moving with them. Similar to the boot camps in which correspondents participate before working as embeds with the military, correspondents are sometimes invited to preparatory trainings run by humanitarian organisations before they travel into crisis areas. Spending time together and sharing the notion that it is 'common sense' to do good and fight for human rights, also encourages a rapprochement of viewpoints (de Waal 1997: 138, 196) between the correspondent and the humanitarian organisation. Mükke remarks in his study:

> To help people in need falls under an existential, non-negotiable value within social cohabitation. Against this background, journalistic investigation that questions the work of humanitarian organisations, or their political and economic backgrounds, is quickly criticised as jeopardising good motives and aims or as relativising suffering.
> (Mükke 2009b: 265)

When correspondents are more emotionally involved, the danger increases that they overestimate the organisation's position in a wider context, and overlook how the organisation follows its own agenda (Franks 2013: 142). Dietrich additionally points out that the information that journalists receive from the party with which they are embedded is "hard to verify, or not at all verifiable" (Dietrich 2007: 74). Although correspondents – unlike journalists embedded with the military – can in most cases use sources additional to humanitarian organisations, it is still difficult to verify data and statistics, which will be further explained in the subsection *Humanitarian Organisations' Prerogative of Statistics*. The journalist can thus become the mouthpiece, the "public representative" (Brandenburg 2005: 235) of the organisation, offering coverage that resembles news instead of professional public relations, which is more effective than material presented by humanitarian organisations themselves.

Visualising the events is very important for war and crisis journalism. "The media and the military equally want to take advantage of pictures charged with emotion" (Fritsch 2008: 18). The same is true for humanitarian organisations, which generate fewer donations for issues that are harder to transmit through the media. Fritsch's following statements on military strategy with regard to the press can be transferred to the relationship between the media and humanitarian organisations:

> Teaching journalists the military trade is supposed to create confidence [. . .] [and] a specific view on military actions. Press conferences and press releases are supposed to accommodate journalists who feel the pressure to always be up-to-date. Photo and video footage such as the [. . .] 'Gun camera footage' appeases the media's hunger for pictures and spectacle. Facilitating the travel of journalists to the areas of operation, organising media days with troop unions and symposia [. . .] on military conflicts [is supposed to create proximity and mutual trust]. Supporting the journalists intensively on the ground makes [. . .] a certain control of coverage possible.
>
> (Fritsch 2008: 20)

The relationship between humanitarian actors and media actors takes on varying forms. I assume that in extreme cases a form of reciprocal dependency has developed between humanitarian organisations and foreign correspondents, which can be structurally compared to embedded journalism. In conclusion, in the words of Bodine Williams, the director of the media service department of the IFRC: "Sometimes it feels a bit like an arranged marriage [. . .]. We need each other, but our different perspectives can put us into situations that make us both a bit uncomfortable. The important point being that we have to make it work" (Gibbon 1996).

The news audiences, however, often do not know enough about the conditions of news production, which is problematic (Franks 2010: 80): it makes it difficult to distinguish which journalist is working as an embed – regardless of the fact that the audience largely does not know what embedded journalism means – and what effects it may have on the resulting coverage. The audience thus cannot contextualise the coverage within its genesis. Studies found that 70 percent of British citizens did not know what the term *embedding* meant after it had been conceptualised in the Iraq War in 2003, even though the term was used very often with reference to reporting then (Lewis et al. 2004: 28). Additionally, studies of audiences in the United States and the UK show that among the audiences who were informed about the concept of embedded reporting, the British were rather critical whereas only very few Americans feared biased reporting as a result. Almost 60 percent of respondents agreed that embedded reporting was good, and eight out of ten were of the opinion that reports by embeds were fair, impartial, and *unbiased* (PRC Pew Research Center 2003; Lewis et al. 2004). In fact, they were worried about the military's security due to information published by embeds (PRC Pew Research Center 2003). In contrast, according to Dietrich's study, German recipients were rather sceptical about embedded reporting in the Iraq War (Dietrich 2007: 178). Dietrich's survey, however, consisted of interviews with students of media and journalism studies, so I assume that due to their education they were more likely to recognise reporting when it was biased, and more critical towards embedded journalism. The audiences' lack of knowledge about embedded reporting is comparable to the lack of knowledge about the interactions between humanitarian organisations and the media and the coverage that results from them. In this book I thus investigate whether the claim that the dependency between correspondents and the military is comparable on a larger scale to the dependency between correspondents and humanitarian organisations is tenable, and what that means for the coverage on sub-Saharan Africa.

I now want to conceptualise what embedding means detached from its original military sense, and explain why drawing a parallel between a correspondent embedded with the military and a correspondent working with a humanitarian organisation, in certain circumstances is reasonable considering the results of this study. This section on aid embedding mainly focuses on the journalist's dependency level; more information on the dependency of humanitarian organisations on media can be found in section 4.4 and in Chapter 6, section 6.2. The term embedding in this sense detached from the military sense describes the journalist and his or her level of personal, physical, and psychological involvement with the humanitarian organisation, and his or her level of dependency on the organisation.

I understand embedding, detached from its original military sense and generalised, as journalistic work under difficult conditions relying on infrastructure, logistics, and information that a structured party, with which the journalist is embedded, provides and controls. It involves a very strong dependency on the assistance and goodwill of this embedding party, which is including the journalist in its operations in the field, i.e. embeds the journalist. Embedding in theory comes with a mutual form of dependency because the other party also needs something from the journalist: it hopes to gain influence over the coverage and get good publicity as an outcome. However, it usually displays an uneven power relationship, with the other party having power over the embed's well-being, access to places, information, and contacts. Future cooperation can be denied if the embed disobeys rules made up by the other party. And equally, the coverage that results from the embedding can cost future cooperation if it disappoints the embedding party's expectations. Embedding in this sense has the following three dimensions with these characteristics:[45]

(1) Logistical dimension with the following aspects
- (a) Low cost for journalist
- (b) Reduced work time for journalist as embedding party organises the visit in the field
- (c) The journalist's safety is increased
- (d) The journalist gains access to otherwise difficult to access areas
- (e) The journalist uses existing facilities that the embedding party controls or has access to
- (f) The journalist gains access to the embedding party's contacts
- (g) The journalist gains access to the embedding party's information and expertise

(2) Social dimension with the following aspects

- (h) The journalist is together with representatives of the embedding organisation that he/she is embedded with over a certain amount of time in a confined space, and in a difficult and potentially dangerous environment
- (i) The journalist is likely to feel responsible to fulfil expectations as relationships under difficult conditions often become personal
- (j) The journalist is likely to identify with members of the embedding party, but not necessarily with the party as an abstract entity
- (k) The journalist assimilates his/her perceptions to a certain degree to the perceptions of members of the embedding party
- (l) The journalist is at risk of self-censorship due to social desirability when the embedding party is generally seen to 'do good'

(3) Consequential dimension with the following aspects

- (m) The journalist is dependent on the embedding party in terms of all aspects under the logistical dimension
- (n) The journalist only has limited perspectives on the bigger picture due to his/her limited radius of movement, and due to the fact that he/she is shown around by the embedding party
- (o) Interview partners may react differently to the journalist if he/she is in company of the embedding party
- (p) The journalist is confronted with explicit or implicit expectations that the embedding party has regarding the output of the embedding, that might conflict with his/her own expectations
- (q) The journalist operates on the embedding party's goodwill
- (r) The journalist can experience censorship or indirect censorship followed by sanctions if he/she 'misbehaves' in the embedding party's view, which has consequences for future cooperation

The aspects under the three dimensions accumulated lead to different levels of dependency. The more aspects apply, the more dependent is the journalist. Not all aspects weigh the same way; the most important are access (to locations, information, contacts), budget economisation, implicit and explicit expectations, goodwill, limited perspective, and censorship/consequences for future cooperation.

Aid embedding I understand as a situational concept, which means that the journalists' dependency on the humanitarian organisation varies from context to context. However, it does not mean that there are no routine interactions. Situational is not to be understood in the sense of unreliable, it rather means that it depends on the situation whether the interaction can be classed as aid embedding. Agreements between journalists and humanitarian organisations are in most cases only considered valid as long as they cover both parties' interests, and – unlike with military embeds – there are hardly any regulations; arrangements are made by individuals and can vary from case to case, which requires flexibility. Regarding both sides' expectations, these loose agreements about interactions also need openness and transparency, which from the humanitarians' perspective journalists often do not obey, leaving both sides dissatisfied, often without either realising that their expectations did not match in the first place. Aid embedding is a form of *unbalanced resource dependency*, or a "trade in scarce resources" that is asymmetrical to one side (Fengler & Ruß-Mohl 2008: 672–679). It takes place in situations where the journalists' dependency on a humanitarian organisation is stronger than the humanitarian organisation's dependency on the journalist. Journalists' scarce resources are time, budget, expertise in specific areas, and the value of quantity and quality of sources. Humanitarians' limited resource is public attention leading to donations and political interventions. The public relations departments of humanitarian organisations thus 'trade' information that is valuable to journalists, access to certain places and partners and logistical support, against public attention. In these "trades of resources" mutual benefits are the favourable outcome. From a journalist's perspective, the network with humanitarian organisations is very important, especially strategically chosen individuals that work for large humanitarian organisations with budget to spend supporting journalists' travels, that are knowledgeable and have exclusive information, and that ideally understand the journalists' perspective. The bigger this network, and the better quality the sources and partners within it, the more options for the journalists. A larger network can make the correspondents' work easier, quicker, cheaper, can provide valuable information, or help to identify it, and provide logistical support in areas where access is otherwise restricted or difficult and expensive to gain (Fengler & Ruß-Mohl 2008: 672–679). Data of this research shows that the larger the network consisting of trusted individuals working for humanitarian organisations, the more journalists on small budgets can travel nevertheless, the more stories they can get out, and – if they are freelancers – the more they get paid. Aid embedding, however, is an asymmetric trading relationship. This form of dependency takes place when the correspondent is more dependent on humanitarian organisations' resources than the organisation is dependent on the public attention. The journalists in these cases rely on the organisations' contacts and information in the field that are not otherwise accessible, or rely on the organisations' budget or facilitation of their trip. Aid embedding also takes place when the journalists do not depend on the organisations' information alone, but are restricted in movement and independent research for security reasons. Or, when freelance journalists also work on assignments for aid organisations and rely on these financially. The humanitarian organisations can "exploit" the journalists' high demand (Fengler & Ruß-Mohl 2008: 677) for these resources, and dictate the conditions under which they assist, which leads to a loss of journalistic independence, despite the fact that humanitarian organisations have no official control over what the journalists publish in the end. It is not only the journalists' decision to pre-emptively react to this dilemma with coverage of which humanitarian organisations approve, but humanitarian organisations can also take active steps threatening to impose sanctions on the journalists, which can minimise the journalists' options to act. The imbalanced power and dependency relationship in the trade interactions can result in the journalists' having too much to lose when they cause disruptions in the relationships with humanitarian organisations that are crucial to their work. It is justifiable to speak of aid embedding to describe interactions between humanitarian organisations and correspondents in dangerous areas or regions with poor infrastructure, where extensive logistical help of humanitarian organisations is often the only way to get to places and to get information.

So far in this book, I have given an introduction into the topic, an overview of the literature, and explained the theoretical concepts that I used to understand the cooperation phenomenon between journalists and humanitarian organisations in sub-Saharan Africa better. I also laid out assumptions on the media and aid sector, and explicated their respective working environment and framework defining their work, and thus also their cooperation with each other. In the last section, I explicated the tightest form of cooperation between journalists and a second party: the military, and asked whether this relationship could be transferred to journalists embedded with the aid sector. In the next chapter, I will explain, based on the information provided in the past chapters, how I designed the research and what methods I used to gather data on these types of cooperation.

Notes

1 While humanitarian organisations are aware of the issue, mainly the large organisations, such as Save the Children, still use images that are perpetuating the idea of suffering Africans (Crisp 2011: 32).
2 By actor categories I mean e.g. 'rebel', 'warlord', but also much broader categories such as 'civil society'.
3 For criticism on the discourse of development, see Ziai (2010).
4 Richard Munz, for example, who worked for many years as a doctor for national and international humanitarian organisations and also operated as a coordinator of emergency missions, says: "The great danger at the moment is surely that these two groups [the media and humanitarian organisations] meet on-site and shape the picture of international catastrophes and the resulting humanitarian missions in the media" (Munz 2007: 34). For the general debate about to what extent the picture of Africans is constructed from a Western perspective, see Fanon (1967).
5 Cited after mediaculture-online.de [12.10.2010].
6 This figure is taken from a study on German foreign correspondents in 2008.
7 The same is true for journalists working on a *retainer*. In contrast to *freelance journalists* who work for several media outlets at the same time, the journalists working on a retainer receive a monthly payment in addition to a payment for every article, and they are expected to be loyal to their paper, even though they are not staff. The same is to a certain extent true for *stringers*, journalists who provide content for correspondents based on regional knowledge, or do facilitating work such as making appointments on site if the correspondents travels to the stringer's patch him- or herself (Stricker 2004: 19).
8 This includes, in the case mentioned, the special *timing*; the pressure of competition from another broadcaster planning to do a piece on the same issue, Buerk having a lot of time to edit his thus high-quality report, Buerk presenting his report personally to his editors, the editors deciding to broadcast the report at full length, and the fact that the famine was portrayed in a simple, causal relationship as a sudden natural disaster (Abbot 2009). "The complicated political nature of the famine was dropped in favour of a simple story about failing rain" (Franks 2013: 32–37). Instead of the complex explanation that a mix of wrong policies, economics, and the role of civil society had been the cause, this incorrect portrayal of the situation sprang not only from media reports but from how humanitarian organisations, who also profited from the natural

disaster being easily communicable via the media, represented the situation (Franks 2013: 90).
9   See for example Jakobsen (2000), whose main reason for his position that the CNN effect is of secondary importance, is that the media mainly report on the violent period of conflict, instead of continuously, also at the stages before and after the conflict. Jakobsen concludes that this results in recipients considering conflicts as desperate and hopeless, and in political actions taken that are not sustainable but rather emergency relief. What kind of reaction follows from the coverage is not relevant for this study though, as long as it can generally be assumed that a reaction follows.
10 For Mükke's research, multiple references were possible, which is why the numbers do not add up to 100 percent.
11 See subsections *What reality does journalism display* and *The editorial headquarters*.
12 The role of news agencies is described more in-depth in the subsection *The Journalist and News Agencies*.
13 Primary sources are cited with quotation marks, and, in favour of readability with larger line spacing.
14 See subsection *Working conditions of correspondents*.
15 For references in regards to the self-referentiality of the media system, see e.g. Esser & D'Angelo 2003.
16 Mükke's study revealed that the German press agency dpa only uses one source in 67 percent of its contributions. Twenty percent of the dpa wire copies refer to two sources. Only seven percent refer to three or more sources (Mükke 2009b: 124, 125; see also Franks 2013). That the wires only refer to one source could of course mean that the agency journalist had more sources but only mentioned one in the published text.
17 Research on the perception of the African continent is not the focus of this study. Mükke (2009b: 39–50) provides a short but good overview of the state of research about German coverage of Africa and the dominating image of Africa in it.
18 *Heart of Darkness* by Joseph Conrad (2007 [1899]).
19 In this context the recent change in coverage is important, which I subjectively perceived without quantifying it. The series of the German magazine *Der Spiegel* that portrays a new African self-confidence and the change of the continent is one example (Part I: "Die Löwen brechen auf", Part II: "Im Silicon Savannah", Part III: "Die Zukunft ist weiblich", Der Spiegel 2013 (47: 106f; 48: 118ff; 49: 106ff)).
20 In Mükke's study this was 48 countries, but South Sudan did not exist when he carried out his study, so I included it into the number as it lies in the patch of correspondents covering sub-Saharan Africa.
21 See Chapter 6, section 6.3.
22 This I will explain further in the sections *Public relations* and *Professionalising PR and fundraising*.
23 In the order of the mentioned concepts: Bentele, Liebert, & Seeling (1997); Ruß-Mohl (1994); Merten (2004); Altmeppen, Röttger, & Bentele (2004); Bentele & Nothhaft (2004).
24 Baerns did not coin the term *determination hypothesis*. Others who followed her named it thus.
25 This information resulted from interviews conducted in 2011 in Nairobi, which were scheduled to sound out the research field.
26 This is further explained in Chapter 5.
27 I selected one year as an example. For more recent numbers, see the OECD website, e.g. ODA to sub-Saharan Africa was USD 52.3 billion in 2013 (OECD 2013).
28 What the German media referred to as "the Unicef scandal" resulted in the German Committee for Unicef losing the Charity Seal of Approval of the Deutsches Sozialinstitut für Soziale Fragen (DZI). The determining factor for that was that the German committee for Unicef had made false claims about not paying commission for acquiring donations. By paying commission, the examinant of the DZI seal found that Unicef "offended against the principle of economic viability and thrift" (press release

by DZI on 20.2.2008). Although the asserted misappropriation of donations could not be proved, the so-called scandal inflicted great damage not only on Unicef but the whole aid sector since many donors withdrew their donations also from other organisations. The public indignation over the payment of commissions illustrates the balancing act that humanitarian organisations must perform between their reality as part of a large aid apparatus with its own economic interests, and the perception of the individual donors, which does not reflect the professionalisation of the aid industry. For a criticism of referring to these events as a scandal, see Parth (2007). On the balancing act just mentioned, see also Benthall (2010: 56–91); de Jonge Oudraat and Haufler (2008: 17f).

29 On the development of humanitarian organisations from "sacred cows" on a mission that should not be criticised, to being carefully criticised, see Franks (2013:149).
30 Often used synonymously with *development policy*.
31 See also Millennium Development Goals of the United Nations from 2000 (e.g. www.undp.org/content/undp/en/home/sdgoverview/mdg_goals.html, or www.un.org/millennium/declaration/ares552e.pdf [3.2.2013]).
32 On the high expectations and demands of this occupation, see Lieser (2013: 297–298).
33 In Chapter 6, sections 6.3 and 6.8 I will give more detail about this grey area and the results of the empirical study on personal relationships.
34 On the role that the nationality of the respective humanitarian organisation plays, see Riddell and Robinson 1992: 124–172.
35 For example the European Code of Conduct on Images and Messages (Concord 2006), Red Cross/Red Crescent Code of Conduct (ICRC 1996), Code of Conduct by Australian Council for International Development (Australian Council for International Development 2014) etc.
36 For the discussion of humanitarian organisations pursuing political interest without a democratically approved mandate, see Macrae 1996; Slim 2011.
37 Interview with interviewee I_65 who holds such a position.
38 Possibly Waisbord's focus on local South American NGOs with small budgets led him to different conclusions.
39 E.g. UN (n.d.) *UN Photo Library*, URL: www.unmultimedia.org/photo/photo_library.jsp [2.10.2015].
40 See, on the use of the term 'embedding' to refer to the dependency of journalists and humanitarian organisations, e.g. Benthall (2010: xvii), Franks (2008). However, none of these studies explains the reference to the term conceptually or compares its use with its original context.
41 Of course relationships between the military and the media existed prior to 2003. I do not understand them as *embedding*, however. They were mainly shaped by tensions and mistrust. The military restricted journalists' access to conflict areas, censored the messages going out, and controlled the journalists constantly. They revised and bowdlerised, and in the end established media pools to make the reporting more difficult. The relationship between journalists and troops can be divided into different phases: from journalists' uncritical support of the military in World War I and World War II, to a general anti-military attitude in the Vietnam War, to the critical anti-military coverage resulting in mistrust towards the press on the part of the military after that. After the First Gulf War, the US government understood that the success of operations also depended on media coverage, so they started cooperating more again. This led to an institutionalised form of embedding in the Iraq War in 2003 (Brandenburg 2005: 227ff, Dietrich 2007: 17ff), which I perceive as the beginning of *embedding* as it is understood here: institutionalised, with working routines, and as a broadly-spread concept.
42 The limited freedom of movement is not perceived as censorship by German embeds (Dietrich 2007: 168). I nevertheless assume that it has a major influence on the coverage.
43 See on this issue also Weichert & Kramp 2011: 208f.

44 This finding refers to the study of Paul and Kim (2004) of the American media during the Iraq War in 2003.
45 I distilled these characteristics from the mostly descriptive literature on embedded journalism, categorised and detached from the military context. I added some characteristics, confined them, and then structured them under the three dimensions. Journalists with extensive experience in embedded reporting advised on this process, and help to specify some of the points.

References

Abbot, Kimberly (2009) "Working Together, NGOs and Journalists Can Create Stronger International Reporting", URL: http://www.crisisgroup.org/en/publication-type/commentary/abbott-working-together-ngos-and-journalists-can-create-stronger-international-reporting.aspx [19.12.2012].

Adamson, Peter (1993) "Charity Begins With the Truth: Too Much Bad News About the Developing World Gives a Distorted Picture", *The Independent*, URL: www.independent.co.uk/voices/charity-begins-with-the-truth-too-much-bad-news-about-the-developing-world-gives-a-distorted-picture-says-peter-adamson-2323657.html [2.2.2015].

Al Jazeera (2015) "Al Jazeera's Peter Greste Back Home in Australia", in: *Al Jazeera Online*, URL: http://www.aljazeera.com/news/asia-pacific/2015/02/al-jazeera-greste-arrives-home-australia-150204152533647.html [15.11.2015].

Al Jazeera (2016) "Foreign Journalists Among 17 Arrested in Burundi Swoop", *Al Jazeera Online*, URL: www.aljazeera.com/news/2016/01/foreign-journalists-17-arrested-burundi-swoop-160129045924385.html [29.1.2016].

Alam, Shahidul (2007) "The Visual Representation of Developing Countries by Developmental Agencies and the Western Media", in: *Policy & Practice – A Development Education Review*, 59–65.

Albrecht, B and Albrecht, C (2004) "Das Afrikabild in der Spendenwerbung", URL: http://spendeninstitut.at/download/SE_Afrika_Albrecht_SS04.pdf [15.1.2013].

Alesina, Alberto and Dollar, David (2000) "Who Gives Foreign Aid to Whom and Why?", in: *Journal of Economic Growth* 5, 33–63.

Altmeppen, Klaus-Dieter (2004) *Schwierige Verhältnisse Interdependenzen zwischen Journalismus und PR*, Wiesbaden.

Altmeppen, Klaus-Dieter (2007) "Journalismus und Macht: Ein Systematisierungs- und Analyseentwurf", in: Thomas Hanitzsch, Klaus-Dieter Altmeppen and Carsten Schlüter (Eds.), *Journalismustheorie: Next Generation: Soziologische Grundlegung und theoretische Innovation*, Wiesbaden, 420–447.

Altmeppen, Klaus-Dieter, Bentele, Günter and Röttger, Ulrike (2004) "PR und Journalismus. Eine lang andauernde und interessante 'Beziehungskiste'", in: Klaus-Dieter Altmeppen, Günter Bentele and Ulrike Röttger (Eds.), *Schwierige Verhältnisse: Interdependenzen zwischen Journalismus und PR*, Wiesbaden, 7–16.

Altmeppen, Klaus-Dieter, Röttger, Ulrike and Bentele, Günter (2004) "PR und Journalismus. Eine lang andauernde und interessante 'Beziehungskiste'", in: Klaus-Dieter Altmeppen, Günter Bentele and Ulrike Röttger (Eds.), *Schwierige Verhältnisse: Interdependenzen zwischen Journalismus und PR*, Wiesbaden, 7–16.

Andersen, Uwe (2011) "Entwicklungspolitik/-hilfe", in: Wichard Woyke (Ed.), *Handwörterbuch Internationale Politik*, Opladen, 100–111.

Avenarius, Horst (2008) *Public Relations: Die Grundform der gesellschaftlichen Kommunikation*, Einbeck.

Baerns, Barbara (1979) "Öffentlichkeitsarbeit als Determinante journalistischer Informationsleistungen. Thesen zur Beschreibung von Medieninhalten", in: *Publizistik* 3, 301–316.
Baerns, Barbara (1985) *Öffentlichkeitsarbeit oder Journalismus? Zum Einfluß im Mediensystem*, Köln.
Baerns, Barbara (1991, 2nd. edition) *Öffentlichkeitsarbeit oder Journalismus? Zum Einfluss im Mediensystem*.
Barnett, Michael (2011) *Empire of Humanity: A History of Humanitarianism*, New York, NY.
BBC (n.y.) "Editorial Guidelines", URL: http://www.bbc.co.uk/guidelines/editorialguidelines/page/guidelines-external-relationships-other/#charities and www.bbc.co.uk/guidelines/editorialguidelines/edguide/war/editorialprinci.shtml [30.11.2012].
Bengelstorff, Anja (2002) *Auslandskorrespondenten in Afrika südlich der Sahara. Eine qualitative Kommunikatorstudie zu Rollenverständnis und Arbeitsrealität*. Magisterarbeit. FU Berlin, Berlin.
Bentele, Günter, Liebert, Thomas and Seeling, Stefan (1997) "Von der Determination zur Intereffikation. Ein integriertes Modell zum Verhältnis von Public Relations und Journalismus", in: Günter Bentele and Michael Haller (Eds.), *Aktuelle Entstehung von Öffentlichkeit: Akteure – Strukturen – Veränderungen*, Konstanz, 225–250.
Bentele, Günter and Nothhaft, Howard (2004) "Das Intereffikationsmodell. Theoretische Weiterentwicklung, empirische Konkretisierung und Desiderate", in: Klaus-Dieter Altmeppen, Ulrike Röttger and Günter Bentele (Eds.), *Schwierige Verhältnisse: Interdependenzen zwischen Journalismus und Public Relations*, Wiesbaden, 67–104.
Benthall, Jonathan (2010) *Disasters, Relief and the Media*, Herefordshire.
Bickel, Markus (2008) "Krisenberichterstattung im Ausland – der Krieg schärft die Sinne", in: Oliver Hahn, Julia Lönnendonker and Roland Schröder (Eds.), *Deutsche Auslandskorrespondenten: Ein Handbuch*, Konstanz.
Birrell, Ian (2013) "Media Short Changes the Poor with its Soft-Soap Aid Coverage", *The Guardian* [17.3.2013].
Blackmore, Chloe (2009) "Responsible Wellbeing and its Implications for Development Policy", in: *University of Bath*, Working Paper Series WeD 09/48.
Blair, Tony. (1999) "Doctrine of the International Community", Speech by Tony Blair. In Economic Club of Chicago.
Bogert, Carroll (2011) "Whose News? The Changing Media Landscape and NGOs", Human Rights Watch Wolrd Report.
Bourdieu, Pierre (1986) "The Forms of Capital", in: John Richardson (Ed.), *Handbook of Theory and Research for the Sociology of Education*, New York, NY, 241–258.
Brandenburg, Heinz (2005) "Journalists Embedded in Culture: War Stories as Political Strategy", in: Lee Artz and Yahya Kamalipour (Eds.), *Bring 'em on: Media and Politics in the Iraq War*, Lanham, 225–238.
Brooks, Jeff (2011) "Sad Face Makes Better Fundraising", URL: www.futurefundraisingnow.com/future-fundraising/2011/07/sad-faces-make-better-fundraising.html [22.5.2015].
Bücher, Karl (1926) *Gesammelte Aufsätze zur Zeitungskunde*, Tübingen (Reprint).
Bütler, Hugo (2004) "Kriegsberichte auf Augenhöhe", in: *Cover-Medienmagazin* 4, 50–52.
Chouliaraki, Lilie (2012) *The Ironic Spectator. Solidariy in the Age of Post-Humanitarianism*, Cambridge.
Clark, D. J. (2004) "The Production of a Contemporary Famine Image: the Image Economy, Indigenous Photographers and the Case of Mekanic Philipos", in: *Journal of International Development* 16, 693–704.

CONCORD (European NGO Confederation of Relief and Development) (2006) *Code of Conduct on Images and Messages*, Brussles.

Conrad, Joseph (2007 [1899]) *Heart of Darkness*, London.

Cooley, Alexander and Ron, James (2002) "The NGO Scramble: International Security and the Political Economy of Transnational Action", in: *International Security* 27(1), 5–39.

Cooper, Glenda (2011) *From Their Own Correspondent? New Media and the Changes in Disaster Coverage: Lessons to be Learnt*, Reuters Institute for the Study of Journalism.

Cottle, Simon and Nolan, David (2007) "Global Humanitarianism and the Changing Aid-Media Field. 'Everyone was Dying for Footage'", in: *Journalism Studies* 8(6), 862–878.

Cottle, Simon and Nolan, David (2009) "How the Media's Codes and Rules Influence the Ways NGOs Work", Nieman Journalism Lab.

Crisp, Lucy (2011) *'The Danger of a Single Story': How Fundraising Images Used by INGOs Continue to Perpetuate Racism in Development*, Anthropology Department, MA: University of London.

Darby, Seyward (2015) "Global Thinkers: What are Africa's New Missionaries Peddling?", *Foreign Policy Online*, Podcast, URL: http://foreignpolicy.com/2015/10/13/global-thinkers-what-are-africas-new-missionaries-peddling/ [30.10.2015]

Davies, T.R. (2006) *The Rise and Fall of Transnational Civil Society. Paper for the 31st Annual Conference of the British International Studies Association held at University College, Cork, from 18 to 20 December 2006.* Paper presented at the 31st Annual Conference of the British International Studies Association. URL: http://users.ox.ac.uk/~magdo788/RAFOTC.pdf.

de Jonge Oudraat, Chantal and Haufler, Virginia (2008) "33 AICGS Policy Report." *Global Governance and the Role of NGOs in International Peace and Security*, Baltimore: American Institute for Contemporary German Studies, Johns Hopkins University.

de Waal, Alex (1997) *Famine Crimes: Politics and the Disaster Relief Industry in Africa*, Bloomington, IN.

Dietrich, Sandra (2007) *Embedded journalism. Ursprünge, Ziele, Merkmale, Probleme und Nutzen von ‚Embedding' am Beispiel des Irak-Krieges 2003*, Saarbrücken.

Dilg, Ute (1999) "Schwarzafrika: Weißer Fleck auf dem Nachrichtenglobus. Die Berichterstattung über Afrika südlich der Sahara in der überregionalen deutschen Presse. Eine Inhaltsanalyse", in: *Communicatio Socialis. Internationale Zeitschrift für Kommunikation in Religion, Kirche und Gesellschaft* 32(3), 241–260.

Eilders, Christiane and Hagen, Lutz (2005) "Kriegsberichterstattung als Thema kommunikationswissenschaftlicher Forschung. Ein Überblick zum Forschungsstand und den Beiträgen in diesem Themenheft", in: *Medien & Kommunikation* 2–3, 205–221.

Esser, Frank (1997) "Journalistische Kultur in Großbritannien und Deutschland. Eine Analyse aus vergleichender Perspektive", in: Marcel Machill (Ed.), *Journalistische Kultur*, Wiesbaden, 111–136.

Esser, Frank and D'Angelo, Paul (2003) "Framing the Press and the Publicity Process", in: *American Behavioral Scientist* 46, 617–641.

Europäische Kommission (2012) "Spezial Eurobarometer 392. Solidarität weltweit: Die Europäer und die Entwicklungshilfe", URL: http://ec.europa.eu/public_opinion/archives/ebs/ebs_392_de.pdf.

European Commission (2012) "Solidarity That Spans the Globe: Europeans and Development Aid", *Special Eurobarometer*, 392, URL: http://ec.europa.eu/public_opinion/archives/ebs/ebs_392_en.pdf [24.4.2015]

Fanon, Frantz (1967) *Black Skin, White Masks*, New York, NY.

Fechter, Anne-Meike (2012) "Introduction. The Personal and the Professional: Aid Workers' Relationships and Values in the Development Process", in: *Third World Quarterly* 33(8), 1387–1404.

Fengler, Susanne and Ruß-Mohl, Stephan (2008) "Journalists and the Information-Attention Markets: Towards an Economic Theory of Journalism", in: *Journalism* 9(6), 667–690.

Fisher, William (1997) "Doing Good? The Politics and Antipolitics of NGO Practices", in: *Annual Review of Anthropology* 26, 439–464.

Franks, Suzanne (2008) "Getting into Bed with Charity", in: *Brisith Journalism Review* 19(3), 27–32.

Franks, Suzanne (2010) "The Neglect of Africa and the Power of Aid", in: *International Communication Gazette* 71(1), 71–84.

Franks, Suzanne (2013) *Reporting Disasters. Famine, Aid, Politics and the Media*, London.

Frantz, Christiane and Martens, Kerstin (2006) *Nichtregierungsorganisationen (NGOs)*, Wiesbaden.

Franzke, Michael (2000) "'Aber die Agenturen haben nichts gemeldet . . .' Das Problem, über Probleme der ‚Dritten Welt' zu berichten", in: Stefan Brüne (Ed.), *Neue Medien und Öffentlichkeiten. Politik und Tele-Kommunikation in Afrika, Asien und Lateinamerika*, Hamburg.

Fritsch, Alexander (2008) *'Angriffskrieg' oder 'Friedensmission'. Vom Verhältnis von Public Relations und Journalismus in Kriegszeiten*. Paper presented at the Medien und Wirklichkeit. 2. Studentische Medientage Chemnitz 2006.

Gabler Wirtschaftslexikon Online (n.d.).

Gibbon, Joanna (1996) "Aid Meets the Press", in: *The Magazine of the International Red Cross and Red Crescent Movement* 1.

Glennie, Alex, Straw, Will and Wild, Leni (2012) "Understanding Public Attitudes to Aid and Development", in: *ODI and Institute for Public Policy Research & Overseas Development Institute*, URL: www.odi.org/sites/odi.org.uk/files/odi-assets/publications-opinion-files/7708.pdf [23.8.2015]

Göhler, Gerhard (1995) *Macht der Öffentlichkeit – Öffentlichkeit der Macht*, Baden-Baden.

Green, Andrew (2016) "The Thorny Ethics of Embedding with Do-Gooders", *Columbia Journalism Review*, URL: www.cjr.org/first_person/the_ethics_of_embedding_with_do-gooders.php [8.2.2016]

Greshoff, Rainer (2013) "Strukturtheoretischer Individualismus", in: Georg Kneer and Markus Schroer (Eds.), *Handbuch Soziologische Theorien*, Wiesbaden, v.

Grill, Bartholomäus (2007) "Auf verlorenem Posten? Als Korrespondent in Afrika", in: Gerhard Göhler, Cornelia Schmalz-Jacobson and Christian Walther (Eds.), *Macht und Medien: Über das Verhältnis von Politik und Kommunikation*, Frankfurt/M., 119–136.

Grill, Bartholomäus (2013) "Die Zukunft ist weiblich", *Der Spiegel*, 49, 106–110.

Grunig, James E. and Hunt, Todd T. (1984) *Managing Public Relations*, New York, NY.

Guillot, Claire (2012) "Photographes en terrain miné", *Le Monde* [6.10.2012].

Hafez, Kai (2001) *Die politische Dimension der Auslandsberichterstattung*, Baden-Baden.

Hamilton, John Maxwell and Jenner, Eric (2003) "Redefining Foreign Correspondence", in: *The Joan Shorenstein Center of the Press, Politics and Public Policy*, Working Paper Series.

Horsti, Karina (2013) "De-Ethnicized Victims: Mediatized Advocacy for Asylum Seekers", in: *Journalism: Theory, Practice & Criticism* 14(1), 78–95.

ICRC (1996) "Annex VI: The Code of Conduct for the International Red Cross and Red Crescent Movement and NGOs in Disaster Relief", in: *International Review of the Red Cross*, 310.

ICRC (2012) "Protecting the Witnesses", *The Magazine of the International Red Cross and Red Crescent Movement*, 2, URL: www.icrc.org./eng/assets/files/publications/1134-magazine-red-cross-red-crescent-2-2012-eng.pdf [2.4.2015]

ICRC (2015) "Key Data Appeals 2016 Breakdown and 2015–2016 Comparative Data", *ICRC Appeal Online*, URL: http://reliefweb.int/sites/reliefweb.int/files/resources/2016_appeals_keydata_rex2015_609_final.pdf

Jakobsen, Peter Viggo (2000) "Focus on the CNN Effect Misses the Point: The Real Media Impact on Conflict Management is Invisible and Indirect", in: *Journal of Peace Research* 37(2), 131–143.

Junghanns, Kathrin and Hanitzsch, Thomas (2006) "Deutsche Auslandskorrespondenten im Profil", in: Institut Hans Bredow (Ed.), *Medien & Kommunikationswissenschaft*, Vol. 54(3), Baden-Baden, 412–429.

Kamber, Michael and Arango, Tim (2008) "4000 US Deaths, and a Handful of Images", *New York Times* 26.7.2008.

Kennedy, Dennis (2009) "Selling the Distant Other: Humanitarianism and Imagery – Ethical Dilemmas of Humanitarian Action", *The Journal of Humanitan Assistance*, URL: https://sites.tufts.edu/jha/archives/411 [2.3.2014].

Kent, Randolph and Burke, Joanne (2011) "Commercial and Humanitarian Engagement in Crisis Contexts: Current Trends, Future Drivers", London: Humanitarian Futures Programme King's College, URL: http://reliefweb.int/sites/reliefweb.int/files/resources/commercial-and-humanitarian-engagement.pdf [10.10.2013].

Kepplinger, Hans (2004, 2. edition) "Problemdimensionen des Journalismus. Wechselwirkung zwischen Theorie und Empirie", in: Martin Löffelholz (Ed.), *Theorien des Journalismus. Ein diskursives Handbuch*, Wiesbaden, 87–106.

Kevenhörster, Paul and Boom, Dirk van den (2009) *Entwicklungspolitik*, Wiesbaden.

Klose, Fabian (2013) *Human Rights in the Shadow of Colonial Violence*, Philadelphia.

Kohn, Melvin L. (1989) "Introduction", in: Melvin L. Kohn (Ed.), *Cross-national Research in Sociology*, Newbury Park, 17–31.

Krems, Olaf (2002) *Der Blackout-Kontinent. Projektion und Reproduktion eurozentristischer Afrika- und Afrikanerbilder unter besonderer Berücksichtigung der Berichterstattung in deutschsprachigen Massenmedien*. Dissertation at the Westfälischen Wilhelms Universität zu Münster, Münster.

Kuhn, Marco (2000) *Humanitäre Hilfe in der Europäischen Gemeinschaft. Entwicklung, System und primärrechtlicher Rahmen*, Berlin.

Kumar, Priya (2011) "Foreign Correspondents: Who Covers What", in: *American Journalism Review (AJR)* (December/January).

La Fleur, Jennifer (2003) "Embed Program Worked, Broader War Coverage Lagged", in: *The News Media & the Law* (Spring), 4.

Leigh, Tamara (2015) "Aid Workers or Journalists: Who Should Report the News?", *IRIN*, URL: http://newirin.irinnews.org/extras/2015/2/11/aid-workers-or-journalists-who-should-report-the-news [2.1.2016].

Lewis, Justin, Threadgold, Terry, Brookes, Rod and et al (2004) *Too Close for Comfort? The Role of Embedded Reporting During the 2003 Iraq War: Summary Report*, Cardiff.

Lieser, Jürgen (2013) "Humanitäres Personal: Anforderungen an die Professionalität", in: Jürgen Lieser and Dennis Dijkzeul (Eds.), *Handbuch Humanitäre Hilfe*, Heidelberg, 295–304.

Lieser, Jürgen and Dijkzeul, Dennis (Eds.). (2013) *Handbuch Humanitäre Hilfe*, Heidelberg.

Lilienthal, Volker and Schnedler, Thomas (2012) "Zur sozialen Lage von Journalistinnen und Journalisten", in: *APuZ* 29–31, 15–21.

Löffelholz, Martin (2003) "Distanz in Gefahr", in: *Journalist* 5, 10–13.
Löffelholz, Martin (2004) "Krisen- und Kriegskommunikation als Forschungsfeld. Trends, Themen und Theorien eines hoch relevanten, aber gering systematisierten Teilgebiets in der Kommunikationswissenschaft", in: Martin Löffelholz (Ed.), *Krieg als Medienereignis II. Krisenkommunikation im 21: Jahrhundert*, Wiesbaden, 13–55.
Luger, Kurt and Pointner, Andreas (1996) "Die 'Gesichter Afrikas'. Ein Kontinent in der Konstruktion österreichischer Printmedien", in: Österreichischen Gesellschaft für Kommunikationsfragen (Ed.), *Medien Journal*, Vol. 4, Salzburg, 4–29.
Lünenborg, Margreth (2012) "Qualität in der Krise?", in: *APuZ* 29–31(Qualitätsjournalismus), 3–8.
Macrae, Joanna (1996) "NGOs: Has the 'N' Gone Missing?", *The Magazine of the International Red Cross and Red Crescent Movement*, 3, URL: www.redcross.int/EN/mag/magazine1996_3/18-19.html [10.2.2014].
Madianou, Mirca (2013) "Humanitarian Campaigns in Social Media", in: *Journalism Studies* 14(2), 249–266.
Martens, Kerstin (2002) "Mission Impossible? Defining Nongovernmental Organizations", in: *Voluntas: International Journal of Voluntary and Nonprofit Organisations* 13(3), 271–285.
McIntyre, Peter (2002) "Child Rights and the Media. Putting Children in the Right. Guidelines for Journalists and Media Professionals", Brüssel: UNICEF.
Meldrum, Andrew (2010) "Africa – Revealed on Global Post Through People-Oriented Stories", in: *Nieman Reports: The Nieman Foundation for Journalism at Harvard* (Fall).
Merten, Klaus (2004) "Mikro, Mikro-Makro oder Makro? Zum Verhältnis von Journalismus und PR aus systemischer Perspektive", in: Klaus-Dieter Altmeppen, Ulrike Röttger and Günter Bentele (Eds.), *Schwierige Verhältnisse. Interdependenzen zwischen Journalismus und PR*, Wiesbaden, 17–36.
Mikich, Sonia (2003) "Geistige Provinzialisierung. Eine Zustandsbeschreibung", in: Claudia Cipitelli and Axel Schwanebeck (Eds.), *Nur Krisen, Kriege, Katastrophen? Auslandsberichterstattung im deutschen Fernsehen. Dokumentation der 21; Tutzinger Medientage*, München, 117–127.
Mohan, Geoffrey (2003) "All is Vanity", in: Bill Katovsky and TImpthy Carlson (Eds.), *Embedded: The Media at War in Iraq. An Oral History*, Guilford, 257–263.
Moore, Phil (2016) "On My Arrest in Burundi", *philmoore.info/blog*, URL: http://philmoore.info/blog/2016/2/on-my-arrest-in-burundi [5.2.2016]
Mükke, Lutz (2003) "Einzelkämpfende Allrounder. Eine Studie über Korrespondenten in Nairobi", in: *Message. Internationale Zeitschrift für Journalismus* (2), 82–87.
Mükke, Lutz (2004) "Schwarzweißes Afrika: Über das Entstehen Afrika-bezogener Nachrichten im Zerrspiegel deutscher Massenmedien", in: *Africa Spectrum* 39(2), 277–289.
Mükke, Lutz (2009a) "Allein auf weiter Flur: Korrespondenten in Afrika", in: *APuZ* 34–35, 39–45.
Mükke, Lutz (2009b) *'Journalisten der Finsternis'. Akteure, Strukturen und Potenziale deutscher Afrika-Berichterstattung*, Köln.
Munz, Richard (2007) *Im Zentrum der Katastrophe: Was es wirklich bedeutet, vor Ort zu helfen*, Frankfurt/M.
n.a. (2013) "Die Löwen brechen auf", in: *Der Spiegel* 47, 106–107.
Neudeck, Rupert (1990) "Katastrophen-Hilfe und Katastrophen-Journalismus am Horn von Afrika", in: Stefan Brüne and Volker Matthies (Eds.), *Krisenregion Horn von Afrika*, Hamburg, 321–336.
OECD (2012) "Aid Statistics, Statistics by Region 2012: Aid at a Glance. Africa", URL: www.oecd.org/dac/aidstatistics/ [15.12.2012].

OECD (2013) "Aid to Developing Countries Rebounds in 2013 to Reach an All-time High", URL: www.oecd.org/newsroom/aid-to-developing-countries-rebounds-in-2013-to-reach-an-all-time-high.htm [20.3.2015].
OECD (n.d.) "Detailed Aid Statistics. ODA Commitment 1966–2013", URL: http://oecd-ilibrary-org./development/data/oecd-international-development-statistics/oda-commitments_data-00068-en [2.3.2016]
Orgad, Shani and Seu, I. Bruna (2014) "The Mediation of Humanitarianism: Toward a Research Framework", in: *Communication, Culture & Critique* 7, 6–36.
Parth, Christian (2007) "Ein Herz für Berater", *ZEIT Online*, 21.12.2007, URL: www.zeit.de/online/2007/52/unicef-skandal [20.11.2013].
Paul, Christopher and Kim, James (2004) "Reporters on the Battlefield. The Embedded Press System in Historical Context", URL: www.rand.org/pubs/monographs/2004/RAND_MG200.pdf [22.11.2012].
Perras, Arne (2009) "Flugzeugentführung in Somalia – Mit dem Leben abgeschlossen", *Süddeutsche Zeitung Online*, 4.11.2009, URL: www.sueddeutsche.de/panorama/flugzeugentfuehrung-in-somalia-mit-dem-leben-abgeschlossen-1.137881 [19.5.2010].
Perras, Arne (2010) "Im Herz der Finsternis", *Süddeutsche Zeitung Online*, 29.5.2010, URL: www.sueddeutsche.de/kultur/2.220/afrikabild-im-westen-im-herz-der-finsternis-1.951471 [20.10.2010].
Péus, Gunter (1977) "Afrika: erschwerte Arbeitsbedingungen: Erfahrungen mit Logistik, Krise und Zensur", in: Rupert Neudeck (Ed.), *Den Dschungel ins Wohnzimmer. Auslandsberichterstattung im bundesdeutschen Fernsehen*, Frankfurt/M, 85–94.
Pfau, Michael et al (2004) "Embedding Journalists in Military Combat Units: Impact on Newspaper Story Frames and Tone", in: *Journalism & Mass Communication Quarterly* 81(1), 87–88.
Plewes, Betty and Stuart, Rieky (2009) "The Pornography of Poverty: A Cautionary Fundraising Tale", in: *Ethics in Action. The Ethical Challanges or International Human Rights Nongovernmental Organizations*, 23–37.
Polman, Linda (2010) *Die Mitleidsindustrie. Hinter den Kulissen internationaler Hilfsorganisationen*, Frankfurt/M., New York, NY.
Powers, Matthew (2015) "Contemporary NGO-Journalism Relations: Reviewing and Evaluating an Emergent Area of Research", in: *Sociology Compass* 9(6), 427–437.
Powers, Matthew (2016) "Beyond Boon or Bane. Using Normative Theories to Evaluate the Newsmaking Efforts of NGOs", in: *Journalism Studies Online*.
PRC Pew Research Center (2003) "War Coverage Praised, but Public Hungry for Other News", URL: www.people-press.org/2003/04/09/war-coverage-praised-but-public-hungry-for-other-news/ [23.11.2012].
Puhl, Jan (2013) "Im Silicon Savannah", *Der Spiegel*, 48, 118–122.
Redelfs, Manfred (2003) "Recherche mit Hindernissen: Investigativer Journalismus in Deutschland und den USA", in: Wolfgang R. Langenbucher (Ed.), *Die Kommunikationsfreiheit der Gesellschaft*, Wiesbaden, 208–238.
Redelfs, Manfred (2007) "'Investigative Reporting' in den USA: Welche Strukturen stützen den Recherche-Journalismus?", in: Horst Pöttker and Christiane Schulzki-Haddouti (Eds.), *Vergessen? Verschwiegen? Verdrängt? 10 Jahre 'initiative Nachrichtenaufklärung'*, Wiesbaden, 131–155.
Reese, Stephen (2001) "Understanding the Global Journalist: a Hierarchy-of-Influences Approach", in: *Journalism Studies* 2(2), 173–187.
Ricchiardi, Sherry (2003) "Close to the Action", in: *American Journalism Review (AJR)* 25, 28–36.

Ricchiardi, Sherry (2005) "Déjà Vu", in: *American Journalism Review (AJR)* (February/March).
Ricchiardi, Sherry (2008) "Covering the World", in: *American Journalism Review (AJR)* (December/January).
Riddell, Roger (2007) *Does Foreign Aid Really Work?*, Oxford.
Riddell, Roger and Robinson, Mark (1992) *Working With the Poor*, London.
Robinson, Piers (2002) *The CNN Effect: The Myths of News, Foreign Policy and Intervention*, New York, NY.
Rothmyer, Karen (2010) *They Wanted Journalists to Say 'Wow'. How NGOs Affect U.S. Media Coverage of Africa*, Joan Shorenstein Center Research Paper.
Röttger, Ulrike (2005) "Public Relations", in: Siegfried Weischenberg (Ed.), *Handbuch Journalismus und Medien*, Konstanz, 369–374.
Ruß-Mohl, Stephan (1994) "Symbiose oder Konflikt: Öffentlichkeitsarbeit und Journalismus", in: Otfried Jarren (Ed.), *Medien und Journalismus*, Vol. 1, 313–326.
Salamon, Lester, Sokolowski, S. Wojciech and List, Regina (2003) "Global Civil Society: An Overview", Baltimore: John Hopkins University.
Salazar-Volkmann, Christian (1997) "Gutes Tun! Aber wie darüber reden? Zur Öffentlichkeitsarbeit entwicklungspolitischer Hilfsorganisationen", in: Günter Bentele and Michael Haller (Eds.), *Aktuelle Entstehung von Öffentlichkeit. Akteure – Strukturen – Veränderungen*, Konstanz, 251–265.
Sambrook, Richard (2010) *Are Forein Correspondents Redundant? The Chancing Face of International News*, Oxford.
Scharf, Wilfried and Stockmann, Ralf (1998) "Zur Auslandsberichterstattung von 'Weltspiegel' und 'Auslandsjournal'", in: Siegfried Quandt and Wolfgang Gast (Eds.), *Duetschland im Dialog der Kulturen. Medien – Images – Verständigung*, Konstanz, 73–85.
Scheen, Thomas (2007) "Kontinent der gepackten Koffer. Was der Auslandskorrespondent an Afrika kritisiert und wieso er dort bleibt", in: *Der Überblick. Zeitschrift für ökumenische Begegnung und internationale Zusammenarbeit*, 27.
Scheen, Thomas (2008) "Ich hatte Angst um mein Leben", *Frankfurter Allgemeine Zeitung* 17.11.2008.
Schmoll, Anka (1998) "Die Wa(h)re Nachricht über Afrika. Stereotype und Standardisierung in der Fernsehberichterstattung", in: Wilhelm Kempf and Irena Schmidt-Regener (Eds.), *Krieg, Nationalismus, Rassismus und die Medien*, Münster, 89–96.
Scholl, Armin (2004) "Steuerung oder strukturelle Koppelung? Kritik und Erneuerung theoretischer Ansätze und empirischer Operationalisierungen", in: Klaus-Dieter Altmeppen, Ulrike Röttger and Günter Bentele (Eds.), *Schwierige Verhältnisse: Interdependenzen zwischen Journalismus und PR*, Vol. 42, Wiesbaden, 37–52.
Seib, Philip (2002) *The Global Journalist. News and Conscience in a World of Conflict*, Oxford.
Shaikh, Alanna (2011) "Has NGO Advertising Gone Too Far?", *Development Research Initiative NYU*, URL: www.nyudri.org/aidwatcharchive/2011/04/has-ngo-advertising-gone-too-far [3.5.2014].
Shawcross, William (1984) *The Quality of Mercy: Cambodia, Holocaust and Modern Conscience*, New York, NY.
Slim, Hugo (2011) "Principled Humanitarian Action & Ethical Tension in Multi-Mandata Organizations. Observations from a Rapid Literature Review", *World Vision*, URL: www.elac.ox.ac.uk/downloads/Slim Bradley World Vision Paper.pdf [10.6.2012].
Smith, Joe, Edge, Lucy and Morris, Vanessa (2006) "Reflecting the Real World?: How British TV Portrayed Developing Countries in 2005", 2.11.2013, URL: www.vso.org.uk/news/pressreleases/reflecting the real world.asp [15.3.2015].

Stricker, Roman (2004) *Ressourcen, Entscheidungsverfahren, Produktionsoutput – ein Vergleich der institutionellen Bedingungen von Fernsehnachrichtenproduktion bei ARD und RTL am Fallbeispiel der Berichterstattung über den Afghanistan-Krieg 2001*. Universität Köln, Köln.

Szyszka, Peter (1997) "Bedarf oder Bedrohung? Zur Frage der Beziehungen des Journalismus zur Öffentlichkeitsarbeit", in: Günter Bentele and Michael Haller (Eds.), *Aktuelle Entstehung von Öffentlichkeit: Akteure – Strukturen – Veränderungen*, Konstanz, 209–224.

Szyszka, Peter (2004) "Manipulation oder Informationsvermittlung? Zum Verhältnis von Produkt-PR und Journalismus", in: *Medienwissenschaft Schweiz* 2, 72–79.

Tuosto, Kylie (2008) "The ‚Grunt Truth' of Embedded Journalism: The New Media/Military Relationship", in: *Stanford Journal of International Relations* 10(1), 20–31.

UN (n.d.) *UN Photo Library*, URL: http://www.unmultimedia.org/photo/photo_library.jsp [2.10.2015].

UNICEF (n.d.) "Principles and Guidelines for Ethical Reporting", URL:. www.unicef.org/esaro/5440_ethical_reporting_guidelines.html.

United States Department of Defence (2003) "Ground Rules For Journalists Embedded With US Forces During The Iraq War".

United States Department of Defence (2006) Public Affairs Guidance on Embedding Media.

Voss, Kathrin (2007) *Öffentlichkeitsarbeit von Nichtregierungsorganisationen: Mittel, Ziele, interne Strukturen*, Wiesbaden.

Waisbord, Silvio (2011) "Can NGOs Change the News?", in: *International Journal of Communication* 5, 142–165.

Walter, Jonathan (2006) "World Disaster Report", URL: http://www.ifrc.org/Global/Publications/disasters/WDR/WDR2006-English-LR.pdf [12.10.2015].

Wanene, Wilson (2005) "An American Correspondent Brings Africa Out of the Shadows", in: *Nieman Reports: The Nieman Foundation for Journalism at Harvard* (Summer).

Weichert, Stephan and Kramp, Leif (2011) *Die Vorkämpfer. Wie Journalisten über den Ausnahmezustand berichten*, Köln.

Weichert, Stephan, Kramp, Leif and Matschke, Alexander (2012) "Überlegungen zur Qualität im Krisenjournalismus", in: *APuZ* 29–31(Qualitätsjournalismus), 22–28.

Weischenberg, Siegfried (2005) *Handbuch Journalismus und Medien*, Konstanz.

Werker, Eric and Ahmed, Faisal (2008) "What do Non-Governmental Organisations do?", in: *The Journal of Economic Perspectives* 22(2), 73–92.

Wu, H. Denis and Hamilton, John Maxwell (2004) "US Foreign Correspondents: Changes and Continuity at the Turn of the Century", in: *Gazette: The International Journal for Communication Studies* 66(6), 517–532.

Zeide, Elana (2005) "In Bed with the Military: First Amendment Implications of Embedded Journalism", in: *New York University Law Review* 80(1309), 1309–1344.

Ziai, Aram (2010) "Zur Kritik des Entwicklungsdiskurses", in: *APuZ* 10, 23–29.

Zitzelsberger, Gerd (2009) "Schweizer Traditionsblatt streicht Stellen", *Süddeutsche Zeitung Online*, 3.1.2009, URL: www.sueddeutsche.de/kultur/neue-zuercher-zeitung-schweizer-traditionsblatt-streicht-stellen-1.376107 [3.10.2011].

5 Research design and methodology

This chapter sets out the research design and methods of data gathering and analysis of this study. In the third section of Chapter 1, I already outlined the combination of micro- and macro-perspectives in the research design. Here I explain it in more detail, including how it was operationalised. The first subsection gives an overview of the study approach, how data was triangulated, and what limits this approach faces. The second subsection explains the sample strategy and how the interview locations were chosen. The third subsection looks into the development of the research tools I used in this study. The fourth subsection sheds light onto processes in the field research, access to interview partners, and shares my reflections on conducting interviews. The fifth subsection delves into the methods of data analysis, followed by a methodical reflection of this form of data analysis.

To obtain data, I used the method of qualitative *semi-structured guideline-based interviews* combined with an *ego-centred network analysis* (Wolf 2004) to reveal processes and patterns in the interactions, and motives for the interactions. I interviewed foreign correspondents (*egos*) using interview guidelines, and asked about their work and relationships with humanitarian organisations (which is not a network in its original sense but a network understood in the sense of "*first/star*", see Barnes 1969). I also questioned them about their humanitarian interaction partners (*alteri*) and partners with which they did not interact(*name generators*). At the same time, I obtained data about interaction partners other than humanitarian organisations. This was important so as to be able to name other possible influencing aspects, and to understand the broader context within which the surveyed interactions take place. After the interviews with the correspondents, staff of humanitarian organisations were interviewed, comparable to control questioning of the alteri as usually done in network analysis – albeit the expression 'control questioning' in this case is not to be understood in its literal sense. I do not believe that questioning both 'sides' gives a picture that is 'more true'; questioning both actor groups rather adds more facets, and provides a more detailed picture in the end, not one that is 'more true'. Having said this, I did not consider it relevant if the statements of ego and alter were congruent throughout. Every interviewee's opinion is bound to be subjective. In this study, I considered subjective networks and subjective opinions on the interactions more important than 'actual' networks or 'facts' about the interactions. In fact, in my opinion the subjective views about the interactions form the actual interactions.

Approaching the research from this perspective meant assuming that actors act in a certain way because they are convinced of the coherence between their actions and a respective issue. Whether or not this coherence exists in form of their action's impact is irrelevant because the actors' assumption shapes their actions anyway. The action thus becomes relevant irrespective of its impact. Additionally, the interviewees were convinced that the interactions between humanitarian organisations and correspondents were essentially based on contacts between individuals. Questioning all actors involved and observing their interactions could best explore these personal contacts. The personal view of both interaction partners thus became more relevant than seemingly neutral third-party observations of the interactions.

Nevertheless, I cannot claim to draw conclusions beyond this method's constraints. I cannot argue that a certain way of covering events has certain effects on the audience by researching the actors involved in the production of news, and by then pointing out plausible consequences of patterns of interaction between the actors involved in the process. Doing so is methodologically flawed. However, several audience studies show that the way media outlets present news has effects on the way the events are perceived. So it is very plausible that, in the case of sub-Saharan Africa coverage where most audiences only know about events through the media, the presentation of events leaves an impression. My study only captures the interviewee's opinions on their interactions, and then distils patterns by comparing statements of several actors involved. I do not 'measure' the interactions and their consequences. Nevertheless, the theory of expert interviews claims that interviewing experts about their view of a specific matter, asking them to describe their actions, and questioning them about their practical experience, reveals patterns, strategies, modes, and conventions that allow conclusions to be drawn from these testimonials about the practice as to the practice itself. The 'control group' – the other side involved in the interactions – may evaluate the interaction practices very differently, and actors within the same group may describe interactions differently as well. Correspondent 'A' might have a different view and different experiences from correspondent 'B', or all correspondents' answers might show different patterns than all humanitarians' answers. I did not look for the 'correct' view in these cases. Instead, I used opposing views to balance single-sided perceptions. Finding similar structures and patterns in many interviews permitted conclusions as to actual practice; and different structures and patterns showed that the practice is multi-faceted. In the view of the interviewed experts, the practice is constituted in the way in which they explained it to me, because the interactions take place on the basis of their subjective perception of them.

Approach to sample strategy

I used a mixture of theoretical and inductive sample selection strategy (Ritchie, Lewis & Elam 2003: 78). The theoretical sampling took place on the basis of criteria that enabled answering the research questions and ensured that I could comparatively study correspondents covering sub-Saharan Africa for German-speaking, American, and British media in different kinds of employment situations. The humanitarian organisations were sampled inductively based on interviews with correspondents and supplemented by an additional pre-selection from a theoretical sampling, ensuring all kinds and all sizes of organisations were included. Besides these, I interviewed a few editors with extensive Africa experience to gain a better insight into the editors' views, correspondents with extensive embedding experience to find out to what extent we could speak of *aid embedding* when correspondents are dependent on humanitarian organisations, and fundraising experts.

Based on the interview guidelines, I conducted overall 71 qualitative in-depth interviews, including correspondents of German-speaking, British, and American quality media outlets, and news agencies. Among those were staff correspondents, freelancers, and journalists working on retainers. I included all quality newspapers and television broadcasters of record, but also – because many freelancers worked for different outlets – others for which the freelancers I interviewed regularly provided content, for example Al Jazeera, even if they did not fit the sample strategy. Applying the same method, I interviewed staff of those humanitarian organisations (mainly communications staff, programme managers, regional directors, and country directors) that the journalists interviewed in the first step had referred to as important partners or sources. I took into account all major organisations working in the relief and/or development sector. Other organisations were included when journalists repeatedly said they would try to avoid them. I used the term 'humanitarian organisation' in a very broad sense, as one aim of the study was to find out to what extent correspondents differentiate between faith-based, politically-affiliated, and independent organisations, as well as between their respective mandates.

A few correspondents were additionally interviewed (not counted in the interview total) that had extensive experience working embedded with the military in Afghanistan, and with armed rebels in Libya and Syria, who also had experiences of trips facilitated by humanitarian organisations. They were also involved in the process of applying characteristics for military embeds to journalistic dependencies on humanitarian organisations, and asked to add, delete, or specify aspects of embedding, and to point out aspects that could equally be applied to interactions with humanitarian organisations. This process added facets during the analysis process beyond searching for patterns resembling theoretical considerations on military embedding in the data. Also, two correspondents well known for their foreign reporting outside of Africa were interviewed on the assumption that they could reveal general journalistic trends and more abstract views of working processes. Following this idea, I additionally interviewed employees in strategic fundraising positions at the organisations' headquarters. The fundraising experts were questioned about their organisation's processes, interests, general fundraising strategies, and the connection between their communications and fundraising departments to reveal aspects, about which actors in the field might not have known.

Overview of interviewees according to sample strategy

Among the people I interviewed, several correspondents also had experience working for humanitarian organisations, and several humanitarian employees had experience working as journalists. The information each gave about their experience working for the other sector was added to the data together with those who exclusively worked in that other sector. Forty-seven interviews yielded data about humanitarians' perspectives, and 49 about journalists' perspectives. This accounts for the number of interviews classified as yielding data about each sector being larger than the number of interviewees from each sector, and means that the overall data set is larger than the number of the total interviewees with regards to each sector, see Figure 5.1. Another reason for inconsistent totals is that some correspondents worked for different news outlets, or spoke about their experience as staff and as freelancers in different positions.

Many interviewees were asked not only about their current position, but also any former positions with different organisations if relevant, and encouraged to compare the positions with reference to a certain issue. I interviewed correspondents and freelancers working for the media in Table 5.1, and those humanitarian organisations that these journalists said played a role in their work, see Table 5.2. The lists are in alphabetical order.

I acknowledge the limits of the statistical significance of this sample size and strategy. However, correspondents of all major news outlets, and employees of all humanitarian organisations that were identified as relevant in the interactions were interviewed. Of around 80 journalists working for British, American, and German-speaking news outlets for quality print and TV covering sub-Saharan Africa, I interviewed 50, which is more than 60 percent.[1] If a correspondent of a particular outlet was not available, I included the outlet through freelancers' experiences. The views and descriptions of the interactions can be seen as

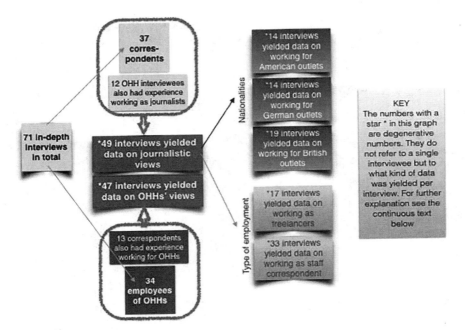

Figure 5.1 Numerical breakdown of interviewees

Table 5.1 Media outlets included in the study

MEDIA OUTLETS	
Agence France-Presse (AFP)	Neue Zürcher Zeitung (NZZ)
Al Jazeera English	Reuters
The Associated Press (AP)	Schweizer Radio und Fernsehen (SRF)
Arbeitsgemeinschaft der öffentlich-rechtlichen Rundfunkanstalten der Bundesrepublik Deutschland (ARD)	Der Spiegel
British Broadcasting Corporation (BBC)	Süddeutsche Zeitung (SZ)
Christian Science Monitor (CSM)	Die Tageszeitung (taz)
Cable News Network (CNN)	The Daily Telegraph
Deutsche Welle	The Economist
Die Zeit	The Guardian
Frankfurter Allgemeine Zeitung (FAZ)	The Independent
Foreign Affairs	Daily Mail
Foreign Policy	The Observer
Global Post	The Times
Irin	Voice of America (VOA)
The New York Times	The Wall Street Journal
Newsweek	Zweites Deutsches Fernsehen (ZDF)

Table 5.2 Humanitarian organisations included in the study

HUMANITARIAN ORGANISATIONS	
Adeso	Oxfam
Cafod	Save the Children
Care	Terre des Hommes
Echo	UNDP
HRW	UNHCR
IRC	Unicef
ICRC/IFRC	WFP
MSF	WHO
Ocha	World Vision

representative for the interactions on the African continent south of the Sahara, and revealed enough information to replicate the study (O'Reilly & Parker 2012). To saturate the data, I followed the view that data ought to be deep, "rich and thick" (Dibley 2011; Burmeister & Aitken 2012), that is multi-faceted, nuanced, and intricate, rather than only considering a large sample size as adequate. Open questions ensured richness and thickness, while the interview guidelines ensured comparability. The end of coding in the analysis and data saturation was reached when the coding no longer brought new information, concretely no new themes, and more coding was no longer feasible (Guest, Bunce & Johnson 2006).

Selection of interview location

Nairobi is, besides Johannesburg, the main base for correspondents covering sub-Saharan Africa. Kenya is also considered – apart from post-election violence in

2008 and recent terrorism attacks – relatively stable and secure; since a belt of less developed, instable countries surrounds Kenya, nearly all international humanitarian organisations coordinate projects from Nairobi in neighbouring countries, and in conflict countries with poor infrastructure. Oxfam even moved its global headquarters to Nairobi in 2017. Furthermore, the UN, which has an important role in information brokerage for media representatives, has a major presence, and two of its agencies have their global headquarters permanently in Nairobi. The tight microcosm of Nairobi's 'international community' was an ideal place to research interactions between correspondents and humanitarian organisations. That some correspondents consider South Africa "less African" than Kenya, shaping the coverage (Mükke 2009b: 211), also spoke for Kenya. Content analyses have shown that humanitarian organisations in South Africa appear less often in the reports (Mükke 2009b: 118). This might be due to South Africa perceived as not being the 'proper' Africa needing Western help. The Foreign Correspondents' Association of East Africa (FCAEA) based in Nairobi provided an easy entry point for interviews. However, since some media outlets had their only correspondent in Johannesburg, some interviews were conducted there, and in other places across sub-Saharan Africa.

Development of interview guidelines

I developed semi-structured interview guidelines (Schnell & Hill 1995: 352ff; Helfferich 2005) for this micro-macro study. To enable the maximum variance of potential answers for methodical control, I used open questions to limit the researcher's influence on answers. The questions were designed to generate narration targeting key areas including a multitude of subordinate aspects. These are the key areas:

(1) Description of the as-is state of the interactions
(2) Motives and target-state of the interactions
(3) Data and motives of the actors of both groups individually
(4) Description of the market and competition
(5) Formal aspects of the interaction
(6) Cost-benefit analysis
(7) Alternative scenarios and trends

Specific questions were only posed when the interviewees did not of their own accord touch upon predetermined topics while narrating their experiences. To guarantee no information was missed using this open type of interview format, which is based upon the natural flow of conversation, the guidelines structured the interviews systematically according to central topics while they were flexible enough to provide "the interviewees with ample space to express their views" (Littig 2009: 105). The guidelines were developed according to the "SPSS-principle" (Helfferich 2005: 1822ff, the following proceeding as suggested by Helfferich): in the first step I gathered as many questions as possible, almost resembling brainstorming. Next, the number of questions was rigorously reduced, and the questions structured and examined with regard to their openness, their implicit expectations, and relevance to the research questions using specific testing questions. In the next step, content-related aspects sorted and prioritised the remaining questions. The last step entailed gathering the bundled aspects under a guiding question or invitation intended to encourage the interviewee to narrate. The remaining questions were entered into a spreadsheet: the first column contained the guiding questions; the second listed subordinated points to help the interviewer to keep track whether essential topics had been touched in the natural course of conversation; the third column contained direct questions on topics to use when the interviewee had not addressed them. The fourth column contained meaningless motivational questions, and general questions requesting to specify what had been said to keep up the conversation. This setup of the interview guideline generally supports the self-reflection and "impulse control" (Helfferich 2005: 12) of the interviewer. It encourages reflection and restrains spontaneous reflexes to interviewee statements.

Since I interviewed two different 'groups' – journalists and staff of humanitarian organisations – two interview guidelines were developed that were nevertheless comparable. Some interviewees worked for both the media and the humanitarian sector, mostly in that order. In those circumstances, I asked questions from both guidelines. Due to limited interview time, however, I often had to make a decision for one or the other, and then chose the sector in which I considered the interviewee to be the greater expert, or for which proficiency I thought he or she might have the more divergent views to share compared to those I had already interviewed. A considerable amount of interviewees had worked for more than one organisation. If their experience differed noticeably and the other employer also fitted my sample strategy, I asked the interviewees to draw comparisons between both.

I assume that every interview is an interaction (Warren 2014). It is therefore necessary to defer to the respective interviewee, their prior knowledge, and their choice of terms, all the while applying specific conversation techniques and keeping general control of the interview to the benefit of quality criteria. During the interviews, I generally aimed at avoiding any kind of value judgement, or terms with a value connotation. For example, I used the term 'contact' instead of 'cooperation'. Overall, I adjusted my behaviour to the respective interview partner. On rare occasions, I intuitively found it helpful to provoke the interviewee with leading questions to create contradiction or agreement. I only used this technique if I was confident that this interviewee would contradict my question or statement if he or she did not have the same opinion. On a few occasions I found it necessary to create rapport by taking the interviewee's standpoint, and/or their respective attitude about a topic they had mentioned, even if it contained value judgement. I then repeated what they had said, adapting to the interviewee's tone (see also Dexter 2006: 33). In case I was not sure whether I had understood something correctly, I paraphrased back to the interviewees what they had said (Yeo et al. 2014: 198), or described neutrally what I observed, asking whether this observation was correct, for example: "You look a little uncomfortable as you are describing it, how is it making you feel?"

This handling made it possible to respond to the respective interviewee's needs. It meant that an interview with a person who was able to think reflectively and in abstract terms was akin to a process in which an issue and set of facts was acquired together with the interviewee, whereas another meeting was more strongly structured and guided by the interviewer. Some interviews were held in a completely open form. The interview guidelines nevertheless guaranteed the validity and comparability of the data, and the openness towards the interviewee's view. I took notes reflecting my own behaviour and the dynamics of the overall interview interaction. These notes made it easier to double-check individual statements, taking into account the entire context of the dynamics between interviewer and interviewee.

The majority of the interviewees referred to nearly all topics listed in the interview guidelines after they were confronted with a verbal stimulus. In addition to asking the actors to share their opinions and experiences, I asked for 'third party opinions'. This meant asking the participants of one actor group how they imagined the other actor group saw the phenomenon. What does actor x think are actor y's motives for acting in a certain way? What does actor x think is actor y's opinion about actor x? And so on. This method of data triangulation can show more facets of phenomena, and reveals a lot about the general attitude and opinion of the actor who was asked. It provides information about issues as well as the actors themselves.

In addition, questionnaires were handed out to the interviewees asking for essential background information that was not part of the interviews, such as age, years of experience, type of employment, patches, and estimated time spent travelling on work throughout the year. The following assumptions explain why the age, years of experience, type of employment, the area covered, and travelling time were ascertained in the questionnaires: pre-interviews in 2011 with journalistic key players indicated that the correspondents' attitude and interactions with humanitarian organisations changes with the amount of years that he or she works in sub-Saharan Africa. The provisional results pointed towards the idea correspondents with more work experience have less contact with humanitarian organisations. The type of employment is insofar relevant, as I assumed that staff correspondents had more financial security and more back-up from their editors, and thus did not have to rely on their contact network with humanitarian organisations providing them information, contacts, logistical, and sometimes financial support. The criteria time spent travelling and the area that one correspondent covers are linked, and I assumed also had a correlation with the interactions with humanitarian organisations: the bigger the area that one correspondent has to cover, and the less time he or she spends travelling, the smaller the travel budget that the correspondent has at his or her disposal. I therefore assumed that correspondents, who covered a large area and travel little, relied on their contacts with humanitarian organisations when they travelled. The questionnaire also contained questions about the intensity of contact between journalists and humanitarians – including a scale asking for the perceived dependency – and questions regarding the importance of contact with the other actor group in comparison to other partners. Finally, the questionnaires asked for the role model with which journalists could mainly identify, in order to detect whether the journalists' understanding of their own role and task influenced the way they interacted with humanitarian organisations. I used the models Mükke (2009b) identified as applicable to German correspondents in Africa, and tested whether correspondents of British and American outlets identified the same way. The humanitarians were asked instead with what role model they thought journalists would mainly identify, in order to gain a better understanding of the self-concept in comparison to the understanding of the other.

Access to interviewees

The data was gathered in two research trips. The first trip to Kenya took place in December 2010 and January 2011 to sound out the field and to conduct pre-study background interviews with key players, such as the chair of the FCAEA. The goal was to revise and refine research questions. The second trip took place from March to September 2014, and a few additional interviews were conducted in 2015. The then chair of the FCAEA was an important door-opener for contacts. Apart from this, interviewees were approached on the basis of internet research about correspondents covering sub-Saharan Africa. I also used private contacts in the media and in the film business, who knew journalists, as well as contacts with UN organisations to gain access to interviewees. Using a 'snowball system', I then asked people I had already interviewed for contacts of further interviewees. A pre-selection was made deciding to study media outlets and news agencies categorised as German, American, and British quality media and media of record. The interviewees were approached via email and telephone. The response rate to the first contact was good: only very few correspondents did not answer. Surprisingly, a few journalists replied very quickly to my first approach and agreed to be interviewed, but never responded to attempts to arrange a meeting. I tied that to a busy schedule, not to a disinclination to take part in the project. Most interviews took place face-to-face in the actors' work environments since this can directly influence the quality of the interviews as interviewees feel more comfortable and connected to their work when interviewed in their working environment (Hannerz 2004). With journalists working in other places across Africa at the time I arranged Skype interviews, met them when they passed through Nairobi, or in other locations.

Conducting interviews

The interviewees, experts in their field, were expected to have technical knowledge about operations, rules, and routines, and to know about the processes and sequences of interaction routines (Littig 2009: 52). Expert interviews generally allow for detailed insights into interaction processes (Tansey 2007). In regard to the journalist's role and self-conception, I did not want to predetermine answers and thus followed the method of Mükke (2009b) and Lange (2002), using qualitative interviews in addition to questionnaires to encircle the self-conception via indirect questions about it, instead of asking via standardised quantitative questionnaires (Weischenberg, Malik & Scholl 2006).

Limits of semi-structured guideline interviews do exist. An interview situation is always an interactive process of generating data between the interviewer and the interviewee (Yeo et al. 2014: 178ff). In the following, I will give insights into how I handled these interactions. One potential problem can be that the interviewee might answer according to social desirability, or anticipates the interviewer's point of view and answers accordingly. As the interviewer, I took a neutral but empathetic standpoint to create an open interview atmosphere and to obtain reliable data (Legard, Keegan & Ward 2003: 156). I principally proceeded from a willingness of the interviewees to answer all questions; they would otherwise not have agreed to meet for an interview in the first place, since I explained the research topic when I approach them. In addition, I already had the impression in pre-study interviews that the topic was generally regarded as important and as a legitimate subject for debate. I anonymised the interview data, unless the interviewee voluntarily opted to waive that option. Interestingly, most interviewees favoured anonymity. I conclude that interviewees spoke openly once they were guaranteed anonymity. I assumed that journalists and humanitarians have a socio-economic status comparable to the interviewer, so the hierarchical decline or incline between interviewer and interviewee is negligible. Occasionally I received feedback that the change in perspective was interesting for the journalists I interviewed, as normally they were the ones interviewing people, not the other way round. Through the very open interview form, it was possible to guide the interviewee rather than direct him or her, which would have influenced the data negatively. The open questions made sure that the interviewees could say what they wanted to say, so that the data could speak for themselves (Yeo et al. 2014: 190ff). To avoid interviewees worrying about their answers, or anticipating my viewpoint and answering accordingly, I said explicitly that there was no right or wrong answer, but that I was interested in learning about their personal views, attitudes, and individual experiences. Some employees of humanitarian organisations seemed initially reserved, answered unassertively, and asked questions about my personal background. I interpreted that as precaution. In the subsequent interviews, I added to my introduction to humanitarians that I had in the past worked for Unicef, which seemed to ease the interviews (for thoughts on the practice of introductions see also Dexter 2006: 50ff).

The first interview minutes were used to establish a relationship of trust. Careful and active listening ensured I was flexible enough to defer to what was said (Legard, Keegan & Ward 2003: 143). This passive role while actively listening is a "key part of interviewing" (Yeo et al. 2014: 184). In my experience, an interview situation – especially at the beginning – is always also a negotiation process between the interviewer and interviewee about who takes on which role during the interview. During this process, I endeavoured to remain open and to adapt to the interviewees' needs. For some interviewees, it seemed important to show me they were more experienced than me through leading the interview. Sometimes they would turn to topics in the beginning that were not listed as 'checks' in my interview guidelines at all. In some cases, I let the interviewee take the lead in the beginning, and took it back myself later on, once the phase of negotiating the roles was over. This always worked when I was patient enough. On very few occasions, I intervened to re-direct the interviewee back towards the topics that I wanted to talk about straight away, when the conversation completely went off-topic.

In very few interviews I observed that my own role was different from other interviews; instead of asking open questions as usual, I asked leading questions. I took notes about these observations and analysed after the interview why this had been the case. In each case, I separately came to the conclusion that the role that had implicitly been 'negotiated' at the beginning of the interview was based on a decline in hierarchy; the interviewee was very experienced, and did not want to answer broad questions triggering him or her to narrate, but get to the point instead. Furthermore, since these interviewees tried to appear as experts much more than the majority of other interviewees, and open questions that did not state clearly what I wanted to know seemed to dissatisfy them. Some literature exploring what I had observed, suggested that too open questions are not appreciated in expert interviews. I will take I_04 as an example here to illustrate what I mean.[2] I_04 had a strong personality and many years of experience as a journalist working in Africa. When I encouraged him to tell me about his experiences, he was deeply dissatisfied as that was much too unspecific a question to him. During the interview he then mentioned that "not even the foreign minister" could mislead him and that he would prove him wrong if necessary. I_04 disagreed when I suggested a certain answer via a leading question, and agreed when he was of the same opinion. He always added to my points. From this, I concluded that the data were still valid, even if I had posed leading questions, because the specific interview situation had required it. After every interview, I noted observations made during the interview about the interviewee's attitude towards discussed topics, and 'between-the-lines' impressions. These notes also contained observations about my own attitude during the interview, and dynamics of the interview. I also took notes of what had been said before I started recording and after the official interview part was over, because these "doorstep data" (Yeo et al. 2014: 189) can be very important. These notes were included in the analysis.

I met many journalists and humanitarians outside the official interview contexts during my research and in the following year that I spent in Nairobi during the analysis process. During this time, I noted down all observations ("participant observation", Schöne 2003) to use as background information for the analysis. For *data triangulation*, I applied a combination of qualitative and quantitative data analysis methods that complemented one another (Foley, Farmer & Petronis 2006; Whitney 2007), as I will discuss in the following subsection. Additionally I researched 'third party opinions', asking the participants of one actor group how they imagined the other actor group saw a phenomenon, or how they saw the other actor group. This method also added more facets of phenomena and helped data triangulation.

Methods of data analysis

This subsection is dedicated to making the process of data analysis transparent, and to explicate, and thus validate, conclusions from the data (Barbour 2007: 131ff). The first part of this subsection lays out how the data were handled, and gives a short overview of the software used; the second explains the approach to deductive and inductive category building; and the third describes the analysis process, including the strategy of organising and documenting the analysis with the qualitative software MAXQDA.

Professional transcription services were used to transcribe the interviews, according to transcription rules that followed the version of "simple transcription" with some extensions as per Dresing and Pehl (2013: 22ff). I added a few specifications, and excluded others; in principle, I preferred to have more information that would later turn out to be dispensable, than the other way around. All interviews were transcribed in their full length and word-by-word to reduce information loss. The transcripts captured the content of what was said, as well as to a certain extent how it was said, to enable the reconstruction of the communicative sense of the interview later in the analysis process if necessary. Apart from spoken words, the transcripts also contain "pauses, laughing, and other features of talk such as sighing or coughing, interruptions [. . .], emphasis" (Rapley 2012: 547) to capture actual meaning. All interviews were anonymised, and given a number to trace statements from the same speaker, to connect the interview content with the respective questionnaire and with the interview notes. The organisation that the interviewee worked for remained only if other available information did not make it possible to identify the speaker this way.[3] All other information enabling the identification of an interviewee was removed or generalised.

Relying on the software MAXQDA for qualitative data analysis made it easier to keep the analysis process transparent since it allows for organising, documenting, and commenting on the process. The software assists in organising the coding of texts, and allows for two different types of 'variables' to be applied. It permits you to choose which documents and which codes should be included in singular analysis steps, features *retrieval tools* in order to search for patterns and coherences within the data, and can display results graphically to make it easier to see coherences at a glance. It also facilitates establishing links between texts, which simplifies drawing conclusions from the data. The interview transcripts, interview notes on the interview situation, background information received during the interviews, and the questionnaires were uploaded into the software. In so-called *memos*, I added inductive remarks and ideas that occurred to me while reading the interview transcripts during the analysis process. All these materials were then coded with the help of the software. *Coding* in this context means applying keywords to certain text passages, like indexing a text. In qualitative analysis, this entails undertaking an interpretative exploration of the material in a search for categories, which in the beginning phase remain preliminary, and are understood as a provisional rapprochement to issues in dialogue with the data. Coding the data, and assigning abstract concepts, key categories, and terms to certain segments of the data, enables you to later on search for and find these segments that are relevant for a certain research question or a certain issue, even if this issue does not exist literally within the data itself. I attached a *code-memo* to each *code*. This means that each code was supplied with a short explanation when this code should be applied to a section in the text; for example, 'use this code whenever an interviewee talks about his or her motives for the interactions'. The code-memos were updated if necessary during the process of applying the codes to more data. To stay with the example given, when I later on split the general code 'motives for interaction' into several more precise codes naming the type of motives, each of those was provided with their own code-memo on when to use it. One sub-code under 'motives for interaction' was, for example, 'security'. I then attached the code-memo explaining when to use this code. A code consists of a string of up to 64 characters, and can have several *sub-codes*, and *sub-sub-codes*, building a *code tree*. A code that encompasses sub-codes is similar to a *category*, summarising several sub-codes under a subordinating term. Having said this, a category is normally more abstract and not as close to a text as a code; the latter *indexes* the data. In MAXQDA, each code can be evaluated on a scale from 0 to 100, which makes it easier to keep track of the importance of some codes in comparison to others in relation to research questions. The evaluation of a code, and its position within a code tree, can be changed at any time during the analysis process. Several code trees can be generated for several sets of data.

Apart from organising the data with the help of codes, the software allows for extended lexical search within the original data itself. At the same time, the researcher can choose which type of documents are to be searched – for example, all interviews with journalists only, all interviews with staff correspondents only, and so on. You can exclude or include certain 'document variables' that you attributed to the documents during the analysis, such as 'working experience of the correspondents', 'type of employment', 'nationality of the media outlet' etc., which then narrows down the lexical search again. I used document and code-memos within the software to summarise general thoughts on interview passages, or to bring together quotes from different interviews about a certain issue, which – incorporated in various text passages – I had earlier grouped under a certain code.

Generally, I applied a mix of an *inductive and deductive open coding* strategy to develop categories (*codes*). I read the interview transcripts systematically, marking all passages that seemed especially interesting, to then read those more closely. On the basis of theoretical assumptions laid out in the theory chapters of the study, I developed a category system that I applied in form of codes to all other material. Most codes were inductively derived from the data, and remained preliminary in the beginning, while they were applied to the transcripts to check if they were sustainable when applied to a larger set of data. They were confirmed or revised during the ongoing analysis process. The open coding process meant that certain issues and arguments were followed and others were dropped if the comparison with other text segments, and segments in other interviews, made them appear implausible explanations for issues observed. At the same time, I generally coded as much material as possible to ensure that in the final analysis of the material that I had pre-sorted in this way, I could speak of singular cases as well as patterns that were revealed from cases that repeated over many interviews.

Some *deductive* codes were used, derived from presumptions developed in pre-interviews and the theoretical reflections, which already informed the drawing up of the interview guidelines. In case the data material contradicted the deductive codes or added more dimensions to them, I always gave the data predominance, and revised codes when necessary. Many issues did not fit any deductively developed codes. In these cases, I inductively created new codes according to the data's messages. This way, many categories and sub-categories (*codes* and *sub-codes* as explained earlier) were inductively derived from the data, and specified during the coding process when applied to larger set of data. Statements that completely opposed each other were categorised under the same code. For example, the code 'importance of interaction' was applied when an interview passage contained a statement that the interaction was seen as very important from the interviewee's perspective and when it was not considered important at all. This ensured that the full perspective on a phenomenon could be revealed. Some of the codes applied only to either aid workers or journalists. Others applied to both. To many sections in the interviews, several codes were applied at the same time. To give a concrete example: in one transcript, a correspondent explained in one paragraph how a field visit to a humanitarian project took place, why, and to which one. In this example, the code 'description of interaction > sub-code: field visit' could be applied, as could the code 'motives for interaction > sub-code: convenience', and 'motives for interaction > sub-code: time pressure'. When the interviewee expressed that he or she could not have gone without the humanitarian organisation facilitating the visit, the code 'importance of interaction > sub-code: dependency' was applied as well. The same paragraph could also include the journalist's opinion of his or her own role, to add the code 'self-perception of role and behaviour/motivation for the job', and so on. All relevant codes were applied to a section to include this information in all topics for which it could be relevant. These steps resemble Gläser and Laudel's methodology of identifying and sorting raw data by structuring the material according to pre-assumptions and theoretical background, and structuring the data by indexing, that is linking the text to research questions and themes via categories (Gläser & Laudel 2013: 25ff), that is *codes* speaking in MAXQDA terminology, see Figure 5.2. Gläser and Laudel also suggest applying a mix of data- and theory-driven categories that are adjusted as information is gleaned from the data, and to keep the indexing process open in order to be open for unexpected information (Gläser & Laudel 2013: 27).

The described process of coding helped organise and structure the data in a way that made it easier to detect within the material general patterns of actor behaviour and attitude, formulas, strategies, modes, and conventions. MAXQDA allows all statements regarding an issue, or passages that could help answer a certain research question, to be available at one sight. With the software, conclusions can become more evident, for example by the option of searching for codes in a defined proximity of another certain code. During the coding process, for example, I applied the code 'interviewee feels uncomfortable' to transcript passages

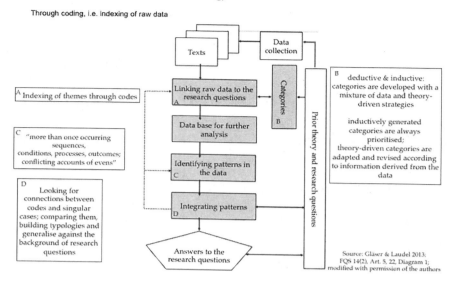

Figure 5.2 Data analysis

where the interviewee suddenly referred to the anonymity of the interview, said that this part should be off record, or if I had observed that the interviewee showed signs of nervousness. That way I could at a later stage ask the software to show me what other codes had been applied in the proximity of this code, and from that conclude which issues generally made interviewees feel uncomfortable, when I suspected patterns. The software also helps to draw conclusions by adding or subtracting so-called *document variables*. Document variables are aspects that characterise the interviewee. They can be applied to a certain document, in this case an interview transcript, for example, the type of employment, the interviewees experience etc. Later on in the analysis process, you then have the option to use these document variables to detect differences in the material according to the respective aspect (*variable*). You can thus use the software to show whether interviewees' answers regarding a certain research interest vary with regards to a certain document variable. To give some practical examples: since I wanted to know whether correspondents' employment status affected the way they dealt with humanitarian organisations,[4] one document variable I applied to each transcript was 'type of employment'. I differentiated between 'staff', 'freelancer', and 'working on retainer'. The latter was in doubt and rather counted as a freelancer because the monthly prepayment was often not enough to make a living. During the analysis, the software could then show whether interviewees' answers on any topic obviously differed between freelance and staff correspondents. I assumed that there would be differences between correspondents of American, British, and German-speaking media outlets, with their different traditions and guidelines, so I applied the document variable 'nationality' to all transcripts; and since I wanted to find out whether it made a difference how long a correspondent had been working in Africa, I applied the document variable 'experience' and differentiated the number of years.[5]

For the analysis I used a mixed-methods approach. The interviews provided an insight into the interviewees' interpretation and perception of their own actions and interactions, as well as their view on thematic issues that were analysed with computer-aided content analysis, applying thematic categories with an inductive open coding scheme to the *qualitative* data. At the same time, I *quantified* some data to supplement the qualitative results and to test some of the hypotheses (Beck 2003). The questionnaires handed to the interviewees also produced some quantitative data. Those were quantified with MAXQDA via document variables applied to interview transcripts, for example experience, which was rated according to the number of years the correspondent had been working in sub-Saharan Africa, in order to then analyse answers interviewees with varying experience gave to various thematic issues. In this given example, it served to prove the hypothesis that the years of experience of a correspondent working in Africa does influence how he or she perceives the dependency on humanitarian organisations. Other quantifiable data collected included:

(1) The estimated time correspondents spent travelling for research
(2) The type of contacts interviewees named, chosen by ticking boxes
(3) The frequency of contact
(4) Binary questions such as "do you consider it easier to publish a report if it features a humanitarian organisation"[6]
(5) The perception of the intensity of some identified categories, such as the dependency of humanitarians and correspondents on one other, rated from 1 (little) to 10 (very much)
(6) The intensity of importance of the interviewee's contact with the other group for his or her work, also rated from 1 to 10
(7) The intensity of the importance of private contacts for successful public relations
(8) The importance of contacts for work in relation to contacts with other partners
(9) With which role models correspondents mainly identified, which was surveyed by ticking boxes with several predefined options

The latter results could then be compared to the choices of role models with which humanitarian workers thought journalists would mainly identify. Interestingly, they differed significantly. In combination with qualitative material from the interviews, this could lead to a better understanding of each sector's approach to the other, by comparing the self-perception of one group with how the other group thought the first perceived itself. The scoring system is subjective due to the respective interviewee's perception. However, this perception leads to the interviewees acting in a certain manner, and thus can be interpreted as practice-relevant.[7]

The questionnaires were used to gather background information on the interviewees, such as the amount of years they had worked in a certain position, the amount of years journalists had worked in Africa overall, with what journalists the aid workers were regularly in contact, and the other way around, which ones they tried to avoid and why, which ones they considered especially important to their work, and what these contacts were mainly about. Some ordinal measurement questions aimed at gathering data on the perceived dependency and importance of interaction for both sides. Most interviewees were asked these questions during the interviews. Only the ones where interview time was very limited were handed the questionnaire. The questionnaires were analysed through coding, and certain sub-groups were filtered. The questionnaire results were then combined with interviewee's answers regarding specific issues in the interviews if the same person had also filled in a questionnaire. In case the interviewee had not filled the questionnaire, in 90 percent of the interviews the questionnaire questions were asked during the interview. Substituting the questionnaires, then interview answers were coded accordingly. This meant that although questionnaire returns were not high, the combination with answers from the interviews enabled me to gather representative results.

Already during the coding process of the interviews, some patterns were revealed that needed proving through the analysis of a wider set of data. These first observations, and all questions arising during the coding process, were captured in so-called *free memos* in the analysis software. In the analysis, in order to detect patterns of actions, or to understand a certain phenomenon, I instructed the software to display all sections that shared a certain code that I assumed would give more insight into that phenomenon. Additionally, adding or subtracting document variables could filter these coding lists. The software then created a list of all the relevant coded sections, so-called *codings*, allowing me to go through them one by one and to cluster similar or opposing answers. This process made it possible to get a quick overview of the data, and to draw conclusions from it. Whenever possible, I grouped statements and quantified them. In all cases, examples from the interviews were added to the newly created clusters. I always made sure that the examples given in my final results were not one-sided but that all different opinions were included. This process of searching for patterns and identifying procedures and practices, as well as conditions under which these occur, is followed by the attempt to summarise patterns that can be grouped under one single mother-pattern, and the study of data that does not fit that scheme (Gläser & Laudel 2013: 37).

In the process of conceptualising the phenomenon of embedded journalism and detaching it from the military sense to apply it to interactions with humanitarian organisations, I filtered out characteristics of the mainly descriptive research on military embedding and then discussed this with journalists who have extensive experience with both embedding with the military and interacting with humanitarian organisations. With these journalists, I also discussed which of the characteristics from their experience they felt could be applied to interactions with humanitarian organisations. These discussions were held over the phone or via email, and only concerned the analysis regarding the conceptualisation of embedding. They are independent of the interviews in the general interviewing phase, during which I also asked all interviewees to what extent they would consider the interactions comparable to embedding with the military.

Reflections on the data analysis process

Qualitative studies and quantitative studies look at phenomena in a different way. Whereas quantitative research puts emphasis on – as the name says – quantity, leaving little room for depth and exploration, qualitative studies dig deeper into phenomena, exploring cases of individuals standing representatively for their kind. It may seem that qualitative studies are less objective than quantitative studies and analyses because they lack the sample size that seemingly makes the data more robust. However, in my view the distinction mainly lies in overcoming difficulties in different phases of the research. Due to the nature of quantitative research, questions are usually close-ended or multiple-choice options for answers that are given, which brings up the challenge of pre-defining answers and thus data. In contrast, qualitative research does not face this problem with the same intensity, since – if done diligently – it is much easier to minimise biases by asking open questions and triangulating data through different methods, e.g. ethnographical observations. The challenge then rather lies in eliminating biases during the analysis process. I handled this challenge through applying a mix of deductive and inductive codes, and by keeping the coding process open throughout the analysis process. Whenever data did not fit any of the categories applied so far, I added a new category and in the following went through all material again to see whether this new category applied to any of the earlier data. The analysis process consisted of a constant back and forth between close reading, making up categories to which the material was applied, adapting these categories whenever necessary and then going back through the material, see also Figure 5.2. At the same time, I created very broad categories in the beginning, identifying overarching themes in the material and defined them more and more throughout the analysis process. The categories did not carry any of my value judgement but were mere descriptive headlines that could summarise the material. However, the interpretation of qualitative data overall is a reflexive process that *creates* meaning based on data, comparing cases, rather than *finding* meaning in the data (Mauthner & Doucet 2003). Since every researcher brings pre-existing ideas to a study, even if he or she is trying to minimise biases as much as possible, it is even more crucial that all hypotheses and proceedings are made transparent. This is why I listed all hypotheses in Chapter 1, explained my constructivist perspective, and laid out my view on what role journalism *should* play in Chapter 4. This is also why this Chapter 5 is lengthy: its aim was to explain as detailed as possible how I proceeded developing the research tools, gathering the data, including the handling of interview situations, and analysing the material. The next chapter will now present the findings of this study, look at reporting conditions, journalists' experience in Africa, editorial policies, journalists and humanitarians' views on each other, the background and perspective from which humanitarian organisations come to the cooperation, and look into details of the interactions between journalists and humanitarians in practice, giving individual accounts and generalising wherever the data allowed for a broader perspective.

Notes

1. The estimated overall numbers of journalists working for the outlets relevant for this study was received through the correspondents' associations where journalists who are staff or regularly work for international outlets are registered. The headcount only included the journalists fitting the sample strategy.
2. The interviews for this study were all anonymised. I stands for Interview and the randomly given number replaces the interviewee's name.
3. For example, if I cited someone as the spokesperson of organisation x, it would be easy to identify this person, even if I did not state his or her name. Due to the reduced number of correspondents, the same is true for many of them. If I said the correspondent of The New York Times states xyz, I could equally state his or her name, as there are only very few correspondents working for this newspaper in Africa. In cases like this, I then referred to the interviewee as 'a correspondent of a large US-based media outlet', or something similar.
4. See presumptions in Chapter 4, section 4.1.
5. Foley et al (2006) used a similar mixed-method approach, conducting semi-structured interviews and combining them with quantitative methods to explore the variation of topics according to type of cancer, age group etc. per interviewee, which can be compared to this study's approach to explore variations in answers according to the applied document variables (experience, type of employment etc.).
6. A similar attempt combining qualitative and quantitative analysis was undertaken in the study on community leadership by Whitney (2007), determining themes in the qualitative interviews and the understanding the correlation between certain themes quantitatively by applying binary coding.
7. See also the argumentation in the beginning of Chapter 5.

References

Barbour, Rosaline (2007) *Doing Focus Groups*, London.
Barnes, John A. (1969) "Graph Theory and Social Networks", in: *Sociology* 3, 215–232.
Beck, Cheryl Tatano (2003) "Initiation Into Qualitative Data Analysis", in: *Journal of Nursing Education* 42(5), 231–234.
Burmeister, Elizabeth and Aitken, Leanne (2012) "Sample Size: How Many is Enough?", in: *Australian Critical Care* 25(4), 271–274.
Dexter, Lewis (2006) *Elite and Specialized Interviewing*, Colchester.
Dibley, Lesley (2011) "Analyzing Narrative Data Using McCormack's Lenses", in: *Nurse Researcher* 18(3), 13–19.
Dresing, Thorsten and Pehl, Thorsten (2013, 5th edition) *Praxisbuch Interview, Transkription & Analyse: Anleitungen und Regelsysteme für qualitativ Forschende*, Marburg.
Foley, Kristie, Farmer, Deborah and Petronis, Vida (2006) "A Qualitative Exploration of the Cancer Experience Among Long-Term Survivors: Comparisons by Cancer Type, Ethnicity, Gender, and Age", in: *Psycho-Oncology* 15, 248–258.
Gläser, Jochen and Laudel, Grit (2013) "Life With and Without Coding: Two Methods of Early-Stage Data Analysis in Qualitative Research Aiming at Causal Explanations", in: *FQS* 14(2), Art. 5.
Guest, Greg, Bunce, Arwen and Johnson, Laura (2006) "How Many Interviews are enough? An Experiment with Data Saturation and Variability", in: *Field Methods* 18(1), 59–82.

Hannerz, Ulf (2004) *Foreign News; Exploring the World of Foreign Correspondents*, Chicago.
Helfferich, Cornelia (2005) *Die Qualität qualitativer Daten: Manual für die Durchführung qualitativer Interviews*, Wiesbaden.
Lange, Silvia (2002) "Auf verlorenem Posten?", *Deutschsprachige Auslandskorrespondenten in Lateinamerika. Eine qualitative Kommunikatorstudie zur Arbeitsrealität und Rollenverständnis. Magisterarbeit*, FU Berlin.
Legard, R., Keegan, J. and Ward, K. I. (2003). "In-depth Interviews", in: Jane Ritchie and Jane Lewis (Eds.), *Qualitative Research Practice – a Guide for Social Science Students and Researchers*, 138–169, London.
Littig, Beate (2009) "Interviewing the Elite – Interviewing Experts. Is there a Difference?", in: Aleksander Bogner, Beate Littig and Wolfgang Menz (Eds.), *Interviewing Experts*, Houndmills.
Mauthner, Natasha and Doucet, Andrea (2003) "Reflexive Accounts and Accounts of Reflexivity in Qualitative Data Analysis", in: *Sociology* 37(3), 413–431.
Mükke, Lutz (2009b) *'Journalisten der Finsternis'. Akteure, Strukturen und Potenziale deutscher Afrika-Berichterstattung*, Köln.
O'Reilly, Michelle and Parker, Nicola (2012) "Unsatisfactory Saturation: A Critical Exploration of the Notion of Saturated Sample Sizes in Qualitative Research", in: *Qualitative Research Journal* (May), 1–8.
Rapley, Tim (2012) "The (Extra)Ordinary Practices of Qualitative Interviewing", in: Jaber Gubrium, James Holstein, Amir Marvasti and Karyn McKinney (Eds.), *Sage Handbook of Interview Research. The Complexity of the Craft*, Thousand Oaks, 541–554.
Ritchie, Jane, Lewis, Jane and Elam, Gillian (2003) "Designing and Selecting Samples", in: Jane Ritchie and Jane Lewis (Eds.), *Qualitative Research Practice. A Guide for Social Sciences Students and Researchers*, Thousand Oaks, 77–108.
Schnell, Rainer and Hill, Paul B. (1995, 5th. edition) *Methoden der empirischen Sozialforschung*, München.
Schöne, Helmar (2003) "Die teilnehmende Beobachtung als Datenerhebungsmethode in der Politikwissenschaft", in: *Forum: Qualitative Social Research* 4(2).
Tansey, Oisín (2007) "Process Tracing and Elite Interviewing. A Case for Non- Probability Sampling", in: *Political Science and Politics* 40(4), 765–772.
Warren, Carol (2014) "Interviewing As Social Interaction", in: Jaber Gubrium, James Holstein and Amir Marvasti (Eds.), *SAGE Handbook of Interview Research: The Complexity of the Craft*, Thousand Oaks, 129–142.
Weischenberg, Siegfried, Malik, Maja and Scholl, Armin (2006) "Journalismus in Deutschland 2005", in: *Media Perspektiven* 7, 346–361.
Whitney, Richard (2007) *What Community Leaders Say about the Leadership Process: A Mixed methods Study of Identity, Resilience, and Self-Efficacy*, University of Nevada.
Wolf, Christof (2004) "Egozentrierte Netzwerke. Erhebungsverfahren und Datenqualität", in: Andreas Diekmann (Ed.), *Methoden der Sozialforschung. Sonderheft der Kölner Zeitschrift für Soziologie und Sozialpsychologie*, Vol. 44, 244–273.
Yeo, Alice, Legard, Robin, Keegan, Jill, Ward, Kit, McNaughton Nicholls, Carol and Lewis, Jane (2014) "In-Depth Interviews", in: Jane Ritchie, Jane Lewis, Carol McNaughton Nicholls and Rachel Ormston (Eds.), *Qualitative Research Practice. A Guide for Social Science Students and Researchers*, Los Angeles, London, 177–208.

6 Research findings

In earlier chapters, I have occasionally referred to some research results when they matched the theoretical assumptions or the general subject of the chapters or sections. Now, I will present the results of the research in a compact form. The first two sections, 6.1 and 6.2, discuss the findings regarding the framework that defines the journalists' and humanitarians' work and the conditions under which they operate. This implies both the general framework their sectors entail, which define the individuals' actions to a certain degree, and the conditions that working in the special regional context of sub-Saharan Africa brings for both sectors. Wherever possible, I will make the connection between these conditions and what they mean for the interactions with the other sector and its individual actors. So sections 6.1 and 6.2 essentially answer the question how the interactions take place and why they are necessary from both sectors' perspectives in the first place. The third section, 6.3, is devoted to the interactions themselves, answering questions of their nature – what the interactions are about, how they take place, and how individuals make contact with each other. The forth section, 6.4, then highlights what challenges the interactions bear, and how they are viewed from both perspectives. The fifth section, 6.5, explores the overall importance of the interactions, and their tendency for dependencies. The sixth section 6.6 contextualises the interactions within embedded journalism. It argues that under certain circumstances we can speak of *aid embedding*. Section 6.7 lays out how the framework of both sectors generally, and the regional context of sub-Saharan Africa, forces the media and aid sector to interact, and how these interactions influence the media coverage to an, as I argue, worrying extent. Section 6.8 finally highlights a general trend towards the blurring of lines between the media and aid sector.

6.1 Framework and conditions defining the interactions – journalists

This section sheds light on the conditions that lead to interactions between humanitarian organisations and correspondents in the first place, and explains how these conditions influence the correspondents and editors. First, the large size of the patches that correspondents working in sub-Saharan Africa are covering is thematised. Following and directly liked to this, the next subsections explore the amount that correspondents travel, their working experience, and their budgets. The fourth subsection elucidates the editorial policies, guidelines, and editors role affecting the correspondents' work and their interaction with humanitarian organisations. The last subsection explores the correspondents' self-perception, and its role in correspondents' interaction with humanitarian organisations.

Common geographic division of Western media coverage of Africa

Africa is the world's second-largest continent by area. In 2015, sub-Saharan Africa counted 949 million inhabitants and by 2030 it is estimated the population will have increased to 1.4 billion; yet the gross national income per capita in 2015 was only USD 3,480 (Population Reference Bureau 2015: 11).[1] This partly explains why the aid and development sector is still growing in sub-Saharan Africa. The correspondents surveyed for this research cover on an average 17 countries. Of those people who responded to the question how many countries they cover, seven said 21 countries, two said 37 countries, and four respondents said 49 countries, which is the entire continent south of the Sahara. The remaining correspondents said their patch contained 13 countries or fewer but these patches then nearly always included South Africa, from where traditionally more Western media coverage takes place than from other countries in Africa. There is little consistency in how Western media organisations divide sub-Saharan Africa into different geographical regions and assign a correspondent to cover so-called *patches*: Southern Africa, Central Africa, East Africa, Horn of Africa (usually added to East Africa), and Western Africa (see Figure 6.1). To understand the sheer size of the patches, the following graphic displays other countries fitted into the shape of the African continent (see Figure 6.2).[2] So if one correspondent covers East, Central, and West Africa, which is common among Western media that then also post one other colleague in Southern Africa, he or she is responsible for news coverage of an area equal to Eastern Europe, the United States, India, and large parts of China combined. As I already argued in the introductory chapter and section on work conditions, it is almost impossible for any correspondent to regularly travel to all countries in his or her patch, and some correspondents have never been to some of the countries that they are responsible to cover. In the next subsection I will therefore explore how much correspondents travel, and whether their editors are willing to spend money on travelling. I also investigate the level of correspondents' regional working experience.

Travelling and working experience

The correspondents who took part in my research travel an average of 112 days a year for reporting, which is roughly 30 percent of their time. How much a single correspondent travels ranges from between a few days per month to several months a year. Nearly all of the correspondents said that their editors are much stricter with travel expenses today compared to some years ago. An interviewee said: "Even major media houses tend to send people to Africa or especially Nairobi

120 *Research findings – framework journalist*

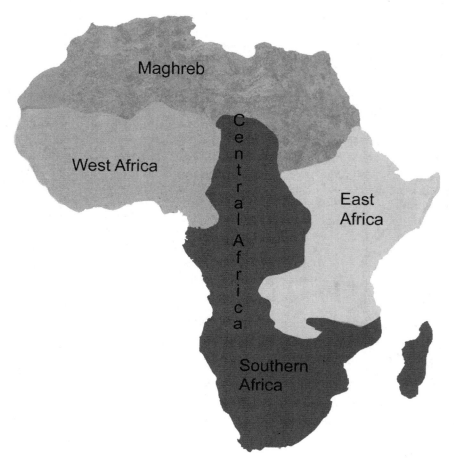

Figure 6.1 Map of common geographic division of Western media coverage of Africa

as sort of a proving ground" (I_41). While it may be true that freelance journalists working in Africa tend to be young, correspondents of major newspapers still counterbalance inexperienced correspondents by the sheer number of years of working experience they have had in sub-Saharan Africa. Most correspondents, that is 58 percent, had been working in sub-Saharan Africa for between four and seven years when I interviewed them; most of those said they had worked in Africa for five years. Another 30 percent had worked between nine and 16 years, and 12 percent have less than four years of working experience in sub-Saharan Africa.

When looking in more detail and differentiating between staff and freelancers (see Figures 6.3 and 6.4, one graph shows freelancers, one staff only), the data show that exactly half of the staff correspondents interviewed have worked in

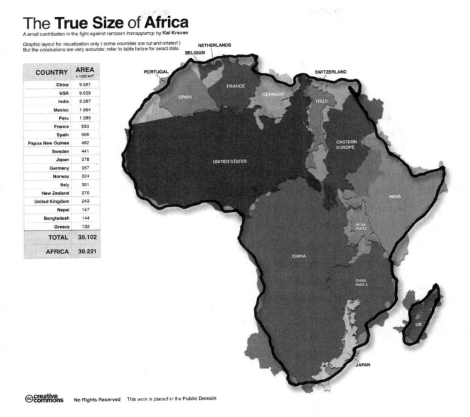

Figure 6.2 The true size of Africa
Source: Krause, Kai (2010), URL: http://kai.sub.blue/en/Africa.html [12.1.2016].

Africa for between four and seven years – most of them for seven – while another quarter had between nine and 16 years' experience, and a fifth less than four. The majority of freelancers, 71 percent, had working experience in Africa between four and seven years – with a peak of 33 percent with five years of experience. Similarly most freelancers – 71 percent – had between four and seven years' experience, almost a third had more than nine years, and nearly a fifth had been working in Africa for 11 years.

Overall, the data do not prove that freelancers are less experienced than staff, which may be because a number of former staff correspondents started working as freelancers. Freelancers, however, are younger compared to most staff correspondents. "The situation of news means there's less and less money, and life is more and more expensive. So it's hard to make a living being just freelance" (I_21). Only after I switched off the recorder after the interview, the same interviewee said: "I've worked for Unicef while freelancing, writing press releases.

122 Research findings – framework journalist

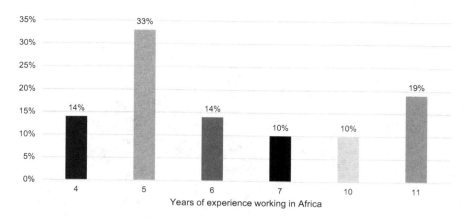

Figure 6.3 Working experience of correspondents working in Africa – freelancers and retainers only

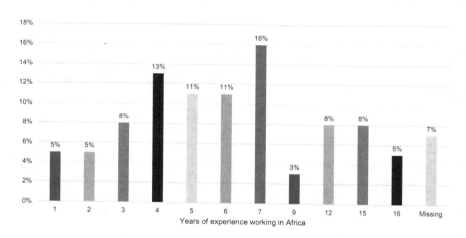

Figure 6.4 Working experience of correspondents working in Africa – staff only

They paid well" (I_21).[3] This phenomenon of freelance journalists working on commission for humanitarian organisations I will describe in detail in sections 6.4 and 6.5. A recurring pattern in my study is that well-paid staff positions have become the exception, and that freelance journalists find it tough to make a living.

Regional experience and understanding of regional context is very important to frame news beyond stereotypes. A correspondent of a German outlet said:

> Even if you did African studies and knew a lot, you would have to revise a lot of things living in the field yourself. Of course, I see and assess things differently than in the beginning. Even if I don't have to completely throw a

former opinion, I see the matter much more differentiated than earlier on in my career here. That clearly is a question of experience on the ground.

(I_26)

A humanitarian working for UNHCR with a long background in reporting herself explained her approach to journalists with different levels of experience:

> In my experience as a reporter, [what] [. . .] made me a better reporter [is] having reported for a longer period of time and in different parts of the world. There's a perspective that you won't necessarily get if [you are] just in one place. But then there's also a level of understanding of a place that comes with spending more time there. So I think your reporting is enriched by more experiences and by fresh eyes. It's good either way and it's just important, I think, [in my position with UNHCR now] [. . .] to understand what that experience level is of the reporter that I'm dealing with. Partly so I can anticipate the kind of things they may ask. Is it someone who has never been into a refugee camp before and doesn't understand that, absolutely EVERYBODY you talk to is going to say 'they don't have enough food?' Or we can check and somebody says, 'We haven't gotten food rations'.
>
> (I_54)

Journalists who have been in sub-Saharan Africa for longer reported they were more concerned with over-close relations with humanitarian organisations, and more clearly saw the issues of too tight a relationship with them. For this finding, I will let interviewees speak for themselves: a regional spokesperson with a lot of experience in the field for a large UN organisation, told me that inexperienced journalists were "more likely to rely on humanitarian organisations for support in a difficult environment" (I_54). Another interviewee, looking back on seven years of experience covering sub-Saharan Africa as a freelance correspondent, said that in her view the motto of the humanitarian sector is: "Never solve the problem that feeds you" (I_08). A correspondent said that as his experience increased, he became more critical with humanitarian organisations:

> I notice that I have a more critical view now what a humanitarian organisation does, how successful they are and how useful it REALLY is what they do. Or to what extent the work of humanitarian organisations [. . .] compensates things that the government should be responsible for. [. . .] The more I see, experience, and understand coherences, the more CRITICAL my opinion becomes. However, critical does not necessarily only mean negative. [. . .] But it has the long-term effect of governments resting on humanitarians stepping in.
>
> (I_28)

Another interviewee told me she attended many humanitarian organisations' press conferences at the beginning of her career in Africa, and the more experience she gained over five years working based in Kenya, the less often she went (I_30). Staff of humanitarian organisations who were more media-savvy noted how journalistic experience affected the correspondents' reporting in crisis areas:

> You could see the differences in age and experience of journalist groups. We sometimes had groups that were very young and not very experienced, [. . .] and they for example filmed a lot inside our [aid] compound, which we don't particularly appreciate.
>
> (I_64)

Data showed correlations between a correspondents' years of experience, their perceptions of humanitarian organisations, and of working with them. I will explain more on this in section 6.5. However, more experience in reporting from sub-Saharan Africa is not only seen as positive. It can also make the reporter 'blind' to obvious things that might interest his or her audience; which is how we come back to the importance of travelling despite shrinking travel budgets:

> It's important to keep travelling because you do become, as a journalist you start to not see the things that are right in front of you because they're not new anymore. And [. . .] I'm not writing for people in Nairobi. I'm writing for people outside Kenya or outside of Africa.
>
> (I_21)

Another interviewee, a consultant for a major humanitarian INGO dealing with children, said that in her opinion some correspondents' inexperience makes for more crisis-focused headlines:

> They've come out of college. They want a few years travelling through Africa. They decide to be journalists. And they can live on USD 100, USD 200 for a story. But they could get very worked up and excited about it. It's their first time ever seeing a drought – they suddenly turn it into a famine. They've seen one skinny baby – everyone's dying. [. . .] Whereas, maybe someone who's a correspondent and has been based here for five years, they've got a proper salary and they're bound by the regulations and rules of their bureau. There would have been, let's say, a higher quality, a more solid form of reporting. But those days are gone.
>
> (I_46)

Budget

All correspondents produce commissioned news only. Either the editors instruct them to produce a certain piece on a certain issue, or the correspondents pitch an idea to the outlet first and wait for the editor to give the green light before they travel for the reporting, or decide against going if the editors do not agree. The small budgets lead to a closer relationship with humanitarian organisations, and the research showed that descriptions of this phenomenon are very similar across almost all media outlets. A correspondent described the situation as follows:

> I mean ultimately I probably go with whoever can get me there and whoever can get me there the cheapest, or for free because the cost of a trip is the difference between reporting a story or not. It's just how it is. It would be great if we had endless amounts of money so we could just say, well, what the hell, there is the place to go for the malnutrition story and I'm chartering a plane, I'll be independent, I'm going to take a guide, I'm going to do my own thing. Never going to happen. [. . .] One of the UN flights to the place we wanted to get to would cost an extra USD 600 return, and that would have [meant] that I wasn't doing the story. So I had to explain that to [this NGO that this was too expensive] to see their clinic and see what is going on there. So then they [put me on one of their flights instead][. . .]. So if you can save USD 200, USD 500, USD 600, USD 1000, then you are going to get the story done, and if you can't, then it won't get reported. [. . .] [The situation also works for the editors] because they don't need to pay for stuff and in the end they get stories for free.
>
> (I_23)

In places that are hard to access, be it because of war, crisis, or simply because the infrastructure is poor, budget constraints and logistical support from outside partners play an even bigger role:

> I think in South Sudan, just logistically, whether you were staff or whether you were freelance, it was tricky. [. . .] Often we are relying increasingly on these [I]NGOs for flights, logistically AND ALSO just expense-wise. [. . .] The WFP commercial [flights] in Juba were – I mean they started off at USD400 return and I think they went up to like USD800, and with the UN peacekeeping mission, they were all free. So, you know, even your editors, even if they're willing to pay, they don't really want to pay USD800 for you to cover a conflict that really no one in the UK or France is going to care about. [. . .] I think it's a, especially as media budgets shrink and as Africa news falls off the radar slightly, especially with what's going on in the Middle East, I think it's very – it's an interesting time to evaluate [I]NGO and media outlet relationships.
>
> (I_43)

As well as flight costs, other logistical help provided by humanitarian organisations can lower the costs of a reporting trip:

> It's a sometimes functional relationship. If media had more money, I think that . . . you would just do these things off your own back. But when someone's offering it on a plate to you and saying: Okay, here's this story. Would you like to come? We'll organise cars, accommodation and this and this. [. . .]

Then it, yeah, I think that a lot of media outlets would see this as a good deal. And if, and the ones that have said that they can't accept any more free things, would look at a story and weigh it up on just its editorial merit and say: No, actually we're willing to pay GBP 2,000 to send a correspondent there.

(I_43)

However, not all correspondents experience such financial constraints. An interviewee of a German-speaking newspaper admitted:

> MY newspaper is still reasonably generous. They accept that I HAVE to travel, and that that costs. And they don't interfere too much. But of course, I still have to be aware not to kick over the traces too much. I'll give you an example: I was in Nigeria, and then one morning you have to quickly decide 'do I do the excursion onto the delta?'. The boat is USD 400, I have to take four people protecting me, and otherwise my fixer won't come. That is USD 200 on top. Then I have to pay the stringer USD 200. [...] So I have to spend a lot of money, just because I am travelling in a group. [...] It can get quite expensive for one day only. In cases like that I just have to hope that my headquarter will understand.

(I_17)

The few people financially comfortable enough to turn down offers by humanitarian organisations, said they were grateful for this not very common freedom:

> Sometimes reality is restricting. In South Sudan I heard that there was no way to travel up north by land. So you have to take a UN flight, and so it is useful to get in contact with organisations that have access to these flights. The Echo bureau then asked whether I needed funding, whether I wanted those travel costs paid. And I was in the luxurious position to say: 'No, my paper will cover the costs.' And I'm grateful for that. Then I don't feel the obligation to mention the organisation but have the freedom to say: 'Fine, I will cite them [but only] if they have something relevant to say about the issue'.

(I_28)

The interviews show that people working for humanitarian organisations are well aware of the budget restrictions on foreign reporting, and confirm that correspondents who can afford to travel by their own means are the exception to the rule. For example, here is one humanitarian's response regarding the situation in Somalia, which reporters can access on their own only at great cost:

> So the journalists who want to cover Somalia have very, very limited options. If they come from a rich organisation they can stay in the city and use these private security guards, and move around a bit like that. [...] So yeah, Somalia is an extreme case where the aid agencies don't control the access, but there isn't much of an alternative unless you're extremely wealthy. So [the

correspondent] from the Wall Street Journal was one of the few I met who came and said, 'Yeah I'm just coming, I'm going to see what I find', and her organisation is rich enough to let that happen. The others have to assemble 19 different strings [that is commissions] in order to justify the costs of the bodyguards and private security. Or they stay on the base and they are sort of embedded. And they see what they can get from an embedded perspective.

(I_22)

The question of budget constraints then also becomes a question of differentiation in reporting, and independence because it is often cheaper to feature humanitarians. A very experienced German television correspondent said:

An important factor is whether you have an employer who is willing to spend money on independent reporting. That's one thing. Then experience is important. Younger colleagues are an easier catch, you could say. Then I think it plays a big role to what extent you still perpetuate your own stereotypes. I have to say, a lot changed in recent years but still it is difficult – especially in crises situations – to broadcast a piece from sub-Saharan Africa with only residents as protagonists. Instead, we tend to – and that is different from Asia, Eastern Europe, or Latin America – look for a white person to disseminate the story. Employees of humanitarian organisations are ideal for that. This trend has declined a bit though. But I have to say that I got the best feedback for stories in which white people played a role, or people from sub-Saharan Africa who had a very strong ties to Germany. That is kind of normal on the one hand, but it is on the other hand the case because we still labour around the stereotype – or let's rather call it racist prejudice that black Africans cannot speak for themselves.

(I_15)

The majority of the correspondents feel the pressure to minimise their travel expenses, while at the same time stating that Africa is an expensive continent to cover, and that their editors mostly do not show a lot of interest in the continent, possibly, because they do not have much knowledge about it. The conglomerate of these factors, with the financial constraints being the major one, makes it hard for the majority of correspondents in remote places to work without the help of humanitarian organisations. I will elaborate the influence of decreasing budgets on the coverage in section chapters 6.7 and 6.8.

Editors, editorial policy, and guidelines from the correspondents' view

One of my hypotheses was that one aspect influencing the interactions between humanitarian organisations and correspondents would be editorial guidelines and the general policy that the respective news outlet had towards dealing with actors that have their own agenda. Recommendations and guidelines on how to interact with humanitarian organisations can be helpful for correspondents. For example the BBC's *Editorial Guidelines* include a section on conflict coverage and the editors' expectations about how the outlet's journalists should behave when interacting with humanitarian organisations.[4] The absence of editorial assistance in German media is remarkable. The German outlets SZ, FAZ, and Der Spiegel do not have guidelines specific to challenges interacting with humanitarian organisations. Der Spiegel refers upon enquiry to the general press code of the German Press Council, which could be understood as guideline but has no explicit editorial approval. The state broadcaster ARD does not have explicit guidelines comparable to these of the BBC. Upon enquiry, the director of the ARD stated in an email that there are *best practice* instructions, based upon general principles such as "journalists should never advocate for an issue, even if it is for good reasons". The director told me that exceptions were granted when covering catastrophes and when interacting with subsidised organisations that have the German Charity Seal of Approval (Deutsches Spendensiegel), and that act according to widely accepted quality standards for disaster relief (e.g. ICRC 1996; The Sphere Project 2004 [1998])" (email from the ARD programme director on 7.2.2014). Charity appeals should only be made if "adequate use of donations" was guaranteed (ARD 2010). Additionally, the general guiding principles of the ARD state that the separation of advertisements and content should be clearly visible, and advertisements must not influence content (ARD 2013: 104). The state broadcaster ZDF clarifies in its guidelines for advertisement and sponsoring that the sponsor must be mentioned clearly and must not influence content (ZDF 12.3.2010: §12). Exceptions are granted if the "economic benefits fully or mostly serve charitable purposes" (ZDF 12.3.2010: §17). Charity appeals are accepted if the donations serve widely accepted humanitarian and social purposes, and if the use is appropriate (Intendant des ZDF 2010: §17). How the use could be monitored and what basic principles could be applied for that, is not mentioned, nor what either outlet considers appropriate, or who makes that decision. One aim of my study was therefore to research whether correspondents knew whether their outlet had editorial guidelines regarding interactions with humanitarian organisations, and whether they consider them helpful. I also wanted to investigate whether American and British outlets are more critical of and less dependent on humanitarian organisations because they, for example, are guaranteed more support by their editors, or because they follow guidelines and rules of conduct.

The large majority of the correspondents report that their news outlet either does not have any rules regulating the interaction with humanitarian organisations or sections in their guidelines on commercial entities including humanitarian organisations, or that they do not know about them. Nearly all freelancers have generally never seen or read any of the guidelines of the outlets for which they regularly produce. How much financial and logistical help for a reporting trip is accepted from humanitarian organisations seems to be a grey area, and handled differently from case to case. Many correspondents state that their news outlet wants them to pay their own flights as a general rule but that beyond that all facilitating help from humanitarian organisations is accepted. Some admit that this is rather 'bon ton' than a general rule, and that exceptions are made; if the flight is run by a humanitarian organisation and went anyway, they would take it without compensation. Even colleagues within the same news outlet handle the issue differently. A few outlets have no general rules but instead require their correspondents to ask for editorial permission to join a media trip beforehand when the trip is completely financed by any commercial entity. More outlets do not accept trips that are fully financed by another entity, but accept partly financed trips. Some of these latter outlets then make the support transparent by naming the respective organisation at the bottom of the article, but that is not always the case. Only one ZDF correspondent and one BBC correspondent said their outlets would not accept a partly financed trip, and that they would always try and stay as independent as possible, renting their own cars, not sleeping in compounds of humanitarian organisations etc. At the same time, the German public broadcasters ZDF and ARD have so-called 'pools' of humanitarian organisations that are endorsed by the outlets as per policy of the broadcasting company. Committees, which lobbyists of humanitarian organisations are also part of, decide which organisations are generally supported, and then also featured in their correspondents' work. Apart from VOA, all American outlets have much stricter rules, and do not accept any so-called *freebies*. They always pay their own way. A correspondent of an American outlet explained the differences between British and American outlets handling the issue:

> We have certain ethics guidelines. But there is a lot of grey area. [. . .] And I recognise that there's a nationality difference because for example I was going on a trip with the EU and I [asked] 'Okay, can I pay for the plane ticket?' And they [said] 'Nobody has ever asked us that before'. [. . .] With my American colleagues we sort of compare, what's your rule on this? You know. And they [say] 'Oh, my rule is this.' But I interact with a lot of Brits too and they're like 'Rules?!'
>
> (I_34)

Confirming this experience, a journalist who worked for the British Daily Telegraph stated:

> We as the Telegraph certainly have no qualms at all about having aid agencies pay for us to go anywhere with them, or [to] provide accommodation, translators, vehicles, or everything. You tend to find that we pay our own flights to the beginning of a story. But beyond that, things are covered by an aid agency, no problem.
>
> (I_27)

The question one may raise is why editorial policy often treats humanitarian organisations differently from any other commercial entity. And why some outlets even directly support and endorse humanitarian organisations,[5] despite the fact that all of these organisations having grown to operate as highly professional and commercialised outfits with hundreds of employees and large budgets at their disposal. One correspondent who worked as an editor for several British outlets for many years, and who has now become very critical of humanitarian organisations, shared this thought: "If you go away with Shell, then you're going to say you went with Shell – there shouldn't be any difference then when you go with Save the Children" (I_10); however, the practice shows big differences.

I had assumed that guidelines influence the way reporting takes place, and that is the case. American news outlets have the strictest rules and guidelines. I found that correspondents working for these outlets comply with these rules, and most often then have their travel expenses financed by their editors instead. In comparison to correspondents of British and German outlets, a smaller percentage of correspondents working for American media outlets said they felt very dependent on humanitarian organisations.[6] However, American correspondents still have to rely on logistical support of humanitarian organisations, even if they pay their own way. Also, many correspondents interviewed did not know whether their outlet had any rules regulating their interactions with humanitarian organisations.

Other than these regulations, correspondents said that another strong aspect determining their work is their editors, who most correspondents considered neither to be very Africa-savvy, nor generally supportive. In the correspondents' views it is clear that the less experience an editor has, the more experience and better standing the correspondent needs, to convince him or her to cover issues that are not being covered by most other news outlets already anyway. This feeds into crisis-focused reporting following issues that other news outlets or the news agencies have already published. Nearly all correspondents would like to have more feedback and editing input from their editors. At least 61 percent said their editors did not have a good understanding of African issues, and little knowledge about the continent; in comparison, only 39 percent described their editors' understanding positively (see Figure 6.5).[7] Among the fewer correspondents who described their editors' understanding of Africa positively, and trusting their correspondents in their opinions, a correspondent of a German-speaking outlet said: "Their attitude really is okay: 'If the correspondent says it is one way or another, then we will

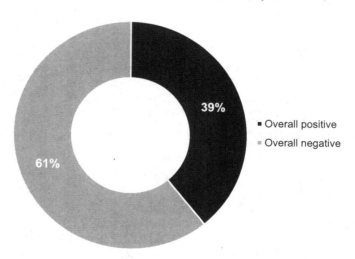

Figure 6.5 The editors' understanding of Africa

print it, no matter what.' But I can't make a huge mistake though, a blunder. Then I'm gone" (I_04). Another correspondent of a German-speaking outlet said:

> If I compare my situation to other newspapers, or to how freelancers often have to accept being patronised, and having to react to silly whims of their headquarters, then I am in a very comfortable situation. Generally, our correspondents decide themselves what will be published in their newspaper. I don't have to consult beforehand. That means I give notice in the morning about what I want to do that same day.
>
> (I_17)

One correspondent working on a retainer said that the relationship to the editors was so important to her that she would rather change the job if the editors were not good.

> For me it is very important that my colleagues in Germany understand my work. That they know that there can be power cuts. The internet doesn't work all the time. And some things just cannot be solved immediately on the ground.
>
> (I_05)

A correspondent of a news agency reported:

> The editors themselves are extremely knowledgeable because they started off doing my job at the age that I started doing it, in most cases. And they worked their way up. [. . .] To be an editor at [a large international news agency], certainly in the time that I spent there, often they'd have a lot of experience in other regions of the world as well, but the ones I worked with, had long standing relationships with Africa and took their jobs very seriously.
>
> (I_16)

One interviewee working for a British news outlet was content with his editors, but at the same time stressed he felt that he was an exception:

> My main point of contact is actually [from an African country]. But all of them are very interested. And again, from what I hear, I think I'm pretty lucky compared to other newspapers in that we don't have an agenda of 'it's only interesting if there's a British angle or there's a British person involved.
>
> (I_09)

Of the 61 percent who described the knowledge of their editors regarding Africa as poor, I picked some of the most telling examples. A correspondent of a German-speaking outlet remarked resignedly:

> When I suggest stories and say 'that is important to me' – it is always a battle to get stories into the paper. And often you suffer a defeat as a correspondent

who is far away. And at some point, you adapt and rather write stories that the editors suggest to you because then it is much more likely that they get published than if you suggest stories yourself and say 'but no one has written about it so far'. The editors will then say: 'We have never heard about that. Well, is that really that interesting?' So at some point, after two, three years in my case, you start pleasing the editor's needs instead of suggesting other things. I consider that a very bad development but it is inevitable.

(I_07)

A correspondent of a British news outlet answered the question, how knowledgeable he considered his editors with regards to Africa: "NOT at all, not at all. Embarrassing, really embarrassing" (I_27). A correspondent of another German-speaking outlet described the contact to the newspaper as follows:

Somewhere like Eastern Congo they would say: 'Can't you just go there quickly?' So I already have to explain: 'Yes, Congo. Okay. On a map you might think that is as if I quickly drove from Germany to Southern France. But in reality that is much further away. And BY THE WAY, in Eastern Congo the situation is such-and-such'. So sometimes you really have to explain a lot.

(I_30)

The lack of knowledge is attributed to editors not having been to Africa:

It's definitely that they've never been to Africa. On my foreign desk, which is five people, one of them has been a foreign correspondent and he was correspondent in Milan and then New York. So there's nobody who has been a correspondent in Islamabad or Kabul, Delhi, Nairobi – any of the places, which are traditional for foreign correspondents. So therefore they don't really know.

(I_14)

A freelancer working mainly for British media was mostly satisfied with her editor but confined it to the specific individual she was working with at that time. Otherwise, she had made negative experiences, too:

I've seen examples of people who've been in charge of foreign desks and have barely travelled outside of Western Europe or North America. And I think that's worrying, not least of all because people don't understand the logistics around reporting and that it's much more complicated in countries that aren't as efficient in terms of logistics, be it transportation or money or, you know, just getting things done can take a lot longer in some places. Or can be more difficult and more DANGEROUS.

(I_47)

A correspondent working for German television described the editors' lack of background knowledge:

> When the conflict in the Central African Republic started for example – no one [in the editorial headquarters] had an idea where that country even was. And what the capital city was called and what they were doing. Like 'What? Christians, Muslims?' Never heard of it so far. So it took a while until we could communicate that this is important. That it means that many people are suffering at the moment. I think if something similar happened in the United States – well, we don't even have to speak of the States as coverage of the States sometimes is even treated like domestic policy [. . .]. But even countries like Mexico, which is far away too, or say India. They are closer in a way and better known than many countries in Africa. I do think that that can hinder decisions sometimes. But in the end actually it is the correspondent's role, to press the point.
>
> (I_29)

Despite the negative experience that many correspondents have had with their editors, many still believe that good reporting is not only down to them but that the editors play an important role. One of these I will cite here:

> Editors play a primary role because a reporter can be good but a good editor can make a reporter much better. And an editor has to know what questions to ask, has to pull things out, has to be able to see things in larger perspective and unfortunately . . . this kind of editor is becoming a rare beast. Why? Because editors get older, they don't want to/ [. . .] I think they'll work for humanitarian agencies <<laughing>> or something else if they can find another job. But very few papers really will work hard to get good editors.
>
> (I_50)

Communications staff of humanitarian organisations who are media-savvy or who have a media background themselves also stress the importance of editors. A spokesperson of a UN organisation told me:

> [The report is] both responsibility on the part of the editor, [and] of the journalist [. . .] I think that editors should look at things and ask questions and that's one of the places where I think that there's a bit of a failing on Africa reporting is that the editors don't ask questions about reporting or evidence that they WOULD in any other part of the world.
>
> (I_54)

The editors' knowledge and engagement, and editorial guidelines are important to back-up the correspondents' work, especially when it comes to dealing with humanitarian organisations. However, more often than not, correspondents working in sub-Saharan Africa say they lack this back-up for their work and coverage.

Correspondents' self-perception and role, and partner-perception

It is important to understand how correspondents perceive themselves and how they perceive their own role, to get a better picture of the conditions framing their work, and to understand what impact that may have on their interactions with humanitarian organisations. In Chapter 4, section 4.1 I gave some theoretical background and an overview of up-to-date-research on how correspondents see themselves and their work. I raised the question whether the 'role concept' of correspondents of British and American media outlets would match the results of Mükke's study (2009b) on German correspondents, which found the majority of the correspondents identifying with the 'mediating-analytical' role. In order to investigate this, in the questionnaire handed to my interviewees, I listed the nine different roles to which Mükke detected German foreign correspondents related, and asked my participants to note with which they identified, with a final option to clarify if none of the given options seemed to match their self-reflection.

The 'reporter role', the 'informing role', and the 'mediating-analytical role' are dominant roles that all correspondents mainly identified with regardless of their outlet nationality (see Figure 6.6). Other than this, there are notable differences: American journalists are the product of a system that values independent and professional reporting, and that to a degree expects its overseas journalists to explain things to a domestic audience but certainly does not expect campaigning or lobbying journalism written by its correspondents (rather than by op-ed writers). This is illustrated by the finding that four in five American correspondents said they were 'reporters', 'informers', 'investigative reporters', or 'cultural interpreters' and 'mediator-analysts'. Compare that to journalists of British media outlets, who come from a more campaigning journalism background. Although a quarter of all British respondents identified mostly with the role of a 'reporter', it is interesting that among British outlets' correspondents 16 percent – the highest ratio among the three nationalities – said their role was to provoke, to advocate, or to broker issues. No journalist of a German-speaking or an American outlet said their role was to be a 'provocateur'. German-speaking media correspondents take seriously their impartiality, with three in five (59 percent) saying the main goal of their job was only to 'report' or 'inform'. Very few felt that it was their role to 'interpret' news, or to 'mediate or analyse' issues, and even less to 'advocate' for or 'broker' issues. None said they were 'provocateurs'.

Now, even more interesting are the findings when we look at differences in the journalists' self-perception depending on their type of employment, and compare freelancers' answers to those of staff correspondents. This is appealing when we assume that the way a correspondent is employed and paid, bears an influence on the way he or she sees him- or herself, and thus also on the way he or she is reporting. There are two notable differences (see Figures 6.7 and 6.8): first, no freelancer chose the role 'provocateur', whereas three percent of the staff correspondents did; second, a significantly larger number of freelancers saw themselves as 'interpreter between cultures', with 14 percent choosing this role, more than twice the six percent of staff correspondents who did so. One may raise the question whether freelancers cannot 'afford' to be provocative, and whether they feel more responsibility to explain the contexts of their stories more clearly to their home audiences in order to have their stories commissioned.

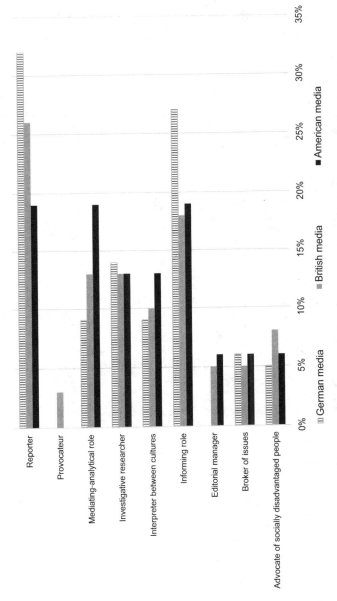

Figure 6.6 Correspondents' self-identification with roles – different media nationalities

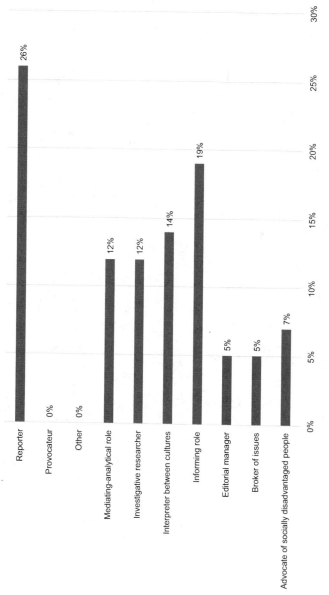

Figure 6.7 Correspondents' self-identification with roles – freelancers and retainers only

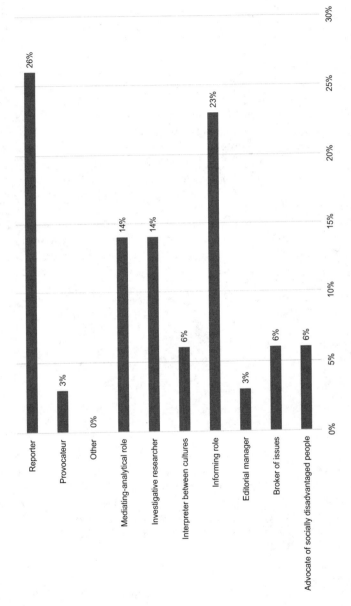

Figure 6.8 Correspondents' self-identification with roles – staff only

I also asked humanitarians with which roles they thought journalists would identify – a common method of triangulating perceptions, by asking one group what it thought the other's ideas of itself were. The humanitarians in this study correctly suggested most correspondents saw themselves as 'informing' and 'reporting'. But they strongly overestimated the number who said they were 'investigative researchers' – they thought a quarter would say this, whereas it was only a little over 10 percent. Over judged was also the role 'advocate for socially disadvantaged people'. These two differences in self- and external perception may explain first, why many humanitarians are wary of media who they believe see one of their key roles to investigate into all the dark corners of everyone's business, whereas that does not reflect reality. And second, why a significant number of humanitarians think that they are sitting in the same boat as journalists, wanting to promote the rights and needs of the poor, whereas correspondents do not share that perspective. It may also explain why many humanitarians express frustration about failed media approaches; possibly they simply started from a wrong impression of what drives the correspondents, and what they see as their task.

In my more in-depth research into how correspondents see their roles, I did not give them predefined categories from which to choose, as in the questionnaires, but instead asked towards the end of each interview about their motives for doing the job they do, and how they understand their role. From their responses, the correspondents I studied can be grouped into four different motivations. The first group wants to inform and educate about faraway places in a way to which audiences can relate. I will give a few examples from these interviews here:

> The responsibility of journalism [. . .] is [to care about these places and issues] where there are great deficits and little knowledge on the reader's side.
>
> (I_01)

> Creating awareness, responding not campaigning, report to people things that they can't see themselves, making sense of things.
>
> (I_23)

> Of course it is about bringing the world in every corner all over the place outside of Germany closer to people there. To explain to them what is happening here. How people think here. Also what connection that has in relation to everyday reality in Germany. To interest people for realities of life that are not in accord with their reality of life. And to again and again explain why they SHOULD be interested.
>
> (I_26)

> [Journalism for me is] mainly about connecting, making Mr whatever his name is sitting at a coffee table in London understand what life is like for Mr whatever his name is in South Sudan who is hungry. [. . .] It's not just describing stuff, it's making sense really. That's why we are kind of fucked when editors start telling us we must only write 300-word news stories

because we can't make any sense of anything and it becomes just a catalogue of obscure horrors in strange places, which is actually pointless, I think.

(I_23)

The second group wants to change something with their reporting. Among those are correspondents who started off far more idealistic than they became over time, like the first one quoted in the following:

> Without any sort of idealism, this would be the wrong job. [. . .] I can shine a light on an issue but what policy makers make out of it – I don't think I can influence that. It's not a helpful motivation for a journalist to want to change the world, I don't think.
>
> (I_28)

> The reason [journalism] helps is because it shocks and surprises the reader who then, or even government in some cases, who then hold people who have power to account for the things that they are doing.
>
> (I_23)

> That means that if it is about showing how universal human rights are violated in certain African societies, it is logical that we also interview advocacy groups who have our undivided admiration. Because they try to enforce human rights in really hostile areas. I feel bound to this universal canon of values.
>
> (I_26)

Two interviewees wanted to make a difference, and change something by investigating and researching into issues that "go wrong"

(I_08, I_21)

One interviewee wanted to show "the other Africa"

(I_30)

Another journalist said he started wanting to make the world a better place, "like everyone", and wanted to push things with his coverage into a certain direction to achieve this goal, but he at the time of the interview considered his job to be about information purely.

(I_04)

The third group wants to depict reality as accurately as possible, with all its complexity, while still rendering it comprehensible to readers at home. These correspondents want to "get to the truth" (I_33), and see their main role in selecting and evaluating events (I_28). One journalist remarked:

> Investigative journalism is a tautology. Journalism is by its very nature investigative. You want to find out what's going on, how this is happening, then you obviously start from some kind of base.
>
> (I_50)

Finally, the fourth group mainly does their job out of curiosity, or because of an "affinity with language and storytelling" (I_47):

> One journalist was only interested in and curious about the continent, did not want to change anything, neither on the ground, nor with the readers but wanted to give a picture of Africa beyond clichés and crisis focus. She viewed herself as "observer" and "collector of opinions", commenting every now and then.
>
> (I_05)

One journalist liked being in different places, meeting different people in developing countries he found exciting, in contrast to developed countries where everything had already happened, which he found boring:

> Here in the developing world, things are CHANGING, things are happening. There's CONFLICT but not just conflict in terms of WAR but also conflict in terms of ideas, in terms of CHANGES. There's RAPID change happening. I just think it's an exciting place to be.
>
> (I_20)

How do these journalists' self-perceptions of their roles now play into the interactions with humanitarian organisations? Interestingly, they clearly play a major role in terms of how regular the contact between the correspondent and humanitarian organisations is. Looking at the two charts in Figures 6.9 and 6.10, the difference is apparent: the journalists who in the questionnaires mainly identified with the roles 'advocate of socially disadvantaged people' and those who in the interviews said they wanted to 'change something' with their reporting,[8] at the same time stated that they had significantly more contact with humanitarian organisations than the ones who identified with any of the other roles.

The data show that two thirds of the interviewed correspondents who identified with the roles 'advocate' or who wanted to 'change something' with their reporting, at the same time said they have contact with humanitarian organisations 'several times per week' or more. None of these reported only 'occasional' contact. By comparison, only 13 percent of the correspondents who identified with all other roles but 'advocate' and 'change', said they were in contact with humanitarian organisations 'several times per week'. None said they were in contact more often than that, and 13 percent said they were in contact with humanitarian organisations 'occasionally'. The highest proportion – 37 percent – said they were in contact 'once or twice per month', and the same amount of people said they were in contact 'every week'. The more idealistic a correspondent is, the more congruent with the goals of humanitarian organisations are the aims that drive his or her actions, and the more contact he or she has with these same organisations. Two correspondents said they were more idealistic at the beginning of their career, when they wanted to change the world with their reporting, but the longer they worked in sub-Saharan Africa, the less idealistic they

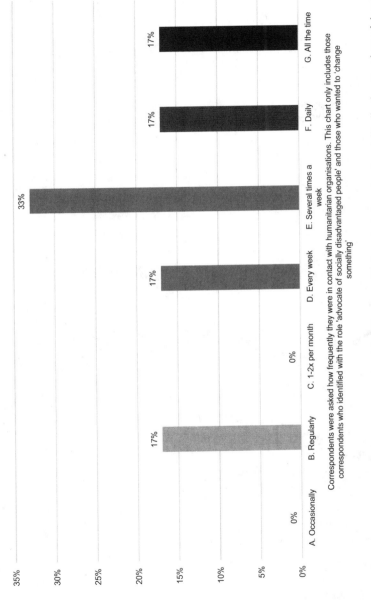

Figure 6.9 Frequency of contact with OHHs – identification with the role 'advocate of socially disadvantaged people' and those correspondents who want to 'change something' with their reporting

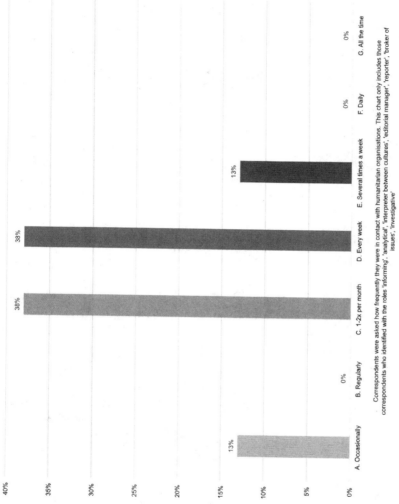

Figure 6.10 Frequency of contact with OHHs – identification with all other roles but 'advocate' and those who want to 'change something'

became. At the time I interviewed them, they mainly identified with the 'informing' role.[9] Since only two correspondents explicitly mentioned this change in self-perception over time, I cannot quantify the phenomenon. However, it seems likely that many of the correspondents undergo this experience that their idealism declines with their growing experience as journalists in sub-Saharan Africa. This suggests the conclusion that the less experience a correspondent has, the more idealistic they are that their role is to 'advocate' for 'change', and therefore the more contact he or she has with humanitarian organisations. Over time, this seems to change.

My research reveals that these role-perceptions play a role in terms of how dependent a correspondent feels on humanitarian organisations. In Figures 6.11 and 6.12, it is clear that correspondents who identified mainly with the role 'advocate of socially disadvantaged people' in the questionnaires, and those who said in the interviews they wanted to 'change something' for the better with their reporting, feel significantly more dependent on humanitarian organisations than those who identified with all other roles. On a scale from 1 to 10, 50 percent rated their dependency at 7 or 8, and the other 50 percent at even 9 or 10, the maximum.

This means that every correspondent who identified their role as being an 'advocate' and those who wanted their reporting to 'change' things for the better, rated their reliance on humanitarian organisations in the four top scales of dependency. By contrast, among the other correspondents who identified with any of the other roles, none rated their dependency on humanitarian organisations at 9 or 10, only 30 percent rated it at 7 or 8, the majority (40 percent) said 4, 5, or 6, and a full 30 percent rated it at 3 or below. The frequency of contact between humanitarian organisations and idealistic correspondents goes hand in hand with the feeling of a strong dependency on the correspondents' side.

Section 6.1 gave an overview of the framework that defines the correspondents' work. The large areas that correspondents have to cover, small budgets, and the lack of editorial support forces correspondents into cooperation with humanitarian organisations, whose framework equally favours cooperation. The next section will give an insight into the conditions defining the actions of humanitarian organisations, and their need for cooperation with correspondents.

6.2 Framework and conditions defining the interactions – humanitarian organisations

Much like the last section on the conditions of foreign reporting, this one highlights the conditions that humanitarian organisations work under, and how they influence the interactions with correspondents. The first subsection discusses the importance of media coverage and good relationships with correspondents from the perspective of humanitarians. The next subsection focuses on humanitarian organisations' competitive struggle for funding, which causes close relations with international media. The last subsection explicates the first two sections leading to professionalised public relations, and how they serve the aid sector.

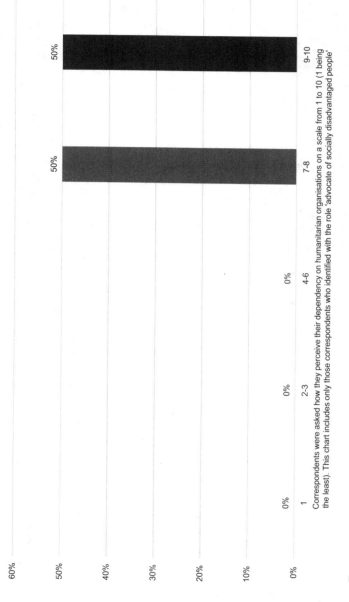

Figure 6.11 Dependency on OHHs perceived by correspondents – identification with the roles 'advocate' and 'change something'

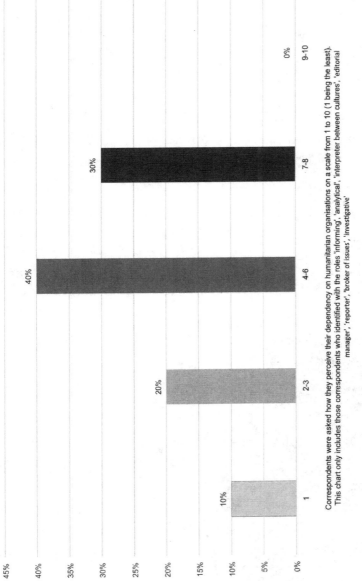

Figure 6.12 Dependency on OHHs perceived by correspondents – identification with all other roles but 'advocate of socially disadvantaged people' and 'change something'

Importance of media coverage for humanitarian organisations

The importance of media coverage for humanitarian organisations cannot be underestimated, as Figure 6.13 shows. Asked to rate the importance of contact with the media and correspondents for their organisation and their work, nearly 90 percent of the staff interviewed working for humanitarian organisations rated the importance at 7 to 10 on a scale from 1 to 10. Only 6 percent considered the contact as not very important, by rating at between 1 and 3.

The new social media have not changed the importance of traditional media for humanitarian organisations, as interviews of my study show. Instead in addition to putting out their own content via their websites, these organisations use social media as a tool to communicate with journalists, or to mediate their messages directly to the audiences. Mainstream media, however, have not lost any of their importance for humanitarian organisations, because they are still seen as an independent voice with significant agency to a wide international audience. They remain crucial for awareness creation, for fundraising, for political and societal advocacy, and for brand building. Social media have, however, changed the way reporting takes place as more and more beneficiaries also have access to social media, and hold reporters and humanitarian organisations to account if they report something that is wildly wrong from their point of view. A communications employee explained that MSF uses Twitter to monitor correspondents' reporting,

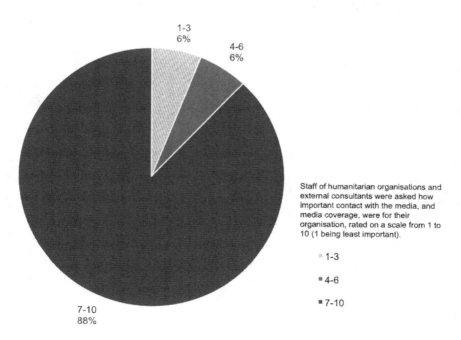

Figure 6.13 Importance of contact with the media from the OHHs' perspective

but also to reach them directly when they cannot interact with them otherwise. Twitter is also used to hold correspondents to account for their reporting:

> At this stage the novelty of Twitter and interacting on it in a dynamic way means that I'll get a quicker response out of a journalist. It ALSO means that I can put a journalist on the spot if I think they're not reporting on an issue and they're also aware that their followers are looking at them [wondering] why is MSF giving you shit on Twitter [. . .] for your poor reporting? And in the same way a member of the public can call me out on something [on Twitter].
>
> (I_63)

However, the interviewed employees of humanitarian organisations do not consider it relevant with which media format they cooperate. Newspapers, magazines, television, and news agencies were rated very similarly in terms of their importance. The outlet choice, however, is considered important. I discuss this in a subsection of sections 6.2 and 6.3. Most humanitarians interviewed think correspondents generally have a positive attitude towards their organisation. The terms that humanitarians used to describe the journalists' perception of their organisation differed. Oxfam and Unicef communications staff both declared they thought journalists had a "very positive" attitude towards them, a perception that was not shared by all journalists. The ICRC and IFRC expected the interactions from the journalists' point of view to be "respectful and professional", which the interviews with the correspondents show to be right. Interviewees working for MSF said that journalists had trust in the accuracy of their information, which interviews with correspondents confirmed. Cafod staff stated their organisation had a low profile, and that few people knew what they were doing, which from talking to correspondents seems true because in comparison to other organisations they were not mentioned as often. Save the Children interviewees thought that correspondents would experience them as producing "credible information", whereas by contrast correspondents reported in interviews that instead they perceived Save the Children as a campaigning organisation, which prioritised loud outspoken messages over implementation of work, which they clearly saw as something negative, and which lead them to trust Save the Children less. UNHCR staff thought correspondents would be rather critical of the organisation and would think it could do a better job, which was partly true. Also Ocha staff said that correspondents had a favourable attitude towards them, especially as "first stop for putting together a story", which correspondents also confirmed in their interviews. UNDP personnel expected correspondents' attitudes to be rather sceptical, and Care interviewees said journalists might describe them as a "logistically-supportive frontline source", which could not be verified in the interviews with journalists. Finally, WHO staff said they were viewed as "persistent", which is correct as many correspondents described their public relations' strategies as aggressive. Overall, the staff of humanitarian organisations seemed to operate in the dark and have surprisingly little detailed knowledge of the media's perception of their organisation.

This may feed into some organisations handling correspondents very cautiously, and trying to control their reporting as much as possible to limit potential damage to their organisations.

Competition for funding and media attention

In this subsection I will explain another aspect of the framework defining interactions between the media and aid in sub-Saharan Africa: how the humanitarian organisations' competition for funds and for media coverage dictates their interactions with correspondents. As I argued in the theory chapters earlier, the increasing number of humanitarian organisations creates a growing competition for funds and coverage. I found that the competition for media coverage mainly springs from the humanitarians' aim to establish their organisations as *brands* and to maintain these brands, in order to increase funding, as well as general reputation.[10] The media coverage helps to "kick back to your donor audience in your country of origin" (I_13), since donor markets are crowded and organisations of different sectors compete for the same money. This is why placing the organisations' logo and name in media reports is crucial to humanitarian organisations in order to outrun the competitors. A WFP consultant explained:

> The press department has a role in raising funds in the sense of keeping visibility high, making sure that a wide range of the projects being carried out by the organisation are VISIBLE in the public eye. Just making sure that in a world where there is a VAST number of humanitarian actors for any crisis, [. . .] your name is still up there.
>
> (I_67)

Since private funding to international development and humanitarian assistance is becoming increasingly important (Stoianova 2012), the branding becomes more important to make an organisation stand out from others. The growing pressure to fund projects amid increasing competition can even be found within large UN agencies that are assured a high percentage of their funds through their donor countries:

> The agencies are scrabbling for money [. . .] that's why you're seeing all this sort of shark practice, you know to be euphemistic, creeping in. Because it really is dog-eat-dog. The UNHCR is in the happy position that we have funding from donor countries [whereas] I mean Unicef have to do this private fundraising [always]. So we're doing private fundraising because times are tight. But I just hope that we don't descend into really infomercial type stuff. But I do fear that UNHCR may end up there as well.
>
> (I_41)

Most organisations in most cases build their brand through media coverage; they get the organisations' name or information about projects, and appeals for donations to wide audiences. This, however, is not the trade-off in all instances. It can also be pursuing other aims, such as policy change through making a certain standpoint public, adding issues to the public discourse to put pressure on policy makers, or similar aims. Organisations which operate mostly behind closed doors, such as the ICRC, sometimes do not want their name in the news; instead they prefer to deliberately place information, or they tip journalists off. Other aims can be more valuable to them than brand-making, because the latter can expose organisations or their staff in situations that are politically critical. A humanitarian now working as a consultant for different organisations after many years as staff for Save the Children described how organisations vary in their media approach:

> The agencies differ in their style. WFP is hyper-aggressive, hyper-vigilant, hyper-generous with logistical help. And they internally definitely see a connection between media coverage and funding. Unicef is a bit more touchy-feely and they see their task is to popularise and advocate certain concepts, trends and pro-policy issues as well as, to raise money and raise their brand. And so, you know, you get competition between the aid agencies for the journalists' attention coming out with, you know, the killer quote or the killer trip.
> (I_13)

Moving quickly to get the media's attention is important, especially in emergency situations that are crucial for fundraising, as many humanitarians told me. An interviewee who worked for CAFOD and Oxfam explained:

> And then being there very fast [is important]. One of the things that you want to happen in an emergency is to make sure that you've got your own people RIGHT in the midst of where the emergency is happening. And they're reporting back to the world. And right now what is happening, because of this cut-throat competition for the attention of media a lot of organisations such as Oxfam, and even ourselves, they're now actually saying 'we need to be there, go, do these stories and then offer them as packages.' Just say [to journalists]: 'We've done this interview, may you want to use it?'
> (I_38)

At the same time many interviewees identified a competition between emergency relief and development assistance organisations for media coverage, even within one organisation. "We used to have a bit more of the monopoly and now we have to face others that are better" (I_58), a Unicef communications employee told me regarding their market place. Reaching out to the media takes place on different levels, which are not necessarily to be understood hierarchical but rather complementing each other. Humanitarian organisations' headquarters often approach editors directly, bypassing foreign correspondents; regional or local offices are more likely to approach foreign correspondents on the ground. At the organisations' headquarters, the public relations strategy can also involve inviting parachute journalists to visit field projects, on trips that the headquarters' communications team often then ask regional offices to facilitate. I found that field staff – that is mainly regional communication officers or program managers – often do not agree with the headquarters' line. One Unicef staff member told me that she despised the now-dominant mentality of competition between organisations, an attitude she believed to be driven not by individuals working in the field but by headquarters:

> For me it was very much driven by New York who were very simple-minded and wanted a Unicef mention and didn't measure anything much besides that, and didn't see the value of not only building relationships with journalists, but also building relationships with other like-minded organisations or allies that were working in your sector. [. . .] You see a lot of ego-driven stuff going on with different heads of agencies and organisations who are very much focused on the brand in a very narrow sense and also their individual egos.
> (I_58)

The competition for coverage and the resulting need for good media contacts create more dependency. The graph in Figure 6.14 shows how humanitarian organisations' staff perceive their dependency on news outlets and their correspondents. Half of all staff of humanitarian organisations interviewed for this study rated their organisations' dependency at 7 and higher, on a scale from 1 to 10; a quarter even gave the highest possible score, 9 or 10. Twenty-five percent rated it at between 4 and 6. Only 5 percent perceived the dependency to be at 2 or 3. None rated below that. This shows that humanitarian organisations feel dependent on the media to a very significant extent. To accommodate this widespread assessment of the media's importance to them, humanitarian organisations developed a range of strategies how to better get the media's attention, and to do so in a more strategised way than this used to be the case only 20 years ago, as the next subsection will explain.

Professionalisation of public relations

The communications departments of many humanitarian organisations used to be sidelined. But as the market has become more competitive, these departments have grown in budget, in number of staff, and in their outreach. Because of the competition for media attention – and remember, the organisations feel very dependent on media coverage – public relations of humanitarian organisations are becoming increasingly professional. This means that most humanitarian organisations have large media and communications departments staffed with editors, photo editors, and video producers, all following a distinct and calculated media strategy often but not always connected closely to the fundraising department. It also means that most organisations create in-house packages offered to the media, including free pictures, footage, and written pieces, and that they publish reports and commission research resulting in statistics. Cottle calls this "institutionalised 'media logic' *inside* aid agencies" (Cottle & Nolan 2009: 866). At the same time they commission professional freelance correspondents to provide content

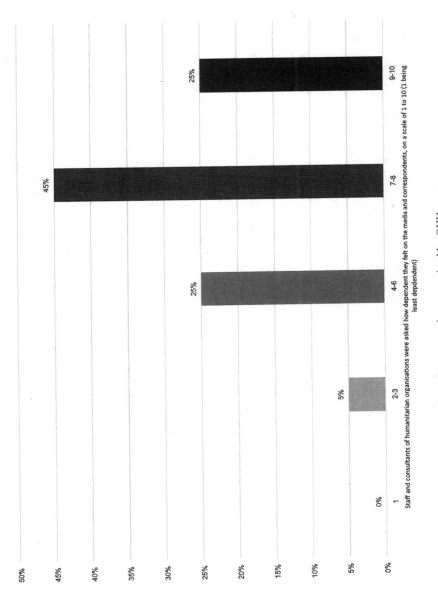

Figure 6.14 Dependency on the media and correspondents perceived by OHHs

directly for use on the organisations' websites and other platforms. All of these things can be witnessed across all different types of organisations.

A humanitarian organisation's choice of which media to target depends on the project or activity they are promoting, the intention for the outreach, on the target audience in terms of creating awareness, and target market in terms of fundraising, as well as on the general interest of the news market. Does the organisation want to raise awareness about a certain issue or crisis? Does it want to stimulate fundraising in general? Or does it want to generate funding in a certain country, amongst a certain readership? Does it want to influence policy makers? Or does it want to communicate the success of a particular project to donors? Is the outcome supposed to generally strengthen the organisation's brand, in the short or in the long run? These are some of many factors defining a humanitarian organisation's interest in a specific media outlet. Overall, the news agencies – AFP, AP, and Reuters – are considered important by all humanitarian organisations as they have a great reach. The large newspapers and TV broadcasters play an equally significant role; most often mentioned were news agencies, the BBC, CNN, The New York Times, The Daily Telegraph, The Guardian, Al Jazeera, and CCTV. The latter two do not play a role in this study since they are not American, British, or German-speaking outlets, and thus do not fall into the research sample strategy. After the news agencies and large news outlets, freelance journalists that an organisation trusts are the next most important propagators from humanitarian organisations' view, as freelancers can place similar stories in several outlets at the same time.

Looking at the strategies mentioned in the introduction of this subsection in more detail, my research shows that the humanitarian organisations' communications departments are not always closely connected to the fundraising departments in terms of an overall strategy. Larger organisations especially, and that includes several UN agencies, do not consider a close connection between their fundraising and communications departments that necessary. They have a media approach, and separately from that, a so-called 'donor approach'. These large organisations, such as, for example, WFP, are mainly funded by bilateral donors that have agreed to fund the respective organisation over a longer period of time, and cannot pull out of these agreements as easily. As a result, these large organisations are less dependent on maintaining constant funding flows, and less afraid of too little media coverage than some smaller and medium-sized organisations and INGOs. The communications departments in these organisations are rather seen as a means to uphold visibility of the organisation, and for advocacy, by putting issues on the political agenda. However, if the communications department does a particularly bad job, I was told by several interviewees, it may very well have a long-term effect on their organisation's funding as it might damage their image, or put their effectiveness into question, and thus affect a potential next grant in the long run.[11]

The communications departments play a significant role for these organisations nevertheless, simply by generating attention, and maintaining the organisation's visibility. The fundraising department, I was told by many interviewees working in communications, always knows what the communication department is planning and doing. This is not necessarily true the other way round. To the contrary, a few interviewees working in communications departments told me that the fundraising departments operate in a black box in their view. The communications departments of smaller organisations, however, which depend far more on individual donors than larger organisations, are seen to play a crucial role in fundraising. They are willing to take greater risks in their interactions with the media, simply because they need to generate more attention to receive any funding. At the same time and for the same reason, damaging publicity can be much more harmful to them, as individual donors might stop funding and encourage others to do the same. That is also true for large organisations that depend on funding from individuals, and who start their budget every year from zero, like Unicef. It makes a significant difference in terms of media strategies whether an organisation mainly depends on fundraising through media appeals or not. In one case you are selling a product, in the other you are communicating a situation, even though these two may overlap. Save the Children, for example, which depends largely on funding by individuals and has a large communications department, is seen as communicating very aggressively by several other organisations and by correspondents. "They're seen as communicating for communication's sake [. . .], and the communications is very fundraising driven", said one interviewee working in another large organisation (I_52). A very experienced interviewee, who has worked for three different major humanitarian organisations experiencing three different media strategies, and heading up communications for all three, said:

> I think it makes a MASSIVE difference. When you're communicating because you need money, there's a tendency to exaggerate; to present a single story, [. . .] the story that is the most extreme, that's going to get you funds. Whereas if you're not doing it for that reason, then you're more likely to take a lot more nuanced reading of the situation. I think [foreign correspondents] [. . .] know very quickly, which organisations are communicating propaganda, and they need to take it with a pinch of salt, and which ones are communicating how they perceive the situation genuinely. Which doesn't mean that they have a necessarily correct reading of the situation. It's still their own perspective, which is often, a very Western perspective of the situation. [. . .] It makes a TREMENDOUS difference if you are fundraising through your communications [department].
>
> (I_52)

Another distinction that I identified in the interviews with humanitarians was whether their communications were publicising development programmes or emergencies. Since it is in the nature of development projects that they are less urgent than emergencies, publicity about them can be planned and strategised to a far greater extent. At the same time, however, development issues tend to be less appealing to the media, are harder to sell, and generate less attention. Humanitarian organisations are willing to take more risks to publicise these development issues, while at the same time feeling that these risks are more controllable than in emergency situations. Most funding is generated from emergency appeals. How strategised emergency communication is, depends very much on the organisation. Some larger organisations, for example Care, have emergency response teams based at and coordinated from the headquarters, or the responsibility for emergency cases rotates between main global offices who then deploy specially-trained staff to the emergency regions for a limited period of time to answer all media queries. In either case, the promptness of the communications departments' reaction is essential, as this statement from an emergency communications specialist of a large INGO shows:

> It is not as important what we say but rather how fast we are regarding certain issues, especially in emergencies. We have to show: 'We are active, we have an interview partner in the field [who can talk to you in the language of your media outlet]. We have published a report about this issue. We can provide pictures'.
>
> (I_65)

The general media strategy of humanitarian organisations' headquarters includes: arranging press briefings, maintaining close contacts to foreign correspondents and their media outlets, publishing and emailing press releases, reaching and informing journalists via Twitter or running social media campaigns, providing as many facts and as much information as possible, supplying photographs and television footage, facilitating access, sharing local knowledge – "even if it doesn't have anything to do with your organisation" (I_59) – linking people, engaging audiences, and finding new angles for chronic crises to overcome compassion fatigue. This could include publishing fresh research or data sheets on anniversaries, arranging celebrity field visits, or clustering several organisations to speak in a combined voice on a certain issue, to reinforce the message, attract more media attention, and encourage more funding than each organisation could have done on its own. Most organisations use a combination of all of the above. An advocacy coordinator who is also responsible for media communications with Care described this mixed approach as follows:

> We use a media piece as one kind of approach in an arsenal of different methods around an issue. So we would have a briefing paper that would go to donors and we would extract a press release from that. We might have a verbal briefing with staff; we might actually do a film or a social media campaign at the same time.
>
> (I_45)

The success of communications is measured in different ways, according to my interviewees. Some count the number of times their organisation is mentioned in different articles, sometimes as compared to other organisations. Some assess whether an issue is reported and framed in a way of which the organisation approves. Some monitor whether the public is engaging with the topic, which can be monitored most easily via social media. Some calculate whether fundraising increases.

A major difference between the organisations I found is the aspect of who is authorised to speak to the media. Organisations that depend on individual funding tend to only let spokespeople or regional directors speak. The same is true for comparatively small organisations such as Adeso, and for organisations that are seen as very politicised, and less implementing, such as for example WHO. The press officers are supposed to "try and control the message to a certain extent" (I_19), not only for fundraising and images but also to guarantee the safety of field staff that might otherwise become targets. Several correspondents told me they find especially UN organisations bad at communications and at understanding how media work, but that it is UN organisations who try to control the messages most. A correspondent for a news agency said:

> MSF might contact us and say, 'we've just started up a new project on the Ugandan border for people coming across from Central African Republic and you know there's some terrible things happening there' and this kind of thing. And if you can go and cover it, it'll be interesting for you. But they won't TELL us what to do. They wouldn't say, you need to write this, this, this. [. . .] You can talk to the people who are on the ground, the nurse, the doctor, the logistician, the administrator, the protection officer and so on. And you can pretty much talk to whomever you LIKE. You do the same thing with the UN and generally a press officer would go with you. EVERYTHING would come out from the press officer. ANY quotes from anybody else [. . .] would be presented to you, 'here are the quotes from so-and-so'. It's much more controlled.
>
> (I_20)

Several correspondents also said that some communications staff, especially those at UN agencies, did not understand what was interesting from a reporting perspective but that they were often the only ones authorised to speak. These correspondents were frustrated that they often received emails about an organisation's headquarters' staff visiting a certain place, which in itself was of no interest. By contrast, programme managers more often knew what stories might interest correspondents, and country directors had "a good overall understanding" (I_31), as a correspondent of an American outlet stated. Correspondents also said they felt that experts in the field could provide better stories, voicing their perceptions of the events on the ground, but often were either media-shy or not allowed to speak out as per their organisation's communication policy.[12] One correspondent with very good contacts to experts of various organisations in the field described how he would call these people to gather information, but then was not allowed to cite them. Instead he was requested to call the press offices, which then instead gave "VERY vanilla statements" (I_27). This is not an individual incident but rather a pattern throughout all data. Some correspondents even described the headquarters as "passive aggressive", refusing to give statements on critical issues that journalists were researching, but pushing hard for coverage of other issues that might not be of any news interest. Even a chief communicator of a UN agency described headquarters' communications departments as "under the challenge of their management and their program colleagues, who are just desperate to keep the money [coming] in" (I_58). By comparison, the majority of interviewees said they saw regional staff as generally helpful, but that it then came down to individuals, rather than organisational strategies.[13]

From the humanitarians' point of view, communications staff of different organisations told me that their field-based colleagues have very little media experience, meaning that journalists were able to control the interactions far more in their favour. For this reason, INGOs, mostly, send communications staff to the field to teach technical staff how to talk to journalists and "which language to use" (I_44, spokesperson for a UN agency). Humanitarian organisations' communications staff mostly agreed that it was key to have a thorough understanding of how the media work to be successful in their jobs. However, many correspondents said in the interviews that in their experience, few humanitarian press officers or communications staff had a clear understanding of how journalists operate, of their needs or priorities. One correspondent in a senior position at a news agency told me his employer received regular requests from humanitarian organisations to attend workshops with their communications staff to brainstorm better ways of working together. His experience is not an exception; other interviewees echoed his point:

> I often get press officers, especially from the UN in particular who are TERRIBLE at press relations. They're disastrous. And here, very regularly we get invited to these seminars of these UN press officers who are paid HUGE amounts of money every month and who are absolutely incompetent and ask us, how can we do our job better? And how can we get you to cover the stories we want you to cover? And this kind of thing. And we don't even know who they are. We go into South Sudan in the field and there are UN people who are generally very reluctant to talk. Everything has to go through one particular press officer, who will stay there. They will be there for three, four months and then they'll get rotated out.
>
> (I_20)

Of the INGOs, Save the Children is seen to have a particularly strategised communications department that, instead of purely providing journalists information, is instead advocacy-focused. Save the Children is very hierarchical and has strict rules on who is authorised to speak. The latter aspect was not only confirmed in interviews with correspondents and staff of other humanitarian organisations, but also by the way my own request speaking with staff in the organisation was handled. Save the Children was the only organisation requiring several clearances, including from a regional communications advisor, before a regional communications officer was authorised to speak to me, despite the scientific interview context and despite guaranteed anonymity. It was also the only organisation where the communications employee spent the first half an hour of the interview reading out statements that the organisation had prepared for this occasion; these statements were typical 'agency speak', hardly containing actual meaning.

By contrast, many correspondents said that MSF often suggests field visits to the agency's projects, where journalists are encouraged to speak freely to patients and doctors; they are asked, however, to restrict discussions to each individual's medical case, and not to ask political questions. The MSF communications department prepares statements, and only the head of section is authorised to talk to correspondents on more general and organisational perspectives, and in difficult situations, I was told by former spokespeople (I_48, I_52). The communications department is seen to have a somewhat outsider role, and critical information is sometimes even withheld from MSF's own spokespeople:

> So you're not even allowed to go to meetings. Information is withheld from you. And you're like: 'But I work for you. Not for the journalists. And I need to know what's going on internally in order to plan the messaging and all of that.' But communications is ALWAYS seen a bit as an outside part of the organisation.
>
> (I_52)

How communications staff deal with this situation varies from individual to individual. An experienced former communications employee told me that he never told journalists that he was not authorised to comment on an issue because he felt that this would make the journalists want to dig even more. Instead, he chose to say he did not know the answer. This, he had experienced over the years, was much better because it kept journalists from probing further, and was additionally seen as an open and honest answer. By admitting his fallibility, he felt he earned greater trust from the journalists (I_61).

Within UN organisations, correspondents said individuals who had been journalists themselves before moving into UN communications were the most capable and trustworthy. During emergencies and humanitarian crises in particular, which can be highly politically sensitive, nearly all organisations send their messaging to the country directors and the headquarters for clearance first before sending it to journalists. A former MSF spokesperson said:

> NOTHING comes out without verification by the headquarters. IN FACT, most press releases are written from the headquarters. There is a complete lack of trust when it comes to having the bureaus in the countries because the head of operations sits in the headquarters.
>
> (I_52)

The headquarters' media strategy and approach can be supplemented by a regional media approach, for example if the same message is brought to the media's attention on different levels: to the editors by the headquarters, and to the correspondent by the regional communications department, "you attack from various angles"

(I_61, humanitarian communications employee with experience in one INGO and two UN agencies). However, the headquarters' strategies often create frustration in the regional communications departments, and even more so with the field staff. An interviewee who has worked as a senior staff member in one large INGO before she started working as consultant for many INGOs complained:

> EVERYONE will tell you the head office is in cloud cuckoo land. And they don't understand what we're doing here. Everyone, I'm sure, will tell you that. One of the biggest headaches of running a country office is dealing with the head office. And as a country director and senior manager, I think one of your STRONG roles is keeping London and their demands under control.
>
> (I_46)

The field staff, often more technically skilled and with regional knowledge, tend to be less media-savvy and have less interest in talking to journalists. They see it as the communications department's responsibility, and get frustrated by media operating on tight deadlines. Additionally, field staff tend to see articles as "too superficial" (I_54, humanitarian communications staff), which is why one of the regional heads of communications of a major humanitarian organisation saw herself as "translator" between the media and the field staff's needs. This is not true for all organisations. A Care advocacy manager said:

> Your key messages have really come from the situation on the ground. [...] They might be polished by the time they get to headquarters level. But you can pretty much guarantee that is what the frontline staff at some point is going to say. Probably in a more credible, rooted, true way that's easier to respond to. So I feel quite safe in letting them [the field staff] speak.
>
> (I_45)

The same interviewee however admitted she is not always satisfied with field-based colleague's answers to journalists, as they may not match the general strategy:

> We are not trying to cover things up as such, but we may also have a very clear kind of message that we want to get across or that we DON'T want to get across. And I've sat next to people where they've been talking to journalists and sometimes I thought 'oh god, no no no, don't say that!'
>
> (I_45)

For fundraising reasons, and to improve the visibility of the organisation, many headquarters and regional communications departments encourage correspondents to visit field projects. Field workers often see these as distraction from their work:

> [The] London office is full of people that are very far from the action. But they feel they are doing a really great job and they're always excited about press releases, and they use them for fundraising [...] and marketing. [...] So

they feel that the more coverage you have in the press, the more your name is mentioned [the more the profile is raised], [. . .] and they totally want to please the press. A lot of that translates down to us at the field levels: have another journalist, have another journalist.

(I_46)

One interviewee working in communications for an INGO explained that their field staff felt correspondents were "disaster tourists" (I_45), and that this caused many discussions between field and communications staff.

The interviews show the pattern that many headquarters instruct a regional communications person to facilitate a correspondent's visit in the field. The humanitarian organisations' headquarters believe that regional communication officers can do all the work. However, they are not based in the field, so while they are designated to be the journalist's main contact point, they will need their field-based colleagues to translate and explain the details, to organise transport, and establish connections with local beneficiaries. All of which means resources are withdrawn from field operations, even though headquarters has dispatched a communications employee to 'take care of' the journalist's visit. Deepening this intra-agency frustration is how headquarters approach journalists when trying to whip up interest in a new crisis:

In 2011 I just found that DISGUSTING that Save the Children was peddling starving children as the main reason for journalists coming out. And literally, I had phone calls, '[. . .] we need to get to the field, and I just need to know, will there be very skinny children, because there is no point in us going out spending a day [. . .] if they are not as bad.' I was really fed up with London, that they hadn't been able to sophisticate the story any more than this. [. . .] This is a bigger issue here, it's not this simplistic, you'll always find a skinny child somewhere here.

(I_46)

The frustration from the field staff towards the headquarters' strategy to send many journalists can render a journalist's field visit of little value. One former regional communications employee with MSF described how, after a lot of encouragement, a correspondent finally agreed to travel to a remote region that was seen as not getting sufficient coverage. But once there, the field coordinator treated the correspondent poorly, which "mortified" the communications staff (I_48).

Interestingly, in larger, decentralised organisations, there seem to be differences in communication strategies on the donor-country-levels even within the same organisation. To give a few examples: within Save the Children, the Scandinavians are seen as more rights-based, understanding of local community dynamics (I_59, former Save the Children communications employee), and having local actors speak instead of taking the front seat and considering themselves as 'legitimate actors' in foreign countries (I_13, former Save the Children programme manager). Save the Children UK is perceived as "involved in advocacy, social change, and more political perspectives" (I_59), whereas the agency's US bureaus are believed to avoid political messages, and instead take an "emotive, dead baby approach" (I_59), while speaking freely on behalf of others (I_13). In MSF's international branches, MSF Belgium is seen as taking a structured, incorporating approach, MSF France is seen as activist and rather militant, and MSF Switzerland as controlling its communications and micro managing (I_52, former MSF communications employee).

Despite the differences in media strategies within larger humanitarian organisations, one trend is apparent across all organisations. An increasing number of communications departments do not rely only on correspondents and their editors to get their message out, but also produce their own multimedia content. "There has been a huge shift in visuals: we break information down a lot more to make it accessible to more people and make it more appealing, infographics, visual information, breaking up paragraphs" (I_68), a high-ranking communications employee working for Ocha said. A Care emergency communication specialist told me: "We are on the ground at the same time to gather stories and material ourselves. Photos, interviews. To then spread them via our own communication channels and publications" (I_63). Former journalists or freelance journalists working on consultancies are contracted to produce public relations material for humanitarian organisations. A German television correspondent told me that these consultants create "in parts spectacularly good reporting on crises. They offer it themselves. Some of the good ones like Human Rights Watch or MSF can afford to pay superb photographers" (I_15). Another correspondent shared a similar view:

> The video offer has become much more professional and comprehensive. These organisations work in regions that are hard to access, and they offer footage in good and broadcastable quality. That means [they are a source for] picture[s] and footage [. . .] one must take seriously. But if we are talking about a trend, then correspondents need to be clear about how they deal with [. . .] [these] sources.
>
> (I_26)

How the organisation's agenda influences the content and what that means in terms of reliability of material, even seemingly unbiased ones such as data and statistics, I will explain in section 6.7. The majority of correspondents do, however, not understand why many organisations spend large amounts of money sending their press teams to produce material that most correspondents will not use masqueraded "as journalism when it is being done by an advocate" (I_23). Instead it will go onto the organisations' websites and reach hardly any audience. A UNHCR communications employee explained that this is where social media came into their equation:

> We would hire a videographer, a cameraman, [when] we don't have the resources. Or would have somebody who can either use the camera as well or edit and direct and produce. Some people say perhaps it's not so good in the sense that you put a lot of money and resources into making a video and then

who sees it at the end of the day? But I think that's where the social media comes in. If you can push it out, then you reach far more people. And even donors now will accept social media mentions as visibility.

(I_41)

The same is true for another trend that my research revealed. I was told by several correspondents and communications staff members that many press releases are written in a more journalistic way than they used to be, formatted as if they were news features in the hope that journalists publish them nearly verbatim. With humanitarian organisations professionalising their public relations, and hiring freelance journalists to produce in-house reports about places that only 10 years ago correspondents would have gone by their own means, a blurring of lines between public relations and journalism is taking place.[14] The circumstances in which reports like this were researched and written are not easily grasped by general audiences, even in cases where the stories' provenance is made transparent by naming its source, which is not always the case. The same UNHCR staffer quoted above revealed:

> What we do and what we've learnt is that you don't heavily brand it. You don't interview ten UNHCR people. You give a story and then it gets used and otherwise, you obviously throw in one interviewee and chances are that person will be used, provided they're not dressed head to toe, like the Smurf [he refers to being dressed in blue UN clothes], it'll get in there. So this is what our unit in Geneva does. They provide all the B-roll, this broadcast role, available all the time.
>
> (I_41)

The more sophisticated the communications work becomes, the more trained staff are needed. A UNHCR spokesperson explained this differentiation:

> UNHCR has previously had the attitude that anybody can do any job. I was not here when it was a very small organisation, but it used to have the approach of the generalist that one day you're driving the trucks, the next day you're doing the registration, the third day you're doing the media relations. . . . And in today's world that just doesn't work. You have to know communication strategy, you have to know does it work better to call somebody, does it work better to tweet this, do you want to use Instagram, should we try to be pitching this to The New York Times or to CNN? So you have to be pretty sophisticated, and you need to be a specialist and I don't think that many UN agencies have really got that.
>
> (I_44)

A WFP spokesperson confirmed that not all colleagues are trained for this more sophisticated communications work, and that some want to produce their own content without understanding the tools:

> Once they start making videos for an office then everybody wants a video and sometimes their like understanding of what a good video is, is not necessarily

what a good video is. So they'll be like: 'We REALLY want to do a video about this' and I'm like, 'What?', and there's no visuals to that. What are we going to film? You know they want to show or do a video about partnership and capacity building and that's difficult to show. So maybe there's a better way we can deal with that than video. They like, you know, they haven't identified like who's the audience for that video. Who are you trying to reach with this?

(I_54)

A senior Unicef employee agreed: "Gavi[15] just thought: 'We'll start the conversation by offering the freebie' and I'd be like: 'No, no, no! You've got to start the conversation by figuring out the angle in the pitch and then you can go to offering the free accommodation and the rest of it'" (I_58). This is why Unicef, for example, teaches field staff to ask basic questions to produce decent captions to go with their photographs. These images and captions can then be used to whet correspondents' appetites to look for similar stories (I_36, a communications employee). Despite the growing trend of humanitarian organisations producing their own material, the mainstream media is still crucial, all interviewees said. A former Cafod communications specialist specified:

> I think we're more able to broadcast ourselves than we ever were before. With our own Twitter feeds, blogs, websites, self publishing groups [. . .] via the Internet. But we still need mass communications. There's still, you know, a huge reach.

(I_37)

While some correspondents use the material humanitarian organisations provide thankfully, this study reveals that equally many are critical of the methods used to gather the information. I already explained how in developing crises the media pressure for quick statistics illustrating the scale of an emergency can force humanitarian organisations to make statements without sufficient evidence. Overstated numbers are beneficial for organisations, but this is not the only criticism correspondents have. Some raise questions over the diligence with which certain organisations carry out their research. Human Rights Watch stresses that it carries out research according to high ethical standards, and many correspondents I interviewed highlighted this organisation as being among the most objective and diligent. However, an experienced correspondent highlighted to me her concerns over a Human Rights Watch researcher stationed in sub-Saharan Africa:

> So Human Rights Watch, for example, has a [researcher] [. . .] who just sits in a hotel and pays [. . .] little helpers who are supposed to go to investigate a rape in village x. [. . .] And these helpers then come back and tell [the researcher] [. . .] what happened. But [the researcher] [. . .] never goes anywhere [. . .] to verify it. [. . .] And I have told [the researcher] [. . .] very often that [he or she] publishes wrong information, or gets FED with false

information, DELIBERATELY. [...] Now, I know these little helpers too and one of them happens to be a friend of mine and has confessed to me on several occasions that he pretends [...] to go to this village, and sits in a bar all day drinking beer. And in the evening he makes up a story what happened in this village. [...] I know this [researcher] in [x], I know [his or her] methods. If Human Rights Watch publishes any report, I re-examine every tiny little bit of it. And I would NEVER just adopt anything Human Rights Watch publishes WITHOUT verifying it. But this is this [researcher in x]. The guy in [a neighbouring country], for example, is REALLY dedicated; he runs around and does everything himself. [...] What he does is close to journalism but he then yields to us and does not claim to know it better than us journalists.

(I_08)[16]

This quote demonstrates that knowing individuals, their methods, and contacts within one organisation can be essential for correspondents to tell whose information they can consider trustworthy. This is, among other reasons, why personal contacts play an essential role in the interactions; I will explore this at the end of the next section, in the subsections *Choosing interaction partners* and in *The role of personal contacts*.

Overall, the findings discussed in this last section make clear that humanitarian organisations have professionalised their communications and public relations strategies significantly in many ways over the last decade. The outreach to media on the correspondents' and the editors' level has been extended, and more strategies have been put in place to attract the media's attention. Additionally, humanitarian organisations now produce material themselves, which they hope to place in the media, or publish via their own platforms. Interviews also showed, however, that the headquarters' and regional and field staff ideas on how to deal with media, are not always matching, and can create dissent. Whether an organisation reaches out mainly to inform the public or to generate funds makes a difference for their credibility in the correspondents' view. The more campaigning an organisation is seen, the more correspondents are wary.

6.3 Overview of the interactions

After explaining the framework in which the interactions take place, I now attend to the interactions themselves. It is important to say that humanitarian organisations are not the only partners and sources relevant for correspondents' work. Correspondents in sub-Saharan Africa rely on a complex network of contacts (see Figure 6.15). However, humanitarian organisations were found to play a major role in this network, and other partners listed above were found overall not to be as important as humanitarian organisations: I asked correspondents not only for other partners and sources, but also how relevant they were in comparison to humanitarian organisations, and the results were surprisingly clear. Eighty-one percent said humanitarian organisations were medium to very important in comparison to other partners, rating the importance between 4 and 10. Only 19 percent of respondents found them not so important, or not important at all in comparison to other partners, rating them between 1 and 3 as shown in Figure 6.16.[17]

In the first subsection of this section I will give an overview of the network of humanitarian organisations that foreign correspondents use, determine which ones are considered important, and how they are generally perceived from the correspondents' perspective. The second subsection gives an overview over the nature of the interactions, answering what they are about, both from the correspondents' and the humanitarians' perspective. The third subsection deals with the question how these interactions are initiated, and how both the correspondents, and the humanitarians choose which partner from the other sector to interact with. The fourth subsection then takes a closer look at this choice, and explains the role

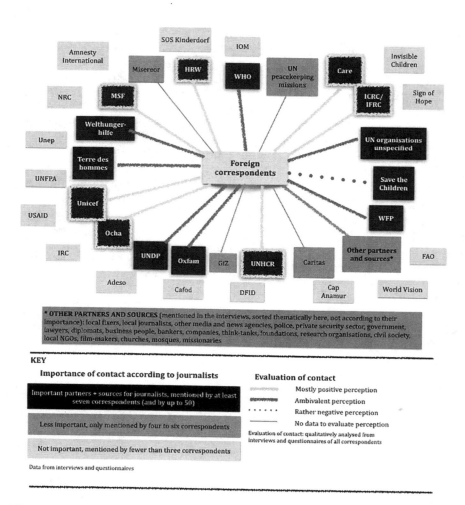

Figure 6.15 The network of foreign correspondents

of personal contacts. I will describe a few individual cases, outline patterns that recur in many cases, give an insight into the perspectives of both the journalists and the humanitarians, and describe in detail how and why the interactions take place, and what consequences they may have.

There is no such thing as the interaction: the questionnaires and the interviews show that the interactions between foreign correspondents and humanitarian organisations take place in many different forms, with differing peculiarities, and are of varying intensity. The manifestation of the interactions depends on various factors and conditions that define work on both sides, and on the underlying motives of both sides, on which the past chapters shed light. The interactions range from emailed press releases or Twitter announcements, to exchange of information on the phone, to cooperative work that can be labelled as embedded journalism due to its obvious dependencies. In hardly any case is the dependency one-sided though – rather, it is a reciprocal dependency. And, of course, in the wider picture also non-interactions play a role when involved actors try to avoid each other.

Overall, the research findings show clearly that humanitarian organisations and correspondents have good working relationships in sub-Saharan Africa; they need each other on many occasions. The surveyed correspondents nearly all bemoaned the shrinking budgets for foreign reporting, with regards to their general wages as well as travel budget. At the same time, living costs in many African cities have risen. The worldwide demand to immediately access all information at any time increases the pressure to report promptly on any incidents. With many correspondents being responsible for all 49 countries in sub-Saharan Africa – a few share the patch with one other colleague – that becomes a challenge under these conditions. Travelling in sub-Saharan Africa is costly and time-consuming. At the same time, some news outlets no longer employ correspondents but instead pay journalists a monthly retainer, plus a 'per story' fee, or use full freelance journalists per story only. Freelancers in particular report that it becomes tough to make a living, and as a result the freelancers become younger, only stay in the job for a few years, and take on different contracts at the same time. These extra jobs often include working as consultants for humanitarian organisations, which I will explain in more detail in the subsection on *Dependency Between Humanitarian Organisations and Correspondents*, in section 6.5.

Many humanitarian organisations feel the need for more transparency in terms of their project funding, achievements, and implementation on the ground because the aid sector has been repeatedly criticised (Moyo 2009; Polman 2010; Foreman 2013; Birrell 2014), and its effectiveness in its current state has been questioned (Riddell 2007). Besides, more and more donors demand reports, and hold the aid projects they fund to account. Some of the criticism even comes from within the sector itself (MSF 2014). Additionally, aid budgets are growing internationally, but not enough to keep pace with the huge expansion in the humanitarian sector. As a result, to claim a larger share of the pie, humanitarian organisations must be a 'brand' in order to sustain their support. For this to generate more funding and to create awareness on issues important to the organisations, it is essential to be present in media reports. Furthermore, humanitarian organisations create their own content, which is presented on websites, in handouts, and films. Since positive presentation became essential for humanitarian organisations and their funding, the communications and public relation departments grew everywhere, in headquarters as well as in country and regional offices.[18] This has happened to such an extent that even aid workers in the field sometimes become annoyed with their communications colleagues for sending so many journalists so frequently that field workers feel they are held back from doing their actual jobs, I was told by several interviewees. One sighed: "The disruption they cause, it's just . . . you know" (I_64).[19]

These two developments, the aid budgets and infrastructure growing, and the foreign reporting budgets and infrastructure shrinking, result in increasing cooperation between the two sectors, and a stable network being established between their actors. The graphic in Figure 6.15 gives an overview of the foreign correspondents' network. Displayed are all humanitarian organisations that correspondents described as partners or sources in the interviews and questionnaires.[20] Organisations not displayed were not mentioned in any of the interviews. Note that no data was available regarding the overall perception of organisations placed in light grey boxes, as they were not mentioned often enough to provide an understanding of how they were perceived. This network is supposed to give an overview of correspondents' contacts and how they evaluate them. It does not display the intensity or frequency of the interactions.[21] The dark grey box underneath the network in the graphic represents partners and sources other than humanitarian organisations, listing all that were mentioned in the interviews; it does not display the relative importance of one partner over the other, or the importance of all of these partners in comparison to humanitarian organisations.[22] This graphic shows the large amount of humanitarian organisations with which an average correspondent is in contact. In the next subsection we will look into the nature of the interactions that spring from these contacts.

What are the interactions about?

In this subsection I will give a short insight into what the interactions between humanitarian organisations and correspondents are about, followed by the next subsection that explains how they take place. Comparing what journalists and humanitarians see their interactions to be mainly about, see Figures 6.17 and 6.18. Respondents of humanitarian organisations rated consulting about information, exchanging data and figures, providing logistical support, and providing or discussing the use of footage, as all nearly equal. In the correspondents' view, however, the use of footage (black colour in the charts) plays only a minor role in the interactions. This mismatch may be due to different motives driving correspondents and humanitarians to interact: humanitarian organisations mainly want to raise funds and awareness through media, which is best achieved by disseminating a lot of information and media material, also in form of free footage. In contrast, journalists ethically prefer their reports to be original, distinct, and

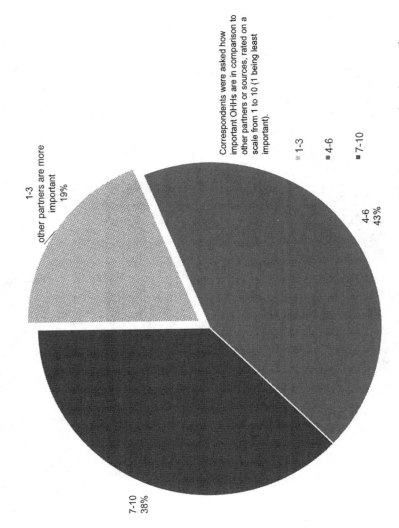

Figure 6.16 Importance of OHHs in comparison to other partners from the correspondents' perspective

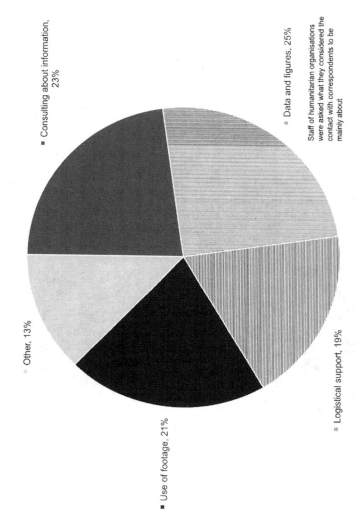

Figure 6.17 Type of contact with correspondents from OHHs' perspective

Research findings – interaction overview 169

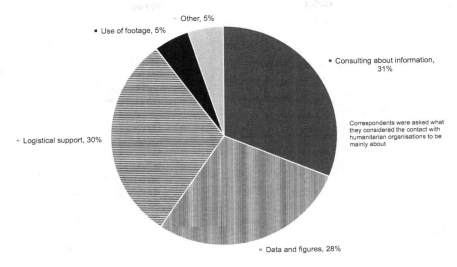

Figure 6.18 Type of contact with OHHs from correspondents' perspective

objective. Using footage by any organisation with its own agenda in supposedly independent media reports is not seen as desirable. Both responses regarding the use of footage are likely more the desired than the actual outcome of the interactions. From the correspondents' view, data humanitarian organisations gather and provide are valuable, whereas producing photography, news stories, or B-roll, are not. It is thus debatable whether the significant number of multimedia packages many organisations produce at great cost and with large teams to offer to news outlets, is economically justified when so few correspondents said they made use of the material, and – as my study reveals – even fewer consider doing so to be journalistically ethical. However, the data in these charts are just an approximate value; the in-depth interviews gave more insight into both perspectives, as the next subsections will show.

How do the interactions take place?

Correspondents and humanitarian organisations have contact in many different forms. Here, I will present the most common ways, mentioned in nearly all interviews by both groups. The most regular contact takes place via humanitarian organisations' emailing lists, or through personal emails if the connection is already established. Correspondents are sent press releases, information sheets, statistics, and figures from the field, case studies, and reports. The hook can be– but does not have to be– new developments in the field, world days, or high profile visits to field operations. Correspondents most often only scan the headlines and first paragraphs. In case anything sparks their interest, or in case they are working on the topic anyway, they contact the organisation for more details, for contacts to field directors or technical staff, or to talk about options visiting the field operations. The more the organisation is trusted to have valuable information and to only send out messages when it actually has something to say, the more likely the journalists said they were to read the email. Equally, when the communication comes from a trusted personal contact with the organisation (see also subsection on the importance of personal contacts), there is a greater chance the correspondent will look at the email properly. Otherwise the journalists either delete the email right away, or – as some interviewees told me – sort them into thematic folders that they browse when they are researching a story about the topic (e.g. I_21, I_29). In many cases, content shared via email is also tweeted, usually with a link to a website with more information or a press release online. Telephone contact usually emanates from the journalist, who may have questions regarding a topic, or be asking for help to arrange a field trip. The correspondents reported that the contact is most successful from their perspective when the interaction partner from the organisation understood what can make the news, stayed away from pushing their agency's agenda too hard, and was aware of journalistic deadlines. This is mostly the case when the communications person is a former journalist. In some cases, when personal contact between the correspondent and an employee of a humanitarian organisation is already established, the communications officer calls certain trusted journalists that have proven to be useful to the organisation, and informs them directly of new events or developments, or gives them story leads and story ideas that spring from events in the field. Correspondents reported that so-called cold calls – when the caller has no prior relationship with the journalist – are hardly ever appreciated, nor are calls proposing what reporters call "non-stories" that the organisation insists are newsworthy, such as a field visit by high-ranking people from the agency's head office. Informal meetings with a few selected journalists over coffee or dinner take place when a humanitarian organisations believes it to be more successful than official press conferences, which are held much less frequently than 10 or 15 years ago as interviews showed.

A very common interaction is the 'field trip' when the humanitarian organisation facilitates a correspondent's visit to their work on the ground to see how the organisation is helping and what impact that has.[23] It can be part of an organisation's media strategy to select certain correspondents and offer them a field visit. These trips offered by humanitarian organisation are either organised to take a number of journalists together to see a project, or for one journalist only, usually when the coverage is agreed upon beforehand. Equally, correspondents often take the first step in reaching out to one of bigger INGOs or the UN to organise travel to remote areas, not full press trips, involving flights in UN or INGO aircrafts, convoys through dangerous areas, or the organisation helping the journalist with visa applications and other necessary accreditation. The latter trips, even though they involve logistical help for the journalists, are often less organised than a 'packaged trip', where the humanitarian organisation plans the whole schedule. During emergency situations, when seats on aircraft or in convoys are limited, some INGOs offer to 'smuggle' correspondents on board UN flights pretending they are their staff. World Vision, I was told several times, does this when it calculates that its best interest is to increase publicity for a certain issue or region (e.g. I_33), but when spaces for journalists are restricted. Once in the field, the humanitarian organisation very often provides the journalist with contacts, translators, vehicles and drivers, and internet access to file stories. In places with bad infrastructure or poor security it is common that they also offer to sleep in the organisation's secure compound. If the location is considered dangerous, the organisation may arrange armed escorts to accompany the correspondents on pre-scheduled tours to interviews. A freelancing correspondent mainly working for British outlets gave an example of how these facilitated field trips often take place:

> The UN and the other relief organisations operate in a quite similar fashion logistically, just the UN can do more and do it bigger. A trip would be arranged and we'd be like: 'Oh look, we really want to get into Mogadishu or Juba.' And we talk to the UN. They say: 'Okay, look, we've got a trip going. We're putting a plane together. You have to be there by 6 am on Wednesday.' And we would all turn up at the airport or turn up at the UN hire cars or the UN hire planes, they would put us all on board and they would take us in. And there would be a press officer who would ride with us, and security, depending on where we were going. And then our trip into the field would be fairly organised by whoever was taking us. We weren't given a lot of freedom. But that was often a really good thing. They would use their contacts. They would find us the evidence we needed for the story we were going to cover. They would have had their people on the ground collect sources for us and accumulate data and information, and know what sites to take us to in order to represent the story that we wanted to. I guess there's a sort of sinister way to view that – that they got to shape the story. But often stories were mutually understood, what the common ground was. If it was a famine or if it was a massacre, going to the site of the massacre and interviewing an eye-witness, is obviously what we wanted to do. There's nothing controversial about that. So having the UN or a relief organisation manage that for us, was something we were comfortable with. And we had to be because we wouldn't have got there otherwise, in those instances. We'd have a press officer with us. They would walk us around. They would introduce us to the people that we either asked to meet or they had thought we should meet or a combination. And then they would [. . .] put us back on the plane or back in the car. If we were staying overnight, we would have had to sign a couple of forms, [. . .] and agree to stay within the confines of a particular compound. And we would join their staff for dinner and for breakfast and we would use their internet facilities, often important when we were in the field, because they would have their own satellite hook-ups and we wouldn't have them.
>
> (I_16)

A recent development is humanitarian organisations send their own communications staff and media teams to areas that are hard to access, and contact correspondents they know to ask whether they are interested in any specific information or angle from that location. Their media staff then gathers the information, photographs, or B-roll, and shares the material with the correspondent upon their return.

I will examine how facilitated trips may affect the journalists' dependency in section 6.5. In nearly all forms of contact between journalists and humanitarians, adaptions to one another's working procedures take place. Humanitarian organisations try to make their stories more interesting, for example by providing hooks such as World Days or bringing celebrities to the field (*adaption effort*, see Chapter 4, section 4.3). Offering B-rolls, purposefully reacting to news demands, anticipating journalists' selection criteria, and choosing topics according to how attractive they will be to the media, can also be grouped as humanitarian organisations' *adaption efforts. Initiative induction* takes place for example when organisations expand their media teams to help facilitate field trips for journalists, or when they produce 'journalistic' material with their staff trying to find story angles that are most likely to interest media – a current practice as I was told by several interviewees. For example, a Care employee described finding photographs and stories for journalists:

> You're also identifying something that might help [the journalist when you are on field trips with them]. There was a small girl doing her homework, she sat outside of a tent, and I saw her, and in MY head the story would be: these people are so resilient that there's still schools, that are still pushing their lives forward amidst this. They're not even living in what you'd call a home. And so I pointed the girl out to the photographer and he's all over her.
>
> (I_45)

In my study, I also observed a new trend that could fall into the category of *initiative induction*: humanitarian organisations increasingly commission so-called scientific research and publish the results in form of reports, including details about how the organisation is already helping to improve the situation. The idea is to drum up media interest in the findings of this 'new report', when the issue that it examines is chronic or long-term, and therefore not newsworthy.

Nearly all humanitarian organisations that were part of this study wanted to understand better how the media work, and accordingly which public relations strategies are likely to be successful. Many organisations invite correspondents to give talks presenting their views on the interactions, and to train their communications staff.[24] A very common practice is also to contract freelance correspondents to produce material for the communications department, blurring the lines between the two sectors to a critical point. I will explain this and possible impacts further in section 6.7 on the influence of the interactions on news coverage. Correspondents on the other hand try to accommodate humanitarian organisations by giving them 'a line or two' in their news pieces, which can be seen as *text induction*. When trips are facilitated by humanitarian organisations, correspondents have to obey the organisations' rules and regulations in the field, and are in many cases dependent on the organisations' estimations of the situation on the ground as the organisation has contacts and information that a visiting journalist might never acquire (*evaluating induction*).

Overall, given the need to cooperate and the established routines between correspondents and humanitarian organisations in sub-Saharan Africa, it is surprising how little detail both know about how the other operates, and how little effort is put into exploring the others' strategies and goals. In the following subsection I will therefore explain how correspondents choose with which organisations to work, and how humanitarian staff decides with which media, and with which individual journalists, to trust and cooperate.

Choosing interaction partners

How do correspondents choose which humanitarian organisation to call, to ask for data, or with which to travel? And how do humanitarian organisations choose which correspondents, or which media outlets to priorities, to invite for a media trip, or for whom to facilitate travels? From the humanitarian organisations' perspective, the answer is much simpler. Large media of record and news agencies are preferred contacts because of their broad reach. The type of media, however, whether newspaper, magazine, television or radio, is not the decisive factor as the interviews illustrate. Mentioned by name by at least 15 humanitarian interviewees were the news agencies Reuters, AFP, and AP, the newspapers The New York Times, and The Guardian, and the broadcasters BBC, CNN, and Al Jazeera. Certain trusted individual freelancers who work for many different outlets, thus apparently guaranteeing a wide reach, also fall into this first group. Freelancers, however, are generally seen as a greater risk as long as they are not trusted individuals that the organisation has either worked with before, or that come recommended. The interviews reveal that a significant number of humanitarian organisations consider carefully what kind of stories a journalist has produced so far and how they are written, before deciding to invite him or her to join a trip or to help them in any significant way. Doing so, they try to evaluate the risk of negative press, of facilitating a journalist who might be after a scoop at any price, or who might put field staff at risk. The second group of news outlets was mentioned significantly less frequently by humanitarians: ARD, ZDF, Financial Times, The Independent, The Economist, VOA, Wall Street Journal, The Washington Post, and Xinhua. BuzzFeed and Vice were mentioned very sporadically. They have evolved to be extremely popular news sites for a young Western audience, which makes them attractive to some organisations. Humanitarian organisations also consider which audience they want to target and for what reason; they weigh up whether the ideal outcome of facilitating a journalist's trip in the organisation's view is to create general public awareness of an issue, whether it is to target a specific fundraising market, or whether the aim is to do advocacy work to influence policy makers or to communicate messages to bilateral donors.

From the correspondents' perspective, the decision of which humanitarian organisation to choose as interaction partner is more complex. The following could be distilled out of the interviews: the choice depends on the issue that is to be covered and whether a certain organisation is known to specialise in it. It also depends on the region the correspondent wants to travel to or wants information about, and how hard it is to access without the help of a humanitarian organisation. Simple things make a difference: which organisation is present in that region, which one responds the quickest to a correspondent's request, and which one is willing and able to help. How outspoken an organisation is and whether its information is considered trustworthy and relevant also plays a role; relevant in this case means that it is either information that the journalist needs for his or her story, 'frontline' information from the ground that is hard to access, or information that is newsworthy in itself (see subsection on news values). Nationality also plays an important role in the decision. The data show that correspondents tend to interview sources that speak their language – this is especially true for television productions – and who come from the same cultural background as their audiences. Portraying or interviewing a person who shares the news outlet's nationality, satisfies the news values 'affinity', 'proximity', 'status', and 'personalisation' at the same time, which is particularly relevant when covering a faraway country to which audiences might otherwise not relate. The correspondents' decision who to contact also depends on the general reputation of the organisation, and its brand recognition in the news outlet's country; Oxfam for example may be known to most British audiences, but not to many Americans. Aside from the organisation's general reputation and its brand recognition to audiences, it is also relevant what journalists commonly know about it ('Unicef equals children', 'MSF is health-related and frontline', 'WFP deals with food issues but is very politicised' etc.).[25] However, the official mandate of a humanitarian organisation is less relevant in the correspondents' view. Few correspondents know the history of many organisations, nor do they know how exactly they are financed, or what their political mandates, and thus political interests are. This includes most UN organisations. Only one journalist talked about "mandates" when asked to differentiate between INGOs and the UN, and more generally between different types of organisations. The UN I found to have an inconsistent role in the correspondents' views: despite being the one that was most criticised – apart from Save the Children – it carries authority. Its agencies are often among the first to receive a call when a correspondent starts researching a story because they are an easy source of information. Another factor is the correspondents' individual and subjective evaluation of which organisation he or she generally considers trustworthy and doing good work. Interviewees stated their evaluations might be informed by whether the organisation's work had long-term effects, how long it had worked in a certain region, whether it ran projects in more rural areas or only in the capital, whether the organisation's staff spoke the local language, whether it only ran sustainable projects or else focused on issues considered to be 'in fashion', and whether they considered the organisation to be self-reflexive and able to acknowledge mistakes. Finally, and this is the most important aspect that is true for both correspondents and the humanitarian organisations, the decision who to reach out to comes down to personal contacts. I will elaborate about this in more detail in the following subsection.

The role of personal contacts

I found personal contacts between correspondents and staff of humanitarian organisations to be of significant relevance. By personal contacts I mean a relationship between two actors who have met in person at least once and who stay in regular, friendly contact. This understanding does not include correspondents on a general email list of a humanitarian organisation, which is used to send out for example press releases without addressing the journalist personally. All interviewees, correspondents and staff of humanitarian organisations, considered personal contacts to individuals of the other group important. Those respondents who said that personal contacts did not play a significant role in their work, at the same time said that they should invest more time in building and maintaining these relationships in the future. Even correspondents who said they tried to avoid interacting with humanitarian organisations if possible, added that it was nevertheless important to know which individuals were knowledgeable and helpful when needed, because due to crises in the region it was be impossible to avoid all organisations. Since I assumed that the personal contacts were especially relevant for communications staff of humanitarian organisations, I asked them explicitly how important they considered personal contacts for their work and their organisation. The results were decisive (Figure 6.19): Ninety percent rated the importance of personal contacts to correspondents on a scale from 1 to 10 at 7 or above. Only 10 percent rated

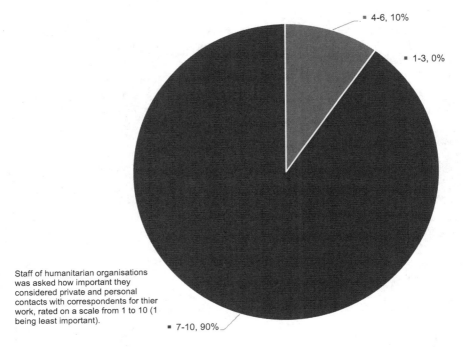

Figure 6.19 Importance of personal contacts with correspondents from the OHHs' perspective

it at 4 to 6, and none at 1, 2, or 3. From the humanitarian organisations' perspective these contacts are very important, because first communications staff find it easier to approach journalists with information when they are not 'cold calling' but when they have made contact with the journalist before. A humanitarian told me that personal contacts were part of their public relations strategy:

> I think it's a really smart move to establish those relationships, especially with the wires but with other people too. Prior to meeting, and then, it's like two ways, you will feel comfortable enough to approach them, and probably get some coverage from them and they will also think of you before they think of someone else.
>
> (I_45)

They consider that their information is more valued when the journalist they are approaching already knows them and their objectives, and has learnt to trust their analysis of situations. By contrast, they think that public relations material and other information sent out without this personal connection, or by personnel who frequently rotate and remain unknown, will most likely not be read at all by journalists. A correspondent of a news agency confirmed this concern:

> We go into South Sudan in the field and there's UN people who are generally very reluctant to talk. Everything has to go through one particular press officer, who will stay there. They will be there for three, four months and then they'll get rotated out. Whereas MSF, you know, they have an office down the road. We'll occasionally sit down and have lunch with them, just have a chat with them about what's going on. The same with Oxfam, same with Care. [. . .] And IF one of these people calls you up and says: 'Ah, there's something REALLY interesting.' Then we'll give them the time. But when you get an email or press release from the UN, which basically says the UN is announcing this, this, and this. I mean, nine times out of ten, I just delete it.
>
> (I_20)

A very experienced spokesperson of a big UN agency who previously worked as a journalist for many years, said she saw it as necessary strategy for successful public relations to establish and nourish these relationships:

> It helps me tremendously, because when I go to meet a journalist for the first time I go prepared for the conversation to go one of two ways or both ways. I go and I just keep it really low-key. 'I just wanted to meet you', because sometimes they're just thrilled to get out of the office and have a coffee and sometimes it's just literally trading stories. I tell them who I am. I tell them what I've done. Sometimes they're really under pressure to produce something. So sometimes they spend two minutes doing that and then saying, 'Well, what story should I cover?' So then I have a press pack and

I'm prepared. Sometimes the last thing they want is another press pack that they're going to throw away. [. . .]. I REALLY personalise the emails and I NEVER write the same email to anybody twice. So I would just write something like 'I completely understand why you couldn't come to the donor meeting. I know it's just not your thing, and I know it's not a new story, but here's some things you might consider for the future'. [. . .] Then when I hear them on the radio, see them on TV, I'll just send them like one line. One of the guys who ended up becoming one of my best contacts and even a really good friend, I went to see him once, [and] we hit it off really well. I don't think he EVER did a story FOR us, but he did a lot of really good stories that kind of touched on issues we liked. I won't bombard him, but when it was relevant I would send him an email about how I saw him on TV whatever. One of the emails that he loved the most I sent him and I said 'love that report on blah-blah-blah.' I said, 'HOW ON EARTH did you manage to look so fresh in that nice blue shirt in that heat?' He loved it.

(I_44)

Sometimes – that same person elaborated – that required to be friendly even if the journalist's request had nothing to do with your organisation:

My approach is unless your desk is on fire or you yourself are on fire, then the correct response is, 'Wow, that's an interesting story, let me refer you to the correct agency that can help you.' Because you earn so many points in your favour by being polite to them because you also could say, 'Are you a complete idiot? Do you not see that I am working for the refugee agency?!', and then they'll never call you again. When you call them [and want to sell them a story then], they're going to say, 'You're the person who was so rude to me.' So unless your desk is on fire, your pants are on fire, the correct response is, 'Wow, what an interesting story. Let me steer you to the right person.' Even if you have to Google it yourself.

(I_44)

However – and this does not seem obvious to less experienced public relations staff – knowing a correspondent well and nourishing that relationship alone does not guarantee coverage at all. It only provides a healthy foundation for a working relationship on a personal level, and that can pay off; but issues must still be newsworthy to get covered, as a very experienced spokesperson of a humanitarian organisation explained:

The way it works in the field, a lot depends on personal contacts. It's way easier if you have met the journalist in person to get your stuff covered. [. . .] But I think criteria number one is still: What is new in your story? Why would I cover it? What's the value? At the end of the day you stay professional as well. You help each other out in facilitating each other's work. But it's not,

'Oh yeah, I like you. Of course whatever you send my way – I'm going to cover it.' No, forget about it.

(I_61)

Second, humanitarian communications staff find it advantageous to know the journalists personally to assess the risk they are taking when inviting them on a trip, or to be able to choose the most ideal correspondent to invite in order to garner the best coverage of the issues they want featured. A communications employee of an INGO told me that they relied on recommendations of colleagues in other organisations in cases where they did not yet know a particular journalist:

> There would be certain people calling and [say] 'this person is a really great journalist and he is going to write something STRONG and he has an understanding of the context'. Because sometimes you get people who might have a nice media behind them, but they are not necessarily good journalists and they are not going to do anything more than just the very basic minimum. And then you would get somebody else who [has had contact with this 'good' journalist and says], 'no honestly, you are going to want to talk to him, [. . .] it will be a strong piece and he is a good journalist'.

(I_48)

Freelance journalists in particular stressed the importance of personal contacts and how those connections could help when a humanitarian organisation was evaluating their work in advance of a potential cooperation. One correspondent who had worked as a freelancer for many years for British outlets, and then worked for a news agency, said:

> A lot of it is personal relationships. I mean if you know someone and you've done a story with them before, and they trust you, then it's easier to call them up and say, 'Look, you know, I did this story six months ago with you. I was FINE. I didn't mess it up'. Because there's always that element of trust and risk. You know especially when you are taking a stranger [journalist] out to a strange place, showing [him or her] what you do. I could write something crazy and incorrect that damages them and so, you know, if you've shown them once you're an okay guy then the next time they'll go, 'Yes, that's good what you did last time. That's okay'.

(I_21)

And third and most importantly, trust emerges from personal contacts. Many of the communications staff interviewed said that only once they knew a journalist, their work, and how they operated, could they be sure 'not to be screwed over', and that the journalist would not publish details that they voiced off record. A correspondent who mainly covers humanitarian issues told me:

> The difference between a good and a bad press officer is [whether they] trust you. They are going to tell you things off the record and want you to

understand the situation and the context and what's really going on. And then at least they treat you like an adult and it helps you understand. The BAD ones are the ones who are very fearful and won't really share anything with you. And then you don't understand what's going on.

(I_56)

From the correspondents' perspective these personal contacts are equally important. This is because first, correspondents find it useful to know who to turn to, and to have that person's private or mobile number to find information quicker, and in a more informal way, than via the official route. A correspondent said:

[Communications people of humanitarian organisation would] reach out and just say, 'Oh, I just read your piece about such and such. Do you want to get a coffee?' And so I think there is very much a personalised element to the relationships that even if you hang out with that person socially, you've kind of met with them in a more casual sort of setting. And so then it does make it a lot easier to reach out, especially when you're on a deadline and you need like information within three hours or something. It's really helpful to be able to call the people that you, at the very least, have had a pleasant coffee date with. And then they tend to be a lot more responsive. And often times, you know, then you have their personal cell phone number, rather than like an office line, or an office email. [. . .] A really important aspect of being a journalist in this region in terms of building like a contact list is using those moments when you're out in the field staying with an organisation because there's nowhere else to stay. And you meet people over at dinner in the canteen area. And it's important I think having those kind of connections, those personalised connections, of we have dinner together for three nights in the middle of South Sudan. And I know what you're doing, and I see what you do day-to-day. And so those would be the people that would be my first preference to call. Someone who I actually have met, who seen in their work environment and then say, 'Okay, I'm starting to look into this particular topic. I know you're based in that area. Do you have information about it, or do you know of anyone who I should talk to?' Because if THAT person doesn't know, if they have a good contact, chances are, that they will really know what they're talking about because they're right there in the midst of it.

(I_33)

How much information is given to a journalist, of what quality, and how frankly, depends not only on the organisation but also on the individual. For that reason correspondents say that it is essential to know which individuals were helpful, especially when on a tight deadline for a story:

It could be that for example that someone of the ICRC in Congo is doing a GREAT job, and I have met someone who is incredibly dedicated. In theory, just to give an example, I could have someone from the same organisation in the Central African Republic who is tough and frustrating to work with. Because there might be someone responsible for press communications who does NOT help but rather blocks everything. If I know a person with whom working together goes well, then I would always call that individual again.

(I_29)

Second, it is only after the correspondent has previously been in contact with the staff of the humanitarian organisation that he or she knows how good that individual's contacts in the field are, and how many strings he or she can pull, "two years ago Unicef helped me in this place therefore I'll try them again" (I_09). Third, correspondents find it useful to know their humanitarian counterpart to assess how well he or she understands how reporting on humanitarian issues works. Not all trips, or requests for information result in news stories or positive publicity citing the organisation's name.

In cities like Nairobi, and even more so in the field, it is not difficult to form these personal contacts, interviewees said. Strong ties between expatriates grow in networks that go beyond a single profession. The expat crowd frequents the same restaurants and bars, and friendships between humanitarians and journalists are common: "A lot of it comes [down] to personal contact. [. . .] You know, we know them. They might be FRIENDS or they might be neighbours" (I_20), an AFP correspondent stated. A former Reuters freelancer explained:

East Africa has a big expat community but over a few years you get to know a lot of these people. We didn't just socialise with journalists. It would be unusual for us to go on a press trip where we didn't peripherally know some of the non-journalists involved, where one of them might be an ex-girlfriend or one of them might be someone you met at a dinner party. That stuff was quite typical and it was all reasonably friendly.

(I_16)

In some cases, the professional contact followed a friendship, in others it is the other way round:

There is around 4000 [I]NGOs registered in Nairobi. That means if you go for drinks or <<sighs>> sit anywhere, then you meet each other. And there are many, many, many employees of [I]NGOs, humanitarian organisations, which ever, that you get to know privately first. So you sometimes have a private contact with them first, and THEN a professional one.

(I_29)

Why a friendship overlapping a professional relationship is both important and valuable is clearly illustrated in this quote of a correspondent:

A very good friend of mine is the spokeswoman for WFP and we were friends from before, from Afghanistan. We have a great working relationship and I'll call her up and she'll tell me what's happening very straight. And then we'll talk about what's going to be on record or off record or whatever. And I know she's not going to bullshit me and she knows I'm not going to screw her over. Because you just don't do that to a friend. [. . .] And some other people earn your respect and a friendship grows out of it.

(I_34)

Personal contacts play an especially significant role in places where living conditions are rough and finding and verifying information is challenging, like in Juba and rural South Sudan:

In South Sudan [. . .] even if you're not personally friends with people, there was always the idea that you knew who was around and that you felt at any time you could kind of just have a chat with them [humanitarian workers] and say oh, by the way what's going on with X, Y, or Z?

(I_4)

A few correspondents criticised the nature of these personal contacts and friendships that result from the 'expat bubble'. A freelance correspondent of a German-speaking outlet who nonetheless considered these contacts important, explained:

I think for many Western foreign correspondents that is a learning process. I had to get through that, too. Of course you automatically run to those who you know, or to those who look like you. That is, Western employees of humanitarian organisations who often live in this famous bubble. That means they clot in the bigger cities where they have the infrastructure they need. And there, of course, social contacts emerge. You would go to the same clubs, or meet in the same cafes, or at whatever events because everyone clucks together. And these are often very tight in-groups with VERY few contacts beyond work to the society in which they live and work. So it does make sense to take a look around who is working for the national scene of humanitarian organisations. If you do that, you often come to a very different conclusion about things.

(I_15)

Nearly all people interviewed for this research said that personal relationships and general trust help in challenging situations, because differing expectations could then more easily be managed. Only two correspondents said that a more personal connection to communications personnel creates more pressure to report positively about their organisation (I_28, I_30), but there could be many more cases where correspondents do not realise indirect pressure. Many freelancing correspondents and some correspondents working on a retainer said that they work on assignments for humanitarian organisations from time to time to earn more money; making a living from freelancing is hard. The potential influence of these relationships on the news coverage I will discuss in more detail in section 6.7.

In this section, I discussed the variety of aspects that influence with which organisations a correspondent chooses to interact. They include: the data and information the correspondent needs; the issue that he or she wants to report about; the logistical support the organisation can provide; its contact network in the field; the accessibility of the country or region where the journalist wants to go; the speed with which an organisation responds to a media request; the policy of an organisation, that is how outspoken it is on certain issues; and on personal relationships with staff working for any of the organisations. How strongly correspondents perceive the dependency on humanitarian organisations depends on their type of employment, the outlet nationality, and the budget they have at their disposal. Which correspondent the humanitarian organisations chooses to approach depends on: the audience it wants to reach and the desired outcome of the communication strategy; the size and reach of the news outlet for which the journalist is working; the credibility and trustworthiness of the individual journalist; and again, personal relationships and friendships, which are enhanced by the tight expat community in many locations where correspondents and employees of humanitarian organisations both operate.

Overall, this last section looked at a correspondent's network with humanitarian organisations and discussed which organisations play a role in it; how the interactions take place in practice; who cooperates with whom; and how these decisions are made. The section also shed light on the importance of personal contacts within the network.

6.4 Challenges in the interactions

What challenges, misunderstandings, or difficulties occur, from both points of view, when journalists and humanitarian organisations interact? For humanitarian organisations, the worry about safety, credibility, and their brand count: I discovered that the challenges mainly occur when correspondents aim to get a scoop at any price; when they hinder field staff from doing their work; and when they threaten to jeopardise the field workers' reputation or security, for example by asking political questions, or by blaming one side in a conflict. The humanitarian organisations also reported a key difficulty was that they can never be sure of the outcome of what the journalist produces, nor do they have a guarantee that the journalist will name their organisation in the news coverage, even if they agency has invested a considerable amount of time, money, and manpower to facilitate the journalist's trip.

From the correspondents' perspective, mainly the lack of independence is problematic when public relations officers push their own agenda and try to influence the reporting. Other recurring problems are public relations staff not understanding journalistic deadlines, presenting 'news' ideas that are not news stories, swamping email accounts with press releases that are of no interest to journalists, and lengthy and bureaucratic decision-making processes in humanitarian organisations that stand in opposition to the fast-moving news cycle, especially in the UN. This can mean that the journalist's deadline to deliver a story to the editor in time to be published cannot be met because, for example, statements still need to be signed off by staff on different levels.

In the interviews, humanitarians frequently said that journalists sometimes need to be more sensitive to the situation on the ground, for example should respect the privacy of hospital patients in crisis areas when the patients have not given consent to be questioned or filmed. Being seen as neutral and not taking sides is crucial to humanitarian organisations in conflict areas, where they operate safely only with the good will of both belligerents. An employee of MSF working in communications said:

> Do not attribute any political statements to MSF because we are here and we need to work here. So in that sense we are always quite strict. When you are interviewing our patients, whether they're soldiers or civilians in a hospital, they are patients. Do not ask them about the war. If you meet them on the street, ask them whatever you want to but NOT in MSF facilities, because then we become a target as well, we're seen to take sides.
>
> (I_52)

Most journalists, however, understand that their work requires sensitivity. A freelance correspondent mainly working for British outlets described a case where she was on a press trip and stumbled across a story that she wanted to investigate but that could have harmed the humanitarian organisations' reputation that she was with among conflict groups. She came to an agreement with the organisation, which was acceptable for both sides:

> I've been away with [a large INGO] on a really soft story about seeds and tools, and then we found out that in the same town, there was a HUGE child recruitment a couple of weeks before. And they really TRIED to stop us doing it, and we said: No way. But we agreed that we wouldn't be seen anywhere near their cars; we wouldn't use their driver; we wouldn't use their translator, and we would make sure that this didn't come back to them.
>
> (I_43)

To understand the consequences of these challenges better, I studied interactions that did not work well, and the sanctions available to humanitarian organisations for journalists who did not meet their expectations. Humanitarian organisations cannot officially censor a correspondent's reporting. However, there are more subtle ways of influencing the journalists. Many communications employees told me that they checked the correspondent's previous work, or asked other colleagues about experiences with that reporter, before they took him or her on a trip. If a correspondent published stories in a way the organisation respected, and if he or she behaved sensitively and was cooperative, the organisation was likely to facilitate further trips in the future. If the correspondent, however, did not meet the organisations' expectations, the public relations department might very well question whether this journalist was worth the time, money, and effort in the future. A correspondent of AFP explained:

> [In cases like this] the press officer would be pissed off and then you knew that the next time you called up and said, 'I really want to go to this remote place, can you fly me around?', and [they] potentially [had to] spend hundreds of dollars on you in terms of aeroplane flights, [and] accommodation, they would not [do it].
>
> (I_21)

In extreme cases, they even blacklisted the respective correspondent. My study found that most correspondents were well aware of this risk, but did not think the threat of blacklisting would compromise their independent reporting in any way. A correspondent for British outlets known for his generally critical view of aid said: "I'm aware that the British aid groups are slightly wary of me, because of my outspoken criticism of them" (I_10). A freelancer who said she would not compromise her reporting, stated in passing when talking about the interaction with a communications employee that facilitated a trip for her: "I didn't want to mess that relationship up, because I needed to go back to her for figures" (I_24). Freelance journalists feel the threat of sanctions more keenly, as their reporting is not as valuable to the humanitarian organisations as the publicity from large newspapers of record or national broadcasters. At the same time, it is freelancers who are much more dependent on humanitarian organisations facilitating and partly paying their travel, as their budgets are especially tight. One interviewee who had been both a staff and freelance correspondent recounted the significant difference his employment status made with regards to his relations to humanitarian organisations:

> The UN could offer so much, they played a bigger part in my professional life, once I became a freelancer, basically because I just needed more favours. I needed to network differently. I needed to reach out in a way that I didn't when I was at Reuters. At Reuters, they would come knocking at your door. Even when I was a stringer in [two different countries in sub-Saharan Africa], the UN would literally come knocking at my door and say: 'Look, you're Reuters. We really think there's a story, we can give you graphs and press packs and everything', and they'd take me out to lunch and try and sell me on a story. And often it was a very valuable story. And if it wasn't, I told them so. Whereas as a freelancer, it's far more . . . the onus is on the journalist to choose a story, verbally sell it to X publication and then go to someone like the UN and say: 'Look, I think I can tell this story in a way that you would think is worthwhile. This is where I want to put it. Can you facilitate my research?' So it was often quite a delicate balance and you had to be very ethically aware all the time of what was appropriate and what was inappropriate. But that was the reality of freelancing in the region, well, being paid

very poorly, and we had to use the resources of the UN, without ever selling ourselves out.

(I_16)

The outreach and brand of large news outlets, however, leaves humanitarian organisations with little choice but to facilitate the correspondents' future trips and field visits, even if he or she did not meet their expectations after earlier missions. During my investigation several humanitarian organisations told me that this was the case for one large American newspaper, whose correspondent everyone tried to please despite negative experiences.[26] The correspondent, however, was not available to present his point of view despite several attempts to arrange an interview. Several correspondents I interviewed reported that UN agencies in particular tended to deny them seats on planes if they wanted to prevent coverage from certain locations that were otherwise difficult to reach, and that they regularly blocked access to the field. A German broadcasting correspondent reported:

> [It happens] that they refuse to cooperate. That means that they do not accredit you in the first place. [In one case] they did not offer us any logistical support but instead said: 'We do NOT want you to come'. We went anyway. And when we got there, they refused to give us access, for example, to food distribution points because we did not have any accreditation. And then we had to argue, face to face. And explain to them that this was not exactly a very good idea.
>
> (I_26)

A freelancer mainly working for British outlets recounted many similar negative experiences with UN organisations, who tried to block journalists' access to the field and to information. The following account of one of these incidents, which turned out to be especially problematic and involved threats over the phone to several journalists, illustrates that freelancers in particular face significant pressures to compromise their reporting to maintain good relations with humanitarian organisations that they know they will need in the future:

> [This high ranking UN person] wouldn't want to give us any information, or allow us access to any information that would make the government look bad. She was in bed with the government and she saw four young freelancers, and I think she knew that she could silence us very easily. One of my friends was even threatened by a [very senior] communications person, that if she kept asking about why the UN hadn't condemned the expulsion of one of its own human rights workers without explanation, that she would suddenly find her access to the UN very, very limited. And in a place where you've got a one billion dollar peacekeeping mission and they operate all the flights, that's quite a statement. [. . .] And there were even meetings that were held about me, after I uncovered a massacre, that I believed and I knew that

UN forces watched and didn't flag afterwards or before either. [. . .] And it was to make the government that had basically sponsored all these massacres look okay. [. . .] I was shown meeting notes by some UN staff about me, that point number ten of many, was that [journalist x] has decided to go after us. And I was told that during a couple of meetings UN staff were told under no circumstances were they allowed to speak to me and tell me anything. [. . .] Anyway, we turned up for about five flights. All of these flights were mysteriously cancelled. We were told that it was bad weather. Then we'd call people there. No bad weather. We were told that you know it was very, very difficult, that only UN personnel could get on flights. And then people within the UN would tell us that flights had left with other aid workers on that were non-UN. So just an extreme catalogue of lies to, basically, cover up for the government. [. . .] And many diplomats agreed with me that this was unacceptable, and [were angry] that the UN was covering up these massacres. A certain large embassy secretly funded a private cargo plane to put three journalists on, under the auspices of one of its contractors, to fly us above an entire area where the whole buildings, and even nearly the UN store, had been either destroyed or razed [. . .], so that we could write about it. And these were routes that UN planes went on every day. So I mean, that was the level. Everyone was just ABSOLUTELY SHOCKED at how much the UN mission was trying to control press. And if they didn't get their way, then they were threatening journalists personally over the phone.

(I_43)

My study reveals that in extreme cases like this, it is common for the humanitarian organisation to then sanction more than just the individual journalist who 'misbehaved', and also refuse to cooperate with the news outlet in general, and sometimes other outlets. A former AP correspondent described publishing a story on aid money disappearing, which infuriated WFP so much that he found himself needing the services of good lawyers. It is the exception not the rule that circumstances go so far. In most cases, if the final story that follows an extensively facilitated field visit does not meet the expectations of the humanitarian organisation and its media officers, they can do little more than feel disappointed, reduce the level of support for the journalist in the future, and write letters of complaint to the editors. A correspondent gave account of the organisations' frustration:

> I have heard many complaints from humanitarian organisations saying: 'We try our hardest to get a TV team deep into the bush to film a village. And they use everything from us. They sleep in our compounds, they eat in our canteens, they use the car with our logo on it. And then we see the report on TV and they do not talk about us once. And even the logo is retouched off the car.
>
> (I_15)

A communications staff member of a large INGO told of the energy it took to take correspondents on a field trip, without knowing whether it would pay off, and without guarantee that it would not jeopardise the field staff's security:

That's the challenge as a kind of media staff. Is to have the confidence and the knowledge not to be pushed [by the journalists]. Because in the back of your mind all the time, it has to be, program security, personal security, long-term risk. It's one of the most tiring things to do, it's the journalist trip because you'll be constantly trying to work out, okay where are they going next, where are they looking. Yes, they tend to live around a bit like toddlers, in they'll take an interest in one thing, they'll kind of go off about it for a bit, and then they'll totally lose interest in that and go in a completely different direction. It's an amazing capacity to explore things, to a level of detail. But also it's quite challenging for somebody who is trying to manage both the logistics and the message and the security.

(I_45)

The same interviewee told of a situation where a journalist's interest could have threatened the operation's security, which left the interviewee in disbelief despite the amount of understanding she showed for the journalists' needs:

I respect them [the journalists] for pushing us [communications people on field visits with these journalists]; it's their job, they are looking for a story, as long as they're doing it openly and directly. There was an instance where we went to our old office in old town [x] whilst we were there, so the frontline staff were in the office. And I sat in the car with the journalists and there was a group of soldiers who sat in the front of the door of another office, which they're now occupying. And the photographer [said] 'oh, do you think they would talk to me?', and I'm like, 'you'll never find out!' <<laughing in disbelief>>. And he is like: 'I can just take off my [INGO's] ID and just go talk to them, leave my cameras and then maybe I come back'. And I said: 'I understand why you want to, but you're here on [our INGO's] good grace, and all I'm bothered about is – if anything goes wrong, you might jeopardise our program, you might jeopardise our staff and [the organisation's] reputation and ability to respond.

(I_45)

An interviewee from Human Rights Watch gave evidence of a level of personal frustration that influenced future interactions with a particular reporter:

[This correspondent] didn't even MENTION Human Rights Watch, and we put loads of reports out on that specific case. But then he never acknowledged. [. . .] It probably makes me a tiny bit, just from a personal point of view, reluctant to, you know, spend a lot of time helping him in the future.

(I_62)

Regarding blacklisting correspondents, an MSF communications employee reiterated the importance of personal contacts in difficult situations:

Then it comes down a lot to the personal relationship as well[, which might prevent incidents like this in the first place]. Because [otherwise] there are some people who are then blacklisted by us [and] we would never work with them again. You know, even if they do come from a big media house: 'Sorry, no way, you are not welcome here'.

(I_48)

Actors from both sectors said that in these cases, it was best to try to understand the other side's point of view. A freelance correspondent for German outlets told of an incident where she published critical accounts of an aid operation but the public relations officer who took her into the field was luckily a former journalist:

> She [the public relations officer] did not find that very amusing. But she has to live with it. She was a journalist herself, so that is why it was ok on a personal level. But if she had been a proper advocacy person – I think she would NEVER take me into a UNHCR car again after a critique like that, you see. So the interaction on a personal level and the mutual understanding for each other's job are very important.
>
> (I_08)

A correspondent of another German news outlet described his mixed feelings when his editor cut from his report the mention of the humanitarian organisation that had helped him during his reporting trip because the information was not necessary story-wise:

> I had to swallow that, but I thought: 'Hm, would have been nice to mention them because they helped me so much'. And they even called and [. . .] said, 'well, that is a shame because we helped you so much in the field', and so on. Oh well. Then I had to explain it to them the same way I did to you now.
>
> (I_28)

A freelancer mainly working for American outlets also reported mixed feelings when she had to stay with a humanitarian organisation on a field trip that she was about to criticise for their work in a different country:

> I definitely felt kind of like I was walking on pins and needles because it was that combination of the sort of practical side of the relationship coming in contact with the functional side in a way that the staff that was working in that office and who hosted me for a week, didn't know I was about to come out with this piece that was pretty much blasting their team in Congo and their comms team for their way of handling the situation in Eastern Congo. But it was definitely a kind of a cringe-worthy moment for me when I realised I would probably have to stay with them. [. . .] [And then] because of the way the [critical] piece [that I wrote] had come out it was no longer in their interest to, you know, be helping me anymore. So that was like a kind of, it was actually kind of a tough lesson because, you know, after having

long interactions with people and feeling, okay we're like we're on the same page, about the importance of getting a story out there and talking about what REALLY happens [. . .]. And then to feel like they kind of turned against me in the end. [. . .] Maybe they wouldn't want me to be around, but I also think they probably wouldn't want any journalists to be around. [. . .] So I don't think it's especially just me being blacklisted.

(I_33)

These insights show that sanctions can be applied on a broader organisational level but also on a very personal level between two people. The account above also shows that many correspondents see the interactions not only on a professional level, but that some feel sorry for having to 'disappoint' the humanitarians with whom they spent time. What implications this may have for the coverage, I will explore in section 6.7.

6.5 Importance of the interactions

To explore relationships, avoidance is also important to investigate. Forty percent of the interviewed correspondents claimed to sometimes avoid certain humanitarian organisations if possible, or at least tried to acknowledge these organisations' involvement in the production of the reporting. A remarkable 60 percent of the correspondents reported not to avoid any humanitarian organisation (Figure 6.20).

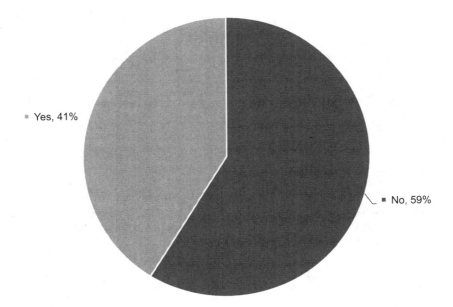

Figure 6.20 Correspondents avoiding OHHs

The 40 percent that claimed to avoid interactions if possible, avoid the following type of organisations for the following reasons (Figure 6.21): the majority, 36 percent, avoid humanitarian organisations with religious backgrounds, especially evangelical ones. Eighteen percent try to avoid all UN organisations if they can; but at the same time many of those said that there were regions where it was not possible to avoid them. One of the correspondents stated:

> Some people just came to despise the UN for all that's wrong with it and refused to work with them. And that was an admirable, moral position but often would hurt their capacity to produce work, even that they might have been proud of. But no, there weren't a great deal of options. It was just the level of engagement with this relationship that you were comfortable with.
>
> (I_16)

Among these 18 percent despising UN organisations, different reasons were given: they were too large and bureaucratic to be adaptable, they were running under an international mandate, were speaking too much jargon, put too much emphasis on events that were not newsworthy, sometimes tried to whitewash that they had not met their targets in order not to lose funding, and paid too much money to their PR departments that produced content that hardly anyone reads.

> I would be reluctant to take, for example, a UN tour of a UN-run camp. Because sometimes the UN does things in ways that are just UNACCEPTABLE. And I wouldn't like to be tied into WORKING with the UN or PROMOTING the UN. With an [I]NGO – they're under no international mandate. They're under no initiative, except for their own personal, private institutional initiative.
>
> (I_20)

Another 18 percent stated that they generally try to avoid any kind of humanitarian organisation that had a particularly strong agenda. Ten percent avoid campaigning organisations, namely Oxfam and Save the Children, with Save the Children having a particularly bad reputation amongst journalists for its pushy advocacy, and little action. And yet another 18 percent said they try to avoid certain kinds of organisations because they either worried they would be manipulated, or because they felt that any dependency on humanitarian organisations hinders their reporting, and results in self-censorship to please the organisation that facilitated their trip.

This detailed picture of the types of organisations many correspondents try to avoid, should not distract from the fact that many of these 40 percent said that on many occasions and in some regions it was not possible to avoid humanitarian organisations even if they tried, and from the fact that the other 60 percent stated to not avoid any organisation in the first place.

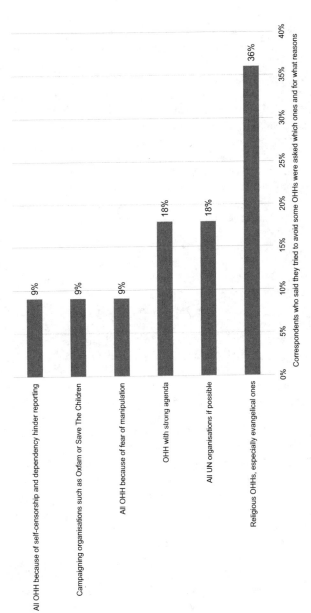

Figure 6.21 Reasons for avoiding certain OHHs

Dependency between correspondents and humanitarian organisations and frequency of interactions

To have a comparison to the importance that humanitarian organisations attributed to journalists, I asked correspondents how important they considered humanitarian organisations for their work, and how dependent they felt on them. The results – shown in Figure 6.22 – are surprisingly clear: 38 percent of the correspondents rated their dependency at between 7 and 10 points on scale from 1 to 10, which shows that they feel very dependent. A further 44 percent rated they were medium dependent, whereas only 18 percent said they were not very dependent by rating at between 1 and 3 only. It is now interesting to look at how the correspondents' perception of their dependency on humanitarian organisations changes with the experience. However, other than assumed, it is not the case that correspondents with longer working experience are less dependent, see Figures 6.23, 6.24 and 6.25. The highest rating of dependency increases with years, from 14 percent rating at 7and above of the correspondents with less than four years of experience, to 50 percent of the correspondents with seven or more years of experience rating at 7 and above. At the same time, the lowest rating increases: from 14 percent of correspondents with less than four years of experience rating at 3 or below, to 37 percent of correspondents with seven or more years of experience rating at 3 and below. In their first years in Africa, the correspondents rated their dependency to be somewhere in the middle of the dependency scale, rating at between 4 and 6. The more experience correspondents had, the more their rating split to the extremes: with seven or more years of experience, some correspondents felt very dependent on humanitarian organisations (50 percent rated at 7 or more on a scale from 1 to 10), and some correspondents did not feel dependent at all (38 percent rated up to 3); the remaining correspondents rated somewhere in the middle of the scale. The assumption that the more experience a correspondent had, the less he or she was dependent on humanitarian organisations, is too simple, and not correct if put that way. My results show that in the beginning of their work in Africa, a significantly higher percentage of correspondents rate their dependency in the middle, possibly because they do not have enough experience so far to give a more detailed assessment. The more experience a correspondent has, the more precise his or her perception of how dependent he or she is on humanitarian organisations becomes, which explains why the rating of the 'middle ground' then drifts apart into extremes. I conclude that the longer correspondents have worked in sub-Saharan Africa, the better they know how dependent they are. This dependency, however, does not correlate with their experience but with other aspects, such as their relationship with the editors, their type of employment (see Figures 6.27 and 6.28 further along this subsection), and their budget. The following quote of a freelancer for German-speaking media outlets explains very well how much the journalists' dependency on humanitarian organisations hangs predominantly on their budget:

> So there are international colleagues who work like me who have a rather sceptical view towards humanitarian organisations, and act rather cautiously

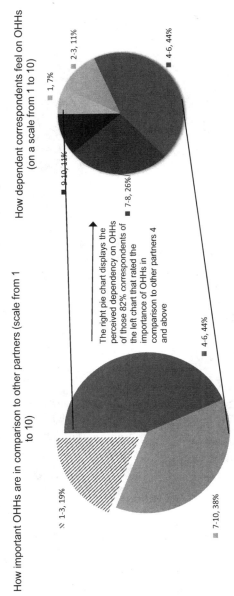

Figure 6.22 Importance of OHHs and dependency on them – from correspondents' perspective

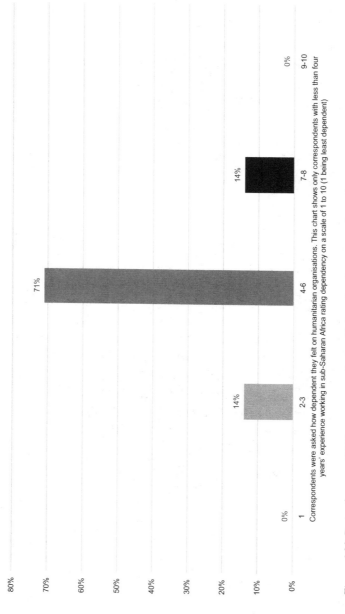

Figure 6.23 Dependency on OHHs – correspondents with less than four years of experience

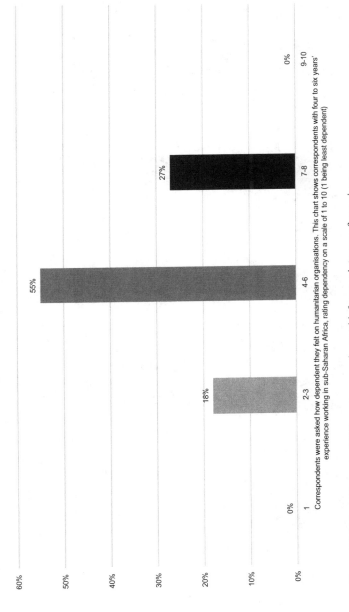

Figure 6.24 Dependency on OHHs – correspondents with four to six years of experience

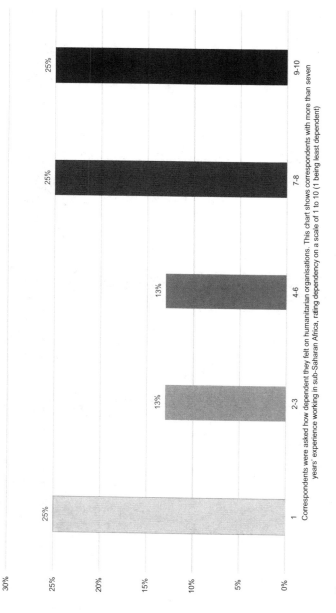

Figure 6.25 Dependency on OHHs – correspondents with seven or more years of working experience in Africa

[. . .], which is healthy. Then there is some from some news outlets, for examples Reuters and Bloomberg. [. . .] They have the policy that they must not, for example, go in a car with UNHCR. [. . .] The car from UNHCR could, for example, go in front, empty, and the journalist has to follow in his or her own, rented car that he or she paid for him- or herself. So there are very absurd in-between solutions how you can solve this problem. So there are correspondents who are not allowed to be invited by humanitarian organisations. And then there are the poorer journalists, like myself, because my outlet has very little money to pay for trips. [. . .] They always HAVE to go with the [I]NGO convoy because they do not even have the money to pay for their own fuel. And then, of course, it is easier to get roped in for all this thingamajig.

(I_08)

It became clear that humanitarian organisations are very important to correspondents and the other way round, and that this can lead to strong perceived dependency. But what does this actually mean? How often are they in contact with each other? Nearly all organisations have a very frequent output to correspondents and media headquarters, but that does not necessarily mean that correspondents actually engage. I asked the correspondents about the frequency of their interaction with humanitarian organisations, and let them describe it in their own words instead of pre-setting answers by a certain set of frequencies that could be ticked by the respondents. I received the following answers that are depicted in the graph in Figure 6.26. Most correspondents answered that they were in contact with humanitarian organisations every week or even several times per week. Some said they were in contact one to two times a month, and more often if a major story was breaking. All journalists of American media outlets said once a week or more often; journalists of British media reported varying contact between daily, weekly, and monthly; and journalists of German media said once per month, apart from one who said once per week. I assumed that journalists of American outlets had less contact but that is not the case, despite their much stricter guidelines as explained in the section on editorial policy. Interestingly, all freelancers (of all different outlet nationalities) fall in the group that claims to have contact one to two times per month. That is notable as my presumption was that it was freelancers who would have the most contact with humanitarian organisations due to their small travel budget. On the other hand, freelancers perceive their dependency on humanitarian organisations as very strong: 40 percent of all freelance respondents rated their dependency at between 7 and 10 on a scale from 1 to 10, which is quite high in comparison to staff correspondents, of whom only 27 percent rated it at between 7 and 10 (Figures 6.27 and 6.28).

I conclude from this that freelancers may not be as regularly in contact with humanitarian organisations, but when they are, the contact is more intense. From the interviews I also know that for freelancers this contact often decides over whether a story that is pitched to an editor will get a green light because the organisation then chips in with money and logistical help.

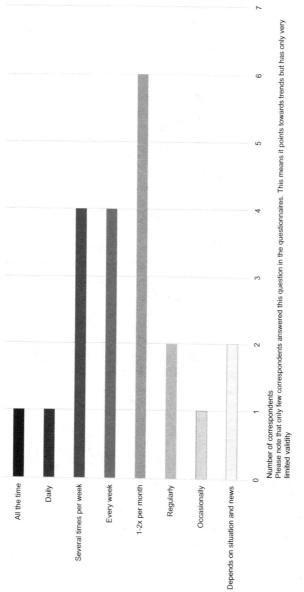

Figure 6.26 Frequency of interactions between OHHs and correspondents

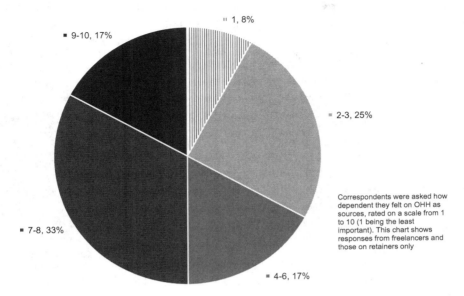

Figure 6.27 Dependency on OHHs perceived by correspondents – freelancers and retainers only

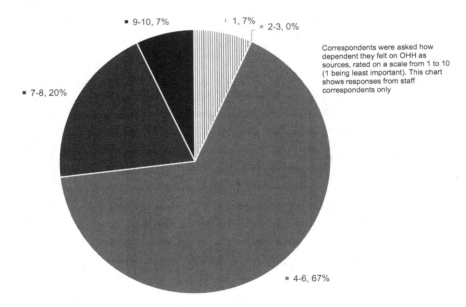

Figure 6.28 Dependency on OHHs perceived by correspondents – staff only

Also, and this is a separate phenomenon, many freelancers work as consultants for humanitarian organisations regularly to earn money, because their freelance writing does not guarantee them income, whereas consultancy contracts with NGOs or UN organisations are well paid and source of a reliable income. Since the correspondents were asked as correspondents, not when during a consultancy, how often they were in contact with humanitarian organisations, I assume that the time they spent as consultants working for humanitarian organisations is not included in their evaluation of the frequency of contact with humanitarian organisations. These consultancy jobs earn them good money, and make it harder for them to be critical with, and independent from, humanitarian organisations, when they are wearing their 'journalist hat'. They may lose consultancy contracts in the future if they act in a way of which humanitarian organisations disapprove.[27]

In short, several reasons make a difference regarding the level of correspondents' dependency on humanitarian organisations: first, the type of employment. Despite very different agreements that freelancers and correspondents working on retainers have with outlets for which they regularly work, half of them rate their dependency between 7 and 10, on a scale from 1 to 10, whereas less than 30 percent rate the same amongst the staff correspondents; another 66 percent of staff correspondents rate their dependency between 4 and 6. Second, the dependency level differs in relation to the journalists' working experience, although very different from the way I had assumed. That journalists become more critical towards humanitarian organisations the longer they have worked in sub-Saharan Africa, is not true. Instead, the journalists with more working experience gave more precise answers how dependent they felt on humanitarian organisations, and the answers of the more experienced journalists were more polarised – either very dependent, or not dependent at all, with little prevarication in the middle. Third, the nationality of the media outlet for which the journalist works does not allow for clear conclusions. American media outlets nearly all have much stricter editorial guidelines on how to interact with humanitarian organisations than British and German media outlets. American correspondents also pay for their trips nearly always themselves, even if that means that humanitarian workers drive in a nearly empty car ahead, and the journalist follows in a second one, hired on the outlet's expenses. Despite these facts, American correspondents often have to rely on the humanitarian organisation's contacts, knowledge, and their assistance with logistics nevertheless, even if they pay their own way. Which makes me question whether they are less dependent in the end, but at least in theory, that is the case. Interesting in this context is also that many correspondents do not know their editorial guidelines, even if their outlet has them.

6.6 Contextualising aid embedding in the light of the research results

In this section, I will contextualise *aid embedding* in the light of the research results as the strongest dependency level between correspondents and humanitarian organisations. Chapter 4, section 4.5 first focused on embedding with the military and then showed a wider perspective on how to use the concept for journalist dependency relationships in general, and then defined what dimensions have to apply for aid embedding. In the sections of Chapter 6 so far, I have shown the research results regarding the framework that humanitarians and correspondents work within, have given an overview of the interactions, why, how, and between whom they take place, and explained the challenges and dependency levels that the interactions bring. This section now uses this background and applies the concept that evolved from putting military embedding into a wider context, and relates it to the research results.

As countries where aid embedding happens very regularly, interviewees named the Central African Republic, Somalia, South Sudan, parts of Ethiopia, and the Democratic Republic of the Congo. In other countries it happens in regions during any type of emergency or conflict, and when other aspects restrict journalists' access to information and places, which in turn only allows the journalists a limited perspective on the events. It also happens when journalists assimilate their perspectives with those of the humanitarians due to working in difficult situations, when journalists feel social pressure to report positively about humanitarian organisations as the organisations are seen to 'do good', or when journalists report in certain ways to please the humanitarian organisation in order not to jeopardise future collaborations. Many journalists and staff of humanitarian organisations described to me trips that were in this way comparable to military embedding.

One correspondent, for example, told me that Unicef facilitated his travel to visit one of its aid projects in Somalia – and this is not a singular case but stands for many other trips, realised in similar ways with Save The Children, MSF, UNHCR, ICRC, and others. Unicef facilitated his trip, booked the flight on a UN plane, organised convoys, visa, and interpreters, set the schedule for the trip, and made sure that the journalist had contacts and interview partners on site (logistical, social, and consequential dimension: a, b, c, d, e, f, g, m, n, o, p, q, and r; from Chapter 4, here and below).[28] Due to the trip's security risk and the remoteness of the area visited, he and other correspondents with him were under the protection of UN troops, not allowed to move freely, and thus not able to investigate freely even if they had wanted. On his own, the journalist could only have been there at great cost and at great risk, so going with a humanitarian organisation was a safer and cheaper option, and the only one to which his editors agreed (I_21) (logistical and consequential dimension: a, c, and m). He felt responsible to 'give back' to the aid workers who had spent significant time organising his stay (social and consequential dimension: m, q). All dimensions of embedding developed in Chapter 4, section 4.5 apply to this case: the dependence on *logistical aspects*, the dependence because of *social aspects*, and the dependence because of *consequential aspects*. In situations like this, the humanitarian staff can decide how they present the situation on the ground to the journalist, and what local people they provide for interviews (logistical and consequential dimension: f, n, o). In company of humanitarian staff, the journalist may also appear less impartial to these affected people on the ground, who may not speak openly, or who may think they will receive more help from the humanitarian organisation if they tell the journalist their stories in a certain way.[29] During my investigation, many correspondents told me about this challenge in their reporting experience (consequential dimension: o). The humanitarian organisation cannot officially influence the coverage, and has no guarantee that the journalist will write about them in a certain way in the end, nor whether he or she will paint a positive or negative picture about the organisation. But interviews reveal that the influence takes place more subtly. Staff of the humanitarian organisation show the journalist around, and present him or her a particular view on events that is often not verifiable (logistical and consequential dimension: e, f, g, n). The staff can introduce the journalist to certain interview partners, and not others, and can brief affected communities on what to say beforehand (consequential dimension: o, p). Apart from this, the organisations can and do threaten to withhold information or not to cooperate with the journalist again, which makes journalists vulnerable that work for outlets that do not have the means to provide security themselves, to pay for flights, to charter private helicopters, or to find other ways to reach remote areas (logistical and consequential dimension: a, c, d, e, f, m, and r). Some journalists have described to me that high-level individuals at an UN organisation have put them under immense pressure to cooperate in a way with which the organisation approved, and threatened to pass information about the journalists to the authoritative government otherwise, which in one case I investigated silenced the journalist, and in another case caused a journalist never to return to this country for security reasons, as the journalist knew she would be left to her own devices if a problem occurred (logistical and consequential dimension: c, m, q, and r). This kind of situation can thus be classed as a classic case of aid embedding as all categories of embedding as developed in Chapter 4, section 4.5 apply, including indirect censorship threatening journalists.

Apart from these cases, where divergent perspectives of humanitarian workers and journalists clash, and an asymmetric relationship gives humanitarian organisations the power to silence correspondents, there are more subtle ways of influencing the correspondents. In difficult, dangerous, or remote areas, and especially in life-threatening situations, a convergence of views between journalist and humanitarian worker can easily occur as my data shows – similar to the embed's fraternisation with the accompanying soldiers (social dimension: j, k). Like embeds rely on troops with which they are embedded in places like those mentioned above, correspondents rely on the humanitarian organisation's goodwill to assist them to reach regions that are hard to access, to facilitate transport on the ground, to provide contacts to local people, to provide safety measures, and have first aid healthcare on hand in case of any incidents. A correspondent for a British news outlet stationed in South Africa recounted (logistical, social and consequential dimension: c, d, e, g, h, j, m, n, q, and r):

> And literally in Central African Republic I was sitting in a vehicle wearing a flak jacket provided by Unicef. And I suppose that was very similar to what I did in Afghanistan sitting with the American army wearing a flak jacket. They protect me. So you know, it has some of the hallmarks to embedding.
> (I_09)[30]

When correspondents travel with humanitarian organisations to dangerous areas, in many cases their ability to move around freely is restricted due to security measures, as it would be when embedded with the military. A humanitarian communications officer working for a UN agency who coordinates many journalist trips reported (logistical and consequential dimension: a, b, c, d, e, h, m, n, and q):

[In Somalia] the foreign white journalists generally do not move around much at all because of the risk of kidnap or assassination. So they often stay in the airport compound, which is UN and EU military protected, or they'd stay in a commercial hotel in the city who provides both accommodation and body guard military escort. And pickups of guys. So the journalists who want to cover Somalia have very, very limited options. If they come from a rich organisation, they can stay in the city and use these private security guards, and move around a bit like that. [. . .] So yeah, Somalia is an extreme case where the aid agencies don't control the access, but there isn't much of an alternative unless you're extremely wealthy. [. . .] If you stay on the base and you go out with EU military patrols and you don't have the resources to move in the city without them, you should probably call yourself embedded, I mean in an aid agency context. If you're in South Sudan and you're 100 percent dependent for your transport, food, water, toilet, electricity, communications, to Unicef or Save the Children or World Food Programme, you're embedded in a way but you can go and talk to other people [. . .]. In the civilian context the embedding is a bit more fluid because you can say, 'Okay,' to the Unicef driver, 'Okay drop me off, I'm gonna go and talk to this guy. And I don't need you in the room.' [. . .] But you need that car to get you to that meeting because there's no cars out there. So yeah, it's a kind of embedding, but it may be less rigid I think than a military embed.

(I_22)[31]

A communications officer explained how a field trip to Somalia with Unicef usually takes place (logistical, consequential, partly social dimension: a, b, c, d, e, f, g, h, m, n, q, and r):

Logistics would involve our staff here in Nairobi and our staff in Somalia, because we have to prepare the airplane and all that, if it's a charter plane or we have to book them on the UN flights. The Unicef staff here and in Somalia would work on what the logistics needed and then we work with the local authorities to prepare for the special protection unit guards, the vehicles and everything. [. . .] They have to stay in accommodations that we arranged. And if we're helping THEM with the logistics, then they become embedded with us, so they're not really allowed to move around on their own and take a taxi and go somewhere and do another story. They have to be with us all the time. [. . .] They don't really have freedom of movement, unless you're in Hargeisa [capital of semi-autonomous Somaliland province, generally considered safer than the rest of Somalia] [. . .]. We wouldn't tie them up or anything <<laughs>> but I mean, it's based on a relationship of trust, really. Normally it's fine. It's a new rule that they have to be completely embedded with the UN and that came about . . . I heard because there were journalists that were taking off on their own and doing their own thing but then that becomes a security threat. So that's why they made this rule.

(I_12)

As my research shows, in many cases – depending on the situation in the field – humanitarian organisations working in dangerous areas have strict safety policies, such as night curfews, regulations on where to stay, where to go, and sometimes even whom to talk to, all of which can get in the way of reporting (logistical and consequential dimension: c, m, n, and r). As opposed to military embeds who usually have to sign contracts, the regulations that humanitarian organisations demand correspondents to meet are usually informal and not written down. My study reveals that correspondents have to stick to these regulations nevertheless; otherwise the organisation's goodwill ends quickly, and future cooperation is at risk (social and consequential dimension: i, n, p, q, and r).

The nice thing about embedding with the military is that you have to sign certain Ground Rules. The ones for the Americans fill several pages on what you can do and what you must not do. [. . .] If you go with the military you have to obey certain rules, which are laid out from the beginning. In opposition to that, when on the road with [I]NGOs that is rather informally managed. You won't have to sign a paper beforehand that you will only publish certain things, and that you will name them. They don't do that because no one would sign that. But de facto that's what it is because you have all these advantages. Because the humanitarian organisations have the advantage for journalists that they are close to the events and that they can show you their projects because they have easy access to people – for example, if they built a school or a hospital or trained midwives. Some, however, do require that you tell them beforehand what you will report about. That's a form of informal cooperation that no one makes visible [to the audience].

(I_02)

This account of a freelancer working for British outlets shows how there can be differences between various international humanitarian organisations even in the same region (logistical and consequential dimension: c, d, e, g, and n):

They have very strict security rules. So when you go with MSF, you kind of know you're not going to be able to wander around. You're in their cars; you use their radios. I was with MSF in Central African Republic in October and I actually LEFT because I just found it so restrictive [. . .] – I couldn't do my job.

(I_43)

In several interviews, correspondents said that they found it hard to criticise humanitarian organisations as they 'do good' and help civilians, which stands in opposition to what the military does (social dimension: h, j, k, and l).[32] Nevertheless, I detected a process of camaraderie in the field working under difficult conditions, and an assimilation of perceptions between the correspondents and humanitarian workers on the ground similar to the one taking place between military and military embeds. Like military embeds who do not necessarily support the military, the correspondents do not necessarily agree with the general work of the organisations, or with development assistance in general. However, military embeds feel close to the troop with which they are embedded, and correspondents are very often sympathetic to aid workers they meet who live and work in difficult conditions trying to 'do good' while assisting the reporter to do his or her job. From this, personal contacts develop that may lead to friendships over time. In contrast to embedding with troops, aid embedding usually happens for a shorter amount of time, which leaves less time to develop companionable feelings. However, military embeds usually do not accompany the same troop twice, whereas personal contacts with aid workers continue, and correspondents tend to call these aid workers again if the initial contact was perceived positively (social and consequential dimension: h, i, l, and r). A correspondent of a news agency explained (social dimension: h, i, and j):

> And often you know you go on these trips with the press officer and you might not have met them before and, you know, they're normally quite intense. It will be two, three days, four days out in the middle of nowhere. Sharing a tent or smelly car and you do become – you have to get on with them.
>
> (I_21)

Many interviewees working in humanitarian communications share this view. A communications officer working for a large humanitarian INGO said (social dimension: h, i):

> On these journalist-trips [. . .] you go out and you spend five days, 24/7 in a difficult location one-on-one. Anyways, you get to know the people. And so the relationship resource becomes very positive.
>
> (I_45)

A rapprochement of views, the so-called *enculturation* (Brandenburg 2005; Dietrich 2007) between correspondent and humanitarian worker I found in many interviews, when interviewees said that they generally thought the humanitarian organisations' employees worked hard to make people's lives better, that they shared the organisations' general values, especially when it came to human rights,[33] or that they sympathised with aid employees working under difficult conditions (social dimension: k, and l). However, many interviewees were conscious that this closeness was awkward, as this correspondent attested (social and consequential dimension: i, o, p, and q):

> If I want to observe a project CRITICALLY, than I find it PROBLEMATIC if I'm accompanied by employees of this organisation all the time when I'm in

the field. They, of course, want to follow THEIR agenda. Maybe even we get on very well on a personal level.

(I_30)

The aid embed very rarely has to fear any form of official censorship. Unlike when embedded with the military, where interviewees described a significant amount of direct censorship, with commanders insisting on reading articles and seeing television footage, the censorship when embedded with humanitarian organisations takes place more indirectly, and is often pushed by different forms of sanctions that hover over the interactions at any time. Any behaviour or coverage that veers from the humanitarian organisation's PR line is likely to be met with refusals to assist in the future (consequential dimension: q, r). That again encourages self-censorship on behalf of the correspondent, as my interviews show. An agency journalist explained the moral dilemma (social and consequential dimension: i, p):

> So you would be using up, I don't know, 150 kilograms that could be used for medical supplies. So, you know, there's also a moral imperative like if you are going to go . . . on an aid flight and take up an extra space then [you have to write about them].
>
> (I_21)

However, some organisations told me of censorship forms that are more direct. An employee of Care told me how they aim to control the message according to the organisation's policy (consequential dimension: m, p, and r):

> In some locations it is a little bit embedded. We don't let them in, unless they expressed a degree of understanding or sympathy with the story that we want to tell.
>
> (I_45)

A former MSF communications employee reported similar practices (consequential dimension: h, m, p, q, and r):

> And you're with them during this visit. You're with them, in a war zone. They don't just get to go on their own. And once they start crossing the line, you say: No, no, sorry. Those questions are not appropriate.
>
> (I_52)

On a more general perspective, I noted during my research a new and increasingly common phenomenon, which military embeds do not face, that very likely also has a bearing on the journalists' independence, and likely causes an even stronger dependency of aid embeds on humanitarian organisations than of embeds on the military: the trend for correspondents, and in particular freelancers, to take short-term assignments with humanitarian organisations.[34] In these cases, humanitarian organisations offer journalists temporary employment in so-called 'consultancies' to use the journalists' skills in-house. The journalists edit reports for the organisations, or are paid to go to the field to write pieces (logistical dimension: m, n, and p). Nearly 60 percent of the freelancers I interviewed, regularly worked as consultants, and my field observations showed that a large proportion of freelancers beyond the ones interviewed regularly get so-called 'gigs' with humanitarian organisations. The material produced this way is then published on the organisations' websites, or offered to news outlets. This practice is very likely to cause the correspondent to employ even stricter self-censorship regarding potential criticism of operations of the humanitarian organisation for which he or she regularly consults, not only while he or she is working on such a consultancy but also when he or she is officially operating as independent journalist (social and consequential dimension: i, p, and r). The correspondent under such circumstances wants neither to endanger journalistic cooperation, nor to risk losing lucrative contracts with this humanitarian organisation in the future (social and consequential dimension: m, p, q, and r). I encountered three incidents within one month, in which news outlets published stories exactly the way they were produced by journalists while on assignments with a humanitarian organisation. In one case only with a small image caption pointing towards the provenance of the material, and in another without the slightest hint to how and under which circumstances the material was produced.

After in-depth research in this field, I take it for granted that a very high number of unknown cases like these exist. In this way a significant blurring of lines takes place between aid and media sector, between aid advocacy and 'independent' media reporting that is not obvious to the media audience. Sometimes the problem with this is not even obvious to editors or the journalists themselves. A freelancer told me (logistical, social and consequential dimension: l, m, p, q, and r):

> That's also the interesting thing, just how many [I]NGOs are using journalists in a freelance capacity to provide them footage or take photos or write stories for them. And everyone does it because the money's really good. [...] I have done some work for DFID here on Somalia, that then another journalist pointed out would make it difficult for me to criticise DFID. The DFID Somalia project, which apparently [needs] criticism. And I thought: 'Oh yeah, I didn't factor that in when I did it'.
>
> (I_43)

The difference between freelancing journalists and staff becomes clear in the following quotation by a journalist who previously worked as staff for a news agency before becoming a freelancer. Only then did the UN suddenly play a significant role in his work, both as a source for newspaper articles and as an employer for short-term assignments (logistical, social dimension, and consequential dimension: a, b, c, d, e, f, g, m, q, and r):

> The UN could offer so much, they played a bigger part in my professional life, once I became a freelancer, basically because I just needed more favours.

I needed to network differently. I needed to reach out in a way that I didn't when I was at Reuters [. . .] And when I went to Nairobi, I became much more of a sort of floating jack-of-all-trades, just to do whatever was available and then that strayed from journalism, often enough, into [I]NGO work and assignments for the UN.

(I_16)

However, it is not only freelancers who are at risk to lose their independence when becoming an aid embed. The majority of staff correspondents share the dependency regarding facilitation of trips, and regarding all of the above points. Some journalists, especially photojournalists, even volunteer for humanitarian organisations if they generally deem the organisation's work good and want to use their journalistic talents to endorse its achievements. A UNHCR spokesperson told me that professional photographers who usually got paid around "250,000 POUNDS PER commercial assignment VOLUNTEERED to work for us to take pictures on assignment" (I_44) (social dimension: l). That the lines blur also shows this phenomenon that I came across: several journalists who joined trips mainly facilitated and financed by a humanitarian organisation, then produced material that won international journalism prizes.[35] And journalists who work on assignments for humanitarian organisations, then often also publish material in news outlets. The provenance of the material, however, is often not declared, or only marked with an oblique reference, as for example with a photo essay on Burundian refugees by a photographer employed by UNHCR that was published with only the image caption referring to UNHCR: "name of the photographer/UNHCR".[36] I witnessed the same procedure in several other cases of the journalists that took part in my study and had assignments with different UN organisations.

All of the above makes it feasible to call the correspondents 'aid embeds' in situations where: they benefit from lower costs by 'riding along' with a humanitarian organisation; they rely on the infrastructure of humanitarian organisations; they rely on their contacts and network for access and for security; they are operating in difficult environments under the organisation's goodwill; they only get a limited perspective because they are shown around by the aid organisation and do not have access to other sources; they often share the organisation's general understanding that 'doing good' is good and necessary; they have to fear censorship or at least fear the organisation to be less cooperative when they need information in the future. Not all aspects apply at the same time and in the same intensity at all times. But because of the unbalanced interactions that the correspondents face when several of these aspects apply which lead to a strong dependency of the correspondent on humanitarian organisations, we cannot speak of a relationship in which humanitarian organisations and journalists enable each other without one side dominating. In these situations, in which humanitarian organisations have more leverage and correspondents strongly depend on humanitarian organisations, I therefore speak of aid embedding instead.

As I already explained in the paragraph above, and in sections 6.3 and 6.5, freelancers are generally more dependent on humanitarian organisations than staff correspondents, because they rarely have an outlet behind them covering all travelling expenses, and because many of them also rely on consultancies with humanitarian organisations to fund their living as freelancers. Figures 6.29, 6.30 and 6.31 however include correspondents of all types of employment including freelancers, to show a general trend that looks different when considering different media outlet nationalities. Comparing the questionnaires with what correspondents told me in the interviews, those correspondents who rated the dependency at 7 or higher were very often the ones who in the interviews spoke of situations that 'were like embedding'. Looking at the figures again with this knowledge, a significant difference is apparent in answers in the questionnaires depending on the nationality of the media outlet for which the journalists worked (see Figures 6.29, 6.30, and 6.31).[37] Sixty percent of the respondents working mainly for British media outlets rated their dependency on humanitarian organisations at 7 or above. This brings me to the conclusion that 60 percent of the correspondents working for British outlets can be classified as aid embeds under circumstances explained earlier.

This is the case for 18 percent of correspondents working for German media, and for 30 percent of journalists for American media outlets. However, it can be remarked upon that none of the American correspondents rated their dependency at 9 or 10, whereas still 9 percent of German correspondents rated 9 or 10. The 20 percent of British correspondents rating 9 or 10 perceived themselves the most dependent on humanitarian organisations. This may be due to the lack of restrictions and ethical frameworks regarding so-called freebies in most British outlets, guidelines that by contrast nearly all correspondents said exist explicitly for American media, and most claim are adhered to. Also, American media outlets still tend to pay more expenses, and value investigative reporting more. However, as I explained earlier, that does not mean that American correspondents do not ride along with humanitarian organisations. It only means that American correspondents tend to pay their expenses themselves, even if they travel with humanitarian organisations, which I assume makes them feel less dependent. The amount of German-speaking correspondents, who consider themselves to be so dependent on humanitarian organisations that I class them as aid embeds, is considerably low in comparison to the British. I ascribe this to the general lack of presence of German-speaking media in Africa, at least relatively in comparison to the number of English-speaking media. Also, those few German outlets that still have Africa correspondents seem to be willing to cover considerable expenses for their correspondents' travels.

All levels of interaction and mutual dependency between humanitarian organisations and correspondents, not just the extreme form of cooperation that I call aid embedding, can leave traces in the journalistic outcome: the news coverage. The closeness of the two professions when working in the field, and the blurring of lines between the sectors, makes it often difficult to detect the provenance of

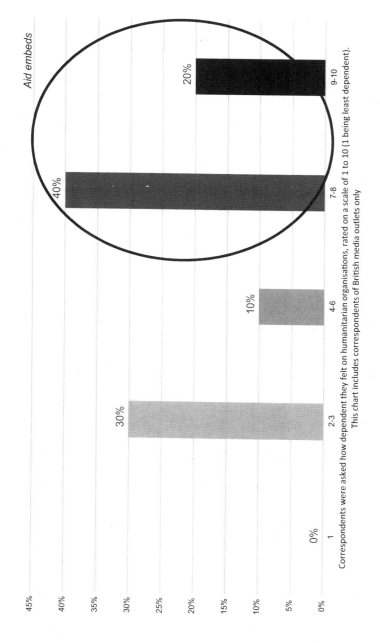

Figure 6.29 Correspondents' dependency on OHHs – British outlets only

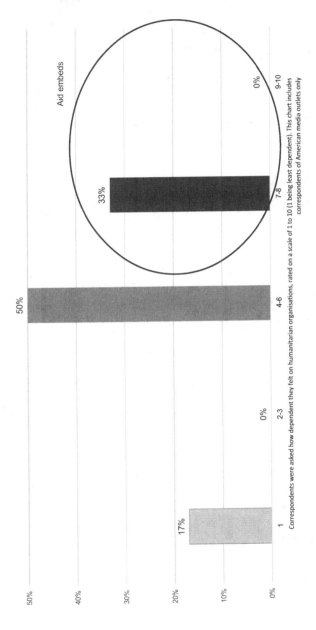

Figure 6.30 Correspondents' dependency on OHHs – American outlets only

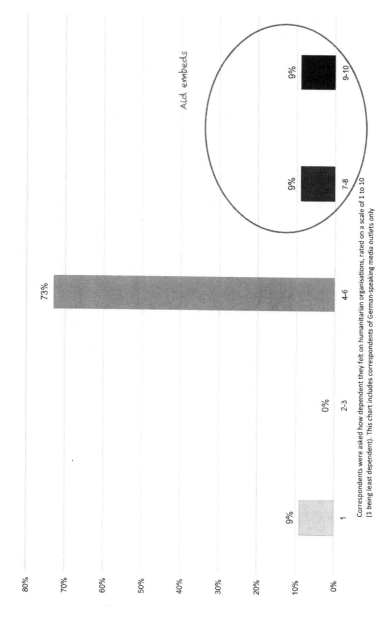

Figure 6.31 Correspondents' dependency on OHHs – German-speaking outlets only

reporting. In the following section I will give an insight into the influence that these interactions can have on the news coverage.

6.7 Influence on coverage

How does all of this now play into the coverage of sub-Saharan Africa and the Western opinion of the African continent? The answer is: to a significant extent. Which reality does media display, I asked in Chapter 3. Can we measure the adequacy of the media's representation of reality, and which and whose interests lie beneath this representation? The media construct a media reality, and define the way this reality is represented to a broad audience, which in many cases does not have a profound knowledge about the places covered in foreign news. Their knowledge about foreign places is therefore mainly based on, and formed by the coverage. In this section, I will examine which aspects discussed so far could determine the reporting, and ultimately the reports. First, I will present the correspondents' perspective on humanitarian organisations' influence on their reporting. Opposing, I will then discuss how likely it is that humanitarian organisations influence the reporting and shape the coverage.

The correspondents' view on the humanitarians' influence on their coverage

Interestingly, my study reveals that many correspondents are of the opinion that their interactions with humanitarian organisations do not influence their reporting and coverage, when asked directly. They said they think they still had the upper hand in terms of how they carried out the reporting and how they framed their coverage. Many correspondents interviewed said that they were aware that humanitarian organisations were often part of their reporting, but that they were not the major part of the stories. One correspondent working for an American news outlet explained:

> I don't feel like they are driving the agenda. And I think that if I felt that they were that would be a problem for me. And you know that's a very kind of personal thing and when . . . you know people sort of attack the media for being like in cahoots with some sort of humanitarian aid lobby or whatever it is. They often say that we are sort of slavishly following an agenda or whatever. I just think from my actual understanding that isn't true. I mean I try to be nice about it, but I feel like I am using them more than they are using me.
> (I_23)

In the interviews, many correspondents echoed the words of the journalist quoted above, and said they felt strongly that the humanitarian organisations were not driving the media agenda, that they and not the aid organisation controlled the interactions; they served the journalists' needs more than the other way around. During the interviews, I also witnessed many correspondents, who had apparently not given much thought to their potential bias, starting to consider it for the first time. Many others said they had discussed this issue at length with colleagues and peers and, while they were aware of the difficulties implicit in their interactions with humanitarians, they took a practical approach that embraced both the advantages and disadvantages, and accepted that the interactions were a kind of necessary evil bringing benefits for both sides. Finally, in far smaller numbers, few correspondents clearly saw problems coming from the interactions and had the editorial support and budgets to steer clear of humanitarian organisations when they could, and chose to be as transparent as possible when interactions were unavoidable. The majority of correspondents, however, were convinced humanitarian organisations did not influence their reporting.

Why this view is to be challenged

Studying the reasons why correspondents and humanitarian organisations interact, and investigating their interactions within their network in detail, it is very hard to agree with the correspondents' opinion regarding the independence of their reporting; several journalists strongly agreed that humanitarian organisations have an extensive influence. Studying the interactions between the actors of both sectors in detail, it becomes clear how strongly correspondents depend on humanitarian organisations on many different levels, and why it is in the humanitarian organisations' interest to use this dependency for "constellations of influence and negotiation" (Kron & Winter 2009: 43). It is, however, understandable considering journalistic ethics and self-perceptions that many correspondents would defend their independent image as reporters. It is therefore likely the correspondents' view is strongly influenced by social desirability – many journalists do not want to acknowledge that they are influenced in their reporting. In practice, in sub-Saharan Africa, however, they very often are. Many journalists, who were confident their reporting was independent despite interacting regularly with humanitarian organisations, later in the interviews contradicted their statements of independence, saying that they regularly had to compromise their reporting, for example, when telling a story in a certain way might jeopardise chances to be offered assistance from the respective organisation in the future. I will sum up briefly the reasons for my conclusion that I disagree with the many correspondents' view that their reporting remains independent; in the subsections after that I will explain this in more detail.

First, previously researched content analyses of news coverage have shown that humanitarian organisations feature in Western news disproportionately often, and are very often only portrayed positively. It is very likely that the actor dependencies that I researched for this book have these repercussions in the coverage. Second, I explored the conditions under which correspondents and humanitarian organisations work in sub-Saharan Africa, that have caused the actor groups to build, rely on, and constantly extend the network between them, with its interactions characterised by strong mutual dependencies. That many journalists think these dependencies do not influence their reporting can also be explained by the so-called "third-person effect" (Davidson 1980, 1983; Dupagne 1999) applied onto the relationship between PR and journalists. This effect says that if people are exposed to persuasive communication – whether it is intended to be persuasive or not – they expect this communication to have a greater effect on others than on themselves. This may explain why many journalists interviewed said that humanitarian organisations influencing journalism was indeed a problem, but that their individual reporting was not compromised. Third, within this network, humanitarian organisations, due to their large budgets and logistical expansion on the African continent, very often hold the monopoly of infrastructure and access, both of which are essential for reporting. Fourth, humanitarian organisations additionally very often have the monopoly of important information – information that is hard to verify for correspondents operating on tight budgets. Fifth, both from a communications and a fundraising perspective, it is in humanitarian organisations' main interest to influence the coverage in a way that suits the organisations' agenda and strategies. For this purpose, results of this study showed, crisis-focused coverage that also mentions the organisation's name and projects is preferred. Sixth, the interactions and the actors' dependencies are often asymmetrical. Despite humanitarian organisations also being dependent on news coverage, they in practice often have the upper hand in the relationship, denying correspondents access, information, or contacts, resulting in the journalists performing self-censorship in order to comply with the organisations' needs and requirements, even if these are not always declared explicitly. Seventh, this asymmetry is further enhanced by a large number of correspondents – mainly, but increasingly not only freelancers any longer – that are financially dependent on consulting jobs with humanitarian organisations, which leads to strong dependencies and a blurring of lines between the media and aid sector in sub-Saharan Africa. In the next subsection I will explicate these points in more detail.

The editor's role in the coverage

As I explained earlier in the theoretical subsection *The journalist as one brick in the whole building*, not only the correspondents but also the editors play a role as to whether a certain story makes the news. Overall, I found the correspondents' gatekeeping role and power to vary significantly between different news outlets, and also between different outlet nationalities. Most British news outlets, especially the newspapers, are driven by editorial direction to do stories that are crisis-focused and have a strong British angle. If the correspondents pitch something different, in most cases the editors reject it. Only the correspondents of two British outlets gave the impression that they could decide to a greater extent which stories were covered. The first was the BBC, because the BBC generally has a larger output on many different channels, and an interest in African stories. The second was The Guardian as it provides long-format stories on the website where articles can still be published online that the correspondent suggests and feels strongly about, but that the editors do not want in the paper. Most German-speaking outlets try to report positive news stories, in theory. However, since there is little space for

African issues generally, more often than not it is negative crisis-focused stories that make the news in the end. Yet, most German-speaking news outlets stand by their correspondents when they have different opinions from the information cycled by the news agencies. The two correspondents of the German-speaking newspapers NZZ and FAZ said that their paper would nearly always print whatever they suggested, regardless of the news value, and also cover travel expenses. One freelance correspondent who mainly writes for other German outlets said that her advantage working as freelancer was that if one outlet did not want a certain story, she could pitch it to others. This freelancer, however, had a second regular income source that was not journalism, and did not rely on her journalism earnings as much as other freelancers. Only one staff correspondent for a German outlet said that he now only wrote the stories his editors told him to write, because in the past his ideas for stories that were exclusive, positive, or not what others were writing about, were too often rejected.

American outlets are very US-focused and favour American angles to stories. Generally speaking, American editors tend to pay more, and give their correspondents more freedom and space to also report about positive stories than British ones. American outlets are also the ones that have the strictest rules regarding interactions with humanitarian organisations. You can ride along, but you always have to pay your own way, is the rule in nearly all outlets. Whether that changes anything in the reporting to the positive, however, is the question. Because even then the correspondents depend on the organisations to take them to remote places, on their local networks and contacts, and the situation on the ground is presented to them through a humanitarian lens.

Aside from editorial differences, another reason for the preponderance of crisis-driven coverage from sub-Saharan Africa is that the patch one correspondent covers is so large that conflicts are nearly always somewhere, which then wins preference over other stories that are less urgent. A correspondent of a German outlet, who covers fewer countries than many of his colleagues, said:

> I'm covering 16 countries. Something is always on. I don't have the chance to look at issues that are at the peripheries, that are not breaking news. I would like to do that, it's not that those stories would not be interesting. I simply don't have TIME to do [positive stories].
>
> (I_05)

In cases where the gatekeeping competence of a correspondent is not so strong, or when the outlet no longer stations a correspondent in Africa, humanitarian organisations try to establish close connections with editors in the headquarters directly. On this level, extra agreements are also made, for example partnerships where a newspaper supports a certain humanitarian organisation over a period of time. A humanitarian who also has experience working as journalist said:

> [There was the] official declaration of famine three weeks before, so it all sort of fed into each other and I think that that was driven very much by good

lobbying to editors in capital cities rather than necessarily editors listening to their Africa-based correspondents. [. . .] In some ways the correspondents were forced to comply with editors that didn't know much about the continent [and wanted] to keep it simple.

(I_58)

A correspondent of a British news outlet, who earlier worked for more than 12 years as an editor for two major news outlets, said regarding humanitarian organisations that only since he reported from the field had he began considering the challenges that come with overly-close cooperation with humanitarians:

Since I stopped being executive, I'm travelling a lot more and I'm covering these stories and I'm seeing them on the ground. So, I guess, that made me have stronger views on it, although, you know, I had the same views before. But I didn't really think through the issues in terms of the coverage and the impact of the coverage until I was going out in the field and seeing how some of these groups operate.

(I_10)

When a newspaper does not have a foreign correspondent based in the region where crises and emergencies take place, the newspaper's main sources apart from news agencies are often humanitarian organisations. Interviews with individual editors seemed to confirm this assumption. However, the sample of editors was not large enough to scientifically prove it. Future studies could investigate this.

Aspects of the interactions influencing reporting and news coverage

The conditions and framework within which correspondents and humanitarian organisations each operate in sub-Saharan Africa resulted in the media and aid sector building a network between them that brings mutual benefits, but also shows mutual dependencies. In the following subsections I will explain in more detail why the interactions within this network influence the reporting. I will first talk about the organisations' monopoly of infrastructure and access, then about their monopoly of information, followed by an explanation how these two often lead to an asymmetry in the relationships – together with a shared Western perspective between correspondents and humanitarian organisations – that hinders unbiased news covering. Then I will consider news coverage from a fundraising perspective. And finally, I discuss how the increasing blurring of lines between the two sectors also threatens independent reporting.

Humanitarian organisations' monopoly of infrastructure and access

How do the interactions between correspondents and humanitarian organisations play into the reporting? In the majority of cases where the media outlets do not provide back-up or budget, humanitarian organisations provide transport and give logistical support, and can, to a certain degree, dictate the terms under which the reporting takes place. With the decreasing budgets of foreign reporting, and the cutting of posts in sub-Saharan Africa, humanitarian organisations with their large budgets, well-established infrastructure, and wide scope of contacts ranging from local communities to high-level politicians, are not only useful partners for journalists, but often essential to realise their field visits. The humanitarian organisation facilitating the travel – not only on fully organised trips – and providing infrastructure and access to the journalists, often present the situation on the ground in a way that suits the organisations' aims. The regional head of an UN agency remarked self-critically:

> A lot of these countries, if you're talking about crisis countries, THAT is the story! You know, there is a war and children are being killed. And people are starving. And women are being raped. And refugees are fleeing across borders. That is the story. The problem is that: Is foreign aid to those people actually the story? And that's probably where it's a little bit unbalanced. [. . .] If you are talking to the foreign press officer [. . .] in fact, what you're reporting on is the aid industry, you're not reporting on the issue itself, on Uganda, you're reporting about the aid industry dealing with Uganda. [. . .] I'm not sure it's healthy that these places are always viewed through an aid agency lens. You know, there's business stories, there's social stories, and art stories, which don't get done. Partly because the aid organisations have such an influence over access for financial and security reasons.
>
> (I_22)

Another aspect of the interactions that plays into the news coverage is that people that are approached for interviews by foreigners in locations of aid intervention sometimes cannot differentiate between aid workers and journalists, and react differently to journalists' questions when they are posed in the presence of aid workers. The monopoly of access is not only referring to access to the field, but also to access to contacts and people in the field, which are often introduced to journalists by aid workers. A correspondent of a German-speaking outlet spoke of the difficulties to explain his job to people in rural areas:

> Many of the people you speak to have no idea what a journalist is. Sometimes you have to explain that and that is not easy. Sometimes you forget, and at some stage you notice: 'That guy thinks I'm from the UN'. And then you have to go back and say: 'Do you know what I'm doing here?' And I often give people the possibility to ask questions. What is that strange person who comes and asks questions, and what does he do with [this information]? I want to give them the chance to ask me that. And that is VERY important. Also, to create a fundament of trust. And to avoid misunderstandings, especially in crisis situations. That I will NOT change their lives, that I will not provide aid.
>
> (I_17)

A correspondent of a British outlet clarified:

> Well, that's the myths of the objectivity, isn't it? Because, exactly, they will take you to this place, and not this place. So you'll get the story that they . . . I know they prepared a young girl or a grandmother or a young boy to tell you that story. The press officer will most likely have gone there the day before and have said: 'Tomorrow a journalist will come and he will ask these fancy questions. What do you think you'll say? Please say this.' And then go back. And then the next day I come and I'm like: 'Hello, I'm an independent journalist. Tell me your story.' And they are like: 'Well, yes, I love Oxfam. Thank you.' So . . . yeah . . . it's a myth that it's objective.
>
> (I_14)

Additionally, the independence of the reporting can be challenged further if the humanitarian organisation provides the translator who adds the organisation's perspective and interpretation of issues to interviewee's quotes:

> If they think you're an aid worker, they will answer the questions in a certain way because they want more money. And they want more help. And they want whatever else. And then it's the [humanitarian] agency that provides your translator. That person knows all the agency-speak and whatever else. So, so many times you're interviewing some grandmother outside the IDP tent in [. . .] wherever. So you say, 'what are the greatest challenges that you're facing?' And she'll gabble away for a minute and then the translator will say: 'Well, there is a need for capacity building, sustainable development of my life, and I need more resources'. And you're like, 'this woman is 65 years old and from Somalia, she did not say 'capacity building' or whatever'. So that becomes frustrating. But then, to do independent journalism is very difficult because the paper isn't going to pay. And investigations and things like that are out the window.
>
> (I_14)

When the trip with the humanitarian organisation requires armed security, people interviewed by journalists are inclined to answer in a certain way, especially when the military is involved. A news agency correspondent described this the following way:

> Reporting in Mogadishu is difficult, it's dangerous. Practically, one of the only ways to go in is with the African Union Peace Keeping, the African Union, Amisom, and that, you know, is a difficulty because they have their own Somali translators. But, for example, when you're on the streets and you're asking an ordinary citizen, you know, 'How do you feel? Is life getting better?' and you're surrounded by twelve guys with machine guns . . . and a military translator. . . . Now, you'd still USE the translator but you would . . .

potentially . . . understand that somebody saying, 'Yes, things are wonderful,' might not be that wonderful.

(I_21)

An open eye for these situations, in which translators or security officers influence sources, sometimes only by their mere co-presence, is thus very important.

I asked all correspondents whether they considered it easier to publish a story when it featured a humanitarian organisation. Generally speaking, that is not the case. While some correspondents said that their editors preferred to have a 'transporteur' of the story to which the Western audience could relate, which often was a Western aid worker, others said that their editors wanted new, surprising stories, and that the 'ever so old aid issue' did not make for good surprises. However, considering the points discussed in this subsection so far, it becomes clear that many reports from crisis areas would not even get to the point where you could pose the question as to whether it is easier to publish an article featuring a humanitarian organisation, because the reporting would possibly never take place without an organisation involved.

Personal contacts between correspondents and the staff of humanitarian organisations, namely people working in communications and in managing positions, make a significant difference as to whether a news story gets covered. "I always tell comms people that they should invite us [correspondents] to dinners more often, cultivate their personal contacts, and that that makes the difference", one correspondent told me in the interview. "They are doing advocacy work, they are salesmen", he added, "and cultivating contacts is the most important thing for advocacy" (I_25). This is mainly because these personal contacts make it easier for correspondents to profit from logistical support. The humanitarian organisations often have a monopoly over the means of transport reaching dangerous or remote places to which correspondents want to go, meaning that they can also, to a certain degree, dictate when and where exactly to go. A humanitarian explained the procedure:

> [The journalists] would only be able to book onto the service if they were actually reporting on humanitarian stories and that could be sworn to by any member agency. So, you know, if you're working for UNHCR, Unicef, or World Vision or whoever, you can say 'this is a journalist who's coming up with us to look at our projects and to report about humanitarian work', and then we could book the ticket. But if somebody who was a member of UNHAS wasn't willing to vouch for that journalist, then the journalist wouldn't fly.

(I_54)

This quote illustrates another potential influence on the coverage. Sometimes implicitly, sometimes very explicitly, humanitarian organisations tell the journalists that if they do not write about humanitarian issues and name the organisation, they will not get a seat on the plane. Most journalists interviewed for this study confirmed that they relied on humanitarian organisations when the circumstances – either financially or logistically – meant that they had no choice but to turn to them. (The same journalists said they were convinced their reporting was independent). Correspondents increasingly face this lack of choice. A correspondent of a German outlet said:

> The only way there is often a means of transport by the UN. And already then I'm embedded in a certain way. Of course, they try to influence my reporting. When I sit in a UN helicopter, it's going to drop me off where they want to, not where I want to. [. . .] Of course I can tell the [I]NGO 'please book my return flight three days later. I will add three days at my own expenses'. Many journalists don't do that because they don't want to operate on their own in areas like this. Often, the humanitarian organisations – I don't want to call it boycott – but they refuse to accommodate these requests, and they say: 'Oh well, we can't rebook your flight now, you have to stay on this one'. Why? Because they can control the journalist better that way.
> (I_04)

Many journalists are not aware of the influence this dependency could have on their work. Asked about the effect the procedures described above could have on his reporting, another correspondent said: "Well, I think at the moment, it has a very positive effect on my reporting because otherwise I would not have the option to go to this place, and the [I]NGO provides this option to me" (I_08). By contrast, other correspondents were aware of the pitfalls. In particular those whose editors provide enough support and budget said they were able to 'afford' to object to a trip if the organisation offering it did not understand that there was no guarantee the correspondent would write about it afterwards. One American correspondent described being able to judge situations like this herself, and could choose how to act according to her outlet's general guidelines, because she could pay her own way if needed. She said: "I've had those conversations before with flacks[38] where they were like, 'Okay well, if we take you out to this, what are we getting out of it?' You know? And that always makes me wary" (I_34). A correspondent for an American outlet remarked: "I think you do end up reporting. . . . I mean you're there, and they are there. And they're part of the story anyway, it's sort of natural that you include them. And [. . .] they're counting on that" (I_31).

Humanitarian organisations' monopoly on essential information

When journalists not only rely on humanitarian organisations logistically but also in terms of information flows, the organisations have a monopoly on information that is essential to the reporting from remote places where journalists cannot go themselves. In the following subsections I will first explain that not only the information itself but also the way this information is interpreted can make a difference and add a bias to the reporting. This is especially the case for statistics that humanitarian organisations generate and that journalists use in their reporting. Then I will speak about the power of images and the use of certain vocabulary with which humanitarian organisations operate, and that find their way into news reporting.

Humanitarian organisations' prerogative of statistics

Every broadcast or story on humanitarian emergencies, crises, or conflicts needs statistics: numbers of victims, numbers of dead, numbers of wounded, numbers of refugees, numbers of IDPs, numbers of children affected, and donations needed to help. High numbers make the news, and even conflict situations often only make the news if the numbers are high enough. A correspondent recounts:

> Well, [. . .] with such an emergency announcement <<laughs>> – everyone goes along. When it is about saying: 'Holy shit! We have three million refugees!' A number like that is a bombshell. Then you get the usual snowball effect – dpa, AFP, all agencies report that. That is a number that has an impact, you can write that in the headlines. You don't even have to explain anything about the conflict. [. . .] And the editor in Hamburg, in Berlin, anywhere, gets that on the desk and thinks 'wow, we have to do something on this crisis'. But crises and conflicts only come onto the news agenda when World Food Programme, UNHCR and so on come with their super hit announcements.
>
> (I_08)

Whether it is in humanitarian organisations' own interest to give out certain numbers, or whether they 'only' interpret numbers in a certain way, is a delicate question. A correspondent working for a German outlet reported:

> They have an interest in higher refugee numbers. [. . .] High numbers mean that it's more legitimate to demand a higher budget. We journalists cannot prevent that the trap snaps shut from time to time and that we make mistakes. But also the editors don't really question these stories because the higher the number is, the more important is the story. And the better you can present it blown up as a big thing. And 'our man is in the field', and, of course, then also the editors have a greater interest in higher number than in lower ones.
>
> (I_07)

Essentially, higher numbers serve both news outlets and humanitarian organisations. A correspondent for a British outlet talked about similar experiences:

> I am aware of instances where aid organisations, you know, have their own agenda, they want to inflate the figures, or they want me to write about what great work they are doing.
>
> (I_09)

The challenge with statistics is not only how humanitarian organisations collect the data, and that the process often remains unclear, but also that the organisations can interpret them in a certain way. Journalists often do not have enough background knowledge to question the data and their interpretation, I was told by many humanitarians. Many refugee numbers, a German correspondent said for a concrete example, are constantly rising although refugees go home; but they are not de-registered (I_08). So a journalist should always check who is included in statistics and who is not. Another thing to check is how often new sets of data are collected and how often numbers get updated. A former freelancer who had regularly worked on assignments for UN organisations explained cynically:

> If our editor says: 'I think 100 people got killed. Go and find out.' And you come back, I can say 'honestly, I talked to a bunch of people; I think it's more like 50.' The editor isn't going to say: 'No, it needs to be 100.' At the UN, they might. The UN or relief organisations, they'll have a series of quotas about: We need 10,000 hungry kids to justify our next budget. You need to go out and find 10,000 hungry kids. And you come back and you say: Honestly, I talked to some people and some people are saying 10,000. But there was this whole, all these other people saying maybe it was more like 5,000. They're going, they're definitely going to be like: Well, just quote the one that said 10,000. So like a journalist gets to be flexible to reality. He gets to come back and try and be even-handed and in the end, use their gut instinct about what is the best representation of reality. Someone working for an aid organisation or the UN, that gut instinct about reality is somewhat secondary to very specific agendas; they're driven by a need to impress donors or justify their own positions. And I know that there is some overlap because Reuters say: 'Shareholders' and whatnot. But having worked internally for the UN, I know how the mechanics of these two things work differently. If I go back to Reuters and say: 'Look, I'm sorry. I know you wanted this. I don't think it's a story.' They'd be like: 'Oh, that's too bad.' If I go back to the UN and say: 'I don't think this is a story.' They'll say: 'No, no, it is a story. Just write it.' It's a very different arrangement.
>
> (I_16)

Another correspondent of a German outlet demanded that in general journalists should look at the aid industry more critically; they should be aware that if communications people reached out at certain times during the year, specifically in the middle and in the end of the year, it meant that they had run out of money and that everything needed to look bad in the news for them to cover operations and to keep their staff employed (I_08).

In order to make such assessments and to be able to evaluate why humanitarian organisations might have an interest in communicating a certain thing and not another, it is crucial that the correspondent has experience with the aid industry, has studied its mechanisms, and questioned its aims. How a correspondent handles facts and numbers published by humanitarian organisations also depends on his or her experience with the humanitarian sector. It affects how he or she might approach the organisations, and how he or she deals with them as sources.

A humanitarian worker in a senior position, with a background in journalism, argued that most people did not know enough about aid to question numbers that in other sectors they would immediately question:

> I used to argue in Irin it was disappointing that people who write about development often don't have the sufficient background. So that if you were writing about the stock market you would know that 100 percent increase in profits is extremely unlikely and what needs to be double-checked. Whereas people would take a press release about food or hunger or famine or malnutrition and they wouldn't know if it had the wrong number of zeros, they wouldn't have a concept of how many thousands of tons of food aid for example would be appropriate. Just in orders of magnitude. And there's a certain amount of education still to happen, I think, about the aid industry. And it's not difficult stuff at all. It's just [that] people tend to trust [humanitarian organisations] because their hearts are thought to be in the right place. Journalists maybe don't dig into the machinery of the aid venture enough. They don't question enough.
>
> (I_22)

A correspondent of a German outlet added to this topic:

> I think you have to do a number of trips and have to have a closer look into several individual projects to see [. . .] potential disadvantages, downsides, or just simply things that the [I]NGO does not necessarily want to read about in the paper. And in order to recognise these things you need a certain level of experience. There are not so many of these types of journalists. After all, that is a niche topic. And editors don't employ a journalist who only deals with development aid, [I]NGOs and emergency relief.
>
> (I_07)

For these assessments the experience of correspondents is crucial, because their home editors often know even less. Andrew Green, a freelance journalist who published an article on the relationship between freelancers and humanitarian organisations based on his own experiences (Green 2016), told me on the telephone that editors often did not ask any questions about stories any more, and that this was the "new norm", the new normal, and considered to be alright. A very experienced correspondent gave an example about the challenges regarding data collection that could only be unravelled when the correspondent had enough experience with humanitarian organisations:

> I am the critical filter regarding these statistics. That's why I find it problematic when the editors in such-and-such decide based on UNHCR information that there is x-amount of refugees and that is why the catastrophe is huge now. But of course UNHCR has to blow up the situation in order to make journalists come. [. . .] And I then know that you have to be cautious with these numbers, right?
>
> (I_08)

However, often these statistics are difficult or impossible to check, and the decision as to which humanitarian organisation is considered to be doing good work, and whose information is generally reliable or not, lies within the subjective view of the individual. Two correspondents, the first of an American outlet, the second of a British one, explained how they handled this:

> I mean it's not that I would check it so much. . . . Because often this stuff is uncheckable, you know. It's more how much do I trust that organisation. You know. Is this an organisation that I've seen try to exaggerate how bad something is in order to get more funding? Or is this an organisation that is pretty reliable in terms of, you know, what they put out?
>
> (I_34)

> No, you double-check where you can. But I think, you know, there's a certain assumption and not necessarily correctly, that when the UN releases a figure, that becomes like a point of FACT. I don't think that's necessarily true and I think there are plenty of cases where it's proven to NOT be the case. But I think often it's probably as close to the truth as you can get, or anyone can get, in that situation.
>
> (I_47)

It became clear that it was only when I interviewed them for this study that some correspondents first began to think about how some humanitarian organisations interpreted data according to their own agenda, whereas other correspondents had discussed this, and how to deal with it, often. The majority of correspondents, however, did not see any way to change this practice, or to verify the statistics properly. Towards the end of an interview, I asked one of the correspondents of a British newspaper, who during the interview struck me as not having put a lot of thought into the issue up to that point: so is there any way you could verify the numbers in, for example, a press release? His answer clearly surprised himself:

> <<Laughing in disbelief>> That's really thrown me, like would I ever do that? [. . .] Would I call, you know, the camp manager and say, 'Is this accurate?' Or call the chief of the elders or something like that? No. I'm really surprised at my own reaction to that. Because it illustrates obviously how much explicit trust we have in what we're fed.
>
> (I_27)

I had the same experience with several other interviewees: "I'm just thinking now . . . what interest a UN organisation could have to operate with wrong numbers . . . but of course: high numbers equal high demands" (I_07). News agencies in particular, whose content is shared with many other news outlets that are themselves very unlikely to check the content provided by the agencies, proved to be very uncritical with UN figures:

> I mean, honestly for us, if the UN says '1.3', then for us it's 1.3. We don't have any means to . . . unless. . . . I mean, the UN has ways of counting and

the UN has ways of doing this. Unless someone comes out and says, no, no, no, this is absolute rubbish. It's MUCH more than that. But the UN wouldn't have any interest in it. . . . If anything, the UN would have an interest possibly in overplaying, overstating numbers. It's possible. But then again, I don't think they would do that. So no, I'm not. . . . I mean, it's a UN figure, like anything other. And if we say there's 1.3 million displaced and we source it to the UN, according to the UN, then that's it.

(I_20)

A Nairobi correspondent of a news agency said that his most important source was Twitter. The first thing he did in the morning was to check Twitter, and what people he followed had written. Whatever they wrote, he mostly took on exactly as it was. He followed governments, media people, and communications people of humanitarian organisations. He hardly ever tried to verify what any of the humanitarian organisations stated. He assumed instead that if someone said something incorrect, that person would be fired, and trusted that meant they would post only accurate information (I_25). A communications officer working for a UN agency, however, stated:

[There are] UN agencies that write a lot of crap as well. I don't name them because I'd get into trouble but, yes, there's still agencies that write absolute [. . .]. Well, never let the truth get in the way of a good story.

(I_41)

This communication officer was not the only one internally raising doubts about the content of some of the press releases, which makes the agency journalist's quote above even more surprising.

American news outlets, excluding American news agencies, appeared more critical of information from humanitarian organisations, especially towards numbers. An example is the following quote of a correspondent of an American outlet who shared this view before I brought up any questions about the reliability of figures:

So the reporting has to go beyond just what the sort of press release says. And maybe [. . .] I'll even find that the information in the press releases is incorrect or is exaggerated or something. And that's something we always look out for and that's why you do that.

(I_31)

Another correspondent working for an American outlet, who wrote a very critical piece about a specific aid operation, in which to her knowledge false information had played a major role in fuelling the coverage of this operation (she and her editors received a significant number of complaints from the organisation for that), said:

And its one of things that has been further alarming to see. [. . .] And I think part of it comes down to just like the speed at which we're expected as

> reporters to get the material together and to get it out, there can be like a laziness of just saying, 'Okay, we need this information and I'm just gonna cite a humanitarian group, and then basically I've covered the bases. If the information is not true – whatever' <<laughing>>. Because they're the ones who said it and I'll just cite them, and then ultimately the criticism falls to them. I really disagree with that. I think that you cannot, just because a source says something dramatic to you – it's not responsible as a journalist to just drop it into your piece and say then you no longer have responsibly because you have a source attached to it. [. . .] There may be a tendency to do that if you are familiar with the organisation and you're kind of like, 'Oh I know these people, [. . .] they seem good. I'll just throw this material in without really questioning it.' [In this case] there were these phenomenal figures from this part of the organisation. But if you just ASKED some people, other people who lived there: 'what the heck happened here' – the whole situation became so much more muddied so quickly. It just baffled me that journalists were able to come out with these absurd statements without questioning.
>
> (I_33)

However, just attaching the source to a figure and then denying responsibility for its accuracy is rather the practice than an exception, as this study reveals. Many journalists said during the interviews that the audiences could then decide themselves what they thought of the information or the statistics. This practice, however, disregards that the general audience knows much less about procedures in the field than many journalists do; the audience therefore simply does not have enough background knowledge to put information and numbers into perspective. Many people additionally assume that all humanitarian organisations are doing good only, and could not imagine why any organisation would bend realities to their agendas, and push a certain interpretation of data that suits these agendas. Most audiences also assume that the information they are provided in the news has been carefully checked, and that the outcome is therefore independent and unbiased.

Humanitarian organisations' prerogative of images and terms

At the same time that humanitarian organisations in many cases have the de facto monopoly of providing access to remote places and the monopoly of data, they also often, as I explained earlier, have the prerogative of terms and images that the media then make available to a broader public. The following quotes show how the prerogative of interpretation over the image of black Africa spread via fundraising posters and crisis-focused news affects the African narrative. Two correspondents recounted:

> Most people in Britain have a very negative view of Africa, as a place of conflicts, and disease, and poverty and hatred. Which in many cases couldn't be further from the truth. And the reason is, I think, because the [I]NGOs and the

aid industry in combination with the government and the media all perpetuate this false image for their own individual purposes.

(I_10)

I think the FACT that the average media consumer in Europe or in Germany is of the opinion that the topics famine, war and diseases are dominating here, is largely because of the aid industry that is massively active in sub-Saharan Africa leading the picture that the public has of this place. And we as correspondents have to try to work against that.

(I_26)

The following quote of an aid worker shows how the drive to find negative pictures can also spring from journalists, and even make aid workers speechless:

[N]othing could prepare me to see [this] [. . .], being in Dadaab, seeing that HORRID, HORRID, HORRID desperation. [. . .] Suddenly the journalists, even though we'd been asking them to go to Dadaab for MONTHS in advance, suddenly the UN declares a famine in Somalia, and phones go off the hook. 200 journalists want to be in Dadaab at the same time, RIGHT NOW, tomorrow. Okay? After months of no interest whatsoever. So I get a call from a journalist that I know well, from a cameraman, who works for an international agency. And he's like: 'You know, I want to go to Dadaab. I hear it's really bad there. Blah, blah, blah.' I'm like: 'Okay. Yeah, let's see how we can help to get you there.' He's like: 'No, no, but what I want to know is, will I get my money shot? I need a child that's ON the verge of DEATH. I mean, like ABOUT TO DIE.' And I said: 'Are you serious?'

(I_46)

News coverage even influences the way Africans see themselves, argued an African INGO worker with a background in journalism:

I mean I think the media, the ones that represent what they see, and I guess obviously how good it's represented to them as well, by the [I]NGOs, matters. And that's why I say, when you need it to raise funds, you're always going to present the worst-case scenario, you know. But it's curious because the sad thing about this is that how journalists or Western media present Africa, doesn't only affect how European's view Africa. It affects how OTHER AFRICANS view OTHER AFRICAN COUNTRIES, because when you're in Ghana, you get your news about Nigeria – which is what? Three countries away? – we're not listening to any Nigerian broadcaster, but to the BBC. So HOW we perceive ourselves as Africans is also affected by the DOMINANT narrative.

(I_52)

Humanitarian organisations often have the prerogative of terms. Should we define this situation as 'civil war'? And what impact would that have? At what stage do we declare a 'famine'? These are questions that actors in the field, together with decision makers in the headquarters are confronted with regularly. A humanitarian communications person working for an INGO, who was frustrated that many of her colleagues and the media were only interested in crises, said:

> We did speak to a couple of journalists to see what they're actually looking for but it is quite difficult because in terms of what we do, we also have the obligation to show that it's not only war. [. . .] According to that person they just want everything conflict-related. So maybe we should put a word in the title 'war', 'war-torn' <<laughs>>.
>
> (I_12)

A correspondent working for a German broadcasting institution explained the challenges that the domination of humanitarian organisations' views can mean for the reporting, which again is similar to military embedding:

> The danger, of course, is, that you adopt the views of the [I]NGOs as your own. They then get the prerogative of what you observe. Because you are with them a lot of time. Or in fact, with their actors in the field. Because you use their help in many ways. And to keep the mental distance and independence during that is a challenge. And because humanitarian organisations are seemingly always doing good. And publicly claim to do so.
>
> (I_07)

The regional head of a news agency explained the role of humanitarian organisations in the process of news making and their prerogative of interpretation the following way:

> I think the skill of good journalism is basically taking LOTS of contradictory or COMPLEX and DIFFICULT information and boring statistics and turning that into a piece of information which tells you something NEW. I mean, that's the interesting thing. And it's all very well having a fact sheet with lots of facts and figures. But in the end, also we rely on the expertise of the [I]NGOs to tell us what exactly this means.
>
> (I_20)

In addition to humanitarian organisations shaping correspondents' views and news content, their communications people act ever more frequently as if they were journalists themselves, as this quote of a humanitarian shows:

> NOW, as a result of the budget cuts, and the less people in the newsrooms or even in the field, the humanitarian organisation as it were, becomes a shadow [news] agency so to speak because then we would have to report what is happening if the newsroom or the news agency doesn't have someone on the ground.
>
> (I_42)

Significant attention is paid – and significant funding follows, with many jobs depending on that – when crises deteriorate, or are declared to be the 'worst ever', or if a 'famine' is declared. Only after the UN has officially declared a famine, a large number of media becomes interested in covering the situation, and only then large donations are made. Thus, much depends on one term, and on the people who decide when to use it. An employee of WFP described how difficult it could be to take back that a famine declaration was to be expected soon:

> You know somebody was making the rounds in the press corps in the last couple of weeks TELLING people or giving them the impression that a declaration of famine is imminent in South Sudan and it's going to be happening within days or weeks. That is NOT true and it was REALLY annoying because I was getting a dozen phone calls a day from people who are wanting to talk. We have to have these long, relatively involved discussions about it because it's a fairly sensitive subject and I'm trying to correct the perception that people have been given about the TIMING and about whether or not we can pre-judge this process that is happening now [. . .]. I don't want to imply that, you know, it's not a crisis but I also need to factually correct the idea. We DO NOT know at this point right now whether there will BE a famine declaration.
>
> (I_54)

How the communications department of a humanitarian organisation describes a situation in the field to correspondents and journalists parachuting in from the news outlet's headquarters to dynamise funding also makes a big difference for the work of field staff and for the media coverage. One former communications officer for Save the Children who was responsible mainly for speaking about developments in the field often had arguments with the headquarters' communications team for telling journalists inaccuracies and exaggerating the situation on the ground to drum up media interest:

> This is exactly how the press office in London of Save the Children will sweet-talk people onto it. 'Come with us. No, we're working in Dadaab. It's fine. Dadaab was where everything's happening. We can get you into Dadaab. And we can show you what you need to do.' So of course, the journalists turn around, what do they want? 'I want skinny children. Where are the skinny children?' – 'Ah, well, let me just call MSF' and [then Save turns to MSF]: 'We're just coming to your feeding centre because they want to see . . . because we don't have a particularly easy-to-show program [ourselves here], you know.' And of course the employees at the field level are going: 'This is nuts. They are coming and they're bringing all these people [to us only because it's easy to fly to Dadaab and they have nothing to show them from their own organisation] and the main problem [of this famine] is not here'.
>
> (I_46)

An employee working in the regional communications department for Care explained the strategy behind this:

> But that's the value of having these kind of trips, that actually if you have a good working relationship with the media team that you're with, you can develop the message yourselves every time. And if they can relate to you as a similar professional in the kind of media sense, then you can sit down at the end of the day and say, maybe this could be a story, or maybe that could be a story, or let me show you a bit more about this.
>
> (I_45)

Of course, this strategy does not guarantee that the journalists take in information without double-checking it. In the field in challenging areas, however, a second source is often just another humanitarian organisation.

An asymmetric relationship and the dilemma of shared cultural backgrounds

The aspects discussed in the last subsections, together with the shrinking budgets in foreign reporting, large budgets in the aid and development sector, and its increasingly professionalised public relations, create an asymmetric dependency in the otherwise mutual dependencies between the media and aid sector in sub-Saharan Africa, as explained in section 6.5. The more dependent correspondents are on the resources that humanitarian organisations provide, the more asymmetric the dependency, and the greater leverage that humanitarian organisations have over correspondents. This is especially the case when humanitarian organisations control the infrastructure, logistical support, and access to the field and to contacts, as well as essential information and its interpretation that the correspondents need for their reporting. Correspondents are then restricted in their movements and independent research, and humanitarian organisations can much more easily guide the reporting according to their agendas, while presenting events in the field through an aid lens.

Additionally, there is a tendency between aid workers and journalists to have similar views on situations due to a shared cultural Western background. Many media houses prefer to quote someone from a similar cultural background as their audience to explain the situation in the field from a 'relatable expert'. A correspondent of a German broadcasting outlet described:

> If I come from a certain cultural background and was educated there, then I do wear certain glasses that make things look a certain way. Also there is the aspect of a language barrier – many journalists tend to want to work with organisations of their nationality who speak French. Or English. Or German. There is an aspect of national affinity. And then, of course, there is a certain perspective of what is important and what is of national interest. And that certainly is a view that many journalists have cut their teeth on.
>
> (I_26)

Different national perspectives also play a role in terms of which humanitarian organisation would be given preference by the correspondent and the media outlet, as the brand recognition is not the same in every country. A communications employee told me:

> Because they just hadn't heard of . . . it's harder to get Oxfam on American media because Oxfam is not as well known there. We still get some coverage but not anywhere near as much as we get in the UK. It's brand recognition basically.
>
> (I_32)

A freelance journalist said: "If I am working for Americans, I'll look for an American [I]NGO, if I work for Brits, I look for a British one because they are more likely to want to hear from them" (I_23). An employee of HRW who had previously worked as a correspondent said:

> I know that [is true] with the British media, but it's similar with the US. It has a link to the country the journalist comes from. And I find that very unfortunate. That, you know, you always have to kind of sell what the UK angle of the story is because otherwise apparently the UK public doesn't care. That very much is something I've realised a lot. [. . .] There are definitely pretty strong editorial policies within individual news outlets as well. And so, you know, why has Al Jazeera been so positive on Somalia? Or why has it engaged as much on Somalia? Well, Qatar is, you know, basically the country that funded the new president, and gave them money for him to win the elections. And so they've got interest in that country doing well. So they've got interest in it getting more attention. I mean of course Al Jazeera is a particular example. But no, it's the same with the BBC.
>
> (I_62)

A news agency journalist told of an official and an unofficial practice:

> I think that [the outlet] practically speaking still has a very strong American interest and American bias when it comes to how it covers stories. It's a global [outlet], we have subscribers on every continent. But our history is American and our headquarters are in the United States. Our board of directors are all American. So especially on the print side it's wise if you choose an American angle from time to time.
>
> (I_25)

An interviewee with journalistic background, now working with the UN remarked:

> Agency X will get a ridiculous run out on certain media because they know somebody or they have connections. And I think – please make sure this is totally anonymous – I think from my experience at the BBC in Britain, I think

there's really something WRONG there, [with] the disproportionate coverage that UK [I]NGOs get in the British media, which is really WRONG in the sense that they just cover them because it's of interest to a British audience.

(I_41)

Only one correspondent working for a US news outlet said that he would try to avoid American organisations that are state-funded because he was afraid that might look bad if they only helped him because he was American (I_31).

Another aspect influencing the reporting is that when the same nationalities stick together, it can create a prerogative of interpretation of events from a Western perspective:

> It's a learning process for many Western foreign correspondents, I had to undergo that, too. Of course, you automatically run to those who you know, or those you look like yourself. That means: to the humanitarian organisations who often live in this bubble. That means they live in the bigger cities where there is a good infrastructure. And there you make social contacts. Usually you'd go to the same cafes and clubs, and meet at the same events because everyone just sticks together. And then this often becomes a VERY strong in-group with VERY little contact apart from work to the society where they live and work.
>
> (I_15)

One former correspondent for the BBC, which makes a policy of employing African journalists to report on Africa, said when stories were for the channel's global output, things changed: "I remember when it was a global audience my editors would say, 'I don't want to hear Kenyans'" (I_24). Another former correspondent for the BBC with African background who at the time worked for an African humanitarian organisation explained how she viewed the difficulties in interpreting events always using Western sources, and how differently people reacted when they saw white journalists:

> A lot of [the correspondents] [. . .] have EXCELLENT analysis of what is going on, <<sighs>> based often on always the same people that they speak to, because they pass contacts on to each other. So it is a limited reading, you know. So for me, it's not that it's an INCORRECT reading of the situation but it is ONE SIDE of the story. [. . .] There are certain things that a local community that I arrive in, when they look at me, if they are able to identify with me, even on a physical level, there are certain things they will tell me [being a black person], that they won't necessarily tell you [being a white person], you know. It's not your fault. BUT if you don't have access to that information, then you can't present that information. And I've seen it many times when taking to foreign correspondents around, that afterwards, you know, when you step back and you're walking behind, there are things that people will tell you, you know, that they will not tell that guy because he's the mzungu.
>
> (I_52)[39]

In summary, the journalists' asymmetric dependency on humanitarian organisations paired with the correspondents' closeness to Western aid perspectives, leads to what I earlier described as aid embedding, and shapes the reporting. In the following subsection I want to add to the arguments that the interactions between humanitarian organisations and international journalists cause reporting that in many cases cannot be called independent journalism, and look into foreign reporting and general media coverage from humanitarian organisations' fundraising perspective.

Media coverage from the fundraising perspective

In the sections so far, I have stressed that it is mainly the journalists' working conditions – their lack of support from head office, their limited travel budgets, the huge patches they cover, their lack of engagement with what humanitarian organisations' agendas might be – that define the need for collaboration between foreign correspondents and humanitarian organisations. I also investigated how fundraising aspects of humanitarian organisations fed into this need. How important is media coverage really for the fundraising? Does it have a direct impact on donations? Do the communications departments of humanitarian organisations, which are usually the main point of contact for journalists, work separately from fundraising departments, or do they follow an overall strategy driven by the organisation's fundraising aims amongst other goals? What would an 'ideal' news coverage from the perspective of a fundraising department be? And do crisis-focused stories really generate more funding?, I asked communications people and programme managers when I interviewed them, and additionally interviewed a few key experts working in senior fundraising positions of INGOs and UN organisations; these were individuals responsible for designing, monitoring, and deciding over overall fundraising strategies at their respective organisations' headquarters.

I asked a communications staff at a large humanitarian INGO who was "horrified" at journalists trying to find "the skinniest babies" what her organisation's head office thought about the request. She said:

> They said 'All publicity is good publicity'. And they said, 'Look, we've done market research on it. It's the only thing people sit up and look at and it breaks their hearts. They're not interested in your development programmes and how much you're arguing for, I don't know, water systems . . . because it just doesn't get the same interest levels'.
>
> (I_46)

A very experienced correspondent described his experience: "I once called the press officer of Caritas, and I was polite and asked 'Hi, how are you?', and the answer was 'Oh well, we could really use a catastrophe'. And there I understood how that works. Just like that. It is a business" (I_04). Asked whether there was a correlation between rising budgets of humanitarian organisations and crisis-focused news coverage, he stated:

Well, that would mean that the [I]NGOs could manipulate the coverage however they want to. That is not the case, I don't think. But there is the tendency to make big crises out of small crises to generate coverage. Definitively.

(I_04)

As much as this correspondent's experience with the press officer sounds like an anecdote, it is not an exception. A former MSF spokesperson explained the difference between outreach that takes place to raise funds, and outreach to raise awareness. MSF shuts down their communication regularly when the situation is delicate and says nothing, he said. The organisations that always have something to say, even if they are not in the field, are the ones who do it for fundraising only:

> I think that makes a MASSIVE difference when you're communicating because you need money, there's a tendency to exaggerate; to present a single story you know, which is the story that is the most extreme, that's going to get you funds. Whereas, if you're not doing for that reason, then you're more likely maybe to take a lot more nuanced reading of the situation.
>
> (I_52)

An employee in a senior position for Ocha explained the coherence of coverage and funding using the famine in Somalia:

> The 2011 famine, [when no one was interested in the coverage in the beginning] [. . .] it was a Save the Children press release that really kicked things off in the early-ish second quarter of 2011. Save the Children had a friendly ear in the BBC newsroom. And they published something about the numbers of people crossing from Somalia. And BBC ran it really hard. And then the BBC went live; they decided to put a correspondent in Dadaab, the refugee camp, and hook them up live which also then gave a second phase of life to the story. And then the UN correctly and on its own terms declared a famine. And the thing became very huge and you can see a direct correlation between the amount of media coverage and the amount of money. After July, August 2011, things became very much better funded for Somalia and the Horn, [so] that you could argue that the correlation was with the declaration of famine, but also I think if you use Google trends you can see how many people were searching for this problem, thanks to the coverage.
>
> (I_22)

An employee working in communications for Save the Children commented on the process following a disaster:

> The next important thing [after a disaster happened] is to capture live the scenes of the disaster [. . .] and to be able to tell those first-hand stories of the affected communities and children. Of course to be able to raise funds, for our response. Perhaps it has occurred in a place that we have a programme

operation so you need to be able immediately to be able to . . . to storm in as it were, raise funds because of the CHILDREN.

(I_42)

An employee for Care said: "[N]o one donates money for an emergency that is not present in the media any more" (I_65). A senior communications person with a UN organisation explained how the media coverage is linked not only to fundraising but also to governmental awareness and policy making:

> You can't deny that there's definitely an aspect of FUNDRAISING, trying to compete for the attention of a limited pool of donors who might hear about something they weren't aware about, or didn't realise the MAGNITUDE of, and so help attract some funding. But there's also the advocacy level of making sure that certain crises stay on the agenda, that they're spoken about, that they're addressed politically [. . .]. So there is a big advocacy role for STATES, for governments, to assume THEIR responsibilities in protecting their populations and providing assistance, and creating an enabling environment so that assistance from [I]NGOs, the UN, the international community can also reach those who need it. So maybe it's a dual role, fundraising but also raising profile.
>
> (I_68)

Fundraising experts told me the role of media cannot be underestimated for funding:

> [I]f there isn't media coverage of that crisis, then the government feels less on the spot to have to deal with it, definitely. And that's just going to increase. And these little forgotten crises are just going to have no, NO, no funding.
>
> (I_27)

For UN organisations like Unicef where only two percent of the overall budget is state-funded, everything depends on good media work. At the time of the study, one in seven of Unicef's health projects in Somalia were going to be closed if not enough fresh funding came in (I_36). The media coverage is necessary to receive funds from individual and institutional donors. A senior fundraising expert for Unicef said:

> I am convinced that media coverage pays off in terms of brand recognition, how well-known is the brand, and all other aspects of branding. Of course, media coverage plays a big role in that. Unicef is mentioned often in top media. That is very important for fundraising. [But] it's rather the background noise and important for the long-term development of a brand, than helping on the short run. [. . .] [But] for example this Christmas we had a massive presence in the media here, within a relatively short timeframe. That, I'm sure, has helped specifically and directly with fundraising.
>
> (I_73)

The coordination between humanitarian organisations' fundraising and communications does not always work smoothly though, as the data shows. Many organisations therefore aspire to closer cooperation, or are even planning to incorporate the two sectors into the same section, as for example Oxfam, which is planning to move towards a model called 'public engagement' combining fundraising, communications, and media, all following one approach.

During my study, I interviewed a few people working for humanitarian organisations who had doubts that their agencies could influence media coverage to a great extent:

> I don't think that [I]NGOs are able to influence the media so strongly [that it would make a difference as to report crisis-focused or not]; they don't write what we want. But they write about the things that they consider to have a news value.
>
> (I_73)

This is a valid objection. Certainly my interviews proved that humanitarian organisations cannot make an event newsworthy that a news outlet clearly thinks is not. A field visit by a high-ranking employee from an organisation's headquarters, for example, has in itself alone little news value in most cases, even if many humanitarian organisations think the opposite. However, in situations that are verging on a crisis, and in emergencies, a humanitarian organisation that is fast enough or even the only one providing information on the ground has a lot of power. For emergency fundraising in particular, media coverage is crucial, and in those same emergencies, media need humanitarian organisations and their help more than in any other case:

> For those types of emergencies the comms team is very active, seeking media coverage for those events, and in particular WFP's response, knowing that that has a direct correlation to emergency fundraising. [. . .] Influencing key outlets to speak about key issues [. . .], [p]ublishing facts about [the emergency] and putting it in front of the public – that's when we see a considerable increase in resources. [. . .] Our positioning is: We are the first on the ground and the things that we do support a larger humanitarian community; not just WFP, not just the UN, but [I]NGOs more broadly. That is positioning and messaging that people like, because they like the idea that we are not all competing against each other but that our response is enabling other organisations to do their job well. That tends to be a unique position [WFP has there].
>
> (I_72)

To give some more examples of the media's relevance for emergency fundraising: Oxfam globally gained 100,000 new supporters through its emergency appeal for Nepal after the earthquake in 2015. Oxfam's aim in incidents like this is not only to raise money for the emergency, but also to develop a good relationship with these new individual donors to turn them into long-term supporters. Oxfam

Australia's team leveraged the good relationship it had created with ABC News to broadcast its appeal so quickly after the earthquake that 37,000 extra Australians joined up. When a typhoon hit the Philippines in 2013, Oxfam New Zealand was so active, had worked on media relations so well, and most importantly reacted so quickly in providing information to journalists that even though Oxfam was not very well known in this market up to that point, it created a huge response:[40]

> Because Oxfam was really first in the media about the emergency, they not only raised a lot of money for the emergency, but they actually doubled their brand awareness because Oxfam was in the news. And this was in a market where Oxfam was not so well known. But because the emergency meant that they were then on the media talking about Oxfam's work and how Oxfam would be responding to the emergency, and it double their brand awareness in that market, even though this was not their priority [. . .]. What happened, was that Oxfam New Zealand were very fast at letting journalists know that if they wanted a response to the crisis that Oxfam would have information. And because then that information is at hand for the journalists, they then turn to Oxfam. Because their mentality is to think, 'oh, I need to cover the crisis, who can I talk to?' And if they've got in their hand 'oh Oxfam New Zealand is there', they'll give me a quote. Then they'll pick up the phone to Oxfam New Zealand first. And I think that's what happened. Because Oxfam New Zealand was very fast at getting to the right journalists and positioning themselves as the agency that would be able to respond and meet what the journalists were looking for – that meant that Oxfam was on the news and then they started the circle of brand awareness and credibility there.
>
> (I_74)

The data show that media coverage is not only crucial for fundraising from individual donors, as one might think, but also for the fundraising from big institutional and bilateral donors, and governments. Many fundraising experts think, however, that single articles or reports do not instantly influence these large donors. But over the longer run, they all say, the coverage adds up to build the brand and the organisation's visibility, which can then influence people's decisions whether they want to cooperate or donate (I_73), to continue existing cooperations or not. A senior person working in fundraising for Oxfam told me that brand recognition and the reputation of the humanitarian organisation was even more important for what Oxfam calls 'unrestricted income': donations coming from big institutional donors such as DFID or Echo that are not tied to a certain project; these institutional donors would want "to have a very deep trust of Oxfam to be able to donate such large amounts of money" (I_74).

In consequence, fundraising and communications have to work together to achieve the overall aims of any humanitarian organisation. The private partnership section of WFP, for example, follows whatever key messages the communications department develops in their outreach (I_72). In non-emergencies, communication with corporate partners is developed with the help of the communications department, providing examples, case studies, and reports to the partner, showing them how businesses can support humanitarian organisations. By providing customised, direct feedback and reporting on projects to the respective partners, the organisation aims to positions itself in the market as the organisation of choice with which businesses should partner, which helps for brand building, but may not directly raise funds. The general brand awareness in a certain market can be measured in surveys, and can make a difference as to whether the media are more inclined to cite this organisation or not. A British newspaper is more likely than an American one to cite, for example, an Oxfam spokesperson on an emergency, as Oxfam is not so well known in the US, interviewees said.

'Ideal' coverage from a fundraising perspective, all organisations say, is that which shows how their organisation helps in difficult situations, and how donations can make a difference. The coverage should be solution-oriented but at the same time should also show the problem and the need because if everything was fine, nobody would donate. A fundraising expert told me that press releases that might be perfect from a communications perspective might not necessarily be perfect from a fundraising perspective. The strategies vary depending on who is supposed to be addressed, and whether it is mainly with the aim to raise funds, or mainly to create awareness. Depending on the people who are to be reached, sometimes releases are created to raise awareness only. Generally, the interviewed people in fundraising positions stated that acute natural disasters and crises have the highest 'perceived' news value. The more desperate a situation, the more newsworthy it is. However, from a fundraising perspective, the coverage should not only be desperate because that causes people to turn away feeling hopeless, a fundraising expert pointed out: instead, a way out of this desperate situation should be shown, and how people at home can make a difference by donating to the organisation (I_73). Large humanitarian organisations then measure their communications output in proxy success indicators, to check whether the coverage was 'ideal'. How much press coverage did we get? How as the quality? How long were the articles? How many key messages were included? Was our brand mentioned? What numbers of audiences do we think that reached? (I_37).

Correspondents and employees of humanitarian organisations agree in their assessments of events or situations that have news value. Crises, catastrophes, emergencies, war, famine, cruelty, sexual violence, stories on animals, stories with a strong national angle – national refers to the nationality of the respective news outlet-new and interesting angles, and generally large numbers, have 'perceived' news value, according to both correspondents and humanitarians in my study. Among that list, 'newsy' crises, catastrophes, emergencies, war, and famine bring humanitarian organisations and correspondents very close together, as they need each other more under these circumstances. The national angle leads correspondents of a particular nationality to prefer cooperating with humanitarian organisations that are a known brand amongst audiences in their country, and to look for humanitarian workers of the same nationality to give expert interviews. Crises have a contradictory status in some editorial headquarters, yet nearly always get priority. A German correspondent described this ambiguity:

> It's always crises [that we are supposed to cover]. On the one hand the editors say 'we can't hear that anymore. Again war, again famine, again drought. Again Islamists'. That's a rather new topos. But then they always reflexively jump on these wagons. That's a given.
>
> (I_07)

Only one correspondent, from a British news outlet, said that because of this editorial disinterest in yet another crisis, good news stories were actually the ones that fulfilled the news value better because they broke with the previous trend (I_09). However, this news outlet overall gave significantly more space to African news than others, and generally had an open ear for humanitarian issues. Also, large numbers do not automatically carry news value, as a very experienced communications employee for MSF exemplified:

> When we try and get journalists to do stories about malaria they're like, 'Oh fuck, malaria who gives a shit?' And in fact actually malaria kills fuckloads of people TODAY in, I mean, if you look at it, [it's] roughly 600- or 700,000 people a year and that's a lot of people, right? Versus a thousand people that have died from Ebola. I mean all those people's lives are important. But we pay so much more attention to this anachronistic, weird, mystique-surrounded disease called Ebola.
>
> (I_63)

The numbers have to fulfil either a cliché about Africa, be it of specific interest to a Western audience, or generate curiosity. A former programme manager for Save the Children summed up:

> We [humanitarian organisations] are not innocent at all, we're talking about media being horny about emergencies, wanting to cover emergencies – talking about international NGOs and the humanitarian sector, the UN agencies, we go up the same road because that's where the money is. So we end up also diverting loads of our resources and attention and time into emergency work, into humanitarian work because that's what pays off.
>
> (I_13)

It is remarkable, however, how little such self-reflection feeds into the communication with the media, and a wider public. In few incidents internal dissent that bears wider consequences leaks to the media, such as in the case of Save The Children's US branch presenting its global legacy award to Tony Blair in 2014, which many staff internally protested against, until a letter leaked to the media.[41] The critical MSF report *Where is everyone?* in 2014 caused a broad media echo,[42] not only because important issues were raised but also because it was one of the rare incidents of a humanitarian organisation speaking out publicly about the industry's systematic and structural failures. These incidents show far greater amounts of conflicting views within aid organisations than the public usually learns about. As correspondents criticised and several employees of international aid organisations admitted during the research for this book, humanitarian organisations regularly 'polish' even internal reports out of fear challenges they face in operations might leak to the public.

In summary, fundraising experts said that news coverage has a direct, quantifiable influence on the fundraising. Coverage with crisis focus generates more funding, as long as it also explains what organisation x does to improve the situation. Humanitarian organisations therefore have a great interest in shaping the coverage accordingly. Due to the often asymmetric dependencies and the correspondents on the weaker end, they regularly succeed. Additionally, most media outlets prefer coverage with crisis focus anyway. An exception is reporting on crises that last for long periods of time. In this case the editors fear their audiences' fatigue regarding the topic, and look for stories that they think would surprise them instead – often success stories within otherwise darkly painted coverage. My study thus reveals that the interests of aid and media sector meet in crises and catastrophes. The actors have created – due to the conditions under which they operate – a system that is beneficial to both media and aid, but not beneficial to the independence of the news coverage.

6.8 Blurring of lines

Several aspects encourage intertwining and blurring of boundaries between the sectors: the asymmetric dependency caused by the journalists' need for provided infrastructure, access, information, and interpretation of this information; humanitarian organisations' strong interest to shape the reporting in their favour to generate funding and create brand awareness; and the professionalisation of the public relations departments that allows for the organisations to provide all of the above. Humanitarian organisations increasingly produce material and news-like articles themselves that they either publish on their own platforms, or push into the media. The media increasingly accept the content happily as it is free and often well produced, even if it is clearly presented through an aid lens.

In addition to this blurring of lines between the media and aid sector regarding the news content, a blurring regarding human resources takes place. Wright and Green already pointed out that freelance correspondents increasingly work as consultants for humanitarian organisations on the side (Wright 2016b; Green 2016). My study confirmed this trend on the basis of a much larger sample; I also found out that this does not only concern freelancers, but also correspondents working on retainers, and some poorly paid staff. Due to humanitarian organisations' increasing hunger for well-produced stories, and as part of their professionalised public relations strategy, they pay journalists to produce news-like stories for them. The journalists' contacts to media outlets help in pitching these stories to news outlets. In theory, the journalists at one time either have the correspondents' hat on or the consultants', and keep these businesses separate. In practice, however, more and more journalists working in sub-Saharan Africa financially rely on these 'gigs' with humanitarian organisations, which means that they carefully calculate the risk of annoying humanitarian organisations that they regularly work with as consultants to secure future assignments. My research shows that the switching of hats between being a journalist and being someone working for public relations has become a widely accepted practice in sub-Saharan Africa. This has consequences. Not only is it hard for news audiences to differentiate between content produced by the same author but under different circumstances – that is, with different hats on – and understand how these circumstances shape the content, but the journalists working as consultants also bear influence on the reporting when they have their journalist's hat back on: it leads them to report in favour of humanitarian organisations' operations and perspectives. However, this coherence and logicality is not obvious to the news audiences that have the opinion that the news is unbiased and independently researched.

General considerations on influence on coverage

Overall, my research proved clearly what started as a hypothesis: in many cases the interactions between humanitarian organisations and correspondents in sub-Saharan Africa are mutually beneficial for both sectors and their actors involved; both sectors have an interest in covering crisis topics; this is also where their interests come together most clearly. A journalist whom I interviewed argued that showing where things go wrong, and highlighting where bad things happen, was a core journalistic task anywhere in the world; it was the journalists' responsibility to shed light on these places and problems, and that this was nothing unique to Africa (I_23). That pointing out problems is a core journalistic task is true. Yet, in no other region in the world do foreign correspondents and humanitarian organisations work as closely together over a very long period of time as they do in sub-Saharan Africa, and humanitarian organisations are so significantly involved in the emergence of news coverage. In no other region of the world must correspondents cover such enormous patches, yet today the global news market only takes notice of events when they are large and devastating. At the same time, no other region relatively draws as many donations to humanitarian organisations over such a long period of time as appeals for sub-Saharan Africa do.[43] What brings all of these phenomena together is the common interest from both media and aid in crisis topics that – putting aside temporary crises and emergencies in other regions worldwide – is most consistently served in sub-Saharan Africa. Following are the thoughts from actors of both sectors regarding this issue:

> I think one point worth mentioning in all this, that is a negative sometimes, is that aid organisations have been known to sort of exaggerate the extent of a crisis and give very high numbers for how many people are facing a famine. There was a controversy about that in Somalia a few years ago. So [. . .] like any organisation they are self-interested, they're trying to raise funds. So

one note of caution here is that the media and organisations can be complicit in the firm writing about how terrible a crisis is. And it serves both their interests.

(I_09, journalist)

I'm only in contact with humanitarian organisations in crisis areas. There we have the room to meet and approach one another. And that is also where we look for each other, and need each other. Under peaceful, normal circumstances that's less the case. It's mostly war, crises, and catastrophes like famines or landslides.

(I_08, journalist)

I mean, especially when we are aiming for the bilateral donors, the member states, and want to raise funds, then international media play a very important role for us. Then this is the journalists who we invite to the briefings.

(I_55, humanitarian)

I don't know how cynical it is like, you know, donors only cough up when they see dead, starving babies on TV. That's certainly a truth.

(I_18, humanitarian)

I mean the itinerary was kind of straight forward, first off, because all they wanted was to say: There is a famine. Look at all of this suffering.

(I_19, humanitarian)

A journalist of a German newspaper who wrote a rare piece questioning why a famine had been declared in a certain region after travelling there to investigate the situation, said:

For this article I was BEATEN up from the [I]NGOs – mainly the German ones. Because I did not only question their statement that there is a famine, which really wasn't true. If someone has to sell their silver jewellery to buy food, that is not a catastrophe, that is something that can happen to anybody, right? I was accused of not having understood anything; these types of articles were harmful to the development of the country. No. This article was harmful to the development of the [I]NGOs.

(I_04)

There are differences as to what extent a foreign correspondent can decide which events he or she wants to cover, and as to how much money the editors are willing to spend on travelling for investigations. Correspondents whose editors invest in their foreign reporting are less dependent on humanitarian organisations. However, they are absolutely the exception. And even then, having a travel budget does not mean these correspondents do not draw on humanitarian organisations to facilitate their travel, to find information quickly, or to share their contacts in the field. The general news value of events always plays a role in the question as to whether an event is covered or not. If an event does not have any news value, a correspondent will not get it past his or her editors to be published, even if humanitarian organisations push the story. However, the humanitarian and the media sectors have greatest interest in negative stories as they have high news value and make the most money. Additionally, humanitarian organisations are a key factor for correspondents' travel, access to data and contacts, and can thus shape the correspondents' investigations in the field, especially in emergency situations. In regions difficult to access, they can deny entry or make it possible, because they have seats on aircrafts, they decide where to go and under which conditions, they point out interview partners, they provide the translators, they are the ones who can explain the situation in the field according to their understanding, and they gather most of the data with which correspondents work. In most cases, all of this is not displayed openly; it happens subtly and sometimes even unnoticed. The correspondent remains the one to decide which stories to pick and how to frame them, and the editors to decide what to publish in the end. However, the humanitarian organisations controlling these things to such an extent, suggests that the situation in the field is likely to be interpreted in a certain way. The correspondent will think twice about antagonising key actors supporting his or her reporting over the long-term. Often, as this study showed, and many correspondents said in the interviews, self-censorship on the part of correspondents plays an even bigger role in mediating the coverage than directly voiced expectations, regulations, or demands from the humanitarians' side about what stories will be produced. Audiences are hardly ever aware of these correlations. As I explained already in Chapter 4, section 4.5 on embedded journalism, audiences were not even aware of, or did not understand, the potential impact on the news of embedded reporting in its original military sense, even though there it is much more obvious than in the case of aid embeds. And the coherences of the interactions between humanitarian organisations and journalists are discussed publicly to an even lesser extent, even though they concern a far larger amount of reporting. They concern not only foreign correspondents responsible for covering sub-Saharan Africa full-time, they also concern journalists generally writing about sub-Saharan Africa, even if from the editorial headquarters. Humanitarian organisations need to raise large amounts of money to keep their operations going, and to pay their staff in the headquarters, in the regional offices, and in the field. Accordingly, naturally, each humanitarian organisation has its own perspective of the reality on the ground, which it will try hard to spread as widely as possible to win attention and earn financial support.

Good coverage according to a humanitarian organisation's view is not necessarily good coverage according to media standards, which causes conflicting interests. This, and it is important to stress this, is not to say that all operations carried out by humanitarian organisations are flawed. It is to say that humanitarian organisations are entities just like any other large companies; they are powerful international players, who carry out their activities in their own and their main donors' interests. The information they gather and give out follows public relations strategies that are supposed to make the organisation and the organisation's projects and activities appear in the best possible light. Nothing is wrong with that. Every company does it. However, it is not neutral information that should feed to a great extent into news reports to inform a broad public without its impartiality being at least questioned. Yet, exactly that is happening, as my study proves by demonstrating how closely correspondents and humanitarian organisations cooperate in the field, with the latter controlling the access to remote locations to a large extent. If the correspondents were to go on a trip facilitated by, for example, an oil company, the editors would never accept reports that did not at least state very clearly that this is how the reporting took place. With humanitarian organisations that is not the case, I was repeatedly told, and I repeatedly witnessed this during my investigations.[44] Of course humanitarian organisations are not 'companies' in the stricter sense, as the majority of them are non-profit organisations. Yet, many of them pay their staff large salaries that are raised through news coverage, and spend large amounts on public relations to get the media's attention to draw more funding. Are journalists uninvolved second-order observers on the ground, I asked earlier. No, they are not. They can influence the situation on the ground with their reporting; they can have an influence on financial flows of aid budgets via their reporting, which again can have significant influences in the field; they can influence how the situation on the ground is perceived by an international audience, which can also influence big bilateral donors; and they can even influence how local governments behave towards their own population's needs when, for example, the UN takes on governmental roles, and the media are either supportive of that, or not.

That the actors involved in the emergence of this coverage depend in many cases and to a significant extent on the aid sector is not problematic as long as it is made unmistakably clear to the audience what that means: this is a sector that plays an important political role, that operates with large budgets, is dependent on economic trends and the political interests of its main donors, and, more importantly, has its own agenda just like any other business-oriented entity – facts of which many people are not aware. It is a sector that additionally spends large amounts on professional communications staff who craft news lines and lay out the red carpet for journalists to report from challenging and newsworthy locations they might otherwise be unable to reach. It is a sector whose employees in the field are, from a moral standpoint, often hard to criticise as they 'do good' in difficult places. Furthermore, it is a sector whose field workers often have a monopoly over information that they pass to journalists with whom they form personal relationships, because they are the only ones on the ground for long enough to develop the kinds of contact networks in remote places that are crucial to the journalists' work, and the only ones with the budget and means to gather data and monitor developments consistently. At the same time, this sector and its employees are highly dependent on the media for publicity, advocacy, and fundraising purposes, which creates the pressing need to win the journalists over, and to be indispensable to them. The reduction in Western media of foreign coverage enables international humanitarian organisations to gain a foothold in setting the foreign news agenda to a large extent. The regional head of a UN agency who formerly worked as journalist said:

> The UN is big, but it's not so big as to justify dominating a development of humanitarian story line, necessarily. In answer to that, the UN is sort of all over the place. And journalists have to be careful not to go with the UN just because they make more noise, and they produce more documents, and they have more planes and they have more data.
>
> (I_22)[45]

But in practice often journalists who need to cover difficult regions have no other choice, as I explained in section 6.5. Bearing in mind how the lines between aid and media sector blur, how close the relationships are between journalists and humanitarians involved in the production of the coverage, and the asymmetry of these relationships in favour of humanitarian organisations – it becomes clear that the reality that media displays is coloured in a way that cannot be called independent.

Overall, this section made clear why and in which cases it is feasible that this key role humanitarian organisations have – both in form of their actors in the field and in their headquarters – can shape news coverage, sometimes even without journalists being aware of it, and clearly without news audiences understanding the context and the implications of news production in sub-Saharan Africa.

Notes

1 For comparison: The European Union (EU) has 510 million inhabitants in 2015, and a GNI per capita of USD 26,280 (the GNI data is from 2014; GNI PPP per capita is the gross national income in purchasing power parity divided by mid-year population, Population Reference Bureau 2015: 19).
2 This map is designed to give an approximation of how Western media divide Africa in terms of their correspondents' attention. Boundaries do not follow exact country borders. The division varies slightly; some outlets include one country in one region that another outlet might exclude from that region, also depending on how many correspondents the outlet has overall.
3 In cases like this, I took notes of all sentences said after the recorder was switched off.
4 BBC (n.d.) *Editorial Guidelines,* URL: www.bbc.co.uk/guidelines/editorialguidelines/edguide /war/editorialprinci.shtml; www.bbc.co.uk/guidelines/editorialguidelines/page/guidelines-external-relationships-other/#charities [1.4.2015].
5 This is for example the case for public German television broadcasters, although the methods of selecting the organisations to be supported are unclear, seem highly subjective, and involve humanitarian lobbyists at the decision table.
6 See section 6.5.
7 These data resulted from asking the correspondents about their relationships with their editors, how knowledgeable they found them with regards to African issues, and whether they felt understood and supported in their role as Africa correspondents.
8 The data for this chart are partly taken from the answers correspondents gave in the questionnaires to predefined roles, and from the interviews where correspondents were asked what they thought their role and task, and what their motivations to this job was.
9 These interviewees were included into the statistics with the 'informing role' as I wanted to depict the self-perception as it was when the interviews took place. However, this shift in terms of the motivation I found important to mention.

10 I discovered this applying a lexical search for the word 'competition' within all interviews and analysing the paragraphs around it, and analysing all text segments coded as text on competition between humanitarian organisations.
11 I_72, I_73, I_74, amongst others.
12 I_33, a freelancer for mostly American outlets, I_35, a staff correspondent for a British outlet, and I_36, communications staff member for a large INGO with a strict media policy, amongst others.
13 I_08, I_33, I_47, I_50, I_57, amongst others.
14 Franks (2008) was one of the first scholars to identify this trend of blurred lines.
15 Gavi, The Vaccine Alliance.
16 Passages in this quotation that could identify the people concerned were neutralised. This is also the case for passages that served for indirect identification.
17 The numbers are rounded. To have the numbers adding up to 100, yet minimising the overall error, and to remain true to actual numbers, the relative to the actual value was introduced before making the decision as to whether to round or not. The number where the relative difference between actual and rounded number was largest, was not rounded.
18 See Chapter 1.
19 More on this issue I will explain in the subsection on the editor's role under section 6.1.
20 The jumps in numbers in the figure attributing an organisation as (un)important partner emerge from the data itself. There is a clear divide between many organisations that were only mentioned once, and very few that were mentioned up to three times, which formed the first category. Then, there were organisations that were mentioned by six interviewees, which formed the second category. Above six there is a large gap. Then, a large number of organisations were mentioned by 30+ interviewees. However, to formally include lesser counts, the distinction threshold nominally had to be seven.
21 For the latter, please see section 6.5.
22 See Figure 6.16.
23 Much seems to have changed since Cottle and Nolan's findings that these field trips "become increasingly rare" (Cottle and Nolan 2009: 867). This is possibly due to more budgets cuts in foreign reporting; and it may additionally be due to regional particularities in sub-Saharan Africa.
24 For example I_38, I_42, I_43, I_45.
25 I_38, I_41, I_44, I_47, I_49, I_67, amongst others.
26 I_43, I_52, I_54.
27 For this double bind situation in which many freelancing correspondents find themselves, and the blurring of lines between the two professions, also see the subsection on personal contacts.
28 For the description of these aspects, please refer to Chapter 4, section 4.5 on embedding.
29 Journalists embedded with the military report about similar experiences as those here embedded with a humanitarian organisation, under the protection of UN troops. A study by Weichert and Kramp revealed that the journalists only had "bad experiences [. . .] contacting members of the civil society when they were embedded [with German armed forces]". The study reports: "It seemed as if the villagers [. . .] could not speak openly and authentically with the crisis reporters in the presence of the military" (Weichert & Kramp 2011: 211).
30 In this case, the interviewee had said that journalists were more and more getting into bed with humanitarian organisations, and he had said so of his own accord. Only after he had mentioned this, I then asked him whether he thought it could be compared to embedding.
31 Much as in the quotation above, also in this case, the interviewee came up with a comparison to embedding unprompted. I then asked him to specify what exactly he meant, and in what way it could be compared to embedded journalism.
32 For example I_07, I_27, I_28, I_56.
33 For example I_23, I_27, I_31, I_57.

34 See also Wright 2016a, 2016b.
35 See for example Marcus Bleasdale's reportage on CAR, which was largely produced by Human Rights Watch: http://lens.blogs.nytimes.com/2015/04/30/marcus-bleasdale-when-photography-campaigns-for-change/?_r=0; www.david-campbell.org/2014/01/14/photojournalism-contributes-change-marcus-bleasdales-work-conflict-minerals/. On his website the cooperation is described as follows: "Since 2000 Marcus has worked extensively in eastern Democratic Republic of Congo documenting a war funded by the extraction of the minerals used in every day electronic products. Marcus has partnered with international advocacy groups Human Rights Watch and the Enough Project to engage US and European politicians and multinational companies to change government policy and working practices. Over the past three years Marcus has been working in the Central African Republic documenting the conflict in the region. His work is recognised internationally and has won a significant amount of prizes, such as the Robert Capa Gold Medal in 2015, and World Press Photo in 2006" (www.marcusbleasdale.com/about).
36 See URL: http://l-instant.parismatch.com/Jour-apres-jour/Les-refugies-du-Kagunga-774620# [2.1.2016].
37 In the case of freelancers, who sometimes do not only work for either American or British media outlets exclusively, I grouped them according to which outlets they mostly work for. That meant in practice that if one freelancer for example, worked for six British outlets on a regular basis, and two American ones less regularly, I grouped him or her under the correspondents working for British outlets.
38 Term journalists use for PR people (as opposed to 'hacks' for journalists).
39 In Africa, 'Mzungu' is the often used Swahili term for 'white person'.
40 All information from this paragraph is from an interview with a senior fundraiser with Oxfam, I_74.
41 Sherwood's article in the Guardian: www.theguardian.com/politics/2014/nov/25/save-the-children-furious-charity-global-legacy-tony-blair [1.3.2015].
42 www.msf.org/sites/msf.org/files/msf-whereiseveryone_-def-lr_-_july.pdf [1.4.2015]; www.theguardian.com/global-development/2014/jul/07/un-ngos-funding-humanitarian-relief-msf-medecins-sans-frontieres; www.telegraph.co.uk/news/worldnews/ebola/11539619/Medecins-Sans-Frontieres-the-organisation-at-the-heart-of-the-Ebola-outbreak.html [1.4.2015].
43 Unicef, just to give one example, one of the main multilateral ODA receivers, spends 55 percent of its average overall annual budget of USD 3.3 billion on sub-Saharan Africa alone (UNICEF 2010, 11, 12; this number is an average of the Unicef annual budgets from 2009 to 2011).
44 Which also makes the argument pointless that influence on coverage could only be proven if detected in content analyses, that means, in news coverage. My point is that the coverage would often not even exist if it was not for humanitarian organisations taking correspondents to remote and dangerous areas – but I will explain this in the following subsections.
45 It is remarkable that this kind of self-criticism is not rare in the humanitarian sector but that it largely remains within the circles of the sector, while the broader public is not aware of the issue.

References

ARD (2010) "ARD-Richtlinien für Werbung, Sponsoring, Gewinnspiele und Produktionshilfe", URL: www.wdr-mediagroup.com/download/spezialmodule/dokumente/ARD-RICHTLINIEN_FueR_WERBUNG_SPONSORING_GEWINNSPIELE_UND_PRODUKTIONSHILFE_2010.pdf [22.2.2014].

ARD (2013) "ARD-Leitlinien 2013/14": Das Erste, URL: www.daserste.de/specials/ueber-uns/ard-leitlinien-2012-100.pdf [22.2.2014].

BBC (n.d.) *Editorial Guidelines*, URL: www.bbc.co.uk/guidelines/editorialguidelines/edguide /war/editorialprinci.shtml; www.bbc.co.uk/guidelines/editorialguidelines/page/guidelines-external-relationships-other/#charities [1.4.2015].

Birrell, Ian (2014) "Aid Agencies Have Become Self-Serving Corporations Dressed in the Clothing of Compassion", *The Guardian*, URL: www.theguardian.com/comment isfree/2014/jul/07/aid-corporations-clothing-compassion-msf-charities-south-sudan-syria?CMP=twt_gu [15.9.2015].

Brandenburg, Heinz (2005) "Journalists Embedded in Culture: War Stories as Political Strategy", in: Lee Artz and Yahya Kamalipour (Eds.), *Bring 'em on: Media and Politics in the Iraq War*, Lanham, 225–238.

Cottle, Simon (2014) "Rethinking Media and Disasters in a Global Age: What's Changed and Why it Matters", in: *Media, War & Conflict* 7(1), 3–22.

Cottle, Simon and Nolan, David (2007) "Global Humanitarianism and the Changing Aid-Media Field. 'Everyone was Dying for Footage'", in: *Journalism Studies* 8(6), 862–878.

Cottle, Simon and Nolan, David (2009, November 16) *How the Media's Codes and Rules Influence the Ways NGOs Work*, Nieman Journalism Lab.

Davidson, W. Philipps (1980) "The Public Opinion Process", in: *Public Opinion Quarterly* 44(1), 91–106.

Davidson, W. Philipps (1983) "The Third-Person Effect Revisited", in: *International Journal of Public Opinion Research* 8(2), 3–15.

Dietrich, Sandra (2007) *Embedded Journalism. Ursprünge, Ziele, Merkmale, Probleme und Nutzen von, Embedding' am Beispiel des Irak-Krieges 2003*, Saarbrücken.

Dupagne, Michael (1999) "The Third-Person Effect. Perceptions of the Media's Influence and Immoral Consequences", in: *Communication Research* 26(5), 523–549.

Foreman, Jonathan (2013) "The Great Aid Mystery. Our Rulers Must Know that Develpment Aid Doesn't Work. So Why Do They Throw Money At It?", *The Specator*, URL: http://new.spectator.co.uk/2013/01/the-great-aid-mystery [20.10.2015].

Franks, Suzanne (2008) "Getting into Bed with Charity", in: *Brisith Journalism Review* 19(3), 27–32.

Green, Andrew (2016) "The Thorny Ethics of Embedding with Do-Gooders", *Columbia Journalism Review*, URL: www.cjr.org/first_person/the_ethics_of_embedding_with_do-gooders.php [8.2.2016].

ICRC (1996) "Annex VI: The Code of Conduct for the International Red Cross and Red Crescent Movement and NGOs in Disaster Relief", in: *International Review of the Red Cross* 310.

Intendant des ZDF (2010) "Mitarbeiterkodex", *Mainz: ZDF*, URL: www.zdf.de/ZDF/zdf-portal/blob/26890782/1/data.pdf [20.2.2014].

Kron, Thomas and Winter, Lars (2009) "Aktuelle soziologische Akteurtheorien", in: Georg Kneer and Markus Schroer (Eds.), *Handbuch soziologische Theorien*, Wiesbaden, 41–65.

Moyo, Dambisa (2009) *Dead Aid: Why Aid is not Working and How there is a Better Way for Africa*, London.

MSF (2014) "Where Is Everyone? Responding to Emergencies in the Most Difficult Places. A Review of Humanitarian Aid System's Response to Displacement Emergencies in Conflict Contexts in South Sudan, Eastern Democratic Republic of Congo and Jordan 2012–2013": MSF.

Mükke, Lutz (2009b) *'Journalisten der Finsternis'. Akteure, Strukturen und Potenziale deutscher Afrika-Berichterstattung*, Köln.

Polman, Linda (2010) *Die Mitleidsindustrie. Hinter den Kulissen internationaler Hilfsorganisationen*, Frankfurt/M., New York, NY.

Population Reference Bureau (2015) "2015 World Population Data Sheet", URL: www.prb.org/pdf15/2015-world-population-data-sheed_eng.pdf [1.11.2015]

Riddell, Roger (2007) *Does Foreign Aid Really Work?*, Oxford.

The Sphere Project (2004 [1998]) "Humanitarian Charter and Minimum Standards in Disaster Response", *IFCR*, URL: www.ifrc.org/docs/idrl/I283En.pdf [14.3.2015]

Stoianova, Velina (2012) *Private Funding. An Emerging Trend in Humanitarian Donorship*, Global Humanitarian Assistance Report, Briefing Paper, URL: https://de.scribd.com/document/287839036/Private-Funding-an-Emerging-Trend [10.3.2015].

UNICEF (2010) "Unicef Annual Report 2009", URL: http://www.unicef.org.hk/upload/NewsMedia/download/international/Annual_Report_2009.pdf [12.12.2011].

Weichert, Stephan and Kramp, Leif (2011) *"Die Vorkämpfer. Wie Journalisten über den Ausnahmezustand berichten"*, Köln.

Weichert, Stephan, Kramp, Leif and Matschke, Alexander (2012) "Überlegungen zur Qualität im Krisenjournalismus", in: *APuZ* 29–31(Qualitätsjournalismus), 22–28.

Wright, Kate (2016a) "Moral Economies. Interrogating the Interactions of Nongovernmental Organizations, Journalists, and Freelancers", in: *International Journal of Communication* 10, 1510–1529.

Wright, Kate (2016b) "These Grey Areas", in: *Journalism Studies* 17(8), 989–1009.

ZDF (2010, March 12) *ZDF-Richtlininen für Werbung, Sponsoring, Gewinnspiele und Produktionshilfe*, ZDF.

7 Summary and conclusion

Prior to the research for this book, I had read that German foreign correspondents in sub-Saharan Africa covered an average of 33 countries, and sometimes even more. I began to ask questions. How is this possible, when at the same time travel budgets for foreign reporting are shrinking? How can we picture the conditions that make work under these circumstances possible? What network do correspondents need to cover these large patches, and who are their most important partners in fulfilling this difficult task? Quickly, the role of humanitarian organisations came into focus, and I wanted to investigate these relationships that have been established between journalists and humanitarians on an individual level, and between media and aid sectors on an organisational level. What are the conditions that brought these two together? How can we picture these interactions? How dependent are the sectors and their actors on each other? What advantages and disadvantages do the interactions bring from both perspectives, and what does this mean for the news coverage on sub-Saharan Africa? This chapter sums up the findings and answers to these questions, and questions posed in Chapters 1 to 4. It highlights patterns and structures detected in the interactions, and their consequences.

One could argue that news tends to focus on negative issues all over the world, and that humanitarians and journalists work together in many locations: so, what is special about the situation in sub-Saharan Africa? There are many aspects to this answer. The coverage of sub-Saharan Africa is focused on crisis news to a much greater extent than anywhere else, and the interactions between humanitarians and correspondents in sub-Saharan Africa investigated in this study are different from the interactions anywhere else, which has an influence on the coverage. In no other region in the world has so much money been raised and spent since overseas aid began to expand, while the institutional growth of humanitarian organisations responding to growing numbers of crises has increased the need for more funding. At the same time, there is no other region that has so few correspondents covering so many diverse countries with such small travel budgets, while the attention of the global public and the editors of Western news outlets is so low as to make the news threshold very high. This combination of conditions of the two sectors makes sub-Saharan Africa a special case. The framework leaves the actors with little choice but to act rationally, choosing to extend their network with the other sector as widely as possible, and keeping good working relationships with individual actors of the other sector that seem to promise benefits.

The data show clearly that the majority of actors of both the media and the aid sector consider interactions with players of the other sector very important. In calls, emails, official press conferences, informal meetings held routinely, and field trips, the correspondents seek information and data, estimation of the situation on the ground, contacts, and logistical help. The staff of humanitarian organisations aim to stimulate positive media coverage on their organisation or singular projects to build their brand, gain international attention, raise awareness for a certain issue, raise donations, or to push policy makers to action via indirect pressure through media reports, and changing public discourses. Not all of these targets are prioritised at the same time, and opinions on how to achieve them best vary. These priorities, interests, and expectations of the correspondents and the staff of humanitarian organisations often do not match, which can lead to misunderstandings and frustration on both sides.

Personal contacts play a major role in all of the interactions, and a significant number of interviewees from both sectors said they purposefully invest in and cultivate contacts with actors of the other sector to be able to draw on them when necessary, and to build a base for mutual benefits. As a consequence, the line is fine between private and professional contacts, and this also intensifies the professional contacts. Many correspondents and employees of humanitarian organisations know each other from private contexts living in expat circles. The better they know each other, the easier it is for correspondents to receive information quickly when needed. Correspondents said that humanitarian workers that they know socially rather than just professionally in most cases understand their perspective better, which lessened the chances of fuelling false expectations, as for example that the organisation would always be quoted in a certain way in their news pieces. The people working in communications for humanitarian organisations expand their personal network to correspondents as widely as possible. When deliberately wanting to place a message, or deciding which correspondent to take on a trip, they choose according to the audience they want to reach, according to the size and name of the media outlet, the expected outreach, the name and prior work of the respective correspondent, and their experience with this correspondent in the past, which also makes personal contacts and recommendations very important. Personal contacts can determine whether a journalist is granted a seat on a plane to a story or not, especially when spaces are limited.

However, not all actors value the interactions. There are three different types of correspondents in terms of how they generally handle their contact with humanitarian organisations: first, the 'avoiders' who try to avoid humanitarian organisations when possible, most particularly organisations with explicit religious backgrounds, UN organisations, or those with a strong agenda. However, in emergencies, and when travelling to remote places in particular, they admit that this is hardly doable. In cases when it is not possible to avoid contact, these journalists try to explicitly acknowledge the involvement of any humanitarian organisation in their coverage if the editors allow for it. Second, the 'unsuspecting', correspondents who have not put much thought into the issue of their interactions with humanitarian organisations, or do not see any negative side to it. And third, the 'pragmatists', the large majority of correspondents, who do not necessarily see the interactions as anything positive, but simply take a practical approach for lack of alternatives, highlighting the mutual benefits that spring from it. Among all these three types of correspondents, the avoiders, the unsuspecting, and the pragmatists, there is hardly any correspondent who differentiates between different mandates of humanitarian organisations when considering the interactions with them. A very few interviewees said they would avoid explicitly religious organisations, or the ones that appear to have a very strong agenda, but could not answer upon request what kind of agenda that might be. Not one journalist considered on a more systemic level that the way an organisation was led and funded, could affect the way it acted and spoke out.

Equally, humanitarian organisations have different ideas on how, and how intensively, to cooperate with correspondents. Headquarters, regional offices, and field staff do not always agree on the media strategies. Communications staff, regional and programme managers have a generally positive opinion of correspondents – some even see them as "natural allies" – but several have had negative experiences finding that the journalists did not value their work enough, that they invested into trips, and did not get any coverage in the end, or that they had shared off-the-record information that was published, and got the organisation into trouble. They revealed that they thought cooperation with the media was necessary and important but that they were generally cautious when dealing with the media. Field staff in particular, who usually have less experience with the media, were very careful about what information they gave and how they voiced it, if their organisation authorised them to speak out at all. Many field staff also disapproved of journalists' field visits mandated by the headquarters because they found them hindering their work.

All humanitarian staff lamented that development projects are very hard to sell to the media, and that correspondents and their editors are not interested enough in covering issues that are, from the humanitarians' perspective, likely to bring about long-term change; this highlights a misunderstanding of the media's role as most correspondents understand it: they do not want to change things with their reporting. The two dominant roles that correspondents working in sub-Saharan Africa mainly identified with – informing and reporting – show that they perceive their task as to neutrally present information. The interpretation of role differs between staff and freelance correspondents. While no freelancer said he or she identified with the role of 'provocateur', some staff correspondents did. Significantly more freelance correspondents than staff identified with the role of 'interpreter between cultures', which suggests that correspondents working as freelancers feel more constrained by the necessity to 'translate' things from faraway places to their audiences' reality of life. I discovered that freelancing correspondents have less frequent contact with humanitarian organisations than staff correspondents, but that the contact when it happens is more intense and the interactions involve more dependency. I found the journalists' role-identification to be a part of what determines how they interact with humanitarian organisations. Regardless of the employment type, the correspondents who wanted to change something for the better with their reporting, or who saw themselves as advocates of socially disadvantaged people, reported at the same time to have significantly more contact with humanitarian organisations, and felt much more dependent on them, than the correspondents who did not identify with these self-perceptions. The interviews show that the majority of correspondents aim to report independently and to inform the public about events without bias. Interestingly, the majority of staff of humanitarian organisations I interviewed presumed that among the roles with which correspondents might mostly identify, the role of an investigative researcher would be one of the top two, and a smaller percentage said that advocate of socially disadvantaged people would be among the top five roles. The journalists' self-perception showed a very different picture, however; Neither of these roles were among the top five preferred, which demonstrates a mismatch of role understanding between the self-perception of journalists and how humanitarian workers think journalists see themselves. It may explain why many actors of both sectors are frustrated with the current situation in the interactions, in which they approach each other with wrong expectations about the other. Despite starting from mismatching ideas of the other's work and self-perception, the actors of both sectors adapt to each other's working procedures in many cases. Humanitarian organisations try to anticipate a journalistic perspective in order to be able to provide stories that are newsworthy and to publicise projects that appeal to the media. Their staff working in communications are trained to provide material quickly to meet journalistic deadlines, and to offer support. Many correspondents who travel with the support of a humanitarian organisation try to see the humanitarians' perspective on taking the journalists to the field, and try to ensure that they get something out of it, too.

From the necessity of both sectors to cooperate in order to reach their aims, and from adapting to each other's needs, a stable network of interactions and mutual dependencies emerged. This network is essential for both the humanitarian and the media sector in order to operate in sub-Saharan Africa. The actors constantly seek to extend their network and improve their position in it. In the interviews and field study I conducted, it became clear that humanitarian organisations think they need the media more than the media need them, but looking at the interactions closely I find that is not the case. All correspondents are dependent on humanitarian organisations to a certain extent, and they are more dependent on them than ever when reporting from remote regions because of shrinking budgets, and specifically decreasing travel expenses, and because correspondents cover ever larger patches. Especially in emergency situations and in regions where access is difficult, the dependency becomes more one-sided. Humanitarian organisations have the de facto monopoly of access and information to and of these places. The correspondents can still decide which organisation to turn to if several operate in the same area. However, most correspondents choose the organisation that they interact with according to very subjective estimations about the organisation's work, simply according to who answers the telephone first, who can take them to a certain place, who can provide important contacts in the field, or – in case the news outlet allows this – who is willing to help (co-)finance the trip when editors otherwise refuse the trip for budget reasons. The correspondents, in theory, have the upper hand in deciding what article they will write and how they will write it in the end. However, in practice, humanitarian organisations can not only often define the angle in which they present information and projects to the journalists and thus influence their way of reporting, but they can and do also sanction journalists if they are not satisfied with their reporting. They refuse to facilitate trips in the future, deny sharing their contacts, or chose not to provide data that the organisation gathers, all of which are often crucial for the reporting when no other option and no other data are available. Some correspondents said that they could not 'afford' to annoy the humanitarian actors because they were very dependent on their goodwill, especially those operating in remote places and under difficult conditions, such as WFP, WHO, UNHCR, Unicef, MSF, HRW, and ICRC.

Generally speaking, the dependency within the network between humanitarian organisations and correspondents is mutual. Both can offer something that the other party needs, and that often only they are able to give. Although that is principally the case, the dependency from both sectors' perspectives is not always even. Apart from wide-ranging reciprocal dependencies within the network, and balanced power relationships, there are many cases of asymmetric power relationships too. The dependency on the journalists' side varies with the journalists' type of employment and their work experience. It increases for freelancers and staff correspondents equally, the fewer travel expenses an outlet pays. Freelancers are at special risk, however, as they lack regular and guaranteed income. The risk of high dependency is even more prominent when correspondents do not perceive humanitarian organisations as agents with their own agenda, and thus rely on them without critically considering the organisations' overall role and motivations, and their role in it, which surprisingly many correspondents do. The more experience a correspondent has, the more detailed information he or she gives on his or her perceived dependency on humanitarian organisations. How correspondents with a lot of experience rated their dependency is also very diverse: some rate it very high, some rate it very low. Correspondents with little Africa experience rate their dependency in the middle of the scale, most probably because they do not know what exactly to answer. The nationality of the news outlet plays a role in the journalists' perceived dependency on humanitarian organisations. Many news outlets do not have editorial guidelines directing how their correspondents should handle interactions with humanitarian organisations, and even among those who do, a significant number of journalists are not aware of their existence. Generally, American outlets have the strictest rules. They regulate that their correspondents must always pay their own way when travelling with any humanitarian organisation, and how to use these organisations' material. At the same time, American outlets cultivate their tradition of investigative reporting, which often comes with more budget for independent travel and research. Editors of correspondents of German-speaking quality news outlets with staff correspondents in sub-Saharan Africa still agree to pay more travel expenses than most British outlets, but their editorial guidelines regarding the handling of interactions with humanitarian organisations and the use of their material are less clear and less strict than those of American outlets. However, the guideline of American outlets nearly always only concern payment, and in many cases not the interactions themselves in practice. American outlets may be stricter in terms of not accepting freebies, but the correspondents for American media I interviewed said they faced the same challenges in the field as the correspondents from British and German outlets when their journalistic working ethics and the humanitarian organisations' expectations conflicted. Even with a larger budget and stricter rules on interactions with humanitarian organisations, American correspondents often have to rely on the organisations' contacts, knowledge, and their logistical assistance nevertheless, even if the correspondents pay their own way. The dependency on the humanitarian organisations' side varies with the media and advocacy strategy, and acute need for funds. All humanitarian organisations, however, are dependent on media coverage and their good image to a certain degree.

The interactions between media and aid in sub-Saharan Africa become asymmetric when the correspondents are more dependent on the humanitarian organisations' resources than the organisations are dependent on the public attention; when the organisations' contacts and information is otherwise not accessible to the correspondents; when the correspondents rely on the organisations' logistical or budget support; and when the correspondents are restricted in movement and independent research, with the humanitarian organisation setting the schedule and guiding them in the field. In the types of interactions that exhibited a strong dependency I found it justifiable to speak of *aid embeds*, as many of the characteristics that apply to journalists embedded with military troops also apply to correspondents embedded with humanitarian organisations in the field.

The power relationship in these cases is unbalanced, and gives humanitarian organisations a greater leverage to play the interactions according to their needs; they consider the media still to be the most important way to generate funding, especially in emergency situations. Both actors invest in social relations and in their reputation with actors of the other sector expecting returns. Both sectors have an interest in crisis topics – the humanitarian organisations to generate funding, and the media because crises have a very high news value. In this context, the editors play an important role as they often ultimately decide which events and which stories to cover. Correspondents deplored that many of their editors did not know enough about sub-Saharan Africa and the working conditions on the continent: they felt left alone and missed their editors' feedback and support, and disliked that this was considered the 'new normal'. There are exceptions, of course, but the majority of correspondents drew a dark picture of their editors. Many of those editors seem to be even more uncritical towards information produced by humanitarian organisations than the correspondents, which feeds into the correspondents' dependency on humanitarian organisations.

I found a strong blurring of lines taking place between the media and aid sector in sub-Saharan Africa, leaving roles and responsibilities not always clear, and forming a large grey area between the two sectors. There are two reasons for

Summary and conclusion 257

this development. First, the communications and fundraising departments of all humanitarian organisations have professionalised and grown significantly within the last two decades. The professionalised PR departments do not only try to push media coverage, but nearly all humanitarian organisations now produce (news-like) material themselves that is published on their websites, and sent to news outlets, or to donors directly. When this material is used in international media, in many cases there is no hint on the provenance of this material. Also, there is a trend to produce pictures, texts, and comprehensive research reports on specific issues with large amounts of statistics that are designed to spark the media's interest, presented as neutrally researched. Here, a blurring of lines between the two sectors is taking place, with humanitarian organisations now also appearing as content producers. The communications departments and the fundraising departments of most organisations work closely together, which reveals the trend of humanitarian organisations shifting from disseminating pure information to using that material to do more advocacy and fundraising work. I call this material *journalistic PR*. Second, many freelancing journalists take on consultancies for humanitarian organisations because they cannot sustain their living with journalism only any longer, which comes in handy for the communications departments of humanitarian organisations and their organisations' increasing need for fundraising, and professional donor communications. The correspondents on consultancies then work to support the organisations' communications team for a limited amount of time before they go back to work as journalists. These consultancies mostly consist of either editing reports that the organisations have produced in-house, or going on missions to report on their humanitarian projects for the organisations' own internal communications or external PR.

Interestingly, the majority of correspondents interviewed for this study stated they were confident that their relationship with humanitarian organisations did not significantly influence their coverage. Several reasons, explored in detail in these past chapters, make it plausible to doubt this view: First, this research overall proved that the interactions between the aid and the media sector on the African continent are so crucial to the reporting that it is hard to believe that they do not shape the coverage in any way. Second, as mentioned in the introductory chapter, content analyses of news coverage show that humanitarian organisations are mostly featured in a positive light, and that their actors generally feature surprisingly often in reports on sub-Saharan Africa. Third, humanitarian organisations are often the only sources for data in emergencies and crises, and often have the prerogative of interpretation of the situation on the ground, which they can present according to their organisation's ultimate aims and requirements. This influence is not explicit, but applies to correspondents of all nationalities and all employment types. Fourth, in regions that are hard to access because of a lack of infrastructure or poor security, humanitarian organisations can dictate to a certain degree where correspondents can go; and in regions and countries where the security risk is very high, they decide over the journalists' movement completely. Furthermore, when the correspondents arrive on the ground, they rely on the organisations' dense network of contacts in the field. Fifth, the blurring of lines between the two sectors hinders journalistic independence, especially when freelancer journalists also work on consultancies for humanitarian organisations (see also Wright 2016). Some of the freelancers interviewed for this study admitted that because they made some of their living from consultancies with humanitarian organisations, they found it especially difficult to point out faults in their projects, both when on contract for an organisation, and even with their journalist 'hat' back on, when they were aware that they might financially depend on contracts with the organisation in the future. Sixth, pointing out flaws of operations and projects is one thing, but choosing to report in favour of an organisation, takes it further. Humanitarian organisations do not expect a direct pay-back in every interaction, and nor is the correspondent officially restricted in his or her reporting in every interaction. However, more often than not, the organisations do expect a favour in return.

In my study I found that even if an organisation does not explicitly voice an expectation about the coverage, some correspondents choose rather to self-censor their own view of faults of the operation in the field, unless it is something major that they consider the humanitarian organisation is doing wrong. In cases of extreme failure of humanitarian projects, I found correspondents would proceed with their story even if it were likely to damage their relationship with that particular organisation, and with many other similar organisations. Staff correspondents are in a better position to do this, as they have the editorial back-up and a guaranteed income, whereas freelancers often have to rely on the logistical and information support humanitarian organisations provide, and on consultancy contracts with the organisations. Having a staff position, however, does not automatically guarantee more independence. I interviewed many staff correspondents whose budgets did not cover significant travel costs on a continent where travelling is very expensive. So then again, they relied to a great extent on humanitarian organisations to provide information and contacts, to get them to remote places, and to arrange their stay and movements there.

The changing nature of foreign news and of aid is forcing humanitarians and foreign correspondents to form an 'unholy alliance' of deep co-dependency, and that is having a serious and largely unnoticed effect on Western news coverage. In some cases the dependency is so strong that it is comparable to embedded journalism. I call the journalists in these cases *aid embeds*. Furthermore, through the interactions between actors of the media and aid sector, the network and dependencies between them have become so dense and strong, that a new hybrid form emerged on the system level: *Journalistic PR*. The dichotomy of PR and journalism dissolves in sub-Saharan Africa more and more, and a new form emerges that overrules traditional journalism, and includes PR. The blurring of lines and emergence of new hybrid forms will increase due to the economisation of the aid and media sector. But even informed news audiences will often not be able to know in which context the information was produced, and thus not be able to understand that what they perceive as neutral information is often not independent but follows agendas of humanitarian organisations that in the public's view are often only perceived as 'doing good'.

For sub-Saharan Africa, this study made clear that humanitarian organisations are so essential for the production of foreign news, and that they influence correspondents and their editors so significantly, that they have a gatekeeper role. For the gatekeeper research this means that we have to re-assess the perception of correspondents as major gatekeepers. The role of other players having a fundamental role in the process of foreign news selection has to be studied in more detail. Follow-up research could identify important gatekeepers and their role in the news selection in other regions of the world. The framework defines the actors' actions and behaviours. The behaviour patterns that evolve through frequent interactions can in turn have feedback effects on the framework. Looking at theories on journalism, journalism is often defined by contrasting it to public relations. This book studied empirically how such a relationship can look like in practice on the actor level, and what consequences it can have for the material that is produced. It is also an empirical example of why the relationship between media and public relations of aid organisations in sub-Saharan Africa cannot be seen as either *determination* – a relationship in which only one side influences the other – or *intereffication* – a relationship in which the actors make each other's work possible.[1] The relationship goes beyond this dichotomy. The borders between the two blur in the aggregated interactions of the actors. For journalism studies this means that we need more actor-focused field research in other regions of the world, to understand better under which circumstances these borders blur, and whether it is still feasible to speak of 'public relations' versus 'journalism'. Or whether new hybrid forms have evolved more broadly and new theoretical concepts have to be developed consequently.

Humanitarian organisations need crises, and the coverage of crises to receive donations. And correspondents need crises to get their editors interested and to pass the high news threshold for Africa stories. The interests of both sectors intersect in crisis topics, fuel crisis-focused coverage and donation appeals that focus on suffering, and thus perpetuate the cliché of Africa as a continent perpetually in crisis in the minds of global audiences. Western news coverage of sub-Saharan Africa is not an unbiased, independent testimony of the events. Instead, the coverage concentrates on the peaks of crises and depicts suffering. As this study of how these actors interact closely with each other in the field shows, the perpetual presence of humanitarian organisations during the emergence of news coverage shapes the presentation of those events significantly, to a point where it is hard to distinguish between news and public relations. However, international audiences are not aware of that but consider the coverage to be unbiased. TV broadcasters and newspapers should have clear guidelines so that PR material or journalistic PR is not only unmistakeably identifiable, but that they also explain to their audiences what it means. Correspondents and their editors should also shine a light on their own role in the interactions. Additionally, correspondents and their editors should be trained to have more detailed knowledge on emergency and development aid and to better understand procedures in the aid sector. They should be encouraged to ask more critical questions, which they are only able to if they understand in detail how humanitarian organisations operate, how their data is produced, and how it can be interpreted. Only with sufficient knowledge and budgets, they are able to maintain certain independence, even if they might still have to rely on the aid sector's infrastructure. This is important as media coverage is key to and helps to drive Western aid and development assistance to Africa. It influences aid flows, development, and political decisions that can define the continent's future. This makes it a normative issue with political consequences.

Note

1 Baerns 1979; Bentele et al. 1997, Bentele & Nothhaft 2004.

References

Baerns, Barbara (1979) "Öffentlichkeitsarbeit als Determinante journalistischer Informationsleistungen. Thesen zur Beschreibung von Medieninhalten", in: *Publizistik* 3, 301–316.
Bentele, Günter, Liebert, Thomas and Seeling, Stefan (1997) "Von der Determination zur Intereffikation. Ein integriertes Modell zum Verhältnis von Public Relations und Journalismus", in: Günter Bentele and Michael Haller (Eds.), *Aktuelle Entstehung von Öffentlichkeit. Akteure – Strukturen – Veränderungen*, Konstanz, 225–250.
Bentele, Günter and Nothhaft, Howard (2004) "Das Intereffikationsmodell. Theoretische Weiterentwicklung, empirische Konkretisierung und Desiderate", in: Klaus-Dieter Altmeppen, Ulrike Röttger and Günter Bentele (Eds.), *Schwierige Verhältnisse. Interdependenzen zwischen Journalismus und Public Relations*, Wiesbaden, 67–104.
Dan, Viorela (2009) *Framing the aid. Deutungsmacht im Politikfeld der humanitären Hilfe als PR-Erfolg oder unerwünschter Einfluss*, unpublished Master thesis at TU Illmenau.
Wright, Kate (2016) "These Grey Areas", in: *Journalism Studies* 17(8), 989–1009.

8 Outlook

During an interview, I asked a CNN correspondent about the prospects for interactions between the media and aid in sub-Saharan Africa in the future. The correspondent said, after some consideration: "It's been fine and it's still fine and I think it will still continue being fine, yeah. I mean, we're working well" (I_35), clearly demonstrating the new normal of the deep co-dependency, and the lack of engagement with what that means. What may the future bring? From the findings of this study, I conclude that it is likely that the number of correspondents will further decrease, and that with no sign of an increase in budgets for foreign news, those who remain will shift from being staff dispatched to sub-Saharan Africa for a long-term posting, to younger freelancers reporting for a limited time before moving to other locations, or other jobs. At the same time, I believe that journalists will increasingly need to look for new working models to finance their living, for example by seeking engagements by multiple employers. One scenario is that there will be more freelancers, and that they will either work for many outlets at once, or for a few outlets and as consultants for humanitarian organisations on the side, or both. If fewer experienced correspondents work in Africa, will that change the way humanitarian organisations approach journalists? So far, the media, and especially the news agencies, have had the upper hand in that the humanitarian organisations have seen them as very important because of their unique reach to global audiences. Might that change with the changing role of foreign reporting? This is hard to tell, and should be subject to future investigations.

Certainly the trend is towards further professionalisation of the communications, public relations, and fundraising departments of humanitarian organisations. In all probability, they will themselves increasingly produce high-quality texts, pictures, and video footage, publish them on their websites and other channels, and offer them to news outlets. These are likely to be accepted when the material comes from inaccessible locations the outlets cannot reach without great expense. This will make it even more essential to counter-check the material, and verify its authenticity where possible. Yet, I anticipate that this will become more difficult and thus less likely. Content from independent correspondents and from humanitarian organisations increasingly appears on the same forums and platforms, often without being appropriately credited, which makes it hard for the audience to understand who produced which material, and I believe this trend will continue.

All of this will blur the lines between the media and aid sector even more than it already happens now. Possibly, this trend will eventually create greater awareness of the challenges the close connections between these two sectors bring, and more correspondents, editors, and even audiences will understand the potential biases in the information they are broadcasting, or watching and reading.

Other new types and forms of media are on the rise, such as Twitter, and online platforms reaching new audiences such as Vice, BuzzFeed, and Medium. A humanitarian worker spoke of the "BuzzFeed-ification" of suffering and how this trivialisation of famine affected its reception: "Raising awareness [has to have] a quality flavour to it. If you just go 'oh my god, oh my god, look at that!', [then] so what? What have you achieved?" (I_22). As well as potentially reaching new audiences, these new forms of journalism might also change the interactions between humanitarian organisations and journalists. Who can most reliably get humanitarian organisations the most coverage that the audience sees as unbiased, will dictate how those organisations reach out, and with whom they cooperate. So far, this has been and still is traditional news media.

How will increasing user-generated content shape the interactions, and the prerogative of terms and images? More of humanitarian organisations' beneficiaries, as well as those who miss out – who are currently rarely interviewed by journalists on aid embeds – will have their own voice thanks to increasingly widespread internet connections and smartphones, and the rapidly emerging social media in Africa. This does not negate the need for foreign reporting. But it can be a way to control and hold to account news coverage and humanitarian organisations' operations, using the crowd's knowledge to check facts and to name poor sourcing. The humanitarian narrative will not only be driven by humanitarian organisations and news media speaking on behalf of beneficiaries any more.

Will the production of content by humanitarian organisations, their ability to broadcast themselves via online platforms, new forms of media, and people's access to social media telling their own stories, together make foreign correspondents disappear? I do not think so. News outlets will remain the most trusted sources. However, I doubt that 'hard news' will be the future of foreign reporting. Instead it will shift towards deeply-researched investigations, well-informed analyses, comments, and opinion that still give enough context to help orientate the reader in the growing flood of information available. But those foreign correspondents who are in sub-Saharan Africa will be less experienced and mostly working as freelancers for many outlets, and there will be more journalists parachuting in to cover crises from headquarters when the interest is large enough. Otherwise, humanitarian organisations will ply their material to reporters based in the head offices. News agencies will play an even bigger role for the coverage of sub-Saharan Africa than they do currently. This is a cause for concern, because my data showed that news agency correspondents in particular were surprisingly uncritical about the proximity between humanitarian organisations and news.

At the same time as the media landscape is changing fundamentally, the humanitarian sector is likely to undergo a change in order to remain sustainable. More local NGOs will implement international programmes, for less money. Some voices, however, are not confident that the humanitarian sector is flexible enough to adapt to these changes, as my interviews showed. Scholars argue that humanitarian organisations must change the way they operate, away from over-using "the emergency model to communicating about [. . .] international development issues", and steer away from seeking "to stimulate intimacy and physical proximity" with beneficiaries in their way of presenting events (Orgad & Seu 2014: 34).

Overall, news media should make clear under which circumstances material that they present originated, and make transparent to the audiences what that means. More staff of humanitarian organisations in departments other than communications and fundraising should communicate to journalists (Leach 2015) to have less 'agency speak', and more real information from the field in the news. Neither journalists nor humanitarians should consider social media a threat but a chance to encourage better quality reporting, and more effective and functional aid. Correspondents and editors should view and interrogate humanitarian organisations as the powerful players that they are, in order to profit from the material they are producing without letting them dominate the discourse. Reporters should understand clearly under which agenda humanitarian organisations' data were gathered and produced, and why these organisations might want to push a certain agenda. This discourse should become public and practices in the field have to become more transparent, so that audiences can adequately evaluate the information they receive. In so doing, as the realisation spreads that Western media coverage of Africa is not as objective and unbiased as it should be, and that humanitarian organisations' campaigns to publicise their work necessitate pushing internal agendas, then perhaps audiences will realise the need to fund quality foreign reporting once again. Why is this important? Because as people from one place emigrate, or flee, to other places, objective reporting of faraway places engenders fair and constructive understanding. In the context of Africa, news coverage presenting it as a place mired in crisis and needing endless humanitarian intervention directly influences aid flows, investment, political engagement, and global expectations. It affects not just how Westerners perceive Africa, but how Africans do, too. If that coverage is not mirroring the reality adequately, and indeed if it is increasingly influenced by organisations whose interests are not served by journalistic accuracy, then how can we expect decisions driving international engagement with Africa to be as valuable as they should? We risk a perpetual misunderstanding of the place that will within a lifetime become the world's most populous.

References

Leach, Anna (2015) "15 Ways NGOs Can Attract Positive Media Attention", *The Guardian. Global Development Professionals Network*, URL: www.theguardian.com/global-development-professionals-network/2015/mar/03/ngos-positive-media-attention-communications-pr [5.3.2015].

Orgad, Shani and Seu, I. Bruna (2014) "The Mediation of Humanitarianism: Toward a Research Framework", in: *Communication, Culture & Critique* 7, 6–36.

Index

actor theory 37–40, 98–99
Adeso 155
Afro-pessimism 1, 227; *see also* crisis focus
Agence France-Presse (AFP) 173, 222; *see also* news agencies
aid agencies, definition of 8, 69
aid agencies and organisations 64–78, 143–162, 213–250; as door opener 218, 171, 173, 201, 208; as logistic facilitator 125,170–171, 183–184, 186, 188, 197, 201; comms for emergency vs. comms for development 153–154; comms HQ vs. field 155–160; fear of press 173, 183, 241; growth and increasing number 69, 71; need for crisis focus 72, 75–79; need to self-perpetuate 71; perception of journalists' view of them 147, 174; public relations 72–75, 76, 77, 85, 159, 146–163; view of journalists 75, 254; viewed by journalists 147, 174, 190–191, 223; *see also* statistics
aid embedding 79–86, 200–212, 234, 256; definition of 83–85
Al Jazeera 173, 232
American journalists *see* American media
American media: audience 61; editorial guidelines 129–130, 255–256; role perception of journalists 4, 134, 143; (un)biased reporting and dependency 82, 129–130, 134–135, 197, 200, 209, 211, 216, 226, 232–233
angle, cultural in reporting 131, 215–216, 231–233, 239
appeals, fundraising 8, 73, 153–154, 237, 242, 259
Arbeitsgemeinschaft der öffentlich-rechtlichen Rundfunkanstalten der Bundesrepublik Deutschland (ARD) 128, 129, 173; *see also* German-speaking media
Associated Press (AP) *see* news agencies
audience: communication with audiences across cultural and knowledge barriers 49, 50–51, 127, 134, 138–143, 174, 231, 233, 253; expectations of news 12, 51; news reporting influencing views 1, 3, 5, 36–37, 49, 50–52, 62, 73, 148–149, 161, 213, 228; understanding of news production 30, 72, 82, 227, 245, 259

blurring of lines between PR and journalism 73, 76, 121, 162, 200, 207–208, 241–250, 256, 259
brand building 52,76, 148–165, 232, 236–238, 252; recognition 174, 238–239
British Broadcasting Corporation (BBC): audience 61; dependency 68, 129, 152, 173; Ethiopia famine coverage 5–6, 53, 78, 81, 235; guidelines 128; leading role of BBC 57
British journalists *see* British media
British media: audience 82; CNN effect 53, 78; coverage trends 4; role perception of journalists 134–135; (un)biased reporting and dependency 209–2010, 215–216, 131, 184–185, 197, 209–210, 232; *see also* BBC
budget: aid budgets 5, 69, 75; news reporting 68, 85, 126, 160, 165, 182, 184, 192, 200, 221, 215, 255, 285

Cable News Network (CNN) *see* American media
Cafod 71, 147; *see also* aid agencies

Index

Care 5, 71, 154, 158, 172, 231, 236; *see also* aid agencies
censorship 80, 85–86, 190, 206–208, 215, 244, 258
CNN effect 1, 49, 50, 53, 75, 87
conflict of interests 73, 122, 185,188, 200, 207, 215, 241–242, 258
correspondents *see* journalists
crisis focus: fundraising and press releases 71, 234, 240, 246; news coverage 3–4, 6, 35, 71–72, 124, 130, 215–216, 229, 236, 240, 242–243, 251, 259

Daily Mail *see* British media
Daily Telegraph, The 129; *see also* British media
danger to journalists 62–63
data analysis, methods of 109–116
Democratic Republic of Congo (DRC) 67, 75, 132, 201
dependency: journalists on OHHs 62–68, 79–86, 140–145, 150–163, 165, 182, 190–191, 192–213, 221, 231, 256; OHHs on journalists 67–78, 71–75, 143–163, 189–199
Der Spiegel 128
donors 5, 74, 76, 78, 236–238, 243, 244–245, 257

editorial guidelines 128–130, 255–256
editors 1, 5–6, 35, 61, 67, 124, 127–133, 149; Africa knowledge 35, 57–59, 130–133, 256; gatekeeping role 55–57; support of correspondents 63, 132; support of crisis focus 130, 240–241
embed *see* embedding
embedding xi, 79–97, 172, 200–212, 229
experience, journalistic 5, 11, 51, 56, 64, 119–124, 130, 192, 194–196, 200, 223–224

famine 53, 78, 124, 216, 228–230, 235, 243
foreign affairs 50, 53–54, 75–76, 152, 173, 174
Frankfurter Allgemeine Zeitung (FAZ) 4, 63, 128, 216
freelance journalists: budget 68, 85, 160, 165, 192, 200, 215, 255, 285; dependency 63, 178, 183–185, 192, 197, 199–200, 204, 207, 209, 255, 285; experience 120–122; guidelines 128; size of patch 62; role perception 134, 136, 253–254; viewed by humanitarians 172–173; working for humanitarian organisations 207, 215, 241, 285
fundraising 8, 73, 75, 152–155, 166, 190, 223, 230, 235; role of comms department 148–149, 150–163, 234–241; role of media 236, 238–239, 243

gatekeeper: aid agencies as gatekeepers xi, 74, 157, 162, 172, 216, 218, 241, 255, 259; gatekeeping theory 34–35; journalists' gatekeeping competence 56, 58, 215–216, 243
gatekeeping *see* gatekeeper
German journalists *see* German-speaking media
German-speaking media: dependency 67, 76, 131, 209, 212, 216, 229; editorial guidelines 128–129; role perception of journalists 54, 135, 212; reporting tradition 64, 231
Guardian, The 173, 215; *see also* British media
guidelines *see* editorial guidelines

Hong Kong syndrome 63
humanitarian organisations *see* aid agencies
Human Rights Watch (HRW) *see* aid agencies

ICRC/IFRC 5, 23, 75, 77, 149; *see also* aid agencies
image of Africa, development of 60–62
interviewing techniques 106–108
IRC *see* aid agencies

journalism, understanding of 2,8, 29–34, 37–38, 51; tradition of reporting 64, 209, 255
journalists: influencing events 245 (*see also* CNN effect); political and social importance 1–3, 31, 49, 52, 64; typology regarding contacts with aid organisations 252–253; view of aid organisations 71, 174, 190–191, 223

Kenya 102–103, 106

media packages 160–161, 163, 169, 172, 190, 254, 257, 261
motivation, journalists 138–140

MSF importance of numbers and figures 71; influencing journalists 155, 174, 187, 204, 226, 230–231; PR strategy 157, 160, 226, 235, 240; use of Twitter 146, 174; workshops for journalists 77; *see also* aid agencies

network theory 42, 85, 164–166
Neue Zürcher Zeitung (NZZ) 63, 216; *see also* German-speaking media
news agencies, role of 56, 57, 58, 59, 67, 152
news value 174, 216, 237, 239–240; theory 35–36
New York Times, The 57, 75, 152, 173; *see also* American media
NGOs *see* aid agencies

Oxfam 5–6, 70–71, 103, 174, 237–239; *see also* aid agencies

patch, size of 5, 52, 119
photography, OHH providing 67, 208
public relations (PR) 23, 64–67, 71–79, 81, 146–163, 176–177, 241–245, 259

Reuters 180, 184, 197, 208, 223; *see also* news agencies
role perception, journalistic 253–254; *see also* role perception of journalists under American media, British media, German-speaking media

Save the Children 71, 74, 147, 149, 153, 156, 159, 230, 235; *see also* aid agencies
self-perception *see* role perception of journalists under American media, British media, German-speaking media

social media 52, 73 146–147, 154, 160, 162, 226, 262
Somalia 67, 75, 126, 201, 203, 235
South Africa 60, 62, 102–103, 119
South Sudan 67, 125, 126, 156, 201, 203
statistics 81, 150, 221–227, 229–230, 257; aid organisations inflating figures 71, 75, 222–224; journalistic diligence in interpretation 162–163, 222–226, 227
Süddeutsche Zeitung (SZ) 61, 63, 128

television 128, 129, 132, 173, 174
terms, humanitarian organisations' prerogative of 50, 59, 228–230
threshold, news 3–4, 75, 251, 259
transparency of sources 75, 161, 207–208, 214, 227, 242, 257, 259, 263–264

UNDP *see* aid agencies
UNHCR 148, 160, 161, 188, 208; *see also* aid agencies
Unicef 5, 121, 149, 153, 162, 201, 203, 236; *see also* aid agencies
United Nations (UN) 174; *see also* Unicef and aid agencies

Voice of America (VOA) 129, 173

Wall Street Journal, The 127, 173; *see also* American media
WFP 148, 149, 186, 237; *see also* aid agencies
WHO 147, 155; *see also* aid agencies
World Vision 71, 81, 171; *see also* aid agencies

Zweites Deutsches Fernsehen (ZDF) 128, 129, 173; *see also* German-speaking media

Annex

The media and aid in sub-Saharan Africa

Whose news?

Inaugural-Dissertation
zur Erlangung des Doktorgrades
der
Philosophisch-
Sozialwissenschaftlichen
Fakultät der
Universität Augsburg
Vorgelegt von
Magdalena von Naso, geboren in
Schwäbisch Hall,
März 2016